D1303791

Global HR

Global HR

Challenges Facing the Function

PETER REILLY
AND
TONY WILLIAMS

GOWER

© Peter Reilly and Tony Williams 2012

All rights reserved. No part of this publication may be reproduced, stored in a retrieval system or transmitted in any form or by any means, electronic, mechanical, photocopying, recording or otherwise without the prior permission of the publisher.

Published by
Gower Publishing Limited
Wey Court East
Union Road
Farnham
Surrey
GU9 7PT
England

Gower Publishing Company
Suite 420
101 Cherry Street
Burlington
VT 05401-4405
USA

www.gowerpublishing.com

Peter Reilly and Tony Williams have asserted their moral rights under the Copyright, Designs and Patents Act, 1988, to be identified as the authors of this work.

British Library Cataloguing in Publication Data
Reilly, Peter A. (Peter Andrew), 1952-
  Global HR : challenges facing the function.
  1. International business enterprises--Personnel
  management.
  I. Title II. Williams, Tony.
  658.3'03-dc22

ISBN: 978-1-4094-0278-7 (hbk)
ISBN: 978-1-4094-0279-4 (ebk)

Library of Congress Cataloging-in-Publication Data
Reilly, Peter A. (Peter Andrew), 1952-
  Global HR : challenges facing the function / by Peter Reilly and Tony Williams.
    p. cm.
  Includes bibliographical references and index.
  ISBN 978-1-4094-0278-7 (hardback) -- ISBN 978-1-4094-0279-4
  (ebook) 1. Personnel management. I. Williams, Tony. II. Title.
  HF5549.R4546 2011
  658.3--dc23

                                                        2011047370

Printed and bound in Great Britain by the
MPG Books Group, UK

Contents

List of Figures

List of Tables

Acknowledgements

The authors would like to thank all of the 70 or so people and organizations that contributed to the content of this book, whether named or unnamed, whether formally interviewed or not.

We have tried very hard to represent accurately individual views and organizational policies and practices. Naturally, over the long gestation of the book circumstances have changed, rendering some of the detail out of date. We beg contributors' forbearance with this fact, pleading that for us there is learning both in what has been done and in what is currently happening inside their organizations.

We would also like to thank those at the Institute for Employment Studies and Royal Bank of Scotland that have helped in various ways, from reading text to drawing diagrams. Colleagues from the universities of Glasgow, Copenhagen and Brighton have also commented on drafts and suggested references to follow up.

Those that have made this book what it is are too numerous to mention, but you know who you are!

Naturally, we accept responsibility for any errors that have crept into the text.

Peter Reilly and Tony Williams

1 *Introduction*

Why the Book?

We wrote our previous book because we were concerned that HR transformation, i.e. the modernizing of the HR function so that it could become a strategic player in the organization, was too fixated on structural and process change. In particular, we believed that the leadership of HR was giving insufficient attention to the capability of HR to meet the requirements of being a strategic player. This book takes this debate a stage further by looking at the challenges of delivering quality HR in a global setting.

It has been written primarily for HR practitioners of organizations that have multinational operations and those that are moving in this direction. Our purpose is to assist organizations to become more effective in their HR management in cross-national settings through better understanding of the challenges facing them and be better able to confront them. Some of these may be familiar problems that appear in a different (global) guise. Others are issues that are new to those operating outside their base country.

What is Global HR?

This leads to the obvious question of what is a global organization. There have been a number of classifications of firms operating outside their national home (e.g. Bartlett and Ghosal, 1989, Trompenaars, 1993 and Hewitt, 2009). The degree of central direction as opposed to collaboration, the way knowledge is transmitted and the extent to which resources are shared seem to be the key determinants in labelling companies as multinational, international, trans-national or global. These commentators can be quite precise in defining types of organization, with a strong sense that organizations pass through a number of stages on their way to a global nirvana. This terminological specificity is not widely adopted or understood by practitioners and we are doubtful of its benefit for our audience.

Moreover, both the Bartlett and Ghosal and Hewitt definitions of 'global' seem to have what to us is an unhelpful slant. They both characterize 'global' as a company where the HQ has worldwide strategies and policies (Hewitt) or heavily regulates/controls subsidiaries (Bartlett and Ghosal). This seems to offer a particular model of what global might mean. In fact, as we argue in Chapter 7, this may well be the method of choice for many organizations growing in international scope, but it does seem to deny alternative approaches to organizations that seek to become global enterprises in a different way.

Despite these reservations some companies, including Rolls Royce and RBS, would not regard themselves as global, using a similar kind of definition. They are UK organizations with international operations. The same is said of many US headquartered firms. Similarly, ANZ told us that they saw themselves as a super-regional not a global company, even though they are represented in North America, the Middle East and Europe, besides Asia Pacific. Their centre of gravity is still in the latter region. There is a sense in some organizations that there is, indeed, a maturity curve, of a corporate progression to being global; whilst within others there is an acknowledgement that they are not (and may never be) truly global. Another third group are secure in their belief that they are global organizations.

So whilst the academics are seeking precision, HR managers are more intuitive in their judgements. In the perceptual mix there is:

- the number/density of expatriates
- the extent of racial/national diversity
- the way the corporate centre sees the world (i.e. by not being ethnocentric)
- how geographically dispersed the operations are, including the relative importance of these operations
- the extent to which there is a global brand
- the way in which the company organizes itself and goes to market on a global rather than regional or national basis.

The question of whether the structure of the organization is a loose federation and loosely managed, or a tightly run and integrated company does not seem to be a particular preoccupation of practitioners in determining the global nature of their organization.

In the end, for readers of this book many of the challenges arise simply through operating outside of the home base, however dispersed their operations, global the business strategy or international their outlook or resourcing strategy.

Is it Becoming More Important?

Not surprisingly given their definition, Hewitt (2009) has found that there are relatively few truly global companies – only 15 per cent of the companies it surveyed had made it as global, but they do see 40 per cent 'transitioning' to this state by adding worldwide strategies and policies.

If one uses a broader notion of global HR, it seems the number of organizations touched by these global questions is surprisingly high. Within HR transformation, for example, adding locations to the scope of change is a noteworthy feature of the change. This is evident in the ADP/HROA (2008) research on HR transformation, where some 40 per cent of organizations expected to extend their geographical scope. Seventy per cent of UK respondents in a CIPD survey (Reilly et al., 2007) felt that globalization was an important or very important driver of change in people management policies and practices in their organization in the next three years. More recent CIPD research (2010c) discovered that 90 per cent of respondents believe that global issues impact their role. Impact of course can have various forms, from being a truly global enterprise to being a national organization that interfaces with global companies, whose business activity has international competitors or simply draws its labour from abroad.

This sense of a progressive move towards greater and greater international contact is consistent with a widely held view of growing globalization through economic, social and cultural integration. It is outside the scope of this book to consider patterns of international trade or supply chain as indicators of this globalization trend, but we believe that it would be wrong to see globalization as something only discovered in the last 20 years. Thomas Friedman (2000) might be right that the 'flattening' of the world is speeding up, but global trade and resource transfers have a long history.

Looking from the Scottish perspective, appropriate given the RBS co-authorship, there is evidence of trade between the Alps and Scotland from 6,000 years ago (a jadeite axe head); there was naturally much trade with the Mediterranean and continental Europe during Roman times and at least temporary transfer of resources (Roman soldiers at the Mumrills Fort on Hadrian's Wall included soldiers from North Africa); and during the ninth and tenth centuries the Vikings moved goods to and from the west – between Newfoundland and Scotland – and to and from the east – including between Baghdad, Tashkent and Samarkand.

Similarly, further afield, from the Bronze Age there were trade routes like the Silk Road that linked the Indian subcontinent and China with the Middle East, East Africa, Java and the Roman and Greek civilizations. A wide variety of goods (food, artefacts and luxuries) and people (including slaves) were transported over a wide geographical area. As much as 7,300 years ago there was a continental trade in Aegean Sea shells centred on Varna on the Black Sea coast. This has suggested to historians that there existed a long-standing 'Afro-Eurasian' economic system.

Alasdair Keith (2010) might be right that there are peaks and troughs in globalization: it has not been a linear movement from local to global. 'Progress' has been affected by war and environmental crises. The current economic 'blip' has slowed global integration with world trade levels not yet back to their 2008 peak, and, if the effects of the downturn are longer lasting than we expect, it may lead towards greater isolationism, restricting the free flow of capital, goods and services. However, in Keith's view globalization will resume, albeit in an altered form.

This suggests that global HR will remain important, but in the areas of knowledge and people (the subjects closest to the hearts of the function) the environment may become more complex, with growing government attempts to control information flows (already true across parts of Asia and the Middle East) and limit the movement of people (especially into western countries concerned about unemployment and national identity).

What is in the Book?

The fundamental question that runs through the heart of global HR management, and is reflected in this book, is how does one manage the global organization, not just in the acceleration phase but now when the socio-economic environment is more complex. We explore this through a number of themes.

We start with business transformation. We are particularly interested in the contribution that HR makes to how global organizations deal with aspects of change, with special reference to mergers and acquisitions. Does HR have an important role to play early in the process; or is it largely a bystander? And does its role depend on whether the acquiring organization imposes its own culture on the acquired organization as opposed to building a new culture together as partners? This issue is particularly important to global companies, not least because the track record in successful mergers and acquisitions is poor even without the added complexity of cross-national attempts.

Whilst these questions are most pertinent to mergers and acquisitions the underlying philosophy applies equally to any form of organizational change.

Another theme of the book is the extent to which there is a convergence in ideas and in cultures that might lead to a universal, global mindset. This is interesting from the HR function's perspective because it bears upon the extent to which it is possible to develop a single organizational culture, employer brand or employee value proposition (EVP). The more people (or at least those employed in multinational companies) are the same the world over, the easier it is to construct that global culture, employer brand or EVP.

There are those who argue against this notion of cultural 'convergence' rather emphasizing the durability of national cultures. There is also the concern expressed that the wish for workforce diversity, to reflect the population of customers and residents in the places of operation, is compromised by this desire for universality. Can you really respect difference if you are trying to meld employees into a common global culture and recruit into the organization those who are attracted by a brand or EVP that represents this culture?

With respect to the brand, how is this created? Is it fair to say that the more it is driven top down, the more it is likely to be part of this enculturization process? What room is there for co-design with employees that offers the chance of a more pluralist vision? The answer to this question also relates to whether there is a single, corporate monolithic brand or multiple brands to underscore the variety of organizational faces to the world.

This leads us to consider the logic of having a global approach to talent management. This can be used to support the common culture, brand or EVP, not least because it should concern the questions of selection and development into this global community. But first, there is a need to define what is a rather slippery concept and then see whether there is anything distinctive about global talent management. The conceptual differences start with deciding who are the talented, but, as we will see, the practical implications of this choice are not as far reaching as one would expect. A definition of talent management such as that by Stahl et al. (2007) as 'an organization's efforts to attract, select, develop and retain key talented employees on a global scale' illustrates the point. It suggests that we are merely scaling up from national to global the activities that form part of the same process. The question remains whether the changing context affects these activities at all. It is obvious that they are different with respect to moving staff across international boundaries, but in what other ways does HR need to make adjustments? Part of the answer lies in who is controlling the resources and whether the staff form a permanent international cadre.

This brings us to the final cluster of questions: how does HR govern itself in a global setting and how feasible is it to have common HR policies, processes and systems across the world.

As we observed earlier, there is a centralized model offered by Bartlett and Ghosal (1989) where the corporate centre directs the business in an integrated manner. Here the emphasis is on corporate control for the benefits of cost and consistency. There is a unitary frame of reference where standardization of policies and practices is the norm. Moreover, a single HR service delivery model, based upon a common technological platform, is seen to best serve the interests of the global corporation. In some cases the form of service delivery and nature of standardized policies and practices is simply the 'home' model exported round the world. In others, there is a wider contribution to the corporate approach that comes from business units or locations.

An alternative approach is that the corporate centre coordinates and facilitates, often with an important role for regional bodies, but with national organizations dealing directly with each other. The corporate centre may provide a set of values, principles and even frameworks to guide the locations, subsidiary or operating companies, but they are free to implement them in a way that fits their domestic business needs.

An even more pluralist model is where power is distributed in a 'polycentric' manner (Trompenaars, 1993) and where there is even more independence of policymaking by local companies. This is more likely to be found in organizations with a holding company type structure loosely bound together with probably quite different people management approaches to reflect different geographies and markets.

To complicate matters, there is not just a simple distinction to be made between global and local, HQ and subsidiary or operating company (or whatever the term might be in any particular organization); there is also the balance between corporate centre and business unit or function. So in some organizations the power rests with the CEO and corporate office. In others, the power sits in the business units or with the functions, which themselves may operate in a more or less directive manner towards other parts of the company outside the business unit or functional HQ. Naturally, in many organizations there is a sharing of power to varying degrees between the various players.

It would be wrong to assume that that even where design intentions are clear that the delivery is straightforward. Many global organizations have real tensions between on the one hand getting the benefits of commonality and of scale, and on the other the benefits of flexibility, empowerment and innovation.

Moreover, there are other challenges with HR governance: how to ensure that staff, especially executives, live by the values of the organization and manage risk in a sensible way. How does HR encourage colleagues to be mindful of the corporate reputation and of the regulatory frameworks under which the firm operates, being aware particularly of media interest in any hint of scandal?

As part of the conclusions, we look at the implications of globalization for the capability of the HR function. What new skills and competencies will be required to succeed in this environment?

Structure of the Book

The book will look at the broad themes of global HR management described above:

- business transformation in a global setting with specific reference to transnational mergers and acquisitions
- organizational culture in relation to national cultures
- diversity issues in a global organization
- employer brand and the employee value proposition and the extent to which it is common across the world
- international talent management: how different is it from national?
- how the function is run via an explicit (or implicit) HR governance model
- the service delivery model in a global setting.

The conclusion tries to summarize our findings and views on the key issues that have emerged in writing the book. It also considers the implications for HR of operating in a global environment.

2 Adding Value to Global Business Change – the Holy Grail for HR?

When businesses combine in an international merger or acquisition, the only safe assumption may be that there will be misunderstandings and knowledge gaps between the managers of the combining businesses. (IPD, 1999)

Introduction

Whilst it has become a cliché to say it, change really is a constant in most organizations, and the frequency of structural change to drive for further performance improvement or react to new business conditions is such that the sort of comment heard in one organization that management 'should resolve the organizational structure once and for all' is risible. Given that change is too big a subject to tackle within the space of this book, we are concentrating on change in the context of organizations becoming more global. Some of this growth is organic, but much of it is via mergers, acquisitions, strategic joint ventures or significant product launches that change the geographical footprint strategically.

The latter is the focus of this chapter: how the globalization objective is met by non-organic means. In the context of global organizations, this is a particularly difficult process to get right. We know from research that many mergers and acquisitions do not meet their business objectives. Three quarters of mergers and acquisitions fail, according to Schuler and Jackson's research (2001) and only 10 per cent were wholly successful in a study by the Hay Group of European deals (Henry, 2008). Thus we can surmise that a good proportion of these failures will come from cross-border mergers and acquisitions. The hard bit, it seems, in getting mergers and acquisitions, or indeed any strategic business change, to work is the people dimension. If the people and cultural challenges derail national mergers and acquisitions then it is likely that success will be tougher to achieve in an international context.

The other main aspect of this chapter is what role does HR play in these strategic business changes, recognizing that contributing to the strategic agenda of the business is, to Ulrich and many other HR commentators, the Holy Grail of HR business partnership. We recognize that, traditionally, HR may be asked to contribute towards the back end of a deal – usually when the lawyers get into the drafting of a sale and purchase agreement and HR is asked simply to comment on employee benefits! In looking at what HR's role should be in business change, perhaps we can also address the issue of what indeed is the role of a business partner as different to other aspects of the functional contribution.

Rationale for Strategic Change (the Why)

So what drives this unremitting business change, especially those drivers relevant to this book? The principal reasons are set out below:

- **Globalization** – this can take many forms, such as the organizational response to the threat of the emergent economies of China, India and elsewhere or creating the scale efficiencies that generate more demand for an organization's products. Whatever the cause, the need for a more global footprint is increasingly an agenda item.
- **Regulatory change** – again this can take many forms and is a fundamental issue for a number of industries, none greater, perhaps, than for financial services, given the very recent economic crisis. Be it the cost of running a bank in the capital charges, the need to avoid bank failures through higher liquidity buffers or operational regulations affecting many parts of how banks are run; these are proving to be major change drivers in the industry.
- **Scale/contraction** – just as many firms are growing scale into new markets to provide ever-increasing returns to shareholders through buying efficiencies (supermarkets are perhaps the greatest example of this), some organizations are also returning to niche activities, having being badly burnt through the financial crisis with highly leveraged balance sheets. Whilst obviously true for financial institutions, this issue is not limited just to banks whose lending books became stressed. Many companies that relied on market funding to support expansion and growth and leveraged debt to support that growth have since had to contract or, worse, fold. Property companies are the most obvious sector affected by this, but a number of retailers have also fallen foul of the unstable financial markets withdrawing funding.
- **Consumerism** – perhaps now considered a dirty word, with the impact of the financial crisis biting deep into the pockets of those in many western economies, but the desire of the consumer for an endless stream of new products has driven many companies to ever-increasing product development and launches. Simply put, we consumers seem just to need more 'stuff' such as global companies like Sony, Samsung and Apple produce. But it also is extended to that second house, the special car, the fabulous holiday and so on. Consumerism is also not limited to direct impact; indirectly it has also fuelled B2B growth and change for those along the supply chain. The drive for global commodities feeding the Chinese machine room has had a dramatic organizational impact for the BHP Billiton, Anglo American and RioTinto's of this world.
- **Market shifts** – further drivers for changing organizational model and presence are created by moving more emphasis to emerging markets as demand for products and services in mature markets plateaus. It is obvious to use the bustling economic growth of China or India over the last 10 years as examples, but there are many other markets that exist with smaller but just as radical shifts for the companies involved. The changing demographic of the Euro Zone has meant some companies have moved eastwards as they follow economic demand.
- **Profitability** – brought into sharp relief as investors chase returns to compensate losses in sectors such as banking or property over the last three years, many companies have to look very carefully at profitability and efficiency in particular as income and growth becomes harder to achieve. This need for efficiency is even more pertinent to

the public sector, as governments across the globe have to trim non-productive spend and radically restructure services. Countries like the UK, Greece, Portugal and Ireland have made severe 'austerity' cuts to services; the USA has passed emergency budgets; the Euro Zone countries generally are on high alert. All of these threats will lead to further cost restructuring driving greater use of operating model efficiency tools such as outsourcing and offshoring.

For us, these are the main reasons for change; but we acknowledge that there are other causes, including environmental and socio-demographic change, that will also cause organizations to adjust their operations.

The Nature of Global Business Change (the What)

Having established why change happens, we need to describe the forms it can take; putting it simply, how organizations respond to these drivers. Again the list below is not exhaustive, but we believe it does set the strategic agenda within which HR's role takes place. In each case we have used some specific examples to illustrate the business context in which some companies have addressed these challenges, drawing particularly on the authors' own experience and on those we interviewed as part of the research for this book. Whilst these are generic themes, we have focused on those that are relevant in the global context beyond domestic change, which, whilst interesting, falls outside the scope of this book.

There are the five forms of global change that we focus on.

1. Mergers and acquisitions
2. Joint ventures
3. Market extension/globalization
4. Disposals
5. Shared services/offshoring

Until the recent recession, international mergers and acquisitions were on the increase, with 172 cross-border deals done in 2006 (Chubb, 2008). We also know that the modus operandi of many deals in the principal emerging BRIC markets is that of the joint venture, where the local company needs expertise and the global firm needs to exploit future demand for its products and services, but lacks local knowledge and relationships. Many global firms look to export their branded products into new markets, perhaps taking them far beyond their historical base, or simply to add more products to an existing footprint, which significantly alter local presence. More recently, we are all aware that financial markets have led to some firms returning to their core businesses, leading to an increase in disposals which can occasionally be significant in their global impact. Finally, the move to offshore and shared services internationally, to drive cost efficiencies, has implications beyond the consumer. Jobs are lost at home and created elsewhere.

MERGERS AND ACQUISITIONS

Mergers and acquisitions take a number of forms. Clearly, there is the difference between a merger, which suggests the coming together of more or less equal partners, and an acquisition where one organization takes over another. In fact, for our purposes a clearer distinction is between imposed and collaborative models. Some acquisitions are executed in a very collaborative way and some mergers actually feel more like a takeover. Another important dimension to understanding mergers and acquisitions is whether there is a full integration of the companies or a 'loose coupling' (Devine and Hirsh, 1998), where the acquired business is left entirely in peace to run its own affairs. Again, whether it is a merger or acquisition does not necessarily give you a clue as which form they will take.

Set out in Table 2.1 below is an illustration of how these factors interplay.

Table 2.1   Types of merger and acquisition deal

	Imposition	**Collaboration**
Integration	Dominant culture pushed through. Old order removed	Taking the best practice from both organizations to form a new common model
Loose coupling	Adherence only to limited requirements (e.g. business principles or ROI)	Synergy sought only in specific areas (e.g. a transfer of some resources permitted)

Take two contrasting examples from history that distinguish an imposed acquisition that seeks full integration from a more collaborative, or at least two-way learning, model.

For the imposed model, look at the Norman Conquest in England. The Domesday Book of 1086 showed that in the 20 years after the invasion there were only 13 Anglo-Saxon nobles out of the 500 listed 'tenants in chief'. The English held less than 4 per cent of the land. Parts of the country had been laid waste for military (defence) reasons. Rents, moreover, had risen substantially such that the peasants had fared nearly as badly as the nobility. What with their castles, cathedrals and foreign customs, the Normans had clearly taken over their new kingdom.

As to the cause of the invasion, the Normans wanted to get their hands on English resources. England was in 1066 a well-administered and prosperous country. The Normans wanted to avail themselves of its wealth and assets, making use of its ordered bureaucracy to achieve these ends.

An alternative model of greater two-way cultural integration comes from the Arabic seventh-century victory over the Persians. On the one hand, for the Persians there was conversion to Islam and the Arabic language dominated the Court; on the other hand in some areas semi-independent Persian rulers emerged who supported the Persian literature and culture. As Adam Silverstein (2010) writes, 'Persians and Persia culture were Islamicized' but so too was 'Islamic culture Persianized'.

This was a characteristic of Arab conquests. After initial subjugation, the conquered countries were either allowed degrees of independence (e.g. mosque architecture reflected local building styles) or seized it. The extent of the occupied areas, limited resources and the nature of communication in the seventh to twelfth centuries meant that imperial 'fragmentation was a matter of time' (ibid).

Figure 2.1 sets out visually how it is the business strategy that determines the mergers and acquisition approach and whether it is an imposed or collaborative model, but this is mediated by the environment or climate within which the organization is operating. The socio-economic context will have an effect, and the legal and political even more so. This may force an organization towards collaboration rather than imposition (indeed it has led to joint ventures in China rather than acquisitions) or facilitate a straightforward takeover.

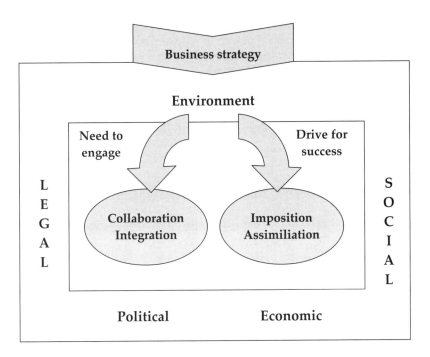

Figure 2.1   Business strategy drives M&A approach

The same distinction between an acquisition that leads to a loose coupling arrangement and one that results in full integration can be seen in the boxed examples below.

Based in Hong Kong, the Cheung Kong Group (CKG), which has business operations in 54 countries around the world and employs more than 240,000 staff, has through its subsidiaries Cheung Kong Infrastructure (CKI) and Hong Kong Electric (now Power Assets Holdings Limited) bought EDF Energy's UK electricity distribution network for £5.8 billon. The nature of CKG's global empire, with its interests in such diverse areas as property development and investment, real estate agency and estate management, hotels, telecommunications and e-commerce, finance and investments, retail, ports and related services, energy, infrastructure projects and materials, media, and biotechnology, means that the Group can only play an oversight role and act as financier to its businesses. To this end, it only has a small corporate office.

So the purchase of EDF Energy's UK network follows an expected path. Although Mr. Li Ka-shing, Chairman of Cheung Kong (Holdings) Limited. is a strong believer in synergy – a fact reflected in the naming of his company after the Yangtze River that 'aggregates countless streams and tributaries' (http://www.ckh.com.hk/eng/about/about_chairman.htm) – his business model allows the acquired businesses to manage their affairs fairly independently. The principle is that those who run their operations know best how to do this successfully. Corporate intervention comes when the subsidiary is not meeting its targets.

During the acquisition of EDF Energy this relatively hands-off approach was evident. A small team from CKI was present to ensure the deal went through as planned, but it did not get involved in questions relating to future operations. More important in that regard was a small team from Northern Gas Networks, another CKG UK asset, acquired in 2004, that was used to support the new subsidiary. The CEO from Northern Gas was appointed as the CEO of the electricity supplier. An Australian, he joined the Group from a previous acquisition in his native country, suggesting that CKG is interested in building its talent from its acquired businesses not just from out of Hong Kong.

By contrast the acquisition of ABN AMRO by RBS and its consortium partners was a far more complicated affair. Essentially, it was a company break-up with different assets going to one of the three consortium banks, each driven by the synergies it foresaw by combining with its own existing operations. Occurring as it did through the credit crisis and subsequent meltdown of the financial services sector, the complexity was accentuated by the need for subsequent iterations of the original plan. In layman's terms, the original deal was that the Spanish bank Santander would combine the operations in Italy and Brazil of ABN AMRO (helpfully separate legal entities) with that of its own, and then exit the consortium at pace. In essence, that is what it did, albeit that it subsequently sold off the Italian operation to an Italian competitor at a good return to shareholders. Fortis, a largely Belgian/Dutch centred bank with considerable asset management and insurance operations, was interested in the core ABN AMRO Dutch and Belgian retail operations as well as the international private client business. This scale acquisition would allow Fortis to combine significant retail operations in both Belgium and the Netherlands and drive synergies through back office consolidations. Unfortunately, the scale of the financial crisis saw Fortis split between Belgian and Dutch state ownership, with the Belgians subsequently selling to BNP Paribas and the Dutch continuing to combine with the ABN AMRO operations in the Netherlands, but retaining the ABN AMRO brand.

For RBS, the aim was globalization. It had long tracked ABN AMRO as a possible target, as it offered RBS a much greater client base across many more geographies in which to do business. It had been interested in the US retail bank that ABN AMRO owned (la Salle) but that had been sold under its nose to Bank of America. With a reputation for extracting value from clients, but limited international capabilities, this provided RBS with a strategic opportunity to combine the Dutch company's global clients and market operations with its own largely fixed-income/balance sheet lending led activities. It also acquired a Global Transaction Services operation that supported the payment needs of many multi-national organizations and a Retail and Commercial business in a number of European and Asian countries. Moreover, ABN AMRO's huge number of international client relationships and unhealthy efficiency ratio suggested high cost and revenue synergies would be achievable from the deal. However, RBS was fully aware that some parts of the company were more attractive than other parts.

This deal was different to previous ones for RBS. This was because of the three companies buying one, and the effect that the acquired company had on the actions of the acquirers because of the powers of the regulator. Nonetheless, from the RBS investment banking perspective, whilst it revised its values slightly to bring in a more international component, it was, in the main, an imposition of the RBS culture. In a wider context, the RBS thinking on acquisitions was 'why have two of something when you can have one'. In the ABN AMRO case this was compounded by its tendency towards decentralization. So RBS pushed for single approaches where ABN AMRO would never have done. For example, RBS implemented a single performance management system across RBS Global Banking and Markets (incorporating ABN GBM acquired businesses) globally, simplifying systems significantly.

The two examples illustrate the complexity of these sorts of deals, especially if there are multiple partners. It reminds us that simple dichotomies of business aims can inadequately describe real life situations. Thus in any one arrangement there may be elements of collaboration, imposition and disposal, and the actors drawn from a wide range of places – organizationally and geographically.

Nevertheless, the drivers behind the different types of model naturally include the business reasoning behind the deal – what is the purpose of the merger or acquisition? This relates to the success criteria set for the arrangement. Is it primarily to take cost out, remove a competitor, obtain economies of scale, acquire expertise or knowledge of a market, etc.? The implementation method should also stem from the objectives, though this does not always follow, with unfortunate consequences. Table 2.2 sets out the preferred alignment.

Table 2.2   Success criteria for mergers and acquisitions

	Imposition	Collaboration
Business drivers	Acquisition of visible assets (physical plant) Take out competitor Channel control	Acquisition of invisible assets (brand, market position, human capital) Extend geographic reach Enter new market Build scale
Due diligence focus	Financial position Asset valuation Market share	Financial position Market positioning Quality and nature of human resources
Implementation	Swift and radical	Intensive communication and reassurance to staff Symbolic gestures of collaboration Talent retention
Success criteria	Financial savings made and other commercial goals met	Financial aims and other commercial goals met Best practice choices made from either party Retention of key skills

JOINT VENTURES

Many of the business drivers for merger or acquisition could also apply to joint ventures; although in the context of this book, the one which has had most recent coverage is where the JV is used for entrance into new markets. This has been particularly prevalent in the last 10 years as 'western' companies expand into the emergent economies where growth offers significant business opportunity. A number of well-known brands have exploited the fantastic rapid economic growth of China, India, and to a lesser degree Brazil and Russia, by partnering with local firms.

Partnering with other firms can be done for a number of reasons:

- **Regulation** – access to regulated markets that existing rules do not allow. RBS did this when it acquired a 4.9 per cent stake in the Bank of China in 2005 as foreign banks were (and still are) limited to a maximum stake in Chinese banking and other financial services activities.
- **Market knowledge** – whilst western manufacturers know their product inside-out, they may not know their new market. An oft-quoted example of this is when a famous German car manufacturer was concerned over limited sales of its mid range executive cars and wondered why the bigger Audi A6 was selling well. Lack of understanding of the market had meant it had not realized that the well-heeled Chinese would not buy their car because it was not large enough to be chauffeured in!
- **Financial risk management** – going into partnership can limit the impact on any individual firm's own balance sheet by spreading the financial risk of failure. A long-established practice in financial firms, where loan partnership helps minimize risk, such collaboration is common to many very large infrastructure projects and public spending.

- **Access to skills** – often used in vertical integration of supply chain, but where limited capital does not facilitate outright acquisition, JV's or partnerships are utilized to maximize the skill-set of different companies or indeed countries.
- **Leveraging scale** – many of the business process outsourcing (BPO) deals of the early 2000s were conducted as partnerships to help the BPO firm utilize one large firm's scale to establish a presence on which it could leverage further scale. Certainly this was the early rationale of the Exult (now subsumed under the AON Hewitt group) outsourcing deal with BP.
- **Dealing with public authorities** – in some countries government bodies have to support organizational activities or they will not be able to operate. This may make a JV an absolute necessity. Yet benefits also flow afterwards when the home organization is able to facilitate government decision making, speeding up processes and ensuring the right result, be it land purchase, health and safety clearance, permits to operate, etc.

The specific challenges with partnerships, over and above those generic issues already described in the M&A section, are in some ways harder to overcome than in a full combination of two organizations. The JV can end up being neither fish nor foul. There is a requirement for a degree of mutuality to secure joint objectives, but also inevitable fissiparous tendencies that relate to dissimilar and separate goals that pull the partnership apart. Due to the added cross-cultural dimension, these differences are often accentuated in JVs operating in a global context. They make it harder to overcome the inherent challenges that exist in any partnership, including marriage!

- **Replication** – there are many quoted examples of local companies setting up JVs with a global partner, learning its skills, copying its product designs, building another factory and then leaving the partnership before the global firm has monetized its investment. As these arrangements are often conducted some distance from the HQ of the global firm, it is difficult for the latter to realize what is happening. The lack of real on-the-ground presence can further hinder monitoring the situation, inhibit communication and fuel the inherent distrust likely between the parties.
- **Margin squeeze** – can occur in a number of forms, be it one partner expects an ever-increasing share of the wallet in relation to its perceived input value. This can relate to supplier price margins where the partnership is integrated across the supply chain. Supermarkets have a bad reputation for this (with active debate on whether it is deserved). One source of difficulty is different views on the need for investment in people. One party may simply want to maximize short-term earnings and is not interested in spending on learning and development, building skills or sophisticated talent management approaches – characteristics often attributed to private equity companies. The other party may see the future prospects being affected by the risk of damage to staff retention and motivation.
- **Personalities** – as with M&A, who gets the top jobs can be a bone of contention, but it plays out in a different way in a JV. Both want the CEO and/or CFO positions to underpin operational control, regardless of who has the better skills. Indeed in our own experience, the COO or CHRO can often be makeweight jobs offered to partners as a sop to the one not getting the CEO/CFO.

- **Culture** – as with the full combination of firms in M&A, a JV can also fall foul of cultural barriers. Whilst technically both an M&A and a JV (as ABN AMRO was separated over time into its constituent parts in line with regulatory approval for the acquisition by the DNB), the consortium approach to the purchase of ABN AMRO highlighted very different cultural issues across the Dutch, Belgian, Spanish and Scottish banks involved.

MARKET EXTENSION/GLOBALIZATION

Whilst it can be achieved through either M&A or JV, market extension in the global context can also be achieved within the existing operating model of some organizations. Having established that a firm has the competence to exploit market opportunities without acquisition or partnership, there should be only a limited number of issues to overcome.

Establishing an in-market presence can be restricted to just a fly-drive sales presence or taken to a fully operational manufacturing, distribution and sales capability. This choice will be largely determined by the financial business plan and availability of resources in all its forms. If the market opportunity is large, such as Du Pont launching a new market-changing product, then the long-term market dynamics should warrant an investment in in-market plant and machinery and resources. The balance between expatriate and local resourcing is both a question of cost and expertise, relating to the complexity of the task and location, and the nature of indigenous talent pool.

DISPOSALS

Another area of significant change for any organization is retrenchment, product line closure or disposal of part or whole portfolios of assets. Exiting whole countries can also have a significant impact on the organization. RBS offers a good example of all of the various examples of disposal, as it has done this with loan portfolios, countries, brands, business lines and combinations thereof. Other firms (especially in the finance sector) are also disposing of bits of their empires; either because regulatory powers have dictated a strategic retrenchment back to core markets; or because damaged balance sheets have demanded repair as the cost of capital increases markedly.

Clearly in these situations there will be staff redundancies with the obvious personal implications and inevitable public relations consequences. This is easier to manage if there is complete withdrawal from the country (though bad publicity travels far and fast where the exit has been badly handled), but the most difficult issue is when there is a partial national/regional disposal. Naturally, it can be hard to insulate the affected area, though clearly this depends on whether it is a line of business going or a section of it. There is a particular challenge in these circumstances of ensuring that the strategic imperative of the change is thoroughly understood. For example, following its ABN AMRO acquisition, RBS has had to repeatedly communicate its commitment to the Asia Pacific region because external commentators kept referencing that RBS was exiting the region and not, as was the case, just the retail and commercial activities obtained from ABN AMRO.

SHARED SERVICES/OFFSHORING

Whilst we look at this matter in the context of the HR function itself later in the book, the emergence of BPO/shared services and offshoring/rightshoring or even nearshoring in the last 10 years has been significant. Without question, the prime rationale in many business cases is that the wage arbitrage has been very attractive such that work that can be done in 'developing' countries at a fraction of the cost in the more developed labour markets of the USA, UK and western Europe. The use of low-cost centres (such as utility company helpdesks) has become a well-debated feature of the twenty-first century.

The implications within the global context are significant:

- **Demographic shift** – skill shortages or work that falls below what many are interested in undertaking in western society, has meant that the workforce and education needs of all affected societies are changing. Allied to migrant worker issues in developed countries, the traditional labour market workforce is changing, affected by both economic and political conditions (e.g. conflict in North Africa and the Middle East has displaced large numbers of people, nationals and migrant workers alike).
- **Wealth creation/movement** – large offshoring deals have led to revenue generation in emergent economies that adds to the vast currency reserves being built up by cheap exports of products. Not only do we see the shift of work, we also see the shift of wealth. Given the financial crisis, the impact of that wealth shift is being challenged as unemployment rates spiral in the same economies which three years ago could support a higher employment cost. With companies having to make cuts to budgets in order to support higher finance charges and with revenues flat or declining, the effects of these tendencies are accentuated.
- **Service quality impact on client satisfaction** – a feature of many early deals, the difference in the quality of service from the original local service provision was very marked and drew strong criticism from consumers. However, as consumers have tightened their belts, the quality of service provision balance with cost has come into sharper focus. Especially with many customers now prepared to use the internet where they would not before, offshore service provision and support is increasingly becoming web based, thereby changing again the economics of business.

There is further coverage of the HR issues in Chapter 8.

HR's Role in Business Change

The context for business change now established, it is pertinent for us to focus on HR's role within that change process and indeed learn from organizations how business change can be embedded and highlight any specific issues that are relevant in the global context.

For us, the possible HR contribution can apply to the business change initiative itself, and/or the implementation of that decision and especially the deployment of HR's technical skills and tools to support business change.

So the HR function can be:

- involved early or late in the process
- party to the key organizational decisions or just to implement them
- making a strategic or tactical impact
- asserting the importance of people and culture or accepting the value accorded to employees given by other leaders/managers
- contributing to broad business issues or be restricted to HR issues.

We would contend that traditionally HR has been asked to do the implementation, but not necessarily become engaged in the strategic thinking or focus on the original 'why' business decision. Too often HR has been told to 'go hire the new India head of a new business operation', but has not been involved in deciding why that is the right solution and indeed how the overall business change is to be managed.

Our interviews have confirmed that the role of HR in the change process varies significantly, depending on the model of the HR function, i.e. whether HR operates in true partnership with the business or in the role of more traditional 'personnel managers' downstream of the main decisions. Research supports this impression (Antila and Kakkonen, 2008).

What is interesting from the Antila and Kakkonen work is that what determines HR's role in M&A above all else is HR's capability and attitude. The required knowledge and skills are both interpersonal and business. HR people need to know their organization's business inside out and be able to influence their colleagues to include them in the necessary decision making and to accept that people management challenges have to be addressed. Having positional authority helps, but the advantage of a formal role still has to be exploited in practice. Management is often overly focused on financial issues and may well neglect the role people and culture play in change success.

Consistent with a theme running through this book, where managers have little respect for HR they will be reluctant to include them in the key discussions. Their role can be usurped by general business consultants, who may give little attention to people management and to the HR function itself, or replaced by specialist HR consultants, thereby also marginalizing the internal HR team. Conversely, if HR is able to assert its value in the change process it will be listened to. So HR can get into a vicious cycle of declining impact or a virtuous one of having a demonstrable effect.

So what can HR managers do to get on the front foot in M&A and similar business change? Clearly, the task of HR will be greater in deals that emphasize collaboration between the parties rather than the imposition of the buyer's business model. Nonetheless, there are a number of things HR can do to obtain a proper role:

- Hire staff into HR with change, and specifically M&A, experience and build that capability internally too.
- Concentrate these skills, probably in a centre of expertise. This is especially important in a global firm because the capability will have to be deployed, possibly in support of business partners, where an acquisition relates to just one segment of the organization, in settings – business unit and location – where HR has to traditionally been excluded from such strategic activity.
- Improve the HR team's understanding of the business issues, where it makes a profit, where its costs lie, where is its competitive advantage, what is its future business strategy (organic growth or through acquisition).

- Build trust in its competence in the eyes of M&A specialists but also of organizational leaders. This can be achieved by consistently good quality performance in a range of areas, but also through networking to build relationships with the key players.
- Point out the evidence of the benefits of HR contribution to deal-making success. For example, Kings College London found that the strategic involvement of HR in mergers and acquisitions led to better absorption of knowledge and innovative practices and expertise (Edwards et al., 2008).
- Push for inclusion in the M&A project team that is evaluating a possible move, ensure that the HR function is represented (and by people with the necessary knowledge, skills and experience in M&A work).
- Emphasize HR's cross-organizational role in using its broad perspective to integrate activities for the greater good.
- Attend to the key HR issues. These might include:
  - harmonizing terms and conditions between the parties
  - consulting/negotiating with trade union or other employee representatives
  - completing all the necessary legal employment processes
  - settling on the most appropriate HR service delivery model
  - tackling systems and process integration.
- But also get involved in every stage of an M&A exercise as they all have a strong people and culture component, including selection of senior executives and the structural design of the new organization. Do not be restricted to the 'HR issues' listed above.

RBS is an example of where the HR Business Partner model is fully employed. Through numerous acquisitions over the period 2000–2008, including NatWest, Charter One, Citizens and First Active, senior HR staff have been involved at the earliest strategic discussions. A 'virtual' 'Business Acquisitions and Disposals Services' (BADs) team of 20–25 senior representatives from the business and across all functions would become insiders to the transaction to quickly establish the business rationale which shaped the acquisition approach. Having such a team reflected the number of difficult deals RBS had successfully concluded, the central role HR was expected to play and any future ambitions it had to meet. These skills are now being applied in reverse to meet RBS's disposal and business transformation requirements. Indeed, Elaine Arden, recently appointed Group HR Director for RBS, believes that the skills learned in numerous acquisitions have been successfully applied in subsequent business changes in the firm, not least the rigour of process, and increased the ability to leverage this to have a rightful seat at the business leadership table.

- Develop a set of tools that can be deployed quickly in the due diligence phase of an M&A – described below under 'Success Factors'.
- Learn from one's mistakes: it is hard to get it right first time and every time. (Wider organizational learning requirements will be described under 'Success Factors'.)

Challenges

GENERAL

Roberts (2006) set out why change often fails in organizations. It is because of:

- not identifying the problem correctly
- adopting an inappropriate change mechanism
- not identifying cultural implications
- underestimating time and effort to change beliefs and values
- not developing a genuine shared vision
- not establishing critical success factors
- not considering impact on the whole organization
- not identifying the human factors.

Most of these challenges are relevant to global mergers and acquisitions and JVs, especially where a collaborative approach is applied, because it points not only to the importance of the people and cultural aspects, but it also emphasizes the holistic nature of change, which, unless a loose coupling of organizations is the aim, is a vital perspective to organizational integration.

COLLABORATIVE CHANGE

In discussing the challenges of mergers and acquisitions it is worth bearing in mind the business drivers. We will tend to emphasize the challenges more in collaborative JVs/ mergers and acquisitions since there are fewer risks with the imposition model because, even if things go wrong in the people domain, they will have less effect on the business outcomes.

Business driven

- **Misunderstanding of the acquired company's business model** Some organizations rush into change without properly understanding how the other party makes its money or services customers. They may not realize how internal processes are linked together. The law of unintended consequences then applies. For example, an IT outsourcing company bought another company for its offshore capability but did not realize its own client base needed on-site help and would not countenance support coming from a distance.

Wal-Mart's German acquisition was not a happy experience. The company made a number of errors. The first one was to buy two businesses, Wertkauf and Interspar, for $1.6 billion, one of which (Interspar) was not doing well. Wal-Mart then compounded this initial error in several ways that reflected its ignorance of the German business and retail culture. For example, it decided to build a new German HQ and in a fair and rational manner it decided this should be sited at neither of the existing HQs. The problem was that key staff, especially buyers, would not relocate to the new location. Wal-Mart had not taken account of the immobility of even professional staff. It then found bringing in talent difficult because the company did not have a trusted brand and its actions in closing the HQs of the acquired businesses led to further suspicion of this American interloper.

To cover the staffing gaps and to deal with the underlying Interspar business problems, Wal-Mart then sent in some 100 American expatriates. This, if anything, made the situation worse rather than better. They spoke no German and did not understand German culture. For example, their concept of service did not accord with the German, especially the distinctive American greeting of customers: it was a switch off to local customers, not a switch on.

Wal-Mart poured money into the German operation. As its first European acquisition it felt it must succeed to protect its reputation and act responsibility with respect to those staff that had stood by the company.

Eventually though it found an elegant exit in selling the business to the Metro Group at a reasonable price.

- **Not recognizing the scale of the challenge** A collaborative approach is harder work than imposed one, especially in people terms. Business managers do not always understand this and do not acknowledge the time and resources needed to make it work. As Juergen Lahr, Vice President HR Governance BASF Group, rightly put it, a true merger is 'like onboarding a whole organization'. What you might do singly or in small groups you do in one massive hit.
- **Short-termism** In a rush to achieve immediate, usually financial, benefits the organization inhibits its longer-term prospects. Whilst elsewhere we argue that speed in the early stages of an acquisition is key to longer-term success, this must not be at the expense of taking people with you on the journey and certainly there should be no attitude of the need for speed for speed's sake. So, an acquisition that was intended to be based on collaboration ends up like imposition because of the impatience of the acquirer. You make the numbers but you are not carrying your workforce with you, and this will be evident further down the line. This is often a reflection that hard measures of success are more visible than softer, people related ones.
- **Thinking this is just another deal** There is a risk that you assume once you have done one merger or acquisition that they are all the same. Whilst some organizations are quoted as perfecting their acquisition model, there is a danger that a one-size-fits-all approach starts to appear. This can lead to a number of inappropriate or, worse, irresponsible actions. Although the use of good, documented processes is necessary they should not to be applied without thought and understanding in the context of the deal. An approach used to acquire a bigger competitor may not be the right approach to utilize when acquiring an 'infill' business of a few hundred staff.

Cultural and institutional

Not surprisingly in transnational mergers and acquisitions, particularly where the aim is to integrate two organizations' business activities, the parties may suffer from:

- **Ignorance of the environment** Organizations do not always seek to find out what is possible, not possible legally or within the mores of the organizations concerned. For example, one company we heard about built its labour supply assumptions on importing people from India without understanding the UK immigration rules.
- **Crass or careless mistakes** that send negative signals to the workforce caused by insensitivity to internal needs. At one organization we know the error was removing the national flag of the company acquired and replacing it, not with the company's own, but of the country of the acquiring company.
- **Insensitivity to local external requirements** If, for example, the acquirer does not invest sufficient time and energy preparing the ground with political representatives or the media, negative publicity may well result that can be brand damaging. This is one reading of the Kraft takeover of Cadburys, where already negative perceptions of the deal were compounded by the absence of the Kraft CEO from discussions with local MPs and trade union representatives.
- **Different world views** Perceptions of presenting problems, and the appropriate solution to them, may differ and stem from competing views of business management. This might relate to different standards in health and safety, attitudes to employee engagement, convictions regarding consultation and dealing with trade unions. These issues have been reported in working with Chinese companies, for example, especially where there has been a division of labour between the partners in management tasks (Allouche et al., 2008).

BP certainly felt the effects of the acquisition of Amoco's manufacturing activities in the USA when the Texas City refinery explosion occurred. It could be argued that the two companies had different attitudes to risk or to the management of safety.

- **Inability to deal with major obstacles**, even when identified as such. This may stem from having very different traditions of decision making and management styles – slow and consensual versus fast and top down – producing misunderstanding and acrimony between the parties.
- **Failure to learn from others** Companies often impose change based on a notion that their way of doing things is best practice, without stopping to see firstly whether the acquisition has better processes. Research suggests (Edwards et al., 2008) that many organizations often do not learn from the acquired business, especially from organizations located in developing countries.
- **A failure of the two entities to cohere culturally** This is obviously more of a risk in collaborative arrangements where building a common culture is a key objective. This may be because of a simplistic approach to cultural change, as alleged in the Daimler-Chrysler case below, or through ignorance of the underlying employment deal in two organizations. As Valerie Garrow said at an Institute for Employment Studies conference: 'You cannot TUPE across the psychological contract.'

The Daimler-Chrysler deal did not succeed partly because of a failure to recognize cultural differences between the two companies, which is odd given that prima facie there were obvious differences in their backgrounds. The problem was that, according to Schuler and Jackson (2001), 'DaimlerChrysler believed two company cultures could simply be put in a blender and poured out as a new synergistic company.' There was some public acknowledgement of potential cultural issues, but no attempt to tackle them. The foundation of mutual respect seemed to be missing, even accepting that there were isolated instances of synergistic actions. The operational decisions that were subsequently made suggested there was little faith in the merger at executive level.

- or due to ignorance of important local context, as is claimed regarding Barclays acquisition of Absa.

According to Dennis Farrell, once General Manager People Management Shared Services at Absa (the South African bank), which was bought by Barclays, the British headquartered bank did not fully understand the impact black economic empowerment had on Absa operations. From his perspective, Barclays did not really recognize that it was Africa they were dealing with – their mental model was too European. There was insufficient realization of the complexity and multiplicity of the cultures within South Africa or of its history. Had the company a better appreciation of the country, Farrell believes there would have been more acknowledgment that the country is quite adaptable.

People related

There are set of more people related challenges that are more acute in a partnership approach but can sometimes be relevant when one business approach is imposed:

- **Perceived or actual favouritism** towards one of the parties in staffing the new organization. If one organization disproportionately provides the resources and casualties are more found in the other organization, naturally this will cause resentment. This will not be as bad if demonstrably the 'best' people have been chosen, i.e. the meritocratic selection process has worked rather than it was biased. In global mergers this is an especially tricky question because conducting a meritocratic process against defined criteria may be seen as the right western way to do this but may not be seen as right in other societies where familial ties, face and other considerations are at work.
- **Multiple cuts** Those who did the deal did not get their sums right or the business environment changes, but either way the expected rationalization is insufficient. We know that employees do not like change through salami slicing. It is bad enough to see job cuts as a result of a merger or acquisition; it is worse still if these are protracted or repeated. In a global context, the twist comes if the chopper falls on particular

countries in the second round of cutting thereby endangering both internal and external support for the deal.

- **Loss of talent** This may occur before, during and after the merger or acquisition. This is a dangerous development in all circumstances, but especially where the takeover was driven by the desire to acquire knowledge, skills and experience. The resignations of employees perhaps signal their disapproval of the acquirer (exemplified if they leave before the acquisition is complete); they do not like the way the new owner goes about their business (resignations start happening during and after the takeover); they do not get the jobs they expect – someone else has got the job or the role design does not suit (this problem is likely to emerge at a critical point in the transition to the new owners); or they are doubtful about their future prospects (something that emerges over time). These challenges do not necessarily happen more in cross-border deals, but they can have additional dimensions. The sort of antipathy born out of history, past experience or myth that will be described in Chapter 3 affects perceptions. So negative feelings are likely to be greater if it is seen as a neo-colonial takeover, as evidenced by the fact that the jobs go to the foreign company.

- **Uninterested but still in post** People may not leave the organization but are not engaged either. They have what is known as 'structural commitment' to the organization: they stay, without enthusiasm, because there is no other suitable employment. This problem can be turned around if the merger or acquisition is seen as a success. If this collective state of mind persists then its consequences will be revealed in poorer customer service (e.g. agreeing with the customer that the organization is not what it was), quality (can't be bothered to get it right) or productivity (why should I push myself for this lot?).

- **Demotivated survivors** Even those who would normally be positively disposed to the new situation may find themselves demotivated. This can arise through the so-called 'survivor syndrome'. When headcount is reduced, the 'survivors' may experience grief and uncertainty, along with increased workloads; morale and organizational commitment may fall and absenteeism increase, with a consequential drop in productivity, distrust of management actions and a tendency to avoid risks. Loss of their old ways of doing things from their previous organization may make individuals nostalgic for the past and resistant to change. Where decisions are made without much employee participation or even decent communication, stress levels may rise leaving employees even less productive.

  Managers are left to manage a disengaged team and a fractured one if the 'survivors' predominantly come from one of the companies. Research amongst senior US managers showed that some 70 per cent who remained in downsized firms reported that morale and trust declined (cited in Ulrich et al., 2009a). Also after downsizing in a major Australian bank, some 49 per cent of 'survivors' felt a decreased sense of commitment to the organization, 64 per cent experienced decreased job satisfaction, and 83 per cent reported increased stress (Ulrich et al., 2009a).

- **Outright sabotage** Whilst some employees may rebalance their commitment to the organization, a small number may seek outright revenge. This is most likely to be a risk at the beginning of an acquisition when feelings are running particularly high. Though most organizations would guard against the possibility, it should be noted that in some societies the chance of this happening is greater, and, moreover, you cannot necessarily rely on the authorities to prevent it.

- **Knowledge depletion** This can come in a number of forms. The combination of a loss of talent, a disengaged workforce and sabotage may mean that knowledge retention and transfer is severely handicapped. Some acquirers favour the decapitation method – to remove the acquired organization's leadership team at a stroke. If your organization bought another one precisely for its wealth of expertise you may well be 'killing the goose that laid the golden egg', as one interviewee so graphically put it and this might apply to the leadership as much as any specialist skills.
- **Saying one thing whilst doing another** happens when statements about how the new organization will be run that are not realized in practice. This may be deliberate on management's part, speaking with forked tongue to persuade acquired staff on to your side without any intention of living up to your promises. This is a dangerous game as it will produce a later reaction when staff realize you have been acting in bad faith. More likely, the dissonance between word and deed is inadvertent. You meant it when you said that both parties will learn from each other, but you had not thought through this statement. You might have meant that your organization will take methods, policies, etc. from the acquired business if they are superior to your own. In reality that would not happen much, since you believe your organization is superior to the other – hence the takeover!
- **Unskilled leadership** The deal may be in the hands of those not well skilled to handle the challenges. Selected perhaps in another context, these leaders may not have the necessary vision, drive or interpersonal skills to make a successful merger or acquisition. These deficiencies can be compounded if there is squabbling for seats at the top table. Deals have never got going or have taken much longer to consummate than they should (including, allegedly, the Glaxo Wellcome and Smith Kline Beecham merger) or they fall apart because of personality clashes. As we have seen, the consequences can be severe if the leadership is not effective.
- **Underestimating the degree of antipathy between the parties** This may derive from personal enmity at the top of the organization or be the result of a history of competitive rivalry. These obstacles can be overcome but need time and effort devoted to them. Resources to do this need to be factored in to the work programme.
- **Unled line** This can translate into impotence for the managers on the ground if the corporate leadership is not giving a clear steer on the direction of travel. This is especially true where decisions on organizational structure are protracted and the new appointments are slow to be made. In these circumstances, expatriates representing the home company as technical experts may have referred, not positional, authority. This may be sufficient to support progress but increases the complexity of their task, especially as management might not be their strong suit.
- **Ignorance not bliss** Leadership failure can also result in poor staff communications, leaving employees uncertain about what to expect next. This increases anxiety levels, causes some staff to jump before being pushed and can lead to widespread loss of productivity if employees are distracted by the change. In the extended lines of communication in global firms, this challenge is all the more likely, especially if account has not been taken of how messages are received in different countries and that in any case those feeling stressed may not hear the communication correctly – engendering an unduly negative or complacent reaction.

IMPOSED CHANGE

Even if imposed change through a hostile takeover has fewer risks, especially where the acquisition is less concerned with obtaining human capital than meeting other goals, there are still issues to be faced that may emerge from a changing business or economic environment, as the RBS case illustrates. These may occur irrespective of how well technically the change has been managed.

The acquisition of ABN AMRO by a consortium led by RBS in 2008 has been widely described as 'the wrong deal at the wrong time'. However, the acquisition and integration process, from an internal RBS perspective, was a prime example of how to take a proven acquisition model and successfully flex it such that it applied to the unique acquisition structure and unparalleled market and regulatory challenges.

This was a complicated deal: three banks buying a fourth. Ultimately ABN AMRO would disappear and RBS had to recognize that this was an emotional cultural issue for people, exacerbated by the fact that it was being carved up by a foreign consortium with all those cultural overtones. Also inevitably the attitude of the partners (and even divisional teams within the partners) differed on whether they were acquiring parts of ABN AMRO to absorb them or dispose of them. These different perspectives affected the different forms of engagement and attitudes to the pace of change.

For RBS, though it was largely an imposition of its culture and business model, it still had to worry about how it was achieving the imposition. It had to spend the time understanding what it was integrating into the RBS business so it would recognise what it had to change.

Again as it played out, RBS had to raise funds twice in the market and subsequently became largely state-owned due to capital and funding concerns as the crisis hit. It has since sold much of the overseas retail and commercial operations acquired in the ABN AMRO deal and had to reduce significantly its investment banking operations in activities no longer suitable for the balance sheet it could fund. The strategic plan to return the company to financial health has led to retrenchment into core bank activities, resulting in a number of disposals and write offs of unwanted assets.

Another illustration is a perspective of someone on the receiving end of an international acquisition.

We talked to Dennis Farrell about his feelings on the purchase and the impact it had on the HR model he had helped to create. From his perspective, Barclays inherited an award winning and successful HR department. Before the takeover it was conventionally organized with a central contact and service centre, together with a 'design and development group' that had expertise in OD, employment equity, learning and development, 'employee wellness' and other specialist areas, supported by delivery staff organized along similar functional lines who operated from five people management centres across the country, implementing strategy or helping line managers in difficult disciplinary cases. 'Account Executives' acted like HR business partners who were assigned to Strategic Business Units to deliver strategic advice.

During 2000–2003 Barclays had also reorganized by centralizing a good chunk of HR, achieving by 2004 a 44 per cent reduction in headcount and a near doubling of the HR/employee ratio to stand at 1:95. It created the standard three-legged stool model of shared services (based at Poole), centres of expertise and business partners aligned to Strategic Business Units and Group Functions. However, the bank has long had a federated structure with a tradition of the individual businesses, like Barclaycard, Barclay Capital, Wealth and the Commercial Bank, as well as a UK Retail operation, operating autonomously. The centralized approach therefore proved not to be wholly successful. In particular, it was felt that the corporate centres of expertise were too remote, lacking the specific business unit knowledge needed to be effective. For example, there were concerns over the treatment of reward by the centres of expertise. The company decided as a result to segment its expertise by business unit.

It was against this background that, when Barclays acquired Absa in 2005, it reviewed the South African company's HR service delivery model.

When Barclays conducted its due diligence exercise its representatives showed little to limited interest in people, culture or value creation, according to Denis Farrell. They were only interested in numbers and redundancy opportunities – i.e. bottom line cost reductions. From their perspective it was a purely commercial transaction.

To begin with Barclays left the Absa's HR approach untouched and indeed there was consideration of Absa's remit extending to cover operating units in the rest of Absa and Barclays' African operations to gain economies of scale. It then toyed with the idea of offshoring HR administration to India but did not go through with the move.

In the end, however, the Absa model was dismantled. Retained at the corporate centre was a small HR team to give policy direction and own HR processes. Transferred to Group Operations was a centralized payroll for South Africa, a responsibility for management information and a contact centre. Administration was transferred back to the 44 business units, as was operational HR (i.e. the activities done by the design and development group). Not surprisingly costs have risen, along with inconsistencies in policy application. According to Farrell the service quality has also slipped.

In the context of this book, it seems an unusual decision to move away from the financial benefits consolidation and standardization brought to Absa. It also is interesting that Barclays eschewed the opportunity to create a regional HR hub for Africa. Having taken apart the service delivery model, Absa has in many ways then been left to handle HR in its own way because of a belated recognition that South Africa has a distinct set of challenges created in part by its labour laws and economic and social environment. So there is little sense of a Barclays' imprint, beyond imposing its view on the preferred service delivery model.

Success Factors

CLARITY OF PURPOSE

As all good change management texts (like John Kotter's *Leading Change*) tell you, the first place to start is being clear as to what the business rationale is for the change.

Our research supports the argument that good learning for organizations has to be based on understanding and applying the change strategy. If the aim is to work together to build on each other's strengths (a collaborative strategy), the approach will be very different from situations where one business or people management model is driven by the stronger party (the imposed strategy). Similarly, if integration is sought the change model is different from only facilitating a 'loose coupling'. In the success factors listed below we will emphasize the collaborative approach that could apply in a true merger, a collaboratively driven acquisition or in a JV. Some aspects will be applicable to an imposed takeover, like well-structured and implemented processes, but the people and cultural challenges are less important to overall success.

Especially when approaching mergers and acquisitions (more than in a JV which can be more temporary in its impact), organizations should consider the clarity of the vision in the context of a large, whole-systems change that is pervasive and deep in its effects. This means attention needs to be given not just to strategic clarity, but also to all the key success determinants; not just to structure, processes and systems, which often receive the most attention, but also to people and culture.

A STRUCTURED APPROACH

Whilst generic to any business change, domestic or international, local or global, the need for a structured approach is invaluable to ensuring the necessary rigour of change management is applied consistently. This means defined plans, clear ownership of each deliverable, a good feel for how the various functional issues connect and, most of all, an aligned team of senior managers committed to the cause. Moreover, a good HR function is the one that acts as a mirror to the leaders of the firm, often looking beyond their own functional deliverables, to ensure that all these ingredients are evident and joined together.

Mergers and acquisitions

If we look at the structured approach applied to an M&A transaction; there are five key stages to a deal.

1. **Strategic exploration**: before a bid is contemplated, the company looks to see whether a merger or acquisition would meet business objectives, and, if so, what might be the right sort of organization to target. Thus, at this stage, the organization should be clear as to its strategic intent, e.g. growth, market expansion, niche consolidation, and this should define the merger/acquisition target and what is sought from the bid, what synergies to look for in terms of scale, geography, markets, etc. A kind of competitive landscape map is also needed, so that if a market move is made, your strategy people can plot how competitors may respond and this will further refine

the approach to the deal.

2. **Pre-bid**: at this point a specific target company is in mind for an acquisition. It is a highly confidential stage because, for quoted companies, it is often market sensitive. This stage of the process tries to ask the simple question of why such a transaction would make sense. Largely a financial exercise (or at least perceived as such by those who lead such deals), running the rule over another organization and how the combination may make for a better company is the prime purpose of this phase. At this point, the organization should be modelling likely synergies and potential risks. If any access to the target company is permitted, it will be extremely limited in scope.

3. **Bid-to-close**: depending on the deal (and described earlier in the chapter), this phase is where much preparation should be conducted as well as verifying and honing assumptions made in the pre-bid phase. In the authors' own experience this phase is where the preparation of plans for 0–30 days, 30–100 days and then through the life of any subsequent integration, can be best planned. It is where HR should be particularly active but is often not involved.

4. **Close–30 days**: this is where the success of the transaction is cast. How the acquirer interacts with the acquired in those first 30 days, and how much speed can be injected into the process to get the key decisions made (that were not already agreed before close), are the key ingredients to setting the right tone for the deal. Important tasks here are to add detail to knowledge gained before acquisition, make senior appointments, assess culture fit, hold leadership and scene setting meetings to communicate sense of direction, set rules of the road and make any necessary changes to governance protocols including authority levels for sign-offs.

5. **30–100 days**: depending on the transaction, the need for quick execution on many aspects of a change is well documented. Lethargy can kill any deal synergies, as individuals often just want to get past the change and into the brave new world, even if that is not with the existing employer. Prevarication over decisions and the uncertainty it fosters in staff morale destroy shareholder value as staff are distracted from managing clients, generating revenues and managing the returns to shareholders. Lower-level management appointments are made at this point, as well as actions taken to retain key personnel either through the change or beyond.

In the case of the RBS acquisition of ABN AMRO (with its partners), the rigour described above was essential to try and manage the complexity down to a number of definable actions/ activities across many locations with clear action parties and measurable goals. Important in achieving this ambition was establishing, in the earliest stages of the deal, a series of Project Management Offices, linked by a global executive steering committee to ensure:

- effective information sharing and optimal communication across the teams
- application of consistent methodology
- documentation completed to consistent standards
- fulfilment of quality gates/checks at key stages per transaction.

In the pre-bid stage, given the deal was essentially hostile, this meant little access to the target. Functional workstreams, led by one of the acquiring banks, were created both at the macro level and the micro level that were carried through the entire lifetime of the subsequent programme of separation/integration. For example, RBS was asked to lead the three banks' approach to HR issues, reporting back to an overall steering committee that transcended the deal both in organizational and country reach. Similarly, within the HR workstream, sub-theme groups headed by one of the acquiring banks were established. Fortis led the staff consultation theme, recognizing its deeper experience in northern European social partner issues. RBS led the compensation issues, driven largely by the fact that it would inherit the lion's share of such issues in the subsequent integration. Santander did not lead on any of the themes, given the very distinct difference of its participation in the business asset carve up and in the full knowledge that it would leave the consortium long before the other two partners.

The eight key people themes addressed by the consortium (and subsequently adopted by ABN AMRO) were:

1.   staffing (headcount implications)
2.   compensation and retention
3.   social partner consultation (essential given the various banks' presence in many European countries)
4.   communication and engagement
5.   organizational design/leadership
6.   reduction and redeployment (a key and sensitive issue in Netherlands and Belgium given the combination of Fortis and ABN AMRO in those countries)
7.   tracking and management information (essential to know what stakeholders would need through the lifecycle of the transaction for the banks' boards and shareholders)
8.   programme management (the interface with the overall business programme and the tool by which the various phases were managed to a single approach pan-banks and pan-regions).

By splitting up the activities both across the deal, and within HR, and by having clear accountability and deliverables across the programme of work, a complex transaction was simplified. By having such a structure, it was easier to ensure that HR's contribution was both proactive and sufficiently well advanced to be able to participate in the key decisions. Interestingly, although all the three banks had prior experience of mergers and acquisitions, the nature of HR contribution seems to have varied between them. For example, RBS has been very methodical and business attuned; Santander has concentrated on implementation; and Fortis, given its Belgian roots, has given particular attention to dealing with social partners and building culture.

The skill of an HR leader is to dial up or down the emphasis of each of these aspects according to the nature of change. The skill of the business leader is to encourage early HR participation and not just ask for execution on transaction parts of the work.

Application of structure to key decisions

Choosing the target company (Pre-bid)

- **Strategic focus** Even before we discuss the process of executing a merger or acquisition successfully and before the formal due diligence process, it is important to emphasize that organizations should seek out the appropriate firm to take over or merge with. External advisers to your bid may raise the human capital 'fit' question, but not give it sufficient weight because it seems less concrete than the financial indicators. However, in certain circumstances, understanding the people characteristics of the target organization is vital to making a good decision. As you move towards focusing on a specific organization and a formal offer, the opportunities for data gathering are likely to grow. The extent to which you can obtain the information you want depends on the access afforded to you and the amount of material you can find in the public domain.

Generally, HR in RBS has not been involved in an open-ended discussion of how the company meets its strategic objectives through acquisition or the choice of target company. HR's participation has tended to begin when a target has been identified and a bid is being considered, but before the bid is made.

At this stage, RBS does general market research on the company, how it is structured, who are its top people, the lines business and, of course, how various parts of the target would integrate into the bank, both in business terms and, if appropriate, people terms. Later on in the process, when it looks like a serious prospect and a project team is formed for the acquisition, RBS ramps up the intelligence gathering.

The approach used is naturally affected by the reason for acquisition. For example, RBS believes it is not worth doing a detailed review of the top team of the company which it is thinking of buying, if it knows that it is not going to keep any of them. A top team review might give some insight into what dealings with them might be like in the early stages, but RBS would not do a detailed analysis.

If the company is not sure whether it will keep these individuals, because the nature of the acquisition (merger of equals or imposition of business model/organizational culture) has not been determined, RBS would gather some intelligence as to which of them it might want to retain. In a true merger, RBS would do a full analysis.

This emphasizes that the business aims must be set out unambiguously because this shapes the HR approach.

For RBS a fuller analysis might mean an internet trawl on the backgrounds of the key individuals and the use of search firms or head-hunters which, within the bounds of confidentiality, give more insight on these people.

Broadening out the review into the culture and operating ethos of the firm, search firms or head-hunters can be helpful here too, as the types of assignment they have been given says something about the target's needs and responses. Some data on staff surveys or salary levels can also be obtained without breaching client confidentiality from the suppliers, but with educated guesses. Things like organizational values and its approach to resourcing are often in the public domain set out on the corporate website.

As an example, RBS reviewed ABN AMRO's strapline and compared it with its own:

- ABN AMRO's was 'making more things possible'

> • RBS's was 'make it happen'.
>
> The positive and negative aspects of the two companies were there for all to see; it just needed attention to this detail.

• **Adding not subtracting human capital** In considering the criteria of selection, besides the obvious business factors, you should consider human capital issues such as the talent capability of the firm and its organizational culture. So are you buying or linking with a company that will add to your talent pool?

> Nomura's purchase of part of the remains of Lehman Brothers was clearly driven by the desire to add talent to the firm. As Stephen Sidebottom, Global Head of Organization Design and Development, explained: 'It [the acquisition] was only ever about talent. We didn't acquire a business.' In simple terms it trebled their payroll costs. It moved the company from a Japanese bank with international interests to a global bank such that 11,000 staff now work outside Japan (*The Grapevine*, 2010a).

• **Consider integration issues** This follows the successful targeting point made above and looks at whether there is a good fit between the way you do things and the way the other organization thinks about the world. Issues of fit to be considered include such matters as:
   - the quality of leadership and the management style
   - decision making capability including attitude to risk
   - work organization – team oriented or relying on individual performance
   - degree of personal autonomy
   - knowledge management
   - cultural characteristics.

A number of HR leaders rate the importance of culture to successful mergers and acquisitions and want to assure themselves that integration of the two organizations will work successfully. For example, it is the view of Satish Pradhan, VP of HR at Tata. 'In mergers and acquisitions this is reflected in a business perspective that thinks "post-merger integration" before "due diligence"' (Chubb, 2008). If the aim is indeed to build a collaborative culture then you need to know whether this will happen in practice. For practitioners like Paula Larson, HR Director at Invensys, if the answer to this question is doubtful then this would for her be a deal breaker (Johnson, 2008). She believes you should use measures of cultural compatibility. You can do an audit to measure the distance between your culture and the target organization's culture. There are tools like OCI that try to establish the nature of cultural differences, be they ones of degree (the relative importance attached to things) or kind (fundamentally opposed visions). These may tap into internal thought processes. Observation of the organization can also reveal visible manifestation of the culture – how the organization goes about its work, its resourcing strategy (particularly make versus buy), what it values, what it celebrates, etc. You cannot hope to understand all the unwritten norms and customs, but, before any agreement, it would allow you to walk away if you thought the organizations were too incompatible.

The sort of information you might want to obtain is set out in Table 2.3 below.

Table 2.3   Pre-deal data gathering for mergers and acquisitions

Area of interest	Information sought	Possible sources
Leadership capability	Who holds the senior/important posts Tenure in role Brief biographies Hotspots in career	Internet, own company website and social network Media search Succession plan
Wider talent capability	Bench and succession strength, and possible external replacements Talent strategy and fit with acquiring organization: • Make or buy model • Selection approach • Development method Potential for change of role in new organization	Search firms, either in general discussion or targeted in due diligence Covert due diligence with risk agenda Succession plan Scan of company recruitment advertising
Management style	Decision making style • Top down imposed • Bottom up consensual • Balanced	Media/internet search Targeted due diligence, e.g. HR consultancy assessments Staff surveys Social partners
Degree of employee engagement/ involvement	Against size of integration task • Nature of legal/contractual requirement to consult • Past corporate practice in degree of employee involvement in change • Usual communication methods (face to face, electronic, etc.) and style and frequency	Internet 'blog' searched to identify 'real' voice on the shop floor Targeted due diligence Staff surveys Social partners
Attitude to risk	Whether broadly risk averse or risk taking, and in what matters Tendency to contingency plan or accept risk Fit with organizational strategy Realism of financial metrics in business case deal	360° feedback Staff surveys Regulatory discussions (e.g. Financial Services Authority if a financial firm operating in the UK)
Nature of organizational culture	Appetite for/ability to change Tolerant or resistant to outsiders Individual or team based	Public statements on policies, e.g. performance related pay philosophy (via speeches, articles, presentations) Customer views on way organization manages its relationships

Table 2.3   *Concluded*

Area of interest	Information sought	Possible sources
HR policies and practices	Potential financial costs, e.g. validity of assumptions on severance costs/ synergy with headcount savings in business case Feasibility of integration, e.g. terms and conditions/benefits Commitments such as in pensions, guaranteed pay increases, etc. Organizational fit and HR philosophy, e.g. centralist/devolved policy	Formal due diligence Information via benchmarking 'clubs' Public statements on policies, e.g. compensation philosophy (via speeches, articles, presentations) Financial commitments in annual reports Social partners
HR systems and processes	Validation of business case for HR Complexity/maturity of HR model/ platform • Single ERP or multiple applications • Vanilla or bespoke • Owned or outsourced	Vendors, e.g. Oracle/SAP Consultancies, e.g Accenture/Aon Hewitt Formal contracts where on public record/accounts Degree of recent expenditure where in public domain, e.g. trade press

Inspired by O'Donnell and Capblanc, 2004

A cultural review at this stage of the deal could reveal the scale of the collaboration challenge. This might alter your plans such that if the two organizations are really culturally incompatible you might want to introduce a federated organizational structure rather than an integrated one. This approach is made all the easier if the two merging organizations are open to cultural exploration.

Another approach, claimed to be easier, is to conduct a 'psychological due diligence' alongside the normal process. This could simply look at whether predominantly employees (number and type) have a transactional psychological contract with the organization, in which case problems that occur may be solved by money or other tangible methods, or whether there is a relational psychological contract, whereby at least some employees have an affective commitment to the organization. The latter group may be harder to win round, as you have to appeal to their emotions.

- **Do your homework on the business model** You need to know how does the target company make money; where are its strengths and weaknesses; how does it operate its key processes (e.g. how does it take decisions); its liabilities in the people area (especially pensions but also pay guarantees); and its attitude to risk or to health and safety policy, etc. Indeed, business compatibility may be more important than cultural in determining whether there is a fit (IPD, 1999).

In 2002 HP acquired Compaq. The two companies were very different in background. HP highly valued product innovation and was strong on values, focusing on long-term staff development, with a strong team orientation. Compaq was more entrepreneurial and commercial, with an individual performance. Opposition to the merger was greater in HP because some staff thought that the merger violated the founding principles of the firm.

Despite these cultural and business differences the merger produced good business outcomes (O'Donnell and Capblanc, 2004).

Delivering effective due diligence (Bid to close)
- **Build a specific project team** This should represent all functions and relevant business areas to drive the change. Staff can be seconded from their normal jobs on a full-time or part-time basis and can be more or less formally managed. What is important is that they have sufficient time and direction to be effective. The team can be aided by the use of online collaboration tools, especially with a globally dispersed team, but this should not substitute for quality personal interaction.
- **Good communication is vital** It needs to be constant and structured, organized to reflect the stakeholder group. In particular, the people directly impacted by the change need particular attention. In a global communication exercise, remote decision makers need to be aware not just of formal and legal communication and consultation rules, but also of cultural expectations and sensitivities. Some people talk of the necessity of 'psychological communication' that addresses the emotional impact on people of change through the demonstration of understanding and compassion in the forms of interaction.
- **Change preparation** The aim should be to get those involved ready for what is about to hit them, and to turn what might be these negative perceptions of the future into opportunities – for short-term challenges, more interesting work, greater responsibility, etc.

Integration and development (First 100 days)
- **Integrate at the right speed** Give yourselves sufficient time to do a proper job, but for the sake of all concerned do not drag it out too long.
- **Manage risks explicitly** Use a risk register, not as a bureaucratic process but as a means of surfacing risks and seeking to address them. We identified in the challenges above the risks of sabotage, losing key staff, disengaging employees, failure to make decisions, etc.
- **Never underestimate the importance of communication** This applies not just to a new audience in the acquired or merged firm that wants clarity of direction, process and timescale, but also to the internal project team and management cadre that will be delivering or being party to the change. They need to know the rules of the game. It should be emphasized this communication should honest and clear such that people can understand and trust its content. It is better not to duck the difficult issues. Be careful to ensure that external messages to customers and shareholders are consistent with the internal communication to staff. It is easy to forget that your colleagues take note of what is in the newspapers and on television or the radio!

To try to deal with the concerns of how ABN AMRO staff would be treated during the takeover, to meet legal requirements to consult and to bind the three parties together in a common approach to the people issues, the partners agreed 10 people principles. It took weeks to settle them reflecting both their different business and cultural perspectives – what they wanted out of the deal and their attitudes to people management and change.

With such a complex, wide-ranging set of issues across the companies, it was only possible to settle on principles below which the detail would be applied by the appropriate company in each jurisdiction. In circumstances where three partners are operating together, especially coming from different business and cultural backgrounds and applying their decisions to 38 countries, it would have been very time consuming to agree every detailed policy.

The Social Partners and staff held the companies to account on the principles during the entirety of the deal.

- **Allow frustrations to surface via message boards and the like** This can feel risky if people criticize management or their decisions, but it is important to know what colleagues are finding difficult so that you can address their issues. An intranet site can be moderated to weed out abusive or personal comments, yet it needs to retain its integrity, so such intervention should be light touch. Decisions have to be taken about the organization's approach to social media since the work/private boundary is often blurred.
- **Offer support mechanisms** These may range from 'job shops' to find displaced staff new roles inside or outside the organization to individual career or personal counselling to pick out both those needing help to find a new direction and those who feel especially under pressure by the changes. These and other practical measures, like retraining programmes, can deliver business benefits in terms of more effective skill redeployment and a faster psychological transition to the new state.
- **Be especially careful in the initial signals the new partner or owner sends** This relates to the first encounters. In particular, be sensitive to highly valued symbols be they of location, language, company name, etc. You should ensure that leaders are particularly sensitive in the language they use, especially in a trans-national setting. Poorly worded or ill thought through statements can have a surprisingly negative effect on an audience that might be overly sensitive and at risk of over interpreting casual remarks. How sensitive the acquirer is to these matters depends on the sort of outcome it wants to the deal. But remember employees will judge the process more by what an organization does than what it says.

RBS had to balance reassuring ABN AMRO staff yet insist on the acquired company moving towards its way of doing things. Its 'Painting it Blue' project combined both elements. There were two-day cultural workshops in Scotland for 250 senior ABN AMRO staff – what it would be like working in RBS, with a strong Scottish sense of RBS'ness which was often well received. A video was produced for the wider audience. Yet RBS also changed the signage on the doors of offices, painted them blue, put receptionists in tartan uniforms and put down the company corporate carpet as soon as it was able to. Whilst this might be negatively seen, it was an attempt to raise standards in the work environment and the quality of service customers ought to expect. However, staff were pretty much left alone, initially at least, in terms of how they were paid, how they were managed, etc.

- **'De-dramatize cultural differences by describing them clearly'** (O'Donnell and Capblanc, 2004). This will help evolving integration. If employees clearly understand the business goals of their new organization and implied culture to support it, and they recognize where there are differences between the parties, these differences can be more easily tackled. This is not to deny the presence of differences but they should be 'worked around' (O'Donnell and Capblanc, 2004), preventing conflict and allowing time for a new culture bed in.
- **Demonstrate your values through the change process** This can be shown both at the level of formal statements (we commit to enact change against these principles) and in practical ways such as a fair selection process (without bias towards either party) against objective and transparent criteria.

Among the ABN AMRO acquisition consortium one of the initial conversations that took place was to confirm that 'people followed the work' so if an employee worked in a private clients activity they went to Fortis as that bank had bought the private clients business. This quickly led to considering in what practical ways surplus people might be managed, such as through the transfer of staff, where there was service continuation, and combined redeployment centres. There was a clear desire to exploit the benefits of working in a consortium, especially the different employment opportunities the partners could offer to meet both genuine business requirements and personal needs.

- **Model the (leadership) behaviours you expect to see from others** Staff new to a leadership team will be anxious to see how they behave, both in word and deed. This will give employees an early and important indication of the way the company will be run. Those staff whose own management team is in the vanguard of change may not be as anxious, but, nonetheless, they will be concerned to see their interests protected.
- **Build relationships** Get people working together across the different companies as quickly and productively as possible. These relationships should be based on mutual respect. This in itself will help meld cultures together.

In the HP/Compaq merger every team had to run a 'Fast Start' workshop. The aim was for the team members to get to know one another and create a team spirit by defining together key elements of their future work (mission, targets, processes, performance measurement, etc.). The issue of culture was addressed head on by reviewing the results of a cultural audit against the corporate values of the new company. The participants were asked to define together acceptable and unacceptable individual behaviour. Through understanding where cultural differences existed, each team was asked to take responsibility for overcoming these differences in their daily work (O'Donnell and Capblanc, 2004).

- **Learn from the other party** This is a practical demonstration of mutual respect. The aim should be to find best practice wherever it might sit. As Stephen Dunn at Scottish Power said (Chubb, 2008), in the context of an acquisition by Iberdola, there should be 'no ego' in deciding what is best. When Nomura took over part of Lehman Brothers, the company drafted a cultural statement that made clear that a new organization was being formed that would improve on the efforts of its heritage components through learning from their efforts (*The Grapevine*, 2010a). Even in a takeover, Wal-Mart demonstrated the benefits of 'reverse learning'.

Wal-Mart learned from Asda, not least because it had bought a successful company for which it had paid a premium price. Its instinct was to leave the business largely alone except where it could add value (in general merchandising and systems management), but to exploit the capabilities that Asda had got. Asda was stronger than Wal-Mart in clothing and fresh food. It was also more sophisticated in HR management. For example, Wal-Mart picked up from the initial acquisition that Asda was 'great' at various people management things. It invited people like David Smith (HR director of Asda) to US internal conferences where he would describe these practices and then a Wal-Mart representative, usually a subject matter expert, would visit to learn in more detail what Asda was doing. So Asda explained its concept of training new retail managers (via 'stores of learning'); the daily 10-minute huddle at the start of the working day where priorities were set; the communication of reward packages and the use of recognition schemes. Asda's business practices were exported not just to the USA, but also to other countries. Staff also followed, with the likes of Canada, Mexico and Japan benefiting from the calibre of UK talent.

No wonder David Smith was able to say that 'it felt more like a merger than a take-over'.

Wal-Mart has continued to search out global best practice with the genuine intent to benefit from experience elsewhere. Not all the learning has been as successful as with Asda – perhaps because the US/UK cultural distance is shorter than in other national cases or because Asda was an innovative and well-run company with plenty to offer. Ideas have not always been as well selected as best practice, but there have been greater problems with implementation, particularly getting a 'good' idea to fit another country. Ideas have, for example, not taken root so well in Japan and China.

- **Celebrate success** Whilst working through the merger or acquisition celebrate as you go through at each successful milestone completed. Do not hold back until the end of the exercise to recognize things that have gone well – the period may be too long to wait, and by then success may look more uncertain than it did at the time. Hindsight distorts accurate recollection of the circumstances of the moment.
- **Search for cultural synergy** This is likely to be easier where the degrees of difference are relatively small with respect to geography, culture, operating model, nature of business, etc. Except where the aim is only a loose coupling between organizations in a federated structure, presumably the goal is to create a shared identity across the merging organizations, but you need to be careful how far to push a common, especially global, culture. There are limits to the extent that national culture will give way, let alone organizational culture. Let a new culture evolve with discreet steering towards one that will align with your business ambitions.
- **Focus on the future not the past** As Hugh Mitchell, the Shell Group's HR Director, told us: 'There is a danger in a change programme that you are solving yesterday's problems, not today's or tomorrow's.' This applies, for example in an acquisition, to making too many assumptions about employees' connection to their employer and its values. Some staff may indeed be fully wedded to the old ways, but it is possible that others may happily embrace the new culture, preferring it to their previous employer's approach. An early task is to find out both a general and specific answer to this question: who and how many will be with us and, if not against us, then very reluctant stayers.

In the first 3–4 months after acquisition RBS came up with structure charts with who it wanted in the key roles – even though this was not going to be disclosed for some time.

Specifically, the investment banking division (GBM) had settled on how to fill the top 140 roles before RBS walked in the door. And within the first five weeks or so, a principal deliverable was to produce retention letters for these people.

Some of the ABN AMRO staff recognized that they probably could secure employment with their new owner. Others (especially in the corporate HQ) recognized that this route would be closed to them. Staff in a third, smaller group were able to obtain work with one of the partners, exploiting the cross-company redeployment efforts referred to earlier.

- **Remember the business logic for the merger or acquisition** If the aim is to improve customer service or drive up quality use that as the lever to effect change. In this way it helps focus on the future and moves away from the current debate about integration. It also gives the new organization a clear and united goal. People like working for successful organizations and this is a sure-fire way of bringing even doubters on board.
- **Be aware of external perceptions of the deal and of its effects** As we said earlier, the Kraft acquisition of Cadbury's exemplifies that in a global merger or acquisition the risk exists that the companies concerned do not know enough about

the local situation – its sensitivities, concerns, interests, etc. These may well be not enough to scupper the deal, but it does mean ramping up the communication exercise both externally and internally. The proposed purchase of the port management businesses in six American seaports to a United Arab Emirates company is another illustration of a contentious cross national deal, as is the killing off by US legislators of an attempt by China National Offshore Oil Corp. to buy Unocal in 2005. This failed deal is still in the news six years later because of the bad blood it produced.

Embedding change
- **Establish whether the change has met its success criteria** Before proceeding further it is a good idea to evaluate what has gone well or not so well in the implementation of the deal. This might mean specific employee or customer surveys, a review of performance metrics, examination of costs against the baseline position, etc.
- **Review leadership and management performance** Given the importance of leaders in setting out a change vision and demonstrating adherence to it, and managers in encouraging staff to follow a new path, then it might be worth specifically testing how well this is happening.
- **Set out an improvement plan** Naturally, the next step is to address the weak areas, be they in the harmonization of terms and conditions, developing a common service delivery model, aspects of company culture, such as in a consistent approach to customers, etc.
- **Measure the performance of the merger or acquisition** Do this through analysis of such factors as:
  - financial targets met within an acceptable timeframe
  - operational continuity maintained during change
  - external customers supportive
  - stakeholder backing kept
  - regulators satisfied
  - brand identification strong externally and internally
  - key talent retention
  - successful executive appointments
  - positive response from employee surveys
    (from employees of both heritage organizations)
  - evidence of synergistic behaviour
  - ability to successfully hire to the new organization.
- **Learn from your past mistakes** In particular do not assume that the next acquisition should be treated the same way as the last one. While there are benefits in a fairly standardized approach to M&A that means that good practice can be regularly applied, each deal needs to be approached on its own merits, especially in a global context. If the aim is to derive benefit from the acquisition, too rigid an application of the company theory can be self-defeating. It is better to keep an open mind on what strategy will work best to achieve the business goal. Those organizations that have been through a bad M&A experience are likely to be more receptive to this point.

Wal-Mart certainly learned from its German *debakel*. It was much more careful about its choice of businesses to acquire, looking more closely at cultural fit. It expanded and professionalized its M&A team, putting good people in these roles, but it consciously chose not to send in the Marines when it was involved in a cross-national acquisition. Two or three people would go over from the States to keep a high-level eye on things, but the emphasis was on using local knowledge to develop local markets. Obviously, this approach is modified somewhat in greenfield sites and where the business problems are more severe, but wherever possible it is a hands-off approach.

The benefits of being a fast learner have been shown in many successful acquisitions in Asia and Latin America especially, as the company has become cuter commercially and culturally.

- **Structure the learning** One way to ensure that learning on complex change, especially in mergers and acquisitions, is maintained is to both preserve useful knowledge in a structured manner and to build expertise as through the BADs team in RBS described earlier. It is important that companies do learn from each deal and try and reinforce this learning through translation into clear processes, templates and other tools that increase readiness for the next deal, but organizations need to be sensitive to the context of what the scale, scope and purpose of the next transaction might be. This means having skilled people to understand and convert the business strategy into the practicalities of the specific merger or acquisition under consideration.

A similar approach to wider change

Whilst a large M&A transaction needs significant amount of resource looking at many different component parts of the deal, there is learning from these situations that can be applied to any significant business change described earlier in this chapter. So the five phases we described relating to M&A transactions can be applied to any change situation. If looked at generically, and applied to HR's role, the five stages can be condensed to:

- **Strategic positioning**: deciding on how the organization can best meet its business goals, this activity should be a broad examination of the options. HR should play a part in this review, focusing naturally on the people dimension and how it might affect the decision. So, it might take in the employee relations implications of outsourcing; the labour market conditions (supply and price) of offshoring; the talent, skills and knowledge loss in a disposal; and cultural challenges of partnership arrangements. Some of these issues may generate concerns sufficient to deter the leadership from a possible course of action; more often they will produce mitigation strategies that lead to delay or extra expenditure.
- **Pre-change announcement planning**: largely driven by answering questions of what the various stakeholders need to be told when announcing the change and thus making sure the pre-work is geared towards answering these questions. If offshoring a major activity to different country, shareholders will want to know what the impact on net bottom line costs are; clients will want to know how service levels will be

maintained or perhaps improved; staff will want to know how many jobs will close in the host location; communities in any offshoring location will similarly want to know how many jobs are created and on what terms.

In an international context, and where the offshored activity is still retained not outsourced, HR will need to know local hiring laws and any customs and practices pertaining to recruitment. What the company does not want to find out at a late stage is unexpected people costs that erode the wage arbitrage benefits that undermine the logic of the deal. Similarly, if the activity being offshored is not in the host country (say an American company transferring work from France to Vietnam), then corporate HR must know not just about the legal aspects of redundancy, but also what will be the public relations implications, especially if there are operations retained in the offshoring country.

If the decision is to dispose of an activity in a transnational setting, the same principles apply: know the context within which you are operating that will impact on timing and costs. Far from the action, the formal legal principles may be easier to establish than cultural norms, but violation of the latter may cause long-lasting damage to corporate reputation. A good HR function will be able to argue that these should be taken into account.

- **Post-announcement, pre-implementation phase**: any significant business change will have a target 'start' date, often a few weeks after any announcement. This period allows digestion by stakeholders of the plans announced, and internally for HR, as with M&A, is a period in which much good work can be achieved. Effective HR will already have been heavily involved in the pre-change phase so this is the time for honing plans and checking assumptions. Key parts of the change can be operationalized such as the search for the operational head of the offshore centre and meeting organizations who can help with staffing (really good HR will have done this in the pre-change phase as a check and balance to the often finance/property led nature of these changes). In a disposal, the important decisions may relate to the terms of transfer of staff moving to the purchaser. European law has specific provisions in this regard, but HR needs to know in Peru, Thailand or Australia what legal provisions apply to consultation, as well as the practical consequences of the transfer itself.

As we argued with M&A, use the first 30 days to get momentum, and the first 100 to try and get as much change executed as possible. This approach applies generically across all business change and fits with Kotter's (2006) injunction to inject a sense of urgency into such activity.

HR'S ROLE

So HR's role in broad terms is to assert the importance of human capital and intellectual capital, making certain that their interests are included alongside financial considerations; to set out good processes by which decision making will occur, especially (but not exclusively) in the people domain; to ensure that the leadership attends to cultural issues and is fully aware of the power of communication, the importance of symbols and behaviour; to deliver the employee aspects of the change in an efficient but sensitive way; and, last but not least, to challenge senior executives on whether the means they are choosing to effect change will meet the articulated business goals.

Figure 2.2 graphically sets out in a hierarchical sense where HR might participate in these processes. If HR has not been able or has not chosen to get a seat at the top table where the strategic decisions are made, then its contribution might be in an advisory role, heavily involved in decision making, but coming to the process after the principal decisions have been taken. If it does not have this role, it may be engaged in the execution of decisions, focusing naturally on the people issues – redeployment, redundancy, terms and conditions, etc. In the ideal situation, HR is involved at all three levels.

In those organizations where HR has been excluded from the strategic decision making processes, functional leadership might well reflect on why this might be so and how the situation can be rectified. For those organizations that are well engaged, the function should not be complacent as it is a very exposed position contributing to the direction setting of the organization. HR should be constantly reassessing its role and whether it is getting the right balance between support and challenge to the rest of the executive team.

Figure 2.2   A hierarchy of HR's involvement in mergers and acquisitions

In some deals HR's role will be given greater primacy because of employee relations considerations. This may be more straightforward in a national context, but can become challenging in international deals where the parent company management may be unfamiliar with legal, institutional and cultural requirements, or in a partnership based deal. RBS's acquisition of ABN AMRO is a case in point.

It would be fair to say that in the RBS acquisition of ABN AMRO, the HR function successfully convinced other business colleagues that more time and effort would have to be paid to formal consultative processes with staff representative bodies than would historically have been the case. Whilst company management might know in theory that continental European law is more exacting than UK law in this regard, the practical consequences had not been appreciated, nor had the effects of working with a continental European partner (Fortis) that was necessarily very sensitive to this point. It should be remembered that this deal involved disposals as well as acquisitions.

CHAPTER 3 *Organizational Culture*

It is absolutely necessary to understand a foreign culture in order to successfully do business with that culture. (Montana and Charnov, 2008)

Much has been written about culture and there is much to write, but our concern in this book on global HR is quite narrow in that our interest lies in the interplay between organizational and national cultures. In particular, we are interested to know whether organizations can create a trans-national, integrated organizational culture. This would transcend the individual national cultures and create something distinctive compared with competitors. This can then be bottled and used as a principal ingredient of the employer brand.

Introduction to Culture

Culture is the deeper level of basic assumptions and beliefs that are shared by members of an organization that operate unconsciously and define in a basic 'taken for granted' fashion an organization's view of its self and its environment. (Schein, 1985)

So culture is about values, beliefs, expectations and goals shared by a particular group (Martin, 2006), in this case an organization or nation, that to varying degrees distinguishes itself from another organization or nation.

It covers such things as visible symbols of our ways of doing things, demonstration of values and beliefs and invisible, underlying assumptions about the world.

Put more simply, culture is 'the way things get done around here' (Deal and Kennedy, 1982) with the interesting addition from Colvin (1997) of 'when there is no one around to tell them what to do'. This introduces the question of whether the culture is formed by an employee perspective of 'how we operate' or a management view of 'the way we should operate'. Usually, there is a tension between the two that can be healthy or unhealthy, but is relevant to our discussion on creating a global culture.

The importance of culture in the context of global business cannot be underestimated. Attributed to the Ford motor company (and to Peter Drucker), there is a saying that 'culture eats strategy for breakfast'. For global organizations this might have gone on to say 'and it might regurgitate it in unexpected ways'. Culture profoundly affects how organizations exercise choice and make decisions against competing options in the way they deliver their strategy. This is even truer in global companies because of the complexity of the cultural map with so many different contributions to it.

National Culture

National culture is an obvious place to start in thinking about how cultures affect global companies, though, as we will see, it is not the only component.

There have been a variety of classifications of national culture. One of the most influential has been from Geert Hofstede (1991). He identified five dimensions of culture (though the fifth one was not always present in his work) that apply in an organizational and other social settings. They are:

- **Small versus large power distance** This describes the extent to which employees accept the unequal distribution of power within the organization
- **Individualism versus collectivism** This considers the extent to which employees feel part of a group and might look to trade unions or others to represent their interests. Individualists, as might be expected, want direct dealings with their employers.
- **Masculinity versus femininity** This distinguishes between an orientation towards male or female values. Putting it rather simplistically, this might suggest that in macho cultures ambition, competition and wealth accumulation are important, whereas feminine cultures put more stress on relationships and the quality of work/life balance.
- **Weak versus strong uncertainty avoidance** This dimension measures how much employees are anxious about change, especially the 'unknown' and therefore seek to minimize uncertainty.
- **Long versus short-term orientation** Here the distinction is between those societies that are oriented to the future compared with the past and present. This manifests itself in, say, deferred or instant gratification – to what extent people are prepared to wait for rewards, say through a career or via job security, as against those who want the rewards now in terms of pay and benefits.

Charles Hampden-Turner and Fons Trompenaars in *Seven Cultures of Capitalism* (1993) also developed a model of culture, this time with seven dimensions. There are five that relate to how people interact. The sixth concerns social attitudes to time and the seventh our relationship with the outside environment.

- universalism versus particularism (general rules bound or exception seeking?)
- analysing versus integrating (do we break down phenomena into parts or seek to see whole patterns, etc.?)
- individualism versus communitarianism
- inner directed versus outer directed (are our actions guided by inner thoughts or by the external environment?)
- sequential versus synchronic time (do we see events one at a time or in parallel?)
- achievement versus ascription (performance driven or predetermined status?)
- equality versus hierarchy (do we respond to colleagues as equals or emphasize the authority of hierarchy?).

If true, these national cultural characteristics can have an important influence on organizational behaviour, especially in the field of people management. This is because managerial frames of reference are set, in part, by their cultural assumptions.

In our organizational discussions and research, some of these issues emerged. This was especially true of those societies that more readily accepted the distribution of power rather than challenged it and put a high premium on social harmony and following rules.

There tends to be greater power distance in the east than is generally true in the west, and eastern managers manage in styles that reflect this sense of hierarchy. In some societies this is reinforced by the fact that senior HR posts are held by ex-military officers or by political appointees (Harry, 2007). There are significant exceptions to the west/east split that Hofstede pointed to: France and many Latin countries tend to favour bureaucratic processes and strong hierarchies. Germany may have the same attraction to rule based systems, due to uncertainty avoidance in Hostede's terms, but not the centralized power. We will see later in the chapter on HR governance, the challenge that decentralized power puts on German international companies, but the global French firms we came across had devolved power more than this cultural profiling would suggest.

The practical effects of high power distance are also felt in how employee involvement mechanisms operate. For example, Bryan Lim, Regional HR Director for BG Energy, has commented upon how surfacing concerns is difficult in Asia (People Management, 2009) and how you have to give colleagues time and opportunity to voice their issues. Similarly, Jonsen and Bryant (2008) report Chinese staff as reluctant to speak up in public, especially if their views differ from those of their seniors. As Garmt Louw, Executive Vice President for Head of Talent Management and Development, from Shell explained, Asians still prefer to argue their points in corridors than in meetings. In a similar vein, in Korea if you ask a good question, the respondent is expected to pause before answering as a mark of respect. This can be misinterpreted by westerners who assume the hesitation relates to an inability to answer and may jump in to help, whilst in fact achieving the opposite.

Certainly, we know that in some other societies employees expect consultation and debate, not simply the imposition of ideas. Mark Jankelson, GM Human Resources, Institutional Division, Group GM Learning, at ANZ bank, talked about this in the Australian context where decision making could easily be slowed because everyone believed they had the right to speak up and be heard. This characteristic, also seen in some European countries such as in the so-called Dutch polder model, is regarded in some parts of Asia as prevarication, not a sign of a well-functioning organization but of one that does not move forward quickly enough.

This is relevant to how organizations manage global change and, within HR, how governance models have been developed and applied. For example, we were told in China that if you present change to a European audience they will need to be convinced of the reasons for the change, the business logic, the fit with their circumstances, etc. In comparison, an Asian audience is less likely to challenge and will be more concerned with the implementation requirements. So the Europeans will concentrate on the 'what' and the Asians on the 'how'. Western run companies, therefore, may misread questions from Asians that are intended to get instructions and treat them as opposition.

Concerning internal versus external control, research has suggested in countries that are not fatalistic about human behaviour, people are more prepared to attempt improvement mechanisms (like performance related pay or job enrichment). Those who are fatalistic assume that staff are not 'malleable' and consequently do not use these improvement mechanisms (Aycan et al., 2000).

Similarly, state-run Chinese firms have tended to be hierarchical and bureaucratic with less interest in talent or development – a product of a fatalistic culture added to a communist ethos. Commercial firms may be different but they come with this heritage.

Both China and Japan exhibit some characteristics of short-term oriented societies, namely taking care to avoid loss of face (*mianzi* in Japan) and respect for tradition and elders in society. In francophone West Africa you would give your boss nothing but praise as any loss of face would be a serious offence. In African tribes of Bantu origin negative feedback affects you, harming your dignity, your family and your ancestors. In parts of South East Asia, too, loyalty to family and clan are of overriding importance.

We saw, too, how attitudes towards careers vary from country to country. Those people from countries with a long-term and uncertainty avoidance orientation tend to favour lifetime careers. This appears to be true in Asian countries. This explains why there is a stress on long-term careers in places like Japan and why those in the east reacted so badly in 1995 to the Shell CEO of the time, Cor Hoekstrotter's, announcement that careers for life in Shell were over. His narrow Eurocentric view of the world, preoccupied by its economic problems, did not go down well in the growing businesses of Asia. Still to this day, the Hoekstrotter faux pas is remembered with disapproval there.

On the individualism/collectivism dimension, Anglo-Saxon countries seem increasingly to have become nations of individualists, a characteristic that Hofstede picked up. Japanese companies emphasize individual responsibility for performance, but also like India and China, the importance of interdependence and teamworking (*danwei* is the work group in Japan). Moreover, they stress the value of employee involvement in structuring work and of consensual decision making. A sense of common purpose is thereby generated, though perhaps one that is not so easy to challenge. As Nissan explained: 'The system of lifetime employment gives employees a sense of security and a feeling of belonging ... It motivates a feeling of unity among employees and a consciousness of sharing the same future as the company' (quoted in Wickens, 1987).

In an example of the importance of the group in some societies, Oxfam used UK and India partnered search agencies to identify candidates for a senior South Asian appointment. However, most of a 'strong' field pulled out because there was a well-known internal candidate and it was culturally wrong to compete against him.

This power dimension added to the collectivist one also affects not just how an organization might run itself but also how it represents itself to the world. So in Indian companies there is a strong sense of internal community with high levels of affiliation to the employer. The fact that even multinational companies are family businesses reinforces this tendency. This communal feature leads to a great emphasis being put on corporate social responsibility in the employer brand because this is an expression of company's commitment to the society in which it operates. A more deferential and class (caste)/hierarchy bound society creates a tendency towards followership in Indian companies and the group orientation to valuing team success over individual. Managers are expected to nurture their staff; employees are expected to work hard for them in return.

As far as relationships are concerned, in some societies the boundary between employment and home life is quite blurred, with the former dominating. People in feminine countries work to live; in masculine cultures people live to work. Think of the traditional Japanese male work culture of spending extensive time together in and around the office, compared with the traditional departure from Dutch offices at 5.30 pm to be home for dinner at 6 pm. However, the word 'traditional' is important here and one we will return to later.

In places like the Middle East it is ill mannered to rush straight to a business topic; you need to discuss non-work issues first such as the health and welfare of the person's children or other familial questions. You are also expected to reciprocate gifts and accept that the asking and granting of favours will be expected, an obligation that extends to the sphere of employment. Family ties are strong in the east and you are expected to look after your own. According to Wes Harry (2007) there are advantages in this culture, namely that social cohesion is built around this network of ties. The downside is that it can be resistant to change, especially from outside the group.

The Director General of the Land Department in Dubai thinks it sufficiently important to engage with staff that he spends an hour every morning shaking their hands. He takes a floor of their building each day and thereby greets each of the 360 staff once per week. Apparently, when he is away on holiday or business, his staff really miss the personal contact (Reilly, 2010).

In China trust and mutual respect govern relationships, not formal contracts like in the USA (the universalism vs particularism distinction). Foreigners attach more importance to the latter, which has led to misunderstandings, especially in joint ventures, and to frustration in multinational companies in dealing with an unfamiliar business approach.

We will now consider these points in the context of whether there is convergence towards a universal set of global values, driven by changes in people's attitudes, or whether the argument in favour of universality is hard to sustain whilst differences remain, not least because of social heterogeneity.

Universalism

There is a sense in which some western multinational companies endorse Francis Fukuyama's (1992) belief in the end of history and humanity's socio-cultural evolution. His argument is that the Hegelian struggle between competing systems is now over and that **market based liberal democracy is the winner**, having seen off fascism and communism (Attar, 2009). Western multinational companies can in many ways be seen as the agents carrying this message of the triumph to all corners of the globe, thereby asserting the superiority of meritocratic, individualistic, democratic capitalism.

This notion appears to have the support of such an august body as the United Nations. Its Global Compact (a voluntary initiative that relies on public accountability, transparency and disclosure that asserts 10 principles in the areas of human rights, labour standards, the environment and anti-corruption) states: 'Never before in history has there been a greater alignment between the objectives of the international community and those of the business world. Common goals, such as building markets, combating corruption, safeguarding the environment and ensuring social inclusion, have resulted in unprecedented partnerships and openness between business, governments, civil society, labour and the United Nations.' This seems to be an appeal to universal values based on a kind of stakeholder capitalist view of the world where the importance of markets is emphasized, but interests beyond those of making money are also legitimized.

In our research we have certainly come across several instances of socio-economic change that have apparently affected work attitudes and pushed them towards an increasingly common set of social and employment mores.

There is a sense that **individualism is growing**, with increased wealth in developing countries and a burgeoning middle class with attitudes more like those found in the UK or US. There appears to be a progress of social homogenization supported by all the cultural exports (films, television, sport, music) and economic exports (brands, products, consumerism) that make operating in Rio the same as Madrid, London or Jakarta. Touring these cities you would notice that the billboards are recognizable; the fast food joints are the same, the technology familiar (different keyboards can be a stress!) and cable television in the hotel offers programmes in a multiplicity of languages.

Leaders in some of the companies we spoke to said that increased mobility, both in travel and jobs, has shrunk the world and that the e-generation is so in touch with its compatriots across the globe that, especially for this group, there is a **convergence in thinking and attitudes**. In an interview with Leena Nair, Executive Director, HR, Hindustan Unilever Limited (HUL), she recognized that increasingly the younger generations are more uniform across country boundaries: so a 20 year old in Brazil, India or China may increasingly be connected to other parts of the world and share common global values and mindsets. As a Nigerian colleague explained, when he was young he would not look his parents in the eye because it would be disrespectful. Now his son, brought up in the UK, has no such inhibitions, but nor do his cousins raised in Nigeria.

One example quoted to us is the apparent growth in the attachment to work/life balance. As Wilfried Meyer, Executive VP HR Asia/Australia of Siemens described it to us: 'A big change in employee views has been the importance now given to work/life balance and integration – from the West Coast of the US to China in one go!' Jing Wang, HR Director at Shell China, made similar points. She sees a change taking place in China where work/life balance has become very important. 'This coming generation has not had the "material crisis" of previous generations. They want work but play too. For the youngsters there is no point having a meeting before 11 am. They work until 7–8 pm, go out for dinner and then get home, go online until 3 am before they go to bed.' For those Chinese managers brought up in another era, the younger generation is very challenging in its consumerist and much more self-regarding attitudes.

Another example of the harmonization of attitudes can, it seems, be seen in the status and salary demands made in cultures where social deference has traditionally been practised. There is a tendency towards wanting reward now rather than in the future. Again, young people in China are apparently demanding immediate personal (including financial) success compared with their forefathers' tradition of thrift and self-denial. It is hard to remember that the post-war government experiment to incentivize rice farmers to grow surplus produce was a failure because the farmers could not see the point of having an extra crop beyond their own needs.

Competing institutions, like trade unions, have become weaker in the face of the individualization of society. Pluralist perspectives have been replaced by **unitarism**: what the company wants it gets because we are all in the same boat together. In some societies the legal framework still balances the interests of capital and labour, but in many others there has been deregulation to give employers more freedom to shape the firm in their interests alone. In this way the world follows the dominant US liberal economic model driven by the need for efficiency and the highest possible return to shareholders on their investment. Management then becomes a technical function to deliver these results. Divergent cultures just get in the way of the corporate juggernaut.

Either reflecting these changes towards social harmonization or driving them is the notion of a **convergence of management behaviour, policies and systems**, centred on the US model. The argument is that the nature of business is the same the world over, so the business function will necessarily be the same, with the American model dominating on the back of its commercial success. As one character says to another in Steig Larsson's (2008) novel *The Girl with the Dragon Tattoo*, 'the Vanger corporation is international, and we could certainly have an American CEO who doesn't speak a word of Swedish ... it's only business when all's said and done.'

This trend in business convergence is encouraged by the fact that many large firms use the same global consultants, who tend towards offering similar business solutions, certainly in structures, processes and systems. Though some of these consultancies claim to eschew best practice methodologies, their attachment to benchmarking to identify 'best in class' leads to convergence in approach. Those leaders trained in western-dominated MBA programmes are likely to be particularly receptive to these international business concepts.

Evidence of these developments comes from research by Budhwar (2010) and Cooke (2010) that suggests that locally owned large companies in places like India and China pursue western approaches to performance management, including performance related pay, even though they may be counter to their traditional cultures, especially elements that reflect social harmony and equality (China) or success through social connections (India).

At ICICI, an Indian bank, staff can challenge anyone in the management hierarchy to justify their decisions or actions. The quality of their response is their only 'protection'. This is a radical concept in the deferential Indian culture (Chubb, 2008).

Similarly, many Japanese companies have been moving towards a more hire-and-fire employment model, even in the bigger companies. The Nomura example illustrates this transition.

The Nomura acquisition of the European and Middle Eastern workforce in the Equities and Investment Banking section of Lehman has had wider implications on the Japanese firm beyond significantly increasing its size. Out have gone lifetime contracts and Japanese style remuneration; in have come the performance management and variable pay associated with the Western world's approach (*The Grapevine*, 2010a).

As the Oxfam boxed example illustrates, this universalization of business practice affects how global organizations operate, as much as local non-western companies.

> In the past Oxfam used to check out if things were culturally acceptable to its global workforce more than it does now. The organization sees a more homogenous world with a greater acceptance of the Anglo-Saxon way of doing business, especially in a company with UK roots. The NGO sector is quite international and follows this common Anglo-centric path.

As globalization reaches all parts of the world, this convergence in business and society (less evidently true in political processes) will wipe out any indigenous practices.

Those in UK and US would also emphasize that **English is the common language of business** and this binds together those who operate in the global sphere, reinforcing the universal business model. Companies like Vestas, a Danish headquartered firm, hold their business meetings in English and the 2008 AGM was held in New York City. Schlumberger, a French international company, decided as long ago as 1947 to move to English as the company language. There are about 330 million to 580 million English speakers (depending on interpretations on first and second languages), i.e. less than 10 per cent of the world's population, yet about a third of the world's mail, telexes and cables are in English and half of all internet traffic. Indeed, Nick Ostler (2010) has described English as a 'predator language' set to dominate the world. Its ease of learning and adaptability gives it an advantage over some other languages. Chinese, in his view, will never become the global norm because its written version is so difficult to learn.

Monolingualism may be a by-product of colonialism with local dialects and languages failing to survive social homogenization, with English again the language of choice for local elites. In fact, the term 'globish' has been coined to denote a kind of cut-down, simplified English that non-native speakers choose to speak, for example in Asia (McCrum, 2010). To illustrate these points, there is the story of a British interpreter acting for the UN in peace talks in Nepal who was left role-less (and speechless) when the negotiating parties switched to English during a particularly heated exchange.

As Martin Kettle has written in *The Guardian* (2010) of the impact of these trends on the UK: 'The online information age, which should, in theory, have been expected to facilitate greater mental and cultural pluralism … has, in practice, had the reverse effect. The power of the English language, at once our global gift and greatest curse, discourages us from engaging with those … outside the all conquering online Anglosphere.'

So, it is not even necessary any more for the Brits or Americans to learn another language. Indeed, the numbers of A level and GCSE students studying foreign languages in the UK is falling year on year.

Finally, these developments would not be a surprise to those who believe that there is a set of **universal values**, and who claim that the needs and motivations of people are fundamentally alike wherever one travels or works. This is expressed via the oft-quoted statement: 'People are the same the world over.' It is indeed what Johnson Matthey found when taking their leadership and employee engagement model around the world – 'People want to work for the same sort of person universally,' according to Operations Director,

Tony Flannigan. Those who argue in this way would no doubt endorse the work of SH Schwartz (1994) with his 'theory of basic human values' that argues that for reasons of biological, social survival there are the same 'values' (e.g. excitement, enjoyment, social justice, honesty) everywhere, which influence our behaviours to seek the desirable and to avoid the undesirable.

And it is not just in the west that there is the assertion of universal values. Dissident Chinese artist Ai Weiwei called for western politicians to stand up for their own sense of democracy: 'Don't believe that these are western values. These are universal values. No one is forcing China to accept values from outside – they are just asking it to listen to its own people.' The same arguments have been heard among protestors on the streets of Tunis and in Cairo's Tahrir Square in the revolt against their governments.

In this view of universalism, where differences occur they are essentially trivial, as Dinesh Mendes, Director of Financial Solutions in Aitken Spence, said: 'The difference between Americans and Sri Lankans is that the Americans drink coffee and the Sri Lankans drink tea.'

Divergence

However, there are counter-opinions to the global convergence argument, though whether they really amount to the contention that we are moving further apart or whether it is more that national and sub-national cultural differences are substantial and enduring is questionable.

Firstly, there is the obvious point to make that business travellers only get a very **superficial understanding** of the places they visit. They move within a cocoon designed for foreigners for the period of their stay that the local business elites enter and leave as they please. The western oriented, well-educated, English speaking contacts are often a small proportion of the local population. Much that has been written about China and India's fast development, in particular, has tended to bypass the point that globalization has touched only a fraction of those countries' inhabitants. Cultural convergence may be occurring in some places or within some groups, but not all at the same speed or to the same degree. Shanghai and Lanzhou in Gansu Province have clearly experienced very different exposure to western ways. Despite the economic vitality of, say, Bangalore, there are parts of India with worse poverty levels than sub-Saharan Africa.

The authors may have more in common, at least initially, with an Indian businessman than a British farm labourer, but it is hard to penetrate below a middle class, outward facing surface, especially without knowledge of local language, history and customs. This is especially true of national subcultures or regional differences within countries. One can be quite shocked as an outsider to discover simmering ethnic or political tensions and all the more surprised if they burst out into civil war or terrorist attacks. Companies have been taken unawares by outbreaks of violence and warfare. One can listen to stories of Britons escaping Argentina when the Malvinas were invaded or smuggling out the family during Idi Amin's time in Uganda.

Secondly, **differences are also complex to understand**. Professor Hora Tjitra of Zhejiang University in China explains how different cultures maintain their principles in negotiation: 'Western managers stand by their convictions like an oak, Asians are as flexible as bamboo.' In other words, westerners tend to believe that being steadfast and consistent in their views is the right way to assert principles. By comparison, Asians believe it to be sensible to adjust one's position so long one sticks to one's ultimate purpose. Similarly, he claims the Chinese seem to harmonize to maximize similarity, whereas westerners seek to integrate differences (spring Messe Management, 2010).

The experience of Western retail companies in Japan is a good example of subtle differences that are hard to deal with. As we remarked in the previous chapter, Wal-Mart has struggled and now Tesco has exited the Japanese market, following in the footsteps of Carrefour and Sephora – French retailers that tried to export their proven shopping model without success. All seem to find it hard to get the offer right and still make an acceptable profit given resistance to product standardization with high rents and personnel costs (http://www.ft.com/cms/s/0/fbacd198-d48b-11e0-a42b-00144feab49a. html#axzz1XTlEEwnf).

Doing a deal with a South American might seem easier to accomplish for a European given the familiarity of language, dress and features compared with an Asian, but the way in which business is conducted will vary within the continent and may be easier to manage in some Asian countries than in some South American ones. Appearances can be deceptive.

The **sensitivities that arise from this social, economic and political backdrop can be missed**. Even experienced global organizations do not always pick up the cues. For example, a couple of years ago, Oxfam, as part of its recruitment advertising and new brand image, suggested using 'change' slogans for recruitment adverts in Zimbabwe. However, it was surprised when the local HR objected. 'Change' signified support for the opposition to Mugabe and this would not have been politically acceptable.

Marx might have wanted all the workers of the world to unite to assert their common interest but it is also important to recognize that **social norms may not apply in the same way to all groups**. Thus Japan's traditional model of lifetime employment, progression on the basis of seniority, and enterprise unions suggests a future oriented, deferential and collectivist culture. This was quite true, but the model only applied to a proportion of the workforce: there was a real core/periphery model operating. The core was strongly associated with male skilled workers in the big firms, not with female, low-skill and low-status workers.

Moreover, people have **multiple identities** that might reflect gender, religion, social class and occupation, as well as nationality and location – which can itself be mixed (e.g. Edinburgh, East Coast, Scottish, British and European). Thus nationality can get in the way of class solidarity; religion can divide countries; and men after all are from Mars and women from Venus!

Next, at the **individual level there are many variations in society**, with people holding views or beliefs that differ from the accepted norms. This is an important point because there are dangers in cultural stereotyping that are easy to fall into. As Peter Honey (2008) has said, 'I've met chaotic Germans, quiet Americans, drunken Swedes, generous Scots and tongue-tied Irish.' In the boxed example we give Eva Akesson's experiences to argue this same point. She is at time of writing Programme Director HR Transformation, Tetra Pak based in Modena, Italy.

'Arriving in the respective countries I have had the opportunity to work within, like everyone, I was equipped with some "cultural prejudices". I was convinced I had to arrive 15 minutes before meetings started to ensure I followed the timely German approach. In fact, I realized that the Germans were actually the ones coming much later than the Brazilian and the Italian colleagues. With the same mindset, I took a diplomatic approach, avoiding some of my most expressive manners to suit the Swedish and South East Asian team members, but found this was not necessary because they were far more expressive than I had ever seen my allegedly outgoing Mexican colleagues be.

'This leads me to underline some of the key learning from the eight years in an international work context – we are dealing with PEOPLE, i.e. there are no written cultural rules, no such thing as expected behaviour or reactions and no shortcuts for understanding each other. The key to common understanding and productive collaboration lies in understanding people as *individuals*, having the interest to *listen* to each person's challenges, concerns and *motivational* aspects. In situations of malfunctioning dialogue, I tend to quote one of my personal inspirational sources (Jordan Bloom) – "What do they have to think, to think like that." There is always a good reason for expression of disagreement – the key is to find the constructive approach to bridge the dialogue with actions that increase the value of the project/activity in question. When the dialogue is constructive, people have forums for dialogue and expression of ideas and feel their motivational aspects are fulfilled; it is amazing what can occur in a diverse team, where different personal profiles are connected with each other to reach a common objective. 1 + 1 does not any longer equal 2, but rather 1 + 1 = 3, 4 or even 5.'

Finally, the failure to grasp what is happening elsewhere may be not just the result of missing social cues, but worse it might reflect an **ethnocentrism** that believes in the superiority of western values over non-western Asian or African ones (as we heard with respect to mergers and acquisitions in the last chapter). Moreover, it may seek to co-opt Asians or Africans to its way of thinking, thereby deculturalizing the nations it deals with.

INSTITUTIONAL AND BUSINESS SYSTEM EFFECTS

Besides cultural and individual variation, there are still important **institutional differences** – the 'social, political, economic, business and labour market features of a country or region' (Martin, 2006) – that need to be recognized and what are called '**national business systems**'. According to Martin (2006), the latter 'comprise the interlocking institutions that shape the markets, nature of competition and general business activity of a country'. These are both largely separate from cultural influences, but overlap with respect to views on fairness and justice, social customs and the moral principles of the State. Indeed the CRA-net survey shows that the country is still the strongest influence on HR practice in **national HR** – though there are aspects of convergence, there are also areas where countries still show differences. If the convergence argument is correct, one might expect to see evidence of the coming together of HR practice within, say, western Europe, where one might anticipate the European Union acting as a centripetal force. Whilst there is some truth in this argument, especially for international companies, which we will describe in relation to the service delivery model and governance, there are still profound differences at both institutional and social level, as the CRA-net survey indicates (Mayrhofer et al., 2004). The Marsden research illustrates the same point.

Research carried out by Marsden and Belfield (2009) shows that prevailing institutional arrangements, especially laws relating to hiring and firing, were the best available explanation for differences in reward and learning and development practice between France and the UK. The relative job protection afforded to French workers encouraged investment in staff by the employer and take up by employees.

Take trade unions; within Europe there is a very varied picture on membership density and this does not neatly correlate with industrial action. By way of illustration, all the Scandinavian countries have high trade union membership, but strike levels are above the European average in Denmark and well below it in Sweden. The French with their 'gréviculture' – relatively early resort to strike action – appear to be responding to social change in a way that contrasts with the UK or Germany, both only a short train journey away. However, France has a very low trade union density and its record on industrial action is no worse than many other European countries.

Moreover, **the legal system** and how it is applied differ (even within Europe between systems that reflect the Napoleonic Code and Common Law). For example, the legal framework is so cumbersome in some places that organizations restrict their investment as a consequence. So it is said that Brazilian labour laws make hiring and firing so arduous that some companies prefer to operate in Argentina or Chile (CIPD, 2010a).

Skill availability and formation also have a big effect on operating in many parts of the world, including discouraging involvement in some countries. Brazil, for example, has difficulties in generating enough trained people owing to failings in its education system. But even where sufficient educated resources exist, which should make overseas investment easier, there are other social and political challenges that put off firms. Libya, Cuba and Sri Lanka all have high literacy rates in their regions, but these countries are good examples where current or historical political problems give organizations pause for thought.

So it is wrong to assume that there is **a single western business model and that this is the only show in town**. Japanese companies, even global ones have, according to Massimo Macarti, a set of 'embedded behaviours' that reflect the strong value system. It is not just Japanese companies that export their values. Indian companies are keen to see their conception of employment rights form part of western PR campaigns and in operational practice. This is true for JSW Steel (a subsidiary of the OP Jindal Group a large steel conglomerate owned and operated from Kolkata, India) as it spreads its reach into places such as South Wales.

Hutchison Port Holdings (HPH) operates in 49 ports in 25 countries from its initial Asian routes into Africa, the Middle East and Europe, with interests in the Americas and Australia, yet according to Francis Tong, HR Director, 'it remains a very Chinese organization': diversity of thought and background are yet to surface, especially at the top of the company.

This attachment to the original culture is likely to happen because 'best practice' **HR policies may be more contextual than you might think.** For example, giving emphasis to redeployment in a business change process may be sound thinking in the UK, but is harder to effect in Japan because of loss of face concerns. Work/life balance may be all the rage for professionals in San Francisco or Beijing, but is probably still seen as a meaningless in the inner cities of Baltimore or Shanghai. Indeed, one company said its Bangladesh female employees found work a haven of stability compared with the uncertainty and threat in the world outside. Work has a different meaning to them.

Change is also not going in one direction towards the western approach. Non-western business education is growing and this may generate new business thinking less dominated by western traditions. Even now, many aspirant Asian business leaders are quite eclectic in the sources of their learning, so the ideas behind the application of policy and practice may have many origins. At the very least this will mean adaptation of western methods or even fresh thinking.

> HCL Technologies is a global IT services company operating in 17 countries. It is of Indian origin, but its people management practices are highly unusual given its background. It believes that managers should be 'accountable' to their staff, not the other way round. This is demonstrated in publicly posting online the results of 360 degree feedback on managers or allowing staff to 'open a ticket' if they have a grouse with internal services and only they have the power to close the case. The European HR director says the company is open to business ideas 'no matter where they come from' (Chubb, 2008).

Moreover, although English language and western values appear to be dominant in some contexts, one cannot assume that Portuguese (with Brazilian spellings, particularly since Portugal adopted this form in 2008), Spanish, Cantonese and Mandarin will also be marginalized: twenty-first century business growth may well occur in Latin America and China. Nor are all organizations the same under their national umbrella and operating within the one institutional framework. Sector, for example, is important in shaping business practice, but so too is business philosophy – as the talent management section will demonstrate, there are hire-and-fire companies as well as build-your-own-timber organizations.

Corporate Global Culture

So should organizations want a global corporate culture and is it possible?

Looking first at the possibility of having a trans-national corporate culture, can one conclude from the previous section that culture, institutions/business systems combine to make working in one country such a different ball game from working in another that a global organizational culture is impossible, or are these differences overrated?

Firstly, the evidence, such as it is, suggests a global organizational culture is achievable. Certainly, a Hewitt survey conducted in Europe (2009b) suggested that although three quarters of respondents see a geographic component to their organizational identity (interestingly more on a regional than national basis), most saw their national roots having a weakening influence on their corporate identity.

Secondly, there have been criticisms of the national culture argument, and of Hofstede's work in particular. Philip Stiles (2007) argued on a reinterpretation of the Hofstede data that survey respondents' values were more affected by organizational than national differences. His own research suggested that, where there were national cultural differences, these were largely ignored. Differences in country-to-country practice where they existed were driven by having to respond to institutional contrasts between nation states in legal and regulatory frameworks.

McSweeney (2002) makes many side swipes at Hofstede's work and concludes by saying, 'The limited characterization of culture in Hofstede's work; its confinement within the territory of states; and its methodological flaws mean that it is a restricter not an enhancer of understanding particularities.' In particular he complains that many of the bi-polar distinctions are simplistic – e.g. 'all of us carry both individualist and collectivist tendencies' – and that Hofstede did not sufficiently acknowledge that IBM's employees (the basis of his research) might be locally atypical, nor did he distinguish between occupational and other differences within the firm that interact with national peculiarities.

Moreover, it has been suggested that his work assumes that societies are homogeneous when in fact they are not. A more pointed criticism is that these dimensions appear to be static, when we know there is change. So, for example, the social norms that produce certain work patterns, like those in the Netherlands we described earlier, may not be maintained in the face of economic pressures, including those produced by globalization.

While there are these criticisms of Hofstede's methodology and doubts expressed about his results supporting the continuing importance of national cultures, Martin (2006) summarizes much other research in favour of Hofstede's broad conclusions, not least from Hampden Turner and Trompenaars's sociological research. He sets out the evidence on national differences in assumptions on the external environment, people management, space, time and language.

Hofstede also defended himself by suggesting that the point about culture is precisely its resilience to change in the face of external threats. As Erla Zwingle (1999) stated, 'When cultures receive outside influences, they ignore some and adopt others, and then almost immediately start to transform them.'

Moreover, Wes Harry (2007) took issue with Stiles in a *People Management* debate, arguing that at least Asian values and social systems are not the same as in the west and this profoundly affects people's attitudes to work and their expectations of management and employment. And the institutional context interacts with these employee views, shaping them and being shaped by them.

The next argument to make is that research suggests, and the boxed illustrations below show, that national cultures interact with organizational cultures in complex ways, especially as inter-country differences are complicated by intra-country ones.

In the workplace, people may modify their 'normal' behaviour to fit in with their employer's view of the organizational norms. Katalin Topcu (2005) reports, for example, how Hungarians working in Austria conform more to rules and regulations than they would do at home. By contrast, employees sometimes may exaggerate their 'national characteristics' to challenge the employer, if what they see as an externally imposed, foreign culture. Indeed, there is evidence to suggest that in matters relating to multinational company ownership, employees can be quite schizophrenic, alternating between being proud to work for a global, major name and demeaned by neo-colonial overlordship.

Their behaviour will relate, not surprisingly, to the positive and negative experiences they have had with their bosses. Some research (Sierk and Hyunghae, 2009) points to the fact that senior host employees are frustrated to a greater degree with foreign firms than more junior staff if they believe their career prospects are hindered by all the top jobs going to home country individuals.

Exaggeration of national characteristics can also go the other way. Katalin Topcu's research suggests how Austrians emphasize their attention to rules and regulations when in Hungary to a far greater extent than they would in Austria or Germany, precisely because of their perception that Hungarians were 'slack' in their attention to these rules. This has the potential to generate conflict if the Hungarians (the hosts in this case) react against both the assumptions made about them by the Austrians and the pressure to conform to outside standards by those who are after all their formal imperial rulers.

To add to the complexity there are differences between people in the same country, and even cultural manifestations that vary according to context – a Syrian woman told us that it was acceptable to challenge your boss at work but not your father or husband at home – that make generalizations about national culture even more difficult. If these differences are valid (and here we do have to distinguish between anecdote and properly undertaken research), then it makes it easier to build a distinctive organizational culture, especially because those round the world attracted to a distinct global offering will self-select.

As to the benefits of a common global culture, from a corporate perspective what are the arguments in favour? The fundamental business driver, as with brands, is to develop 'corporateness'. Organizations want to have a glue that binds employees together and a means to control their behaviour, both within the terms they set. 'Doing things the General Mills way' is a clear description of a corporate ambition of this kind (CIPD, 2010c). A culture defines 'what we do round here' and this also implies what we don't do as well. Asserting a common set of values, business principles and behavioural frameworks acts to inform colleagues of the positive things expected of them (e.g. teamwork, knowledge sharing, openness, etc.) and also those behaviours that will not be tolerated (e.g. dishonesty, buck passing, sexual harassment, etc.). The global organization rightly feels that some of these ethical principles have to be universal because the organization is held responsible by world bodies like the International Labour Organization (ILO) that assert universal human rights or to meet the terms of the UN Global Compact, by stock markets operating to largely the same values set as each other, by western governments (or the European Union) that pursue their vision of good governance outside their territorial area and by the media that claims to reflect public opinion. The organization needs to protect itself from challenge be it over the use of child labour, the payment of bribes, the promotion of relatives or whatever is felt to be contrary to these assumptions about how business ought to be conducted.

Novo Nordisk, for example, reacted to a scandal of improper payments to the Iraqi government during 2001 and 2003 by instituting a company wide training programme that instilled a common approach to business ethics that replaced more local practices. This has been backed by a global business ethics board and three yearly audits of business units of adherence to the Novo Nordisk Way. The aim is to create a unified culture (Smedley, 2011).

British American Tobacco's 2009 Sustainability Report has a whole section on managing human rights, especially emphasizing the avoidance of child labour, including in the supply chain. It further states that their companies are required to operate according to Group Employment Principles that assert equal opportunities and require non-discrimination.

The binding together of organizations comes from the communication of these values and principles, the association with the purpose of the organization (reflected in the brand) and with the shorter-term business goals (profit maximization, cost reduction, innovation, etc.). The organizational aim is to engage employees such that they have a strong attachment to the firm that will deliver results in terms of higher productivity. Put more crudely, the organization wants its whole workforce to be 'on message'.

There are a number of factors working in favour of the global firm succeeding in creating a single global culture.

CULTURAL ASSIMILATION

- **Selection process** The selection process should identify those whose attitudes and values would fit working for a multinational company. Paula Larson of Invensys has taken this further using a modified version of Hofstede's classification (picking out the power distance, collectivism, masculinity and uncertainty avoidance features) to test for individual fit with the organization. She successfully applied the technique to Americans joining a Japanese firm (Johnson, 2008).
- **Induction process** The power of organizational socialization is such that through the induction and management processes, employees learn to accept and then support the organizational business culture. For example, Oxfam explicitly hopes that the induction process will enable new recruits to understand and endorse the organizational values. They use an interactive 'Knowledge of Oxfam' CD in four languages to provide a consistent – and exciting – introduction to Oxfam wherever you are in the world – even for recruits to watch on the plane out headed for an emergency.

- **Cultural familiarization** Training courses, especially management development programmes, are important too in reinforcing and extending this capability of operating in potentially strange and foreign environments with unfamiliar cultural norms. This may also have a strong element of underlining a common set of corporately endorsed values that will be transmitted by a leadership cadre that shares a common perspective. For example, Oxfam has worked hard to achieve cultural familiarization, using training managers to develop the concept of giving honest and constructive feedback accepted across the world.

GLOBAL ORIENTATION

- **Global affiliation** Employees self-select to work for global companies because they are attracted to the brand (which may give status in their local community), accept western business mores, and are excited by the prospect of international communication.

> Hindustan increasingly promotes itself as part of the Unilever global footprint. This is attractive to recruits and employees in India, as many want to be part of a global firm; with the second most quoted reason for joining HUL identified as 'global career opportunities'. In the aspirational culture of Indian society being part of a global firm means higher standards of living and wages.

- **Western culture** Even in non-western companies there may be aspects of western business culture that are seen as beneficial to organizational performance. Thus Francis Tong stressed that he felt HPH had a 'western' style of culture, notwithstanding its traditional Asian senior leadership group, in that there is an ability to speak openly and speak up, which he feels is a 'breath of fresh air' in Asian context. This was at first a culture shock for local supervisors but one they have come to accept.
- **Global mindset** This process is then reinforced through selection of the talented for high-potential development or in succession planning. As with all organizations, those who play the game, as well as those with the requisite competencies, will be picked out. Many international organizations, in particular, will, as we will see in Chapter 6, choose for development those who have the skills and attitudes (e.g. empathy, adaptability) that will allow them to prosper in the global village. These staff can come from anywhere in the world as long as they can develop a global mindset. Trompenaars and Woolliams (1999) argued that those with what they called a 'trans-cultural competence' were not only high performing, but also particularly effective in handling diversity and international working, especially in bridging and reconciling the cultural differences we described earlier.

REINFORCING THE CULTURE GLOBALLY

- **Maintaining consistency** Management then will work on their staff at the formal and informal level, advising, cajoling or directing them to behave in ways that are consistent with the organizational norms.
- **Creating alignment** Formal communication channels through video broadcasts, letters from the CEO, corporate newspapers, recognition schemes reinforce what the organization sees as important. The translation of such communiqués into local languages is key to them being understood by employees and the more personal or 'authentic' they are, the more likely they will be well received by staff wherever in the world they may work.

> The one thing everybody reads in Oxfam is a letter from Barbara, the Chief Executive, which she sends personally every month. She writes it entirely herself, about what she's been doing and what's bothering her, so it has an authenticity that cuts through much better than the more 'professional' communications.

- **Corporate messaging** Expatriates, especially those in senior management positions from the home base, may be a powerful source of transmitting the corporate message in a more thorough going sense, as they may typically have three years of demonstrating the corporate imperatives.
- **Absorbing the corporate way** Similarly, other employees from business units/ subsidiaries going on expatriate assignments, secondments, short-term visits, working on global projects or just attending global meetings are likely to absorb the corporate line on how to do business. This approach was, for example, successfully used to help East Europeans acclimatize to West Germany's business modes.

> Oxfam finds the best learning is by staff visiting around the world. Says HR Director Jane Cotton: 'It is fantastic for those staff who can get out to the programme. And it's great for local staff to visit the shops and meet volunteers in the UK. It makes them determined to be more cost effective. When British based HR staff do secondments and projects, they really feel what it's like to work in places where electricity and water are frequently off and where security is extremely dicey. It reminds us so forcibly why we need to keep HR as simple as possible!'

- **Gen X and Y** Moreover, organizations can work with the flow of the growing homogeneity of younger people, as we reported earlier. For Leena Nair from HUL, global frameworks and people management practices make increasing sense in this context.

Challenges

There are a number of obstacles faced by those engaged in developing a global corporate culture. Some of these are sufficiently fundamental for organizations to give thought to whether such an approach is the right way forward. Several of these objections are similar to those we will discuss under the standardization of HR policies and practices, because they have same roots in wanting commonality.

ETHNOCENTRICITY

- **Reinforcement of the home view** In seeking a truly global organization, one suspects that the organizational default is to refer to the home country model, and indeed research suggests that is particularly true for US companies. Their HR practices appear to be embedded in the American business system and are exported as the approach to follow, sometimes without thought on their applicability elsewhere, thereby demonstrating ignorance of the laws, mores or simple facts of life in other countries.

GTEC, a US company, once operated in a joint venture with Aitken Spence in Sri Lanka. It declared it had a policy that no one employed in the partnership should be allowed to ride a motorcycle in any activities relating to their employment. This seemed a sensible (if restrictive) approach from the US perspective: it reduced accidents and insurance claims. However, globalizing this policy was a step too far. Aitken Spence pointed out that even a Honda Civic costs $100,000 dollars to buy and an accountant, say, is only paid about $6,000 per year. It was possible to operate GTEC's policy but it would be very expensive to apply since the company would have to purchase the vehicles as the employees clearly could not.

- **Imposition of western values** Despite the claims of those who argue for a set of universal values, there are those who believe that we are indeed talking about compelling countries to abide by western ethical model based on the Judeo-Christian tradition. As Timothy Garton Ash observed, the award of the Nobel Peace Prize is based on the appeal to 'universal' human rights, but the Chinese reaction to the award to Liu Xiaobo was seen by them as the imposition of 'western' values as part of a continuing imperialist plot (Garton Ash, 2010). Critics come from two directions: the 'ethical relativists' that would contend that there are different, equally legitimate codes of ethics and it is wrong to impose a particular set on all the others. The other objection comes from ethical absolutists that want to see their vision, not a western one, as the dominant one in their (part of the) company.

Reflecting upon the western objection to nepotism, Paul Ballman argued: 'Why should this perspective be morally superior to the person who puts the welfare of their family or community first instead. Of course, we can always find reasons why our perspective is "better for business", but it will always be hard for us to differentiate between doing something because it is best and doing it because it is what we are used to' (CIPD, 2010a).

- **Difference among neighbours too** These challenges are not restricted to the 'clash of civilizations', west versus east, but also within broadly similar countries. Thus Scandinavia gives higher importance to social equality and consequently tolerates variable pay less than the UK, especially if bonus distribution is very much skewed towards the top of the shop. Poland is a more individualist country than the Czech Republic next door, which has retained a collectivist tradition from Communism. An e-mail based contact centre might work well in Spain, but less well in Argentina where the telephone is favoured for sorting out issues.
- **National stereotypes** These challenges are made all the harder through persistent stereotypes that make cooperative working all the more difficult. During our discussions we heard of the difficulties of doing business with the Chinese (secretive), of the Koreans (untrustworthy), Indians (arrogant) and the Americans (unreceptive). Perhaps being British we did not hear complaints about the UK! There are colonial hangovers to cope with and the alleged neo-colonialism of Indians and Chinese. There are issues that come from past conflicts as well as current ones. This typecasting is not, of course, limited to nationalities but is also found in gender, age, beliefs and sexual orientation. It is not our place to make judgements on these accusations, but to observe that these perceptions exist and they must make the development of global culture all the harder, especially with management spread thinly across the organization, and not all the management cadre is global in its thinking or on message with respect to diversity.

> As Sierk Ybema and Hyunghae Byun's (2009) research into working in international firms suggests, this stereotyping can become deliberate or inadvertent cultivation of cultural differences, mixing self-praise for their own national characteristics (in this research the Dutch showing off their communication skills, flexibility and decision making ability whilst the Japanese emphasize their virtues of 'loyalty and devotion') with denigration of the manifestations of the culture they are exposed to (the Japanese pointing to the Dutch vices of 'imprudence and impoliteness', reciprocated by the Dutch complaining of Japanese slow decision making and hierarchical business management).

COMMUNICATION AND (MIS)UNDERSTANDING

- **Poor performance of the 'cascade'** The corporate message does not get through. British American Tobacco, for example, tested how well colleagues round the world took in a video from the CEO on business direction. It had been mandatory for the video to be shown, but too few a number for comfort had any recollection of the CEO's messages. Oxfam also found that cascade briefings did not work.
- **Reaching non-wired employees** Relying on technology to get your message across may well be unrealistic. Connections between HQ and some locations may be poor. Is every employee linked in to your corporate system, assuming they have access to a computer? Once more, modern communication methods work for the online population but may exclude the offline workers.

- **Your intentions are misunderstood** The aim may be to ensure behaviours are acceptable to a global firm, but it might be misread that you are trying to impose a particular belief set. One UK interviewee faced this problem in a people management training programme where a Korean accused him of trying to change his beliefs.

IMPLEMENTATION

- **Transplant rejection** Assumptions are made that standard management activities that work well in one (western) setting will work in other cultures. The problem may be due to
    - **poor understanding** This may stem from an imperfect grasp of what is being proposed, perhaps because the location has only a superficial understanding of the corporate centre's intentions. So, for example, the holistic nature of Japanese management practices has only dimly been understood in some western countries. Similarly, some Indian companies appear to have over enthusiastically adopted imported business practices without recognition of the importance of organizational context to their successful implementation (CIPD, 2010a).
    - **deliberate misunderstanding** If what is proposed is disliked, either on its own merits or simply because it is a corporate centre imposition, then execution will suffer. This is especially true if those who are expected to implement it (often first line managers) believe the initiative is inappropriate to their circumstances. The result may be half-hearted efforts or complete omission. As an example, quality circles have often been unsuccessful in the UK due to middle management subversion; or
    - **inappropriate export** Organizations may have been ill advised in the first place to transplant ideas because they simply will not work in this environment. For example, mentoring does not appear to operate successfully in China (McCauley, 2008). Oxfam has been found it especially difficult in some countries to use 360 degree inputs. McCauley (2008) reports research suggesting the 'process was found to be most effective in cultures with low power distance and individualistic values'.
        So, processes like the US originated Six Sigma and Japanese just-in-time inventory control and lean systems, are to be found in wide use, but that does not mean they have been successfully applied.
- **Variation in local adoption** There is likely to be uneven execution of putting corporate values into practice. This may have as much to do with management capability and style as to do with location (as Oxfam found), but managerial weaknesses may be more pronounced in some business units or workplaces. Then, as Martin and Hetrick (2006) suggest, 'even if companies are initially successful in implanting their home-grown practices, they can never be sure how these transferred practices will interact with the existing systems to produce anything like the originally intended outcomes'.
- **Different leadership norms** House et al.'s research (1999) suggests leadership will be more effective in going with the cultural grain. Their review concluded that socially learned collective norms concerning the nature of leadership, amongst other things, meant that the greater the fit between leader behaviours and the implicit theories of leadership, the more the leader will be accepted and consequently be

effective. Thus, if for business reasons the leadership wishes to change the culture it will come up against a question of legitimacy.

- **Local differences** Then there are occupational and sectoral differences that emerge in particular forms in individual countries. For example, there is the Japanese propensity for male white-collar workers to see the office as a social place. This means staff tend to stay late as part of work group experience and are dubious about the benefits of remote working. How do you deal with that against the work/life balance preferences of, say, teleworkers living in the south of France or islands of north-west Scotland? Do you ignore these differences or allow national/occupational subcultures to operate? The latter runs contrary to the whole thrust towards a common culture, governed by an integrating set of strategies and structures.

- **Barriers to local diffusion** Even where cultural, communication and linguistic barriers are relatively easily overcome there are issues at country level that restrict organizational integration and the diffusion of a common business approach. As we will describe in Chapter 7, there is the local exercise of power. This is what a Eurasian bank has found. The central functions find it difficult to pursue common approaches because national business leaders want to flex their muscles. This opposition may be dressed up as national cultural particularism, but in fact it may be due to retention of power. The local culture might reflect more the preferences of the local MD than of the corporate centre.

- **Unchanging culture** If organizations need to adapt and change there cannot be a fixed culture. This especially applies to maturing companies. During its early years, SAP's development centred on its founder-led engineering culture, with an emphasis on rigour and thoroughness, together with entrepreneurialism. Personal relationships and values were important also. But trying to export this sort of culture is not that straightforward. Does it fit all geographies and is it affected by business circumstances? For example, does the business philosophy suit a more competitive market place? Should it be adopted by operating companies around the world, whether it fits their current circumstances or not?

- **Multiple markets** Finally, companies themselves do not act as if the world is a single market place. SAP has appreciated that some of its people will not be able to operate in new market conditions with the geographic focus of the business switching to those areas with higher growth potential, i.e. the Middle East, Brazil and China. It understands that it needs staff capable of dealing with the cultural challenges to be faced outside western Europe and North America. This point was put even more clearly by Giovanni Bisignani, CEO of IATA: 'We must recognise that we cannot sell in Mumbai with a Montreal mindset. And we will not convince a potential partner in Guangzhou with a Geneva approach' (Jonsen and Bryant, 2008).

Success Factors

How might organizations address these challenges: how do you try to shape the culture that applies and what determines your thinking? Some possible 'solutions' are offered below:

- **Clear business principles** Define a clear set of business principles and values that are non-negotiable. Toby Peyton Jones (Director HR, Siemens Plc and North West Europe) has described these as 'the rules of the road 'or 'a highway code' that can be understood and acted on across borders and culture. They need therefore to be written at a level of abstraction that makes them accessible to all parties. This means careful drafting and testing with a wide audience to see whether unwittingly any trespassing on cultural sensitivities has occurred. However, there may be times when the organization has to assert principles it wants to uphold in the face of opposition, say relating to ethnic or gender discrimination. For Peyton Jones these are 'the red lines' of organizational life that need to be defended, as in many instances they are strongly linked to the source of long-term competitive advantage.

- **Cultural flex** Operate on the principle 'when in Rome do as the Romans would do' (to a degree at least). This is the cultural adaptation approach that acknowledges and respects the local culture, avoiding ethno centralism. It does not try to impose the home country values or customs, but accepts that the host country legitimately operates in its own way. However, the 'to a degree at least' qualification is important. The Romans had slaves, were at times corrupt – offering and receiving bribes – and participated in gruesome sporting events that might not be widely accepted today. So local adaptation has its limits and the fundamental business tenets of the organization should be upheld wherever the organization operates.

Nomura's values of 'lead, connect, create, achieve' are used worldwide, but are interpreted differently in different places, according to the Global Head of Organizational Design and Development, Stephen Sidebottom. It seems that the importance and emphasis given to these concepts varies, with the Japanese giving more weight to the creativity aspect coming from the leadership and the West (and other parts of Asia) focusing on performance achievement. The company seems untroubled by these variations, perhaps because the basic purpose of the firm is not in doubt. In this it is helped by the fact that investment banking is basically the same wherever it is practised (Grapevine, 2010a).

Schneider Electric tries to find a 'subtle balance' between local culture ('a source of enrichment') and global 'unifying principles' that 'serve as stable, secure guidelines'. Its policy is 'put our trust very quickly in the local team as they won't let you down'. Previously, the idea was to ensure a large expatriate presence because 'it was said that they were the only ones who understood how the business ran' – which whilst 'partially true' stems from a 'neo colonial mentality' that is out of date (Entreprise&Personnel, 2006).

- **Focus on behaviours not beliefs** In particular, organizations might more safely focus on behaviours rather than beliefs in trying to integrate or control. It is not up to the employer to determine what individuals hold sacred, but it is legitimate to legislate against certain behaviours. An obvious example would be sexual harassment: practices which in some cultures are accepted (or maybe just tolerated) would not be deemed allowable in most global companies. This distinction between beliefs and behaviours is easy to say and harder to operationalize. The current debate in France and Belgium on women wearing the Muslim veil illustrates this point. If the behaviour is a representation of belief should the organization leave the matter purely to personal choice? However, if there is legalization that bans its use in public places, presumably the organization would have to comply, and, presumably, there are jobs were wearing the veil might present a health hazard. There was a similar debate in the UK about Sikhs wearing helmets when riding motorcycles. And then there was the BA case and the wearing of a visible cross by an employee at work, which touches on how one implements a diversity policy.

BA said in a statement: 'British Airways has 34,000 uniformed staff, all of whom know they must abide by our uniform policy. The policy does not ban staff from wearing a cross. It lays down that personal items of jewellery, including crosses may be worn – but underneath the uniform. Other airlines have the same policy. The policy recognises that it is not practical for some religious symbols – such as turbans and hijabs – to be worn underneath the uniform. This is purely a question of practicality. There is no discrimination between faiths. In Nadia Eweida's case, she is not suspended and we want her to come back to work. We have explained to her the need to comply with the uniform policy like all her colleagues whatever their faith.'

Interestingly, in a contemporaneous poll, the BBC found that 70 per cent of respondents said yes to the question: *Should there be a right to wear a cross at work?*

- **Both corporate *and* locally customized policies** But this means you can still build in flexibility to HR policies and practices to allow variation to reflect cultural differences without violation of these principles. You can mix your policy suite so that those matters which are essential to corporate integration are standardized, but those where this is not necessary reflect local needs. For example, Saint-Gobain (Allouche, 2008) uses a mixed model in China, insisting upon a common performance appraisal process, but innovating by introducing seniority bonuses to suit local preferences, whilst allowing local customization on other policies like housing aid, transport to work and meal subsidies. By this means, you can demonstrate your commitment to cultural diversity by signals you send that the corporate centre is sensitive to the needs of different groups. This can have both practical and symbolic value. It is easier to flex the 'how' than the 'what'. For example, a company in Sri Lanka allows individuals to pick their holiday package to reflect Singhalese, Tamil, Christian or Muslim festivals. Other ways this may be achieved is through the choice of communication media or diversification of the assessors of your emerging talent.
- **Reward supports culture** Develop reward systems in a way that supports the culture you wish to develop. JSW Steel has used profit sharing to negate the past practice of backhanders and corruption because the staff can share in the company success in a more open way. Attraction and retention of staff has improved as a result. However, the rewards have to fit, or effectively lead, local expectations. Thus a German company offering an improved pension to improve retention might be the right solution at home, but not in those parts of the world where immediate cash is more prized.

- **Deep leadership understanding** Ensure that the leadership of the organization is aware of the power of culture and is sensitive to its influence. This recognition can be both its ability to do good or about the ill effects of having the wrong sort of culture. We have seen and read about the problems of organizations where managers abrogate responsibility for decisions or take undue risks; where there is excessive secrecy or deference; corruption or greed. Appreciation of the power of culture can be developed through formal programmes, coaching, site visits (that are less superficial than the regal tour), attendance at international training courses and informal lunches and teas. This can develop into creating a leadership that encourages organizational agility to restrict rigidity in thinking. Leaders must recognize that organizational cultures that are open to new thinking, new ways of working, new experiences are likely to prosper in the global market place.

- **A role for HR** An important task for HR is to act as the cultural translator particularly between locations and HQ. As a current or past expatriate, or through research and careful observation, members of the HR team can operate as the conduit between different parts of the organization. Useful actions might include explaining 'surprising' behaviour (e.g. an operating company's negative reaction to an 'obvious' policy change) or counselling on whether policy developments will be understood and supported round the world.

- **International communication approaches** Whether internal communication is largely from the centre, or centrally led and with local adaptation depends (like HR approaches) on the organization's philosophy. But many organizations are now realizing the limitations of the traditional cascade, even at a national level. Essentially, this approach suffers from the 'message in a bottle' problem where it is not certain where the message will land, so central communication fails to connect locally and engage even senior regional leaders. Successful organizations ensure that international communication is a management responsibility and one that supports business performance. Even talented local communicators face an impossible challenge if local managers are not onside. Effective central communication teams fully support local colleagues by engaging senior executives with communication that is 'business real' and performance oriented. Together, they facilitate a business dialogue between senior executives and local line managers. For non-wired employees, in retail environments and remote locations, for example, many global organizations still use paper based systems, but do so creatively, such as through as posters with impact. As Shell has found, in some cultures pictures speak louder than words. Organizations also make full use of other channels, such as internet kiosks, video and telephone for their non-wired staff.

- **Organizational assumption tracking** Use culture audits to see what your employees believe the organizational culture to be and how this might contrast with what the organization might want. Variation by grade, function and country would also illustrate how homogenous a culture this is and allow judgement about how much variation is acceptable against the business model. Such audits can also identify variation by business unit, indicating whether there are important subcultures reflecting real or territorial differences. Culture surveys and specific focus groups can be used to capture the employee's perspective. The use of drawing and metaphors can help surface opinion, as shown in Figure 3.1

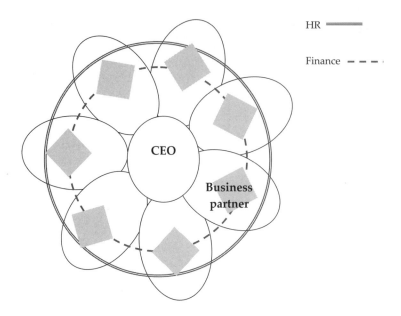

Figure 3.1   A cultural representation of MAS Intimates in Sri Lanka

---

At the time, Shanaaz Preena was Head of HR for MAS Intimates. This is a Sri Lankan international company that makes lingerie for some leading international brands. Asked at an international symposium held by IPMA-HR in Beijing to represent her organisation's culture pictorially, Shanaaz drew her company as like a wheel with the CEO at the centre. The CEO at the hub gives the wheel its discretion but is reliant on the blades to give rotational energy. He operates down the functional strands of the wheel as well as pulling them altogether. These functional strands can be quite distinct from each other because they may be supporting individual business activities for different clients. These lines need to be kept apart for contractual reasons: the clients do not want their activity compromised by any other – they want to retain dedicated resources for their product line.

The very shape of the picture tells us a great deal about the company. Many people conceive of an organization as a top down driven entity where power flows mainly in one direction downwards. In this representation, it is a harmonious structure with all the well-oiled parts working together showing their interconnectivity – a transparent communication network, including the role of the support functions (Finance and HR) and in particular, the positioning of the HR business partner.

- **Support for international networking** Many opportunities for in-organizational cross-national dialogue have been cut back by those who judge meetings on a narrow conception of their costs against benefits or to meet more justifiable environmental sustainability goals. Meetings and events like conferences or social occasions are an excellent way to build understanding between those working in different countries (and sometimes also different business units) and has benefit further down the line in creating camaraderie that can help the organization through subsequent change programmes. Virtual networking may help sustain these relationships, but periodic face to face contact is essential to avoid their ultimate decay.

- **Encourage learning from others** This capacity for knowledge acquisition and deployment can be developed in a number of ways from those outside the organization, e.g. through partnerships or joint ventures with other companies, as the boxed example shows; participation in external learning and development events; study tours or business visits to other organizations in other countries, etc. Rather than resist foreign methods, organizations would be better served seeing what works for others and take from it those tactics that work for them. So you should seize any attempts to get ideas, new practices and ways of doing things from other organizations.

In Malaysia, Shell operates as a competitor to Petronas (the state oil company), as a trainer to its staff; as subject to its regulatory oversight and as a partner in joint activities. This multiplicity of interactions breeds flexibility in the minds of Shell employees and prevents a rigid approach to dealings with it. A simple us against them would be wholly inappropriate.

SAP has US and European HR networking groups of customers to discuss either technical or general HR issues. Moreover, the company organizes customer visits to see either its HR (or financial) systems technology in use or forms of HR (Finance) structure (like shared services) that might be of interest to clients. For example, the company organizes site visits to the shared services centre in Prague.

There are many other networking groups, like Oxen Park, that operate on a national or trans-national basis that encourage learning on HR matters.

- **Assumption alert** Similarly, eliminate cultural stereotyping. One of the principles of Percy Barnevik, the CEO of the ABB Group between 1988 and 1996, is that you should deal with the person not with your assumptions that might flow from their nationality. You should play the ball not the man. This is an issue we will cover again under the diversity heading.
- **Intercultural awareness raising** We will return to this point when considering expatriates, as they are the obvious candidates for such training, but there is a case for raising the general level of cultural sensitivity. This may be picked up in diversity training, but may need to go further in considering cross-national issues. For example, the Hofstede and Hampden-Turner/Trompenaaars research can provide useful frameworks in which people can talk about what they really think about those from other countries. Being aware in a German company that the predominant decision making style is rational and analytical, whereas in other parts of the world it is intuitive and ethical, is useful to know for anyone who interfaces with colleagues in those parts of the world. The number of staff who have international phone or e-mail contact is surprisingly high in global companies and the room for misunderstanding is potentially quite large. As the authors found in writing this book, the nuances

used in one's native tongue (and the underlying cultural norms) are often lost by others not party to these subtleties. One is reminded of the reason why the US army failed to relieve the Glosters at the battle of the Imjin River in the Korean War: they misunderstood the nature of British understatement in describing the extent of the overwhelming odds they faced against Chinese forces.

4 *Diversity*

Why impose conformity when we can benefit from diversity? (Henry Mintzberg)

Diversity has long been recognized as a vital component of healthy organization, a way to overcome the dangers of cloning and group-think. The question remains: 'Just how much diversity do we need here?' While HR professionals push for more diversity and senior executives espouse its value, line managers might feel one can have too much of a good thing. This is a far greater challenge in the global than national context and puts more pressure on those managing to cope with the local implications of a corporate approach to diversity.

In this chapter we discuss the difficulties and success factors in developing and delivering diversity strategies. But in doing this we are also challenging organizations to think much more explicitly about what they are *really* trying to achieve, their motivations and the ultimate benefits they expect.

What and Why Diversity

Many organizations, either for internal reasons or to meet external (legal or procurement) requirements, seek employee diversity.

What do we mean by diversity? There are many possibilities in celebrating difference by:

- gender
- ethnicity
- sexual orientation
- social class
- age
- religious belief or philosophical conviction
- physical disability.

Besides the statutory obligations and some of the more obvious distinctions, HR practitioners are increasingly concerned to see diversity in thinking style, management style, personal beliefs and working preferences. This might be to respond to the cultural diversity we described in the previous chapter, or to recognize the business benefits of difference. This is then reflected in the emergence of diversity and *inclusion* in specialist job titles.

SAP has established diversity networks as follows:

- businesswomen's network
- cultural network
- family and career
- mental and physical ability
- older employees
- sexual orientation.

This leads to the question of whether it is better if firms create these sorts of networks or do they support those created by the various interest groups themselves. The argument for the former approach is that it demonstrates the company's commitment to a range of forms of diversity. The argument for employee created networks is that they tend to have better buy-in from participants and are more trusted and popular than company organized ones. Thinking about this question on a global scale, one can see the practical difficulties of emergent networks and an understandable wish for management to give them some help to get going.

Where organizations are examining diversity to meet their own interests, as opposed to fulfilling legal obligations – 'to use the diversity of the workforce as a strength rather than as a weakness', to quote Massimo Macarti from Canon Europe – there are a number of drivers:

- to reflect the diversity of the customer base
- to exploit the diversity of the workforce to generate a greater range of ideas, insights, experiences, etc.
- to have a greater range of types of people at senior or executive level, either for presentational reasons or to improve decision making
- to develop the corporate image/employer brand
- to widen the labour pool
- to acquire new/different skills (though the suggestion that gender or ethnic diversity offers new skills is controversial).

Many of our case study organizations are actively engaged in broadening their executive or management population, particularly with respect to gender and nationality.

Siemens' aim is to have 'global talent' or globally trained managers represented at all levels in the organization. The company has not yet reached this goal. Locally sourced managers are in place where there is a good person, but not really at sector/cluster CEO level or the global Managing Board. There are only two non-Germans on the board – a Swiss lady and an American man.

SAP's HR top team was, until the recent appointment of a female German, white, male and middle-aged, split between Britons and Germans. There is a wider range of nationalities on the board. There is an American, a Dane, a Belgian, as well as Germans. However, in the top 60 in the organization there are only five woman and two non-whites. Given the expected business growth will be in Asia, this is a disappointing position.

Shell has had a conscious policy over many years of reducing the dependency on Anglo/ Dutch employees, especially at senior positions. So it deliberately tried to encourage both the expatriation of high-potential staff from outside the UK/Netherlands and to create mixed nationality management teams in operating companies. In particular, the company is trying to ensure that all its country heads (an important representative role) are from the country concerned.

Garmt Louw believes the argument on diversity has been won. He feels there is no need for social engineering to effect change because management gets it. The message has been pushed for so long and a new generation takes it as read. At a practical level, as Head of Talent Management and Development he is expected to put forward a 'balanced list' of candidates for consideration for senior jobs, reflecting not just gender but national mix. This has both principled and pragmatic origins. It is principled because Shell believes fundamentally in the value of diversity. Pragmatic because business growth will come in the east, not the west and so the company leadership should have an appropriate proportion of Asians.

There are automatic checks on pay decisions by gender and in some cases ethnicity. However, he admitted that in many ways it is still a male-dominated organization and there are the 'subtleties of culture' that mean that certain groups (especially British and Dutch) are still dominant.

British American Tobacco is seeking to increase female representation in senior management positions. The Management Board Talent Review meetings track progress, which is recognized to be a slow process. There are no women on the Management Board and less than 10 per cent in the top two grades below that level, but half the management trainees are female.

Oxfam is pleased with its recent success whereby half the country directors come from developing countries rather than the west, up from a third two years ago. There has also been a major leap forward in women's leadership at Corporate Management Team level from 1 in 7 to 4 in 7, including the Chief Executive. The organization has also been able to place women in really challenging places in South Asia and even Afghanistan.

What emerges from these examples is that the principal goal and main diversity activity from an HR perspective is to widen the talent pool. This is a good thing in itself as it offers the potential of a greater choice of people and the opportunity to find those with a broad range of skills and abilities, but it is also important from the organizational perspective in that it is another way of demonstrating sensitivity to the variety of customers, particularly in retail operations. The workforce should reflect the population it serves and this applies not just at the checkout till, in the factory or at the sales desk, but also in the offices and executive suites. For example, NatWest used to hire people of Chinese origin into some of its London west end branches given their proximity to Chinatown. The impact of such an approach is all the greater if some of these staff progress to more senior positions in their organization.

A Company of all the Talents

Ensuring your organization has a sufficiently diverse population is even more important for global organizations than national ones. The broader reasoning for the diversity drive in talent management (see Chapter 6) will be covered later, but it is a vital mechanism to ensure having a wider pool of people available to bring a varied set of contributions to bear. This might focus on top talent, on leadership positions or across the workforce, depending again on the talent management philosophy.

Gender diversity has been the principal area of attention. Schlumberger, for example, has sought to grow the proportion of women in senior positions, changing its policies on work/life balance and on mobility to try to bring this about. Many organizations would follow the Allianz challenge: what is the diversity of my management team and pipeline? They might set out their results like Wallenius Wilhelmsen Logistics, which describes the overall proportion of women in the company (28 per cent), the proportion in management (24 per cent) and the percentage of 'top talents' (9 per cent).

Challenges

However, there are challenges for global companies to meet, or at least questions to ask.

- **Lack of clear goals** Do companies think through properly what their diversity goals really are? You might say you have already answered your own question by setting out the list above. However, some companies really only try to conform to their legal obligations in whichever jurisdiction they operate. They may make no attempt to cohere their diversity policies and practices. Another type of organization talks a good game, but it is only in fact a PR exercise. Being strong on diversity is thought to be good for business so it appears as an organizational goal on the corporate intranet. Others may say they want true diversity but not act to make it happen. They think that by having action groups they have solved the 'problem'.
- **Take the case of women** Organizations frequently think they have dealt with encouraging women into senior positions by creating a women's network. The organization may have a policy or even a target for the proportion of women in executive positions, but it does nothing to address issues of flexible working or the dominant sexist and macho culture, both of which deter women from seeking promotion to these roles (unless of course they take on male characteristics). Thus diversity is mere political correctness. The challenge is even greater as companies grow internationally since the position of (working) women varies considerably across the globe, from positive encouragement in labour market participation (e.g. through maternity leave possibilities) to constraints relating to particular jobs or employment after marriage. There are also questions of preference as well as gender stereotyping that draw women towards some careers more than others. Is it that charities, like Oxfam, are successful in appointing women to senior positions because they prefer this kind of work or because the organization is more welcoming of them? Indeed, even in the 'developed' world, one might question whether the gender diversity argument has really been won when the President of the Federation of German Industry told his members, in rejecting quotas, 'in the not too distant future it will

be worth it to have a good reputation in the field of gender equality' (http://www.dw-world.de/dw/article/0,,14953136,00.html). It is hard to understand why this is a future need!

- **Or ethnic minorities** The issue with ethnic diversity is subtler, and more complex in an international organization. There can be an initial intention to ensure that the workforce in any one country is a fair reflection of the wider society, and that minority groups are represented in senior posts. There are, however, in some locations real difficulties in delivering this goal. Minority ethnic groups may be less well educated, or as well educated but avoid jobs in business, preferring work in the professions of law or medicine. There may be a government policy of favouring 'nationals' rather than immigrants, as in parts of the Middle East. There are outright cases of discrimination, e.g. against those of Chinese origin in parts of South East Asia. Women from ethnic minorities may be excluded, or merely discouraged, from studying certain courses preventing their employment in the relevant occupations.

- **HQ-centric** In most multinational companies, whilst there is often a genuine wish to see a wider range of nationalities in senior global positions, unintended obstacles impede progress towards this goal. There are practical issues, which we will more fully cover later under expatriation, such as the fact that in some companies executive positions are largely in the corporate headquarters in the west, and there can be visa restrictions or personal reasons why non-westerners find it difficult to take up these posts.

- **Hard to keep 'minorities' on-side** Even organizations that attach high importance to open and meritocratic processes have often found, for these and other reasons, insufficient women and ethnic minorities being identified as high potential. Since staff often cannot see the succession process for themselves, this does not motivate them to try and succeed, leaving them suspicious of unfairness. This may ultimately cause them to resign from the organization or just limit their ambition, which might lead them to underperform.

- **Ethnocentricity** A more damaging challenge is if the drive towards a corporate culture actually resists diversity or even actively pursues an ethnocentric view of the world, not least through the cloning of the workforce. Perhaps inadvertently, the introduction of standard best practice recruitment processes may limit the range of people employed in that they weed out those who do not fit the notion of the model employee. This is then reinforced whilst in employment through assessment against standard competency frameworks (often derived from interviewing successful managers in the firm); through who is chosen for promotion and through learning and development programmes that instil the corporate values and the way we do things around here. Managers buttress these messages with the informal advice they give to their newer colleagues. This might range from helpful tips on dress code ('we wear suits in the London office') to the more restrictive ('it is inadvisable to challenge the views of your boss in public').

An Institute for Employment Studies project illustrates the effect of cloning. For a global accountancy firm, we looked at the profile of those who joined the company some three years before and then the profile of those who remained. Taking into account factors such as gender, ethnicity, age, qualifications and the like, we identified that the original intake was not reflective of the pool from which it was drawn. It had, for example, higher proportions of men and whites than one might have expected. What was more striking, however, was that by year three, the population had narrowed still further. Non-whites, women, older employees and those who had done non-standard degrees had all left at a faster rate than their comparators. It was a recruitment and induction process that was delivering a perfect representation of the workforce that was already employed.

- **Non-inclusive frameworks and terminology** What is not inadvertent is that companies want people with certain types of attitude that meet their business goals. A lot of these are uncontentious. Many western employers want engaged employees, so they seek people who will be collaborative, 'go the extra mile', communicate well, are trustworthy, loyal, etc. Yet these competency frameworks or behavioural indicator statements/dictionaries may send messages that exclude certain groups. Women in particular may be put off by certain terminology. Some Diversity and Inclusion specialists object to 'gravitas' as a development competency, claiming that it is a very male word. One organization we know criticized itself for always using war-like analogies that discomforted female colleagues. Another found that having a positive behaviour of 'makes sacrifices to meet the organization's needs' was interpreted by some managers to mean that part-time employees or those with domestic responsibilities would nearly always fail this test because they could not easily (or at all) stay on at work late or work extra hours. Then reward systems may be biased against older staff (an assumption that young people contribute more?) or in favour of long-serving staff (through respect for seniority).
- **Historical national prejudices** However much the formal authority of the organization is in favour of diversity it still has to recognize that in a global workforce it will have many nationalities, with their own prejudices that derive from history (e.g. the enmity between Turks and Greeks) or personal experience. So the diversity challenge is all the greater in a global organization when one is trying to meld together people from around the world to support a common viewpoint that might be contrary to the heritage they have grown up with.
- **Complex diversity factors** Take these issues and then multiply them by the 100 plus countries in which some companies operate and the variety of ethnic groups and attitudes to women. Then add issues of sexual orientation, religious belief and disability. And then do not forget national (or sub-national) cultures, or indeed distinctive occupational characteristics. A common set of HR policies ignores all these complexities and delivers a single model of what the corporation wants to see in its employees. The recruitment, assessment and development processes fulfil this goal. Why not, many readers may ask. The trouble is that viewed from Lagos, Santiago, Colombo or Karachi these may be seen as coming from a particular conception of the desirable employee. The further the part of the world is from this western formulation, the greater the cultural distance.

- **Everyone should be like us** Again, practitioners might well say that people themselves select the organizations they feel comfortable with. If they do not subscribe to western values and customs they would not try to get hired by a western multinational company. Or, equally, westerners may be attracted to Chinese or Indian multinational companies and they accept their cultural norms. This is of course true, but the attachment to the firm may only be skin deep. Moreover, the point we are making is that it does not lead to a particularly diverse firm if the people that work for it are exceptions within their own societies. The diversity goal is therefore rather disingenuous: we want a range of people (by colour, creed, gender) but ones that look like us. Diversity becomes tokenism!

- **Simplistic messages** If this sounds harsh, and belittling of the genuine attempts to promote diversity, our response would be that too often organizations are too loose with their language and simplistic in their approach – perhaps organizations do not realize the messages they send out. One senior HR manager, for example, told us with all sincerity that she worked for a Christian and democratic company and that those who do not subscribe to the implications of that fact were not welcome. She was referring to a set of guiding principles that drove the company and had to be accepted by employees. How does that play in Israel, India, Japan, Pakistan, etc.? It sounds excluding and may suggest that devout Jews, Hindus, Buddhists or Muslims are not welcome even if they subscribe to 'western' values.

- **All countries have forms of discrimination** It is not the place here to discuss the universality of these values, even if the Pope expounds the view that there are ethical principles, 'rooted in the natural law' (speech 17 September 2010 at Westminster Hall) or Barack Obama talks of certain values, such as 'human dignity', as 'not English, or American, or western ... [but] universal' (speech to UK Parliament 25 May 2011), but one can observe that these values are not upheld everywhere (even in countries that claim to espouse them). Diversity may be an unknown concept in many societies or has a particular and different meaning to the one that is intended. Discrimination, or at least inequality, may stand out in countries in Africa and Asia on the basis of gender, tribe, social class and religion, but it occurs widely with differences being more or less overt.

- **or troubling social practices** that do not conform to the mores of a western, 'democratic Christian' laws, relating to homosexuality, attitudes to nepotism, treatment of child labour and so on. If a company is operating in these countries does it have to accept some of these practices, however much it dislikes them? Moreover, depending on the sector, the organization may employ a wide range of staff in these countries, from blue-collar to executive – not all would hold what one might call broad-minded views. Does it also exclude from employment those inhabitants of these countries that positively accept, or do not challenge, wife beatings, sexual mutilation, discrimination against immigrants, etc.? Probably not, at least for the non-management cadre, in which case, what does it say about the diversity goal?

- **Societal values are ultimately incompatible** One may have to accept this compromise as a fact of life or decide that doing business in that country is no longer compatible with corporate values. The example of Google in China comes to mind as an illustration of this dilemma. Critics think Google should pull out, and equally condemn BAe Systems for the use of bribes in securing contracts in the Middle East. The critics come themselves from an important liberal and democratic tradition that was inspired by Christian principles. The point is that there is no one agreed set of values even within the Christian faith (e.g. disagreements on the social acceptability of homosexuals) and certainly wide disagreement on the application of these values in practice. As Wes Harry (2007) has argued, not only are certain frowned upon practices normal cultural behavior, they have survived because they are socially useful.

- **The only tool in the box** From a different direction, it may not be politically correct to say it, but is diversity a good thing in all cases? There are circumstances where you want convergent rather than divergent thinking, or you want a routine response rather than a creative response to a situation. In these cases a homogeneous group may be better, certainly for delivering against tight timetables. Is it better to have a set of similar 'completer finishers' than having the mix spiced with some 'plants' (to use Belbin terminology)? It would be puerile to suggest that mixed gender or ethnic groups would necessarily mean discord, but there are circumstances where effectiveness and efficiency suffer because the pressure to be diverse leads to poor (management) selection decisions. Indeed, this is what Vestas has found, albeit as part of a complex picture. On the positive side, women outperform men in the organization, teams managed by women are more satisfied than those managed by men and gender diversity leads to a general sense of employee satisfaction and motivation (which correlates with performance). However, the performance gain from gender diversity comes at a price, as it seems to harm cooperation between colleagues. National diversity similarly seems to have a negative effect on cooperation.

Some years ago in a Middle Eastern country one of the authors had to work with a dysfunctional management team that apparently shared few common perspectives, in large part because national differences combined with functional differences to make a common approach difficult. The management challenge was exacerbated by the poor view the expatriate leadership apparently took of the local staff. The CEO was temperamentally incapable of holding the management team together, not least because he did not embrace diversity of views.

THE TROUBLE WITH MEASUREMENT

A further and significant challenge arises from the fact that many organizations, understandably, want to measure diversity in order to demonstrate progress towards an HR goal, but this is not as straightforward as it might appear.

- **Where does the data come from?** Is it collected at recruitment? If so how do you handle existing employees? If you want to get full coverage do you send out forms to them all? The problem here is what is the likely response rate (in some places it can be quite low) and the quality of the response (which depends upon its perceived acceptability). This is where data can be collected at all: in some countries (for example France) it is illegal to collect information on ethnicity, religion or sexual orientation.

- **Can the data always be gathered on a global basis?** There are real challenges with some of the questions that you can try to obtain. Is it acceptable to ask about sexual orientation in, say, Uganda? Whilst the relevance of religion may be obvious in, say, Northern Ireland, it may not be seen as important in, say, Ukraine. Ethnicity has to be classified and can this be done on an agreed global basis? Does this have to be done on an internal basis, as national or regional measurements vary?

- **What is causing the phenomenon?** Data interpretation is necessary because the facts do not always speak for themselves. Apart from the unreliability of some data and the relation of internal figures to the external labour market, it is important to understand causality. Why are disadvantaged or minority groups not progressing? Is it simply a matter of time for policies to work their way through, e.g. younger women may become more successful than older women? Is it because the glass ceiling is reinforced by a generation of managers who will soon be retiring? Are the problems external to the firm, are the women applying for work in your firm arriving with a traditional set of career assumptions? Is it a reflection of labour market segregation that means that women/ethnic minorities are not choosing the relevant occupations?

- **What might be the right targets?** So, for example, do you try to internationalize your senior management? For European companies three quarters of Board members come from the country of the firm, but this disguises wide variation by location. Switzerland has half its management boards filled by non-nationals compared with 10 per cent in Spain or 11 per cent in Germany. Perhaps, your aim is gender equality. However, a simple statistic may reveal a 50:50 relationship between men and women, but looking at the figures by grade may show that men are concentrated at senior grades, women at junior grades. But in an international context, there are different cultural processes at work. So in some societies women do not move up through the organization. In others they do not work after marriage. Thus in Japan in 2008 less than 1 per cent of executive positions are held by women compared with 44 per cent in Norway. So what might be realistic for a multinational company to aspire to achieve? Policy decisions have to be made about pushing corporate imperatives in the context of local cultural norms or doing as the Romans do. There may be institutional encouragement. In the UK there is a desire to increase the representation of ethnic minorities across the economy as a government objective. There is as yet no permission for positive discrimination, unlike in the USA, or a requirement to have 40 per cent of females on the boards of publicly listed companies as in Norway and as will be in France by 2017: as the Davies report indicates, the UK is still pursuing the voluntary/exhortation route to gender equality, although an EC green paper is floating the idea of compulsion, and public procurement exercises increasingly require diversity statements and actions. It is worth noting, however, that representation on company boards is not the be all and end all. It does not mean that women have made it. As a McKinsey report (2010) indicates, the proportion of female representation on executive committees does not necessarily correspond with non-executive appointments. Indeed, the percentage of women on executive committees is roughly the same in the UK and the USA as in Norway, with Sweden a little ahead and with Russia not far behind.

In other countries the employment of specific groups is promoted, whilst others are held back. So, for example, in Saudi Arabia there is a programme of Saudification – increasing the Saudi nationalities as a proportion of employees to replace expatriates.

And there can be cultural and social influences on employment. In Brunei ethnic Malays benefit from positive discrimination. The Chinese, who comprise about 16 per cent of the population, have often felt (and been) marginalized. In China there is still discrimination against women because they will not be as productive as men (because of maternity absences).

ARE THERE DEGREES OF DIVERSITY?

To illustrate this point, answer the following questions:
Which is the more diverse organization of the options listed below? Or which situation would give you the greatest satisfaction? For the example we are using Vestas in Denmark as the employer, as the question emerged in a discussion between the authors and Thomas Øyvind Lehmann, Director of Analytics, People and Culture.

a)   3 Danes and 1 Swede sitting in Copenhagen
b)   3 Danes and 1 Indian sitting in Copenhagen
c)   3 Swedes and 1 Indian sitting in Copenhagen
d)   4 Danes sitting in San Francisco
e)   4 Swedes sitting in San Francisco
f)   3 Danes and 1 Swede sitting in San Francisco
g)   3 Danes and 1 Indian sitting in San Francisco
h)   3 Danes and 1 Chinese sitting in San Francisco.

The point of the exercise is to illustrate whether from the perspective of a Danish company there is a hierarchy of diversity and what are we really interested in?

- non-Scandinavians or non-Europeans in our workforce?
- is this a matter of ethnic origin or nationality? For example, would it affect your order if you knew in scenarios (b) and (g) that the ethnic Indians were of Danish nationality?
- are you more interested in expatriation than in diversity at home?

Vestas has plans to address this issue by examining their nationalities in terms of cultural distance from each other, using the results of the global employee survey.

We do not believe that these are straightforward questions and we think many organizations have ducked them not least because they take either a superficial or instrumental view of diversity. The organizational objective is too often less to fulfill a genuine celebration of difference and more of a tick box exercise. It has to be said that where diversity does have an impact is where the business benefits and the diversity aims coincide. Take Tata Consultancy Services; it recognized that the company needed to broaden its talent base to seriously compete against the better known (and in the west better branded) consultancies and so it needed staff from a wider variety of countries.

Success Factors

Our argument is that many organizations with global aspirations are failing to think through the implications of diversity. Diversity is not an easy topic. It is hard enough to do it properly in western countries where there is generally social and political support. Especially in the global context, we would advise organizations to take a careful look at what they want to achieve, what is realistic to accomplish and how they can get there.

The big question for us remains what are the bonds that hold the employees together. Do you follow the assimilation or multiculturalism route? This choice has produced a great deal of acrimonious political debate, complicated by arguments about immigration and national identity. In an organizational context, the assimilation option would be the route to a common culture, with the risk of ethnocentricity, and multiculturalism leading to geocentricism (Martin, 2006) where the organization is blind to race or country of origin and sees the advantages of diversity.

Answering this question, we would agree with Toby Peyton Jones from Siemens that the right policy is to 'recognise, understand and embrace national differences rather than work against them' or with British American Tobacco 'our business benefits from the breadth of ideas and experiences they [a diverse workforce] bring'. This for us, like Toby, would define a truly global organization over a multinational company, one that it is open to ideas from around the globe and does not try to impose one *world view* upon the firm. Paula Larson, HR Director at Invensys, expressed it this way (Johnson, 2008):

> *I do not want 'just American diversity' – the colour of your skin, whether you are male or female. My passion is creating an inclusive culture that recognises and respects country of origin realities and identifies an organizational culture that creates a shared sense of 'we', leaving room for what is relatively unique.*

This was after all the approach of the Persian Empire. Diversity was a principle of the empire. It had a striking capacity to tolerate and adopt other religions, dress and customs from the people it conquered. It was happy to issue proclamations in local languages. This multi-faith/multicultural system made it very flexible and successful. It used its approach, its style of conquest (acquisition in a current business context) and control as a positive PR benefit.

In other words, there can be a competitive advantage through diversity and a positive approach to difference. You could argue, for example, that football teams like Chelsea derive benefit from their mix of nationalities, blended together and working to a common goal – if you would excuse the pun! The skills, athleticism, drive and so on that they bring comes from a number of sources and draws on football traditions from both inside and outside the UK.

But there were limits to Persian tolerance – subjects had to accept the oversight – just as Chelsea footballers have to accept the manager's instructions. This is similar to the point made earlier by Peyton Jones about obeying the corporate 'rules of the road'. This still leaves open the question of how tight this definition should be. The British American Tobacco Group Employment Principles are required to be followed around the world, but with the important caveat that operating companies have the 'flexibility to customise their management of employee and development issues in ways that are most appropriate to their local business environment'. Jean-François Pilliard of Schneider talks of 'unifying rules' (Entreprise&Personnel, 2006) and Paula Larson of needing to avoid the chaos of having 'a lot of neat people who disagree about how to get work done'. Here the devil will be in the detail of how the Employment Principles, 'unifying rules' and 'shared sense of we', are interpreted.

Clearly, one would have chaos if people were free to choose whether they drove on the right or on the left, stopped at red or green traffic lights. But if we continue this analogy, how does the organization deal with the driving behaviour of Sri Lankans, Italians or Turks compared with Britons or Americans? Is the answer that in Sri Lanka, Italy or Turkey you can tolerate their overtaking customs rather than impose the more staid UK or US approach? Is the universally applicable requirement that you drive in a way that is mindful of the safety of the driver, passengers and pedestrians, but (and here is diversity at work) you do this according to the rules and customs of the country concerned? And this applies to expatriates, as to nationals?

So would organizations be better to work to establish in the minds of colleagues the common purpose or goal of the organization and then allow fair scope as to how colleagues express this? As Oxfam puts it, the organization wants all its employees to endorse its goal of alleviating poverty but respects and encourages the diversity of the organization, rejecting any notion of cloning – 'there is no standard Oxfam person'. It is certainly successful in the first part of this ambition: 97 per cent of employees agree with the statement 'I believe strongly in what Oxfam is trying to achieve' in the employee survey.

This task is easier for an Oxfam or a Chelsea Football Club than for a British American Tobacco ('who would want to work for a tobacco company anyway' is the opening line in the 'People and Culture' section of BAT's 2009 Sustainability Report) and many other companies. Nonetheless, there are risks in giving managers some degree of free expression in their management style, and, as Oxfam admits, the company has to judge the amount it is prepared to take.

Is there more that organizations can do to make diversity a true reality rather than a cosmetic, PR exercise?

- **Extensive learning** Learn through joint venture and partnerships as the Shell and Petronas example showed earlier and HPH is doing with its various collaborations.
- **Research findings underpin policymaking** Emphasize research that supports the contention that there are business benefits to be found in diversity. Jean-François Pilliard of Schneider is clear: 'Diversity, no matter what the kind, is always an advantage in business' (Entreprise&Personnel, 2006). Reported benefits (Le Boulaire, 2005) include:
  - higher return on the investment due to greater degree of employee commitment and productivity through working in an environment that values them
  - the ability to attract and retain top talent
  - greater scope for creativity and innovation
  - a better understanding of new markets
  - improved business resilience and flexibility.

Moreover, research by Eversheds (2011) suggests that those companies with a higher proportion of women on their boards outperformed those with a lower proportion.

Vestas can demonstrate that an inclusive approach to management, where everyone is treated with respect irrespective of their differences, leads to higher employee satisfaction and ultimately better performance.

The strategy textbooks can point to cases of insular thinking that meant that companies missed market opportunities or persisted with outmoded products that were well past their sell-by date. The answer is to have a breadth of thinking that is unlikely to emerge from the old boys' network, and is more likely to come through a diverse leadership.

- **Diversity at the top** Recognize that a global firm will not be regarded as global if the board/executive team has a narrow composition. It will not be seen to reach out to the diversity of its customers if it appears too mono cultural. But this diversity cannot be seen as a PR ploy.

Rabobank acted on this basis by recruiting a German workforce to match the ethnic composition of the country. It is argued that this helped drive up business performance. Deutsche Bank put its diversity strategy firmly in the context of globalization, 'the need to adapt to an increasingly global market in which companies must integrate the requirements of a multinational, multicultural environment' (Le Boulaire, 2005).

The CEO at Vestas has chosen to publish the rate of women in management in every quarterly stock exchange announcement.

- **Diversity is a feature of employee surveys** If their selection and socialization in the company has meant that for your employees corporate norms override their own personal or background assumptions, they may be more accepting of diversity goals than would be typical for their group. One way to check this interaction is either to conduct a diversity survey of your employees or use specific questions in your regular employee survey.
- **Cultural reinforcement** Build an organizational culture where diversity flourishes. This might begin by emphasizing that diversity is a fact of life. It can be achieved by ensuring all staff are respectful of views and customs of others. It requires expatriates especially, but also short-term visitors, to be sensitive in what they say and do in countries other than their own. The organization can reinforce this message in the care it takes with its language in official announcements, on the intranet and in public documents.
- **Diversity acceptance and promotion is a selection feature** Select managers with their people management capabilities in mind, develop them further and weed out those who cannot work in a diverse world. Take the Middle Eastern management team referred to earlier, all would have benefited from cross-cultural management training and some of those would have not been appointed if cultural (and people) sensitivity had been a selection criterion.

At Shell the Global Leadership Framework is used to select and develop staff. It is based on desired outcomes, including motivating staff, and it expressly values differences. This 'what' is a given. 'How' managers deliver the 'what' is up to the individual, but certain behaviours are deemed no longer acceptable, especially those that involve diversity. The company wants to see 'enterprise behaviours', cooperative actions for the common good, not those driven by a narrow business unit perspective. People are judged both on their behaviour and their business results. Some 3,000 leaders have been put through assessment centres judged on their likely future performance at a higher level, taking account of both aspects of performance.

- **Real diversity learning for managers** Then train your managers in diversity management, not in a sheep dip or going through the motions way, but to expose them to real business issues and how to tackle them.
- **Working together** Develop your project and business-as-usual teams to be effective even if they are diverse. Putting that more bluntly, it is not an acceptable excuse for failure that the group was too heterogeneous. It would be better if diversity was embraced, but even if it is merely tolerated, it has to be successfully dealt with.
- **Workforce plans reinforce diversity** At Shell, as we have said, the east is a key strategic area of business investment, so HR's role is to identify the Asians to manage these operations and this requires a 10-year lead time. Therefore HR will vote down unrealistic business plans that assume an inexhaustible labour supply in this tight labour market and do not take account of the requirement to grow the Asian managerial cadre.

Swiss Re emphasizes the importance of diversity by stating: 'When creating and updating succession plans, line management must consider the corporate commitment to diversity and must therefore exercise due diligence to ensure that succession slates, for all bands, are diverse and that necessary action steps are defined and initiated to ensure diversity is promoted across each division.'

- **Context related targets** Set realistic targets that are achievable in the varied environments in which you operate. Answer the questions posed by Vestas on p. 82 regarding what success would look like. Monitor diversity performance, understand the reasons for failure and be prepared to take action to overcome your problems through positive action of the appropriate kind.
- **Top down goals and bottom up culture** Use performance management processes to align staff with organizational goals and values. HPH embeds a set of firm-wide 'principles' from the top but, aware of local cultural sensitivities, they also build the culture from the bottom up. Their advice is that this process takes times and some failures will occur. HPH focuses on their trainee managers who often will form their international cadre.

- **Mean what you say** The McKinsey survey (2010) referred to earlier clearly demonstrates that with respect to gender diversity, organizations that tackle the issue in deeds as well as in words, including having active CEO support, produce demonstrable results.

5 *Employer Brand and Employee Value Proposition*

If more companies had the answer to the question, 'Why would someone want to work for us?' chances are we wouldn't have the increasingly high levels of disengagement we do now amongst employees in companies around the world. (Minchington, 2010)

The employer brand is an important part of developing and sustaining the organization's overall culture (see Chapter 3). In this chapter we will demonstrate how the employer brand is a key factor in demonstrating to the world what the organization stands for in employment terms. Obviously the idea grew out of the marketing need to represent a corporate image and has found favour with HR teams in many organizations because of its power to attract but also to retain talent already hired.

The employee value proposition (EVP) is also a concept that has grown to be widely used for very similar reasons – to describe to potential recruits and existing employees what the employer is offering to attract and keep talent.

Because of the close relationship between the brand and employee value proposition we will consider them together in this section. After brief confirmation of their meaning and intentions we will look at the issues faced by global organizations in developing these models and describe ideas they have had to make them a successful reality.

Corporate Brand

As explained by Martin and Hetrick (2006), corporate brands look outwards to present to customers a promise or pledge that generates a set of expectations about the company. The brand allows the company to differentiate itself from its competitors, and anyone who has watched American television adverts will have seen this aggressively put into practice. The most effective brands (like Coca-Cola) have been built up over time with growing customer support for their offering, but though new market entrants (like Virgin, Microsoft, Amazon) may have created brands over a much shorter period, they still operate in the same way – introducing a market proposition about their products that resonates with the public. These brands present a very powerful offering to customers.

Some, like Amazon, have focused really on one business proposition (internet retailing of books and similar media). Others, like Unilever, are more like an umbrella description within which products are nested, some of which (e.g. Ben and Jerry's or Persil) have their own separate (and often stronger) brands. Martin and Beaumont (2003) have described this as having a 'house of brands' rather than a 'branded house'. This of course reflects the business model. It does not prevent a Unilever using its core brand to project its corporate and employment image, but other companies either do not use their overall company name, preferring to work with the more meaningful brands of their subsidiaries (like Cheung Kong Group in Hong Kong), or find it hard to get heard with a less well-known name.

Another group of companies that overlaps with the first two categories do not so much promote products as sell a concept. The Body Shop illustrates the point: its brand promotes an ethical lifestyle. The header on Southwest Airlines website is 'More Than a Way to Fly — A Way of Life'. These sorts of brands are aiming to generate a positive affiliation to the company by customers.

The brand is also used to communicate to other stakeholders. Investors may be reassured by investing in a company with a strong brand. They may rightly believe that these firms will be able to ride out any economic vicissitudes more easily than those with a weaker brand. The fall of Lehman Brothers was so great a shock precisely because it was a firm with such a strong brand. Government, too, especially for multinational companies is impressed by branded organizations. It is more likely to take seriously a business proposition from a Rio Tinto Zinc to dig a mine than from another country's national company with only a local reputation. It may give companies the 'social licence to operate'.

> 'The resource industries are accepted by the public at large because of the role they play in society, providing the essential materials for society's needs and well being…. However, at the level of individual projects this acceptance is neither automatic nor unconditional. Today, there is the need to gain and maintain the support of the people that live and work in the area of impact and influence of any given project – to have a Social License to Operate' (http://socialicense.com).

Over time companies have built these reputations about their competence and reliability (like John Lewis), over their price competitiveness (like Wal-Mart or Tesco), flair and innovation (like Armani or Gucci) or, say, excellence in motor engineering (like BMW or Volvo). And these companies trade on these reputations and exploit them to acquire funds or convince stakeholders. Short-term customers' image of the company may vary from reputation. The recent experience of Toyota with its driving problems in Prius cars is a good example of how the image of the company is different from its reputation. So corporate brands depend on a long-term corporate reputation, which may in turn be affected by shorter-term image problems, that, should they last, will ultimately affect the organization's reputation.

Employer Brand

The employer brand uses these same ideas but looks both inward and outward. To the recruitment market it says who we are as an organization, how we differ from other employers and what you might expect if you joined us. Similarly to those already employed, it reaffirms a form of corporate identity: we are all members of the same club because we all have the same goals and we will work together to achieve them. On the competitive point, just like corporate brands, organizations may directly and publicly advertise their strengths (especially in skills and career development and job interest) or in private advance their wares compared with other firms (especially better remuneration or benefits). In the same way as corporate brands, the employer brand can be deployed with governments (e.g. to allow expatriates to be brought into the country or in lobbying to change an irritating employment law) and with investors (in a story line that says that we can attract top talent to the firm). How effective this will be will depend on the reputation of the organization generally, but in the employment market a narrower perception of the brand is evident. Is the employer trustworthy and reliable (is the offer they make going to be delivered in practice)? Is it competent (is this a well-run organization I am joining)? Do its values accord with my own? Is it sexy; does it enthuse – like the concept brands and high-visibility commercial brands described above? The answers candidates have to these and similar questions will depend upon how the organization is perceived, based on its past actions. Employers try to influence these views through their projected image.

As with the business brand, there may be sub-brands used in the labour market because they are more effective in some settings. We will return to this point with respect to Tata Consultancy Services (TCS), but one can see it with holding companies (e.g. though Anheuser-Busch InBev has a Global Management Trainee Program some of its talent acquisition comes via the subsidiaries with more powerful brand names, like Labatt in Canada) or those owned by private equity companies (e.g. employment is with Boots not with its private owners).

Employer brands can also convey organizational values. In our interviews this was an important element in our discussions about the brand. Canon's employer brand, for example, is underpinned by the spirit of *kyosei* – 'living and working for the common good'. Ikea has a similar business philosophy. One important element in the philosophy is that the company seeks to improve the everyday life of not only customers but of staff themselves. Philips' similar message to customers that it offers 'technology that touches people's lives' is reflected in the employer brand: staff can in their daily work 'touch lives every day' (Overman, 2006). Likewise, Panasonic links business performance to customer value. Its basic business principles state 'so long as we manufacture products people wish to buy and that will enrich their lives, that would build their trust and reliability in the company, and profit and sales will come as a result' (Grapevine, 2010a). As a charity, Oxfam's purpose and brand are wrapped together – overcoming 'poverty and suffering'. Unilever's strap line is 'creating a better future every day' and it is considered an iconic brand in India, very much positioning the company as improving the quality of life. In all these cases the employer brand can feed off the organizational brand in saying what the organization stands for and what that means for staff.

There are other subsidiary reasons for employer branding. One is that the organization can define what its business aims are and how it wants them enacted. The brand can covey to employees the selfsame imperatives. For example, an organization may wish to signal that excellent customer service is a distinguishing feature of its USP and the employer brand may support this position in the way it expects employees to behave. Southwest Airlines, for example, makes outstanding customer service the centrepiece of its offer under the banner 'The Southwest Difference'.

'My role is to take the [consumer] brand and make sure that we mirror it internally, that we make sure employees understand how customers see us. We want to make sure employees understand the brand they are delivering,' said Christine Donahue, director of customer communications at Pitney Bowes (Overman, 2006).

These sorts of brands seek to offer an experience, not just a transaction, to customers. So the employee brand has to similarly be an experience, not just delivery on a transactional promise. This places a strain both on how customers are handled (via employees who are supposed to be inspired by the brand and committed to its values) and on how employees are treated. So is the brand projection in tune with the way customers and employees feel about the way it is delivered? It may be easier for retail firms with their specific products to think (and deliver?) in this way than for, say, a manufacturing company that does not naturally generate a consumer brand image. This is why CSR activities can be used as a means of developing a profile where the business activities do not naturally lend themselves to brand projection.

Employee Value Proposition

The EVP is the more specific articulation or reflection of what the brand stands for in terms of what precisely it is offering to the workforce. As such it is similar to, but probably more explicit than the organization's psychological contract. The nature of the deal will vary from organization to organization. It can be expressed in terms of extrinsic reward (pay, benefits, training, etc.) and intrinsic rewards (especially job satisfaction and worthwhile activity).

Though employee centred, the EVP is usually expressed in terms of reciprocity – in exchange for these rewards what the employee is expected to contribute and deliver (i.e. effort, commitment, alignment with goals, etc.). These employee responsibilities may well be implicit rather than explicit. So employees might have to infer what their work responsibilities might be against a company Safety First value assertion in the EVP.

The main purpose of the EVP is recruitment and retention of the requisite skills and talent. As the McKinsey report put it: 'A strong employee value proposition attracts great people like flowers attract bees' (Michaels et al., 2001); though ironically bees will always move away to the next flower – a problem with the hiring of great people, though this is less of a problem in the case of McKinsey whose resourcing model allows the employer and employee to have a great experience together before a no-regrets parting of the ways. The EVP also has a strong employee engagement component to it because it is about having an offer that maximizes the contribution of staff.

The Nature of the Offer

So how do organizations present their brands and EVPs in the sense of its content?

Some are values based with an attempt to convey what are seen as universal values that will bind the organization together. This may be linked to organizational purpose, to the way they want people to behave and the organization to operate.

Not surprisingly, Oxfam has a value based EVP along with the usual reward offerings. Empowerment and accountability are principles in how they run their business both for employees and their 'clients'. In the same way, inclusivity is how they want to operate. As we said, there is no standard Oxfam person, except all are united in working to alleviate poverty.

SAP has also recently attempted to develop a single employee proposition reflecting the core values of openness, empowerment, participation, innovation and integrity.

Greg Horton, Managing Director, Fairbairn Private Bank, believes 'culture defines the brand'. His company is a values driven organization based on:

- humility
- integrity
- quality
- compassion
- development.

The last quality introduces what in this version of the offer comes across as a necessary feature of an employment relationship, but in other settings can be more transactional or possibly reciprocal.

For example, Audi offers 'scope for personal development' as a key element of its appeal. BP talks about careers and global opportunities (open to all), a work/life balance in a 'progressive company' and 'competitive [reward] packages linked to performance' (http://www.bp.com/productlanding.do?categoryId=9031834&contentId=7058274).

Linda Fan said that Schneider Electric offers common employee principles that are valid across the world. These are:

- a focus on the employee career
- an investment in learning and development
- a responsiveness to employees' own aspirations.

This clearly is an employee-centric deal. In other organizations the brand is more a reflection of the goals of the specific firm or even values in action. RBS had a 'make it happen' slogan. Vestas conveys something of this sense in believing that a common 'will to win', the strategic vision of the CEO, Ditlev Engel, unites people in the firm despite their different backgrounds. This shows the important integrative effect of the brand – pulling people together in the same direction – which, here, is shaped by organizational purpose. And it seems to be working at Vestas. Rather than joining primarily for environmental reasons, many people seem to have been attracted to the company because it meant working for a successful and growing industry, precisely what Engel was seeking. As a successful pitch it has echoes of the Shell experience in China. Jing Wang says that being part of a winning team is vital. Especially in Asia a company has to show to the market that it has a track record of high performance and plans for business growth. Thus in India JSW Steel is one of the fastest growing business groups and this is generating strong goodwill among its people, who are proud to be part of a successful growing company (building on the spirit of ambition in the country generally).

ANZ sees its brand as expressing what the company stands for, what it pledges and what it expects. It also conveys where the company comes from – hence the publication of the ANZ Story. So, it combines the reciprocal element with a sense of what the organization is about, its characteristics, culture and values. This is reflected in its statement in the Story about 'new opportunities, enduring values':

> *Acting with integrity needs to be at the core of everything we do. We are committed to doing the right things (our value of integrity) as well as doing things right (through our values of collaboration, accountability, respect and excellence).*

IS IT ALWAYS THE SAME?

Just as there is debate about universal or specific organizational characteristics of the brand, so our practitioners have different views on having a universal or segmented EVP. Those that segment it do so by grade or occupational group. The segmentation may be clearly set out or it may be implicit. Toby Peyton Jones, for example, acknowledges that what is offered for Siemen's 'professional' international staff is very different from what is offered those working in the domestic economy. Part of the reason for this is that project managers, for instance, are globally mobile, are required to have the same skills and are paid roughly the same salary such that there is a distinct and common offer for them.

Members of the same occupational groups may, indeed, have the same characteristics, which link them together across national boundaries, and organizations can tap into these. The sort of description that TCS makes is obviously relevant to a certain category of employees.

TCS' EVP (largely aimed at professional staff) has a number of components:

- Culture – TCS prides itself on having a strong culture promoting flexibility.
- Project rotation – as with many consultancies, it offers graduates structured rotation on projects.
- Overseas travel and experience – key for its home market, tapping into the aspirations of its Indian people, TCS deliberately offers overseas assignments.
- Compensation package – as a large Indian company with a strong growth record, it has been able to pay upper quartile rates for staff compared to competitors.
- Structured and constant learning – a structured approach to learning is offered both to its project and operational teams.
- A strong culture of CSR – see later reference.

Not surprisingly, there may be a different proposition for expatriates. In this case, in exchange for mobility the organization may offer generous terms and conditions. This is usually per single assignment, but this deal could be extended to a whole career basis for those who are expected to move from foreign posting to foreign posting.

Commonly, there is a specific focus on graduates. Unilever, for example, offers the graduate population:

- 'A chance to make a genuine impact on people's lives' through working with its brands
- 'Exceptional exposure and experience' locally and internationally
- 'World class development opportunities in a fast-paced, challenging work environment'
- Opportunities to work together with others to deliver corporate success.
          (http://www.unilever.co.uk/careers/whyunilever/graduates/index.aspx)

The offer may focus on high-potential staff and may be made specifically to them. At Vestas it is to join a global leading company, to save the world and to have an international career. At the next level down in talent terms the EVP is more practical, namely to join a fast changing company, with competitive pay and an informal style of decision making. ABB describes its aim to develop 'a culture of openness, flexibility and inclusiveness to attract top performers'.

These examples interestingly convey extrinsic reward with an offer of purposeful work, something that is thought to characterize young graduates' attitude to employment. So another segmentation that is emerging is a generational one. Some employers believe they have to appeal to the 'iPod generation' in a wholly different way that to a more mature workforce. ANZ uses the business strap line 'we live in your world' to communicate to younger people that its message is in tune with their aspirations. JSW Steel uses the message 'young thinking' in all aspects of values to emphasize innovation and problem solving and this is key to its proposition for staff.

Differences by grade and occupation (and indeed employer) may relate to the time horizons under which employees operate. Is the deal one of organizational investment in the individual for a long-term return to the organization and employee? If so, career management and development processes can operate in that context. A Shell or Tesco would have this grow-our-own-timber approach for its 'professional' or 'graduate' populations. Conversely, if employees want immediate rewards and the organizational expectation is for immediate performance, then the EVP will reflect that reality.

Research carried out at Aegon discovered whilst developing an EVP that the drivers for attraction are not always the same as those for commitment. This introduces the question of whether the brand/EVP is presented in different ways at different points in the employee lifecycle. Aegon, for example, found that, not surprisingly, how staff were managed was a source of motivation but not important for recruitment. Compensation was the reverse. This view on pay has been supported by survey research from Towers Perrin. It found three key attractors that were present irrespective of geography – 'ensuring adequate compensation and financial security; achieving work/life balance; and having relevant learning and career opportunities'. The order of importance varied by country, but everywhere these three items were present (Towers Perrin, 2005).

Aegon's research also interestingly concluded that attraction and commitment drivers were not the same in all cases across the world: some were global (e.g. career opportunities) and some local (a meritocracy was more important in the UK than elsewhere). Again

Towers Perrin (ibid) came to the same conclusion; not only were retention motivation factors different from attraction, there was much less geographic similarity. Furthermore, according to the Kenexa Research Institute (2010), levels of employee engagement vary considerably by country. This suggests that the brand/EVP representation should be adjusted to the geographic context. However, there are those who tend to take the opposite view, based on the sense of universality we described earlier. For example, Jing Wang said to us: 'What people want from work is the same the world over, especially professional staff want a career, profession, learning and skill development, and remuneration'.

The opinions of Linda Fan, Jing Wang and Toby Peyton Jones (at least for one part of the Siemens population) underpin the common brand/EVP principle, which, as we have said, is used by global companies to build a common culture. Whilst the means of presenting the brand/EVP may vary somewhat by location, the underlying philosophy is likely to be same, not least because it is a top down, not bottom up view of the world. This, according to Garmt Louw, is more achievable from the very fact that people are attracted to Shell because of its international nature and develop an 'affiliation with the global rather than the local'. As we have seen, TCS precisely makes this sort of pitch, as demonstrated in the box above.

Garmt Louw of Shell believes what is important to applicants is:

- do I want to be associated with this company?
- what is their reputation as an employer: social, environmental, etc.?
- will my choice be accepted at home by relatives and friends?
- what are the opportunities for professional development (compared with competitors)?

So the brand/EVP have to offer something that people want – something that meets their current needs and future hopes – as well as align with organizational values or goals. How this will be expressed will vary from organization to organization, but there are likely to be a number of common characteristics.

Why Have they Become Important?

Brands in general have become important in business because of the extra value they can add to the company. This became apparent in 1988 when Philip Morris bought Kraft for $12.6 billion, six times its book value. It is evidence of the power of the brand as an intangible asset on the back of the way it can generate profits and higher returns to investors. Similarly, employer brands are now seen as value creators in the people management sphere through their ability to realize employee related business goals.

It is probably no coincidence that the concepts of brand and EVP have come to the fore as the war for talent hotted up. The reason these ideas have been taken on board by organizations is fundamentally to do with recruitment and retention: how can we attract the talent and skills we need and how can we keep them? The term 'employer of choice' was coined to convey this message, and, again, has come into common parlance during this same tight labour market period. So SAP wants to be to be the 'most admired' IT software company in the world and as a consequence to attract their 'unfair share' of the right talent. The causal link that practitioners have accepted is that if your external image improves in the market place and you have a good offer to make to potential recruits, you are more likely to be successful in hiring the people you want. If the brand is strong and the organization delivers on its promises, quality staff are more likely to stay: why would you move?

To grow interest in the organization, just as the corporate brand can project the product message globally, so the employer brand can do this in the recruitment market. For example, Philips explicitly has sought to build its brand in China from a position of limited understanding to one which is better recognized (Overman, 2006).

Perhaps as importantly, the brand can be what holds the organization together. It can be an expression of, or a deliberate attempt to push, its 'corporateness' (Martin and Hetrick, 2006). The brand can convey the EVP to existing employees and act as the internal glue that binds the disparate workforce together in a common cause, despite differences in nationality or culture. Like corporate culture (see Chapter 3), corporate brand, employer brand and the EVP make a significant contribution to that internal glue. Each element can play an important role in increasing organizational cohesion and alignment, while HR is well placed to build these concepts into its strategic approaches. In global organizations there are always fissiparous tendencies: the risk of fragmentation is always there. The strength of the common bond may closely relate to the strength of purpose of the organization. Having a clear goal can motivate, like Vestas's will to win or Oxfam's poverty alleviation. It may relate more to the social aspects of work: a camaraderie among the workforce that is often particularly important where there are a large number of expatriates. Done well, leaders can use the brand as a binding device to help pull the organization together. This can come from personal behaviour so long as it is 'real'. For example, the global CEO of Schneider Electric is French but worked in China many years ago. According to Linda Fan, when he returns he remembers the names of people who used to work with him and this is extremely well received by staff in the same way as it was in the Dubai example quoted earlier.

Challenges

CORPORATE REPRESENTATION AND DESIGN CONSIDERATIONS

- **Many EVPs resemble each other** There is increasing brand competition, as both Unilever and Shell reported to us. How do you really distinguish your EVP as unique in a crowded market place where all the multinational companies are essentially offering the same thing? Every one of them says the organization will give you competitive remuneration, a great career, lots of new skills and experience, work/life balance, etc.
- **Non-transferability of some EVP concepts** Similarly, you conscientiously develop your EVP with all the words that you would expect to see in it relating to learning and development, career management, total reward, etc., but the concept

bombs in some parts of the world. For example, an American company tried to apply an EVP model to China that had been home grown. Their Chinese employees responded to the contents by saying that it sounded as if it was a description of the 'membership of a country club'. What they wanted was to be employed by a 'hard working' company because hard work would mean success. Working for a successful employer would bring rewards of greater opportunities for development, as well as financial benefits. This response chimes with the Shell and Vestas experiences described earlier. The converse also applies: brand images may not be well received in the more cynical west, but more positively accepted in the Far East because they convey aspiration.

- **Global brand representation** Getting agreement of the visual representation of the brand can be tricky, as how different people round the world want to picture their brand can be very different. This relates to colour and selection of images. It is hard to build a consensus – to square the proverbial circle. How this is done, though, does signal the attitude of the corporate centre to the views of colleagues in other countries.

- **Brand perception management** Moreover, the problem is exacerbated if the basic brand image does not work in the employment world. Non retail companies, for example, find it hard to project the employment brand because it may not resonate in the labour market; potential employees have not been customers to form, hopefully, a positive view. SAP has admitted that, though its name is well recognized (especially for a software company), it is also seen as 'boring' in some circles. Likewise, Siemens wants to shift outdated perceptions of the company's products. BASF is working on the employer image in the external and internal labour market. Based on a campus reputation survey, apparently the Shell brand not as strong as before. These companies may be seen as safe and solid to the older generation, virtues that may no longer seem fashionable. Young people might prefer the sexier companies like Google, Apple and Virgin, with modern brand images. (Although, having a low key commercial brand means there is less likely to be pollution of the employer brand, if there are business problems.)

- **Brand recognition varies** Even brands that are strong in one country may be weaker in others. Take two contrasting examples. Tata is a very well-known company in India but is weaker abroad and especially so when its consultancy arm competes with better-known professional service firms. So Tata Consultancy resorts to TCS (Tata Consultancy Services) to prevent it being seen as a manufacturing company. Oxfam has an amazing 99 per cent public brand recognition in the UK but the name resonates much less in other parts of the world. The student campus survey from Universum (a consultancy specializing in employer branding), for example, puts Nokia much higher in the ranking of a desirable employer in India than in the UK, and Proctor & Gamble comes in the top three organizations in China and a more modest 16th in the USA.

- **Differing business circumstances** Business development does not go at the same speed across the world such that some areas may be in growth mode, whilst others are in contraction. Having a single EVP to cover these different circumstances is possible, but it has to be stated at a high level of abstraction to work. In early 2010 one bank we talked to spoke of trying to respond to being a 'three speed company' – New Zealand just out of recession, Australia doing reasonably well and Asia 'going great guns'.

- **Differing EVP applicability** A similar problem exists with how a common EVP is received. Some locations may have more interest in parts of the offer than others. As Jing Wang points out 'the urge for material wealth is perhaps stronger at this stage of China's development' than elsewhere, emphasized by the very competitive labour market that has been pushing up wages. Even within the same geography, groups may feel it resonates with them, whilst others feel it does not apply. This divided reaction may split along grade lines – manual or clerical employees may believe that all the stuff on career management and skills development is not meant for them, whilst professional staff may happily concur. In multinational companies you also see the split between expatriates and locals in a similar way. Or between those who are more global in their outlook and those who are more parochial (by reason of limited exposure or because they live in more insular societies).

How Vestas as a company is seen depends upon where you sit. For someone in the corporate centre: 'It is an international company in a Danish company'. In Australia: 'Everything happens in Denmark' and viewed from the Portland Regional Sales HQ: 'The action is centred on Portland'.

Shell's EVP is global. It works well in Europe and the USA, which is more international than in the past, but in Singapore and Hong Kong the local influence is greater and the divergence from the corporate norm is more obvious, as reflected in the employee opinion results.

VARIATION IN APPLYING THE BRAND

- **Inconsistent global experiences** A real challenge is to deliver a consistent experience of the brand or EVP across the world. The brand experience has to live up to the brand promise. This is not just because the management capability may be lacking in some locations, but also because the interplay between what the company wants to see happening and the local conditions in which it is played out. Thus organizational values might clash with local customs and practice. Alternatively, there could be the challenge of sustaining a single brand proposition in a very devolved business.

Specsavers faces a challenge as it grows beyond its original UK roots into northern Europe and Australasia. It is still a family owned and managed company, and the founders are still very much at the heart of the business. It has a strong set of values that have been recently re-launched. Employees have a powerful affiliation to the firm. Yet it has an interesting hybrid ownership model based on partnership – where those who manage the individual stores have a financial stake in them. This helps drive a focus on performance, but could create a risk of weakening the sense of belonging to the wider business.

The approach at Specsavers is one of 'consistent where possible, different where necessary' and, despite this devolved business responsibility, the need for consistent delivery is held together through partnership and a strong sense of vision, values and brand.

- **Bad news travels quickly** An important point here is that if a young interviewee has a poor recruitment experience with a traditional type of firm, one that reinforces these perceptions, the negative message can be conveyed round the world in seconds via Facebook, blogs and texts. Even word of mouth can be dangerous in spreading harmful corporate impressions across university campuses. Trying to reposition the employer brand is not straightforward. Impressions of organizations can be quite enduring.
- **Over-promise and under-delivery** The EVP may be promised in all sincerity but the delivery falls short. This can be for a number of different reasons. Economic circumstances may mean redundancy has replaced promotion as the experience of the moment. Business volatility makes it hard to transfer people as intended, grow their skills or give them new opportunities as one financial services company we know found in Asia, especially with a very mobile population. The management capability is not what you would wish it to be, so that promises of, say, fair treatment or opportunities for all are not kept, or the promises were all wishful thinking.

DEALING WITH EXTERNAL PRESSURES

- **Customer negativity** Usually these problems are experienced internally and the organization tries to ensure that these disappointments are not felt externally. Sometimes the challenge comes the other way round: the outside view is not as positive as the inside experience. This is the challenge that McDonald's faced: customers had an unenthusiastic impression of employment conditions whereas employees had not. (See boxed case below.)
- **Tarnished public perception** An organization works hard to develop a brand image but this is derailed by an incident that happens in one part of the world, the impact of which is spread round the world. At the time of writing, BP's problems with the oil leak in the Gulf of Mexico had tarnished the corporate image, especially its attempt to be seen as pro-environmental. President Obama kept referring to the company as 'British Petroleum', a prefix the company dropped in 1998 in its wish to be seen as global. The 'Beyond Petroleum' strapline to emphasize its environmental pretensions is hard to sustain against CNN images of beachside oil pollution. This bad publicity is likely to affect the employment brand, especially in the USA, for some time to come. It will be a brave US graduate who tells their friends and family that they want to work for BP. In a more limited way Shell had the same problems over Brent Spar (Shell petrol station owners faced death threats in Germany) and over the execution of Ken Saro-Wiwa in Nigeria. The travails of British Airways (on one of whose planes these words were written) with their cabin staff is a good illustration of the damage to reputation that an employee–employer dispute can have.

Before the banking crisis, RBS was number one on the high street within financial services in customer service, and NatWest, having been taken over by RBS, had moved to number two. After RBS had posted the biggest corporate loss in history and been taken over by the UK government, its position with retail customers had, over a six month period, moved to bottom of the list.

As this book is written, NatWest is now a more trusted brand than RBS, yet is part of the same group. The answer to this apparent contradiction is of course simple: that the RBS brand had been severely damaged, whereas the NatWest brand image, along with the other sub-brands of Direct Line, Churchill, Coutts, Ulster Bank and others within the group have all held up well during this period.

This is a sobering reminder of just how quickly brand allegiance can be lost, having spent years building up the brand qualities and reputation. And these difficulties played out in the labour market as much as in the commercial world, especially where the RBS brand, not sub-brands, had been pushed. It also tested employee allegiance to the brand and industry, affecting the degree to which they would be prepared to be brand ambassadors.

- **External pressure groups** These challenges are growing through shareholder activism, the greater PR skills of the pressure groups and the power of technology to mobilize opinion. 38 Degrees is at the present time organizing opinion against various UK government policies through on-line campaigns that lead to bombarding MPs with letters of complaint. As Michael Porter and Mark Kramer (2006) have suggested, quoting Nestlé and bottled water, not all these attacks are 'fair' or reasonable. But, of course, this does not stop the impressions sticking, especially because it is the high profile firms that are targeted
- **Superficial response** However, the organization may make things worse by their response. As Porter and Kramer (2006) remark, a veritable cottage industry has developed in the USA to produce 'glossy' CSR reports with many charitable actions to support the claims, but the risk is that either these actions are disconnected from the main business or they are superficial public relations exercises. If they are seen to be no more than window dressing they may damage the band still further.
- **Mis-match with the organization's rhetoric** These sorts of problem are particularly acute for those organizations that set themselves up in brand terms with a message that implicitly or explicitly suggests the positive way in which they will treat people. Thus The Body Shop or Oxfam cannot be seen to treat staff in anything other than a 'proper' manner. Achieving that goal across a global operation is a real challenge.

RELATIONSHIPS WITH THE ORGANIZATION

- **Employee–employer relationships** If your resourcing model is one of 'hire and fire' (rather than grow your own timber) then you will have greater difficulties with brand affiliation. Staff will see, and be encouraged to see, that they have a transactional relationship with their employer. The brand and EVP may accurately reflect this deal, but it will be harder to obtain the benefits of any employee alignment with the organizational goals.
- **Work–life relationships** In striving for employee identification with the firm, organizations forget that most people have identities beyond work. The job may be important to them but they have other lives. In some societies this distinction can be blurred, for example in Japan in the attachment to the office or, in a different

way, in workaholic East Coast US companies. Yet even within work, particularly for those professionals with transferrable skills, employees have loyalty to colleagues, their team, even their manager but not necessarily to the organization as a whole. Sometimes branding exercises ignore this point.

- **Centre aspirations at odds with local employee experiences** They can also create an idealized picture of what the management would like the organization to be that is a long way away from the reality of the employment experience. There may be a desire to create an aspirational brand with the sort of features that will appeal to an external audience, but inside the organization this impression is hard to sustain. This is especially true of the sort of motherhood-and-apple-pie brand descriptions. As Martin and Hetrick (2006) argue, 'attempts by corporate communication departments (in conjunction with a willing business press) to create corporate identities which are unrecognizable to employees are counterproductive in the long run; often they generate unofficial, opposed identities and resentment towards heroic leadership ensuring leaders, line managers and HR are "on message" to deliver on these expectations or value propositions'. These dangers are greater in an international firm because the challenge is to deliver something believable in all corners of the world and when the 'corporate communication departments' are a long way away, physically and culturally, from their audience. They can be tone deaf to the variations of expectation.

Success Factors

So what are organizations doing to meet these challenges? If you are developing or reviewing your brand/EVP you should consider the issues listed below, which we have roughly grouped under design and execution.

DESIGN

Follow a good process

- **Clarity** Be very clear at the outset what you are using the EVP for or why you are creating it in the first place. There is a terrible danger in best practice HR that the concept is chasing a business rationale. The important point is that a focus on attraction would lead to a different emphasis in the EVP (and brand) than if they are being deployed principally to motivate an existing workforce.
- **Alignment** The deployed brand should communicate the organizational vision and business goals, not be at variance with it. This means it will appeal to some people more than others. This is not a problem if you are attracting/keeping those that you want to engage with.

Vestas has a 'go, do' culture. Its vision is to be number 1 in modern energy, i.e. going beyond being market leader in wind to compete directly with oil and gas. It wants to move 'beyond green' as a competitive energy. That is perhaps why the company does not seem to attract, nor get 'environmental hippies'. It is a test for those at managerial levels to survive their first year. Those that do are:

- dedicated to the organization
- prepared to work long hours and be online the whole time
- thrive on change.

Those who cannot cope with high degree of uncertainty leave.

- **Fit people strategy** There is also a need for the brand/EVP to be internally consistent not just with the business direction but also in relation to the people strategy and other HR policies and practices. How well do they line up with reward, talent management, work organization, development, etc.? There is no point (indeed it can be quite destructive) in the organization believing its own rhetoric about the sort of employer it is, if it is unable to deliver. Organizations need to be realistic about what they can do. This can be very obvious in global career management: we say we offer international careers but in reality this is only true for a few people.
- **EVP that attracts** Construct a brand/EVP that not just reflects what you want to say about what the organization stands for, but also one that is attractive to potential recruits and existing staff. Consider how the words and pictures will play round the world.
- **Ensuring wide appeal** Test the prototype with your target employee groups worldwide and with line managers, as well as with the executive level, to see whether the design is widely supported and which, if any, types of staff or location are not impressed.

Determine the employee contribution

In designing your EVP/brand you need to decide the extent to which it will be a top down affair with little to no input from your employees, or bottom up with a significant contribution from your staff. As one might have expected, we found differing ways of incorporating employee attitudes to work into the EVP/brand. In global organizations employee engagement in the design process means in effect giving emphasis to operating company input.

1. **Bottom up design** The first option is 'privileging the local' (Martin et al., 2009) which means giving voice to employees in an upward expression of the brand meaning. The boxed McDonald's example later shows direct employee input through the use of employee surveys. But employee involvement might mean even more of a co-creation by staff participation through focus groups in the design of the EVP. This approach can be argued simply on the basis of good practice: if employees participate in the construction of the brand and EVP they are more likely to espouse the message. It also helps deal with the threat of the message being seen as inauthentic. As the

McDonald's example shows, even those adopting a common brand/EVP can follow an inclusive way of generating its contents.

2. The alternative is a **top down decision** on the brand/EVP. For example, Invensys surveyed employees for their views on company values, but though they informed the final outcome, the company wanted something more aspirational and challenging to put before potential recruits. The attraction of the top down method is that it indeed offers the possibility of conveying the corporate message in a consistent manner across the world without either the risk or the reality of being sidetracked by local, employee preoccupations. Those companies with strong brands, especially in certain sectors, might favour this method because they are keen to reinforce the brand image.

Agree extent of local tailoring

A critical question between design and execution of the brand/EVP is the extent to which it is to be standardized across the world or adapted to local settings. We heard differing views, which we boil down to two: differentiated or uniform, as set out below. Neither is right, though taking either position to its extremes is not likely to work; what is necessary is that your choice should be consistent with your business model.

1. **Seek local resonance** Some organizations take the view that it is impossible to present a single view of themselves to the world. Wilfried Meyer of Siemens believes that the 'execution of this new brand proposition has to be local, because different things have different meanings depending upon the place'. Take 'green' for example: it would mean something different in China than in Germany. Professor Tjitra makes the same point with respect to 'profit' and how that concept is understood differently in China compared with the west (spring Messe Management, 2010). So which value you emphasize and how you apply that must be local. These changes can be subtle. We talked earlier that Unilever's 'creating a better future every day' was well received in India, but its understanding in that market is about better nutrition and hygiene, quite a different response to the one that would be found in the North American, European and Australasian markets. This approach is supported by Graeme Martin. He and colleagues (2009) argue for allowing 'employees at local level considerable latitude in creating local expressions of these (corporate) values'. The model is a pluralistic not a unitary one. It has led some to use the term 'glocal' brands to put into practice the 'think global, act local' dictum. If you support this argument, you can in part resolve this dilemma through involving employees, as per option 1 above.

In 2002 HSBC launched a new worldwide advertising campaign to appear in 81 countries 'designed to define the distinct personality of the Group's brand and introduce HSBC as "the world's local bank"'.

'The concept was developed following worldwide consumer research which found that, while people appreciate the value of international organizations and services, they question the prevailing "one size fits all" global model. Consumers want to be treated as individuals, and to feel that companies care about them, recognise their needs and understand what makes their community unique. Underpinning the advertising is HSBC's philosophy that the world is a rich and diverse place in which cultures and people should be treated with respect.' http://www.hsbc.com/1/2/newsroom/news/2002/new-campaign-for-the-worlds-local-bank#top

2. **Or, convey a single global message** The alternative view is that a single message can and should be conveyed. This achieves the benefits we described under top down decision making of consistency and common business alignment. SAP points out that recruitment via the e-portal means that a single corporate message is projected. It is only quite far into the e-recruitment tool before individuals get any local material. Schneider Electric has worked with Universum to define a global EVP. It used inputs from the labour market, candidates, employees and executives. The results were pooled but the input from the big seven countries (including China because of its sales volume) were seen as critical. In fact there was little variation in the messages. The top three were the same even if the order was not.

The single brand approach is exemplified by McDonald's, as shown in the boxed example. Despite its many characteristics, the McDonald's system has:

- **A very strong company brand that the EVP can build upon** It has a very consistent business delivery model: the customer experience should be the same all over the world based on standardized operations and service procedures. For example, the company optimized its kitchen procedures after extensive research and achieved the appropriate balance between quality of products, service speed and high level of cleanliness. As a result, consistent practices increasing customer value are continuously implemented worldwide.
- **The company employs predominantly younger people** While the McDonald's workforce is diversified, most of its crew members are between the ages of 16 and 24 and holding their very first job, which makes them more likely to become brand ambassadors with a shared perspective.
- **Its hiring practices tend to focus on 'attitude' along with the usual qualifications and experience** Hence, most employees share the organization's core values and customer service orientation.

Using a franchising approach McDonald's can also manage difference in product offerings and service styles without affecting the whole organization. This may apply less to the employment proposition, but geographic variation is facilitated here if need be.

Respond to your environment

In designing the employer brand/EVP understanding the nature of environment within which you are operating is crucial to success, both those aspects of the context that might work in your favour and those that you have to work against. In this process, we emphasize the benefits of creating tangible meaning for your whole stakeholder group. Remember, too, that brands are like fashion and change over time, not just in visual representation but in the buttons they are pressing. The employer brand has to keep up with these changes and be periodically refreshed if it is to be seen to be relevant, especially to young people who tend to be more fashion conscious.

- **Exploit the corporate brand** An obvious approach is to exploit the main brand (if it is well known and regarded) by hitching the employer brand to it (e.g. as in the Virgin family). In Siemens there is a global campaign to shift impressions and assert the company's traditional values of innovation, responsibility and excellence in the business fields of their business sectors of industry, energy and healthcare. They want to emphasize reliability, sustainability, environmental consciousness and curiosity in their employer branding – there is lots to explore and they want curious brains to explore it.
- **Maximize business position** Or the organization can make use of its socio-economic advantages. Schneider and Shell have benefited in China from being in the energy sector, which is of national strategic importance, and they can play on having global brands in a society where this has a social cachet.
- **Build a lasting reputation** As we have seen through examples like RBS, BA, BP and Toyota the main brand may be under attack, which leaves the employer brand vulnerable. To protect themselves against this negative publicity and/or to build the image they want people to have of them, there are various actions organizations can take:
  - By stressing corporate social responsibility in their external stakeholder management. This seems particularly evident in Indian and Chinese companies where there is an expectation that corporations play an important role in the community. For example, the Tata Group gives a lot of attention to CSR and corporate responsibility in particular. Indeed, seven or eight years ago TCS launched an initiative designed to target specific CSR and culture programmes. As Francis Tong from Hutchison Port Holdings (HPH) put it, the company is 'very keen to be seen as integral to each and every one of the communities in which it operates and the local economy'.
  - Through putting out a positive message of themselves, presenting their organization in the best possible light by engaging in specific projects and beneficent actions that will help position themselves as valuable to the community.
  - By encouraging positive external behaviour through internal messages stressing its importance to colleagues. Tata Steel has a competency relating to environmental awareness.

JSW Steel is extremely strong on human rights, corporate responsibility and its own values, all of which are heavily profiled on its website. JSW has its own foundation promoting the education, health, livelihood and empowerment of women (the company pays for health check-ups for local women); sports, arts and culture; environment and sustainability; and good works (it provides over 130,000 midday meals every day to schools in India).

HPH says it has long regarded education as the basis for sustainable development. 'Our Dock School Programme is at the forefront of our efforts to ensure children in the communities where we do business have the skills they need to realise their full potential, better their employment prospects and succeed in the 21st Century.

'Under the Dock School Programme, HPH member ports across the globe are encouraged to "adopt" local schools in need of financial and educational assistance. Our ports choose many ways to help their Dock Schools. Past contributions have funded construction projects, scholarships, school supplies and books, computer purchases and educational activities. We continually encourage our business units to come up with creative ways to take part in the programme. Since the Dock School Programme was first implemented at Hong Kong International Terminals in 1992, it has grown considerably in importance. Today, the HPH Group supports more than 20 Dock Schools around the globe' (http://www.hph.com).

- **But ensure its authentic** An important consideration here is whether the CSR initiatives come across as sincere or merely as marketing devices that have more spin than substance. As the late Sir Geoffrey Chandler (creator of Shell's first statement of business principles) wrote in 2002: 'To suggest that doing right [in business] needs to be justified by its economic reward is amoral, a self-inflicted wound hugely damaging to corporate reputation.' Nonetheless, CSR type programmes often work best when they are connected either to the core business or deliver clear business benefits. Developing relevant technical skills in schools is socially and corporately desirable, as it helps develop long-term future talent pools that are strongly connected to the firm. Examples include the opening of corporate universities or education sponsorship in parts of the world that need skill development. Both Philips and Sanofi-Aventis have been trying to build a brand in China using similar means, especially creating a presence at premier universities (Allouche, 2008).

TCS on corporate sustainability: 'In the current climate it is more important than ever for businesses to acknowledge the impact they have on society and the environment and commit to tackling the issues, not just because they should, but because it's good for business' (http://www.tcs.com/about/corp_responsibility/BitC_index/Pages/default.aspx).

The ANZ Story – 'By being the first bank in our region to connect our customers, people, communities and shareholders to this opportunity, we can also play a lead role in building Australia and New Zealand's longer term prosperity … As a bank, we also have a pivotal role to play in society, to support individual prosperity, enable thriving communities and ensure responsible, sustainable growth.'

JSW Steel targets 31 academic institutions in India in the areas of management and engineering, and awards 100 scholarships every year to encourage brand awareness and talent development. Notwithstanding the scholarships, individuals are not bound to join JSW relying as they do on goodwill and the strength of their development proposition.

If the CSR policies are seen as positive locally there can be real spin offs. For example, the Hatton National Bank in Sri Lanka had done a lot of CSR projects, chosen and delivered locally, such as in health, education and the environment. This paid off during 'the troubles'. Tamil branch managers were relatively protected from the worst of the ethnic conflict because of this community activity.

Li Ka-shing (Chairman of Cheung Kong (Holdings) Limited) established the Li Ka Shing Foundation (LKSF) in 1980 as a vehicle for his philanthropic enterprises. According to the corporate website, it has three strategic objectives: 1) nurture a culture of giving; 2) support education reform initiatives that encourage long-term thinking, empowerment, creativity, open-mindedness and constructive engagement with a focus on positive and sustainable change; and 3) help advance medical research and services.

To date, the Foundation has made grants of over $1.45 billion to further these objectives.

He also founded Shantou University in 1981 in China to encourage reform of China's education system. Shantou University has 7,500 undergraduate and 1,500 graduate students.

- **Labour market understanding** To make progress organizations need to understand the labour markets in which they are operating, and how these might change. The expectations of Gen X and Gen Y may be different to their predecessors. The aim is to align your values to the social values and expectations of your target talent pools, which may include a graduate market. This is challenging on a global basis, but organizations have to be sure about where their attraction hot spots are, where the brand is weak and what reception the EVP is getting in the key recruitment locations. You also should understand how the brand is playing internally and externally. Conducting the sort of exercise BASF did will give you a good picture of your strengths and weaknesses, and of any mismatch between your brand aspiration and how it is perceived.

BASF's research involved:

- interviews with more than 5,700 people worldwide, including in Brazil, China, India, Japan, Malaysia, Singapore, USA, Germany, France, the UK, Italy, Spain, Belgium and Poland

- focus groups with key target populations – students, professionals and school children in Germany
- focus group discussions with employees
- adding relevant questions to the global employee surveys.

The global employee survey showed that the following are most important to their employment by the company:

- interesting and challenging tasks
- being treated fairly and with respect within the company
- balance between work and family/other interests
- future career and development opportunities
- competitive compensation.

- **Responding to these data** Labour market insights are not just for inward management consumption, they can be deployed externally. Fact based messages to the market can be very powerful if they are connected to a good reading of the labour market. The Shell example shows how it can be used.

Shell's reaction to the competitive market is to avoid 'arrogant self-confidence' (Garmt Louw) and use data to back up its claims that the company provides opportunities to develop leadership skills. Interestingly, its pitch is to stress its size and scope rather than possibility of international assignments, as it might once have done, being careful not to over-promise. It also emphasizes what it stands for and what it does not.

Make your employer brand stand out

- **Distinctive employer branding** The leadership may seek to reinforce any distinction between themselves and their competitors. The brand may reflect what may be subtly different organizational cultures (e.g. between BP and Shell despite operating in the same sector) or the leadership may engage in a degree of covert cultural engineering that is then reflected in the brand.
- **Distinctive employment offer** Organizations should see what advantages they have compared with the opposition and what makes their offer distinctive. Shell in China cannot offer job security or status like the State Owned Enterprises, nor making a lot of money as in entrepreneurial companies, but it has an 'all round' offer – good pay but especially very strong professionalism, a long-term career, global exposure, intellectual freedom and delivery against the core company values. As a Hong Kong company, HPH is seen as a positive employment choice because it offers a chance to migrate from the home locations for many staff. By contrast, a number of Scottish based companies have promoted homecoming as a positive feature of jobs in Scotland, and Bangalore has seen 'a reverse diaspora' with more than 50,000 IT workers born abroad relocating home in the last five years (Keith, 2010).

- **PR opportunities accessed** Another approach is to participate in competitions like the Sunday Times Top 100 Companies to Work For. This has proved to be very important at company brand level in Business Week and Fortune rankings of successful firms in projecting the right image. Sanofi Aventis has used employer competitions to help grow its brand in China (Allouche, 2008).

In 2007 Tata Consultancy Services won the Golden Peacock Global Award for Corporate Social Responsibility in the 'Large Business' category by the Institute of Directors, the international body of company directors.

EXCELLENT EXECUTION

As with all HR activity, quality design can be compromised by poor implementation. Success in particular comes from doing communication well and getting employees engaged in the process of rollout and delivery. It also relies upon the organization sticking to what it says. Finally, organizations should measure how the brand/EVP is working out in practice.

Effective communication

- **Carefully communicate the brand/EVP** This can be as a promise to the world, a statement of the current reality or as a future aspiration. At a practical level, this can be used as part of a total reward communication or in the performance management process.
- **Employee support** Whatever approach is taken with their formulation, EVPs will not work as recruitment tools if your own employees do not support them. In the past, this obstacle might have become evident if candidates met current staff during a pre-recruitment visit and heard negative stories. These days such dissent can appear rapidly across the web. As the BASF example above shows, organizations really do need to listen to what current staff tell them about the organization and also potential recruits (including those who refuse job offers).
- **Employees as corporate ambassadors** The engagement and support of employees allow them to act as external ambassadors to project the brand for the organization with customers, family and friends. In 2009 British American Tobacco consciously rolled out its new EVP internally first so that employees could become advocates of it when the company was searching for new staff. This provides the opportunity to address any negativity from customers or the wider public. This can build employee loyalty especially in the face of external challenge.

Keeping promises

- **Leading the transmission of corporate DNA** That boxed Shell description emphasizes that the leadership of the organization really does need to live the values if they are to be taken seriously by employees. Authentic leadership is critical because, as Jing Wang again says, it is the most important conveyer of an organization's DNA. Leaders set the tone through what they preach and do, so it is very important who you choose as leaders, how you develop them. As the German saying has it, 'The fish stinks from the head', or as Wang puts it, 'The "shadow" that they cast really does affect how others in the organization behave.'

- **Clear but doable promises** yet these leaders do need to deliver practical results. This suggests the company should be careful not to over-promise. This means being realistic in what can be consistently delivered. For example, you might promise a stimulating job with considerable personal freedom, but the reality is that many jobs have little autonomy and work under close supervision. BASF acknowledged this need in its formulation of the employer brand. Its promise incorporated company competencies, benefits and 'personality'. The latter was described as 'pioneering' (open-minded, foresighted), 'passionate' (dynamic, caring) and 'professional' (competent, reliable).

> Linda Fan at Schneider told us that she herself accepted a job as a national staff manager on the basis that she would do the job for 18 months or she would leave to find a job more to her taste. After she had proved herself in the first year, she was given the business unit job she wanted.

- **Experience matches promise** The same applies to new recruits. The exhaustive interviewing and selection process in Shell China impresses candidates, but has to be backed in practice by the actual experience within the company. Is it as well run/ fair/diverse/developmental as suggested at interview? Greg Horton, MD of Fairbairn Private Bank, meets all new starters and those who have passed their probation to check both that there is still a good match between company requirements and employee expectations, and that they understand that their behaviour, as they put their training into practice, must align with the brand promise.
- **Promise into practice** Whatever the means, organizations should develop action plans directed at their key audiences – the external labour market with its potential recruits and the current workforce – that will put the brand promise or EVP into practice. As we have suggested this is likely to comprise a variety of communication media, practical demonstration through HR policy and practice, and the behaviours of key management participants. As Jing Wang puts it, Shell China's cultural norms are built into decision processes, a sort of 'software inscribed on the company hardware'.
- **Consistency of message** What the market and your own employees expect to hear and see are communications that make sense, that an internal logic applies to them. People lose confidence if they have a feeling that the left hand does not know what the right hand is doing or the story does not add up. Politicians are often rightly accused of this inconsistency and illogicality – their ideology and pragmatism do not always mix. The CEO and HR must instead endeavour to convey the same and believable message.

- **Tap the emotions** This last point re-emphasizes that the brand and EVP do not need to speak just to the tangible and financial benefits of employment, but they should also connect emotionally. This can be:
  - directly through its products (as in the Philips example earlier)
  - through its CSR actions, including the ability to deploy its capability for the common good

    'I am proud to work for a company that makes a difference to the world,' said an Ericsson technician in the light of his work in helping to restore communications in Haiti after the earthquake.

  - or through putting its values into action. See Jing Wang's description below.

The core values of honesty, integrity and respect are difficult to commercialize – it is 'like the air that you breathe'. For example, there are endless opportunities to voice one's opinion, lots of 'love and huddling', a lot of care is taken over terminations (giving people a chance to improve/find the right job, counselling, etc.). There is a lot of staff continuity to nurture/ sustain the culture. The company has long been a big advocate of diversity and inclusion and has a good reputation in this area. It has moved beyond the broad diversity concepts like gender to inclusiveness and micro issues of cultural sensitivity. For example, some US companies arrange calls to suit Houston time – i.e. very late for China – whereas in Shell there is an attempt to accommodate the needs of those in different time zones. It helps that the Shell's population is very diverse and that most of the senior people have themselves been expatriates.

Rick Brown, at the time Vice President – HR Functional Excellence, similarly talked about the fundamental right at Shell to query and expect a decent answer. As he said, if you get one then you are expected to follow the agreed position. 'The CEO accepts the challenge because it means the people care, and he has to respect that.'

Measuring progress

- **Outcomes tracked** Organizations should then track the performance of their brand/EVP. This is what ABB did, having rebranded the organization. It looked to see whether its actions had a positive effect on its target groups. Its conclusion was that it took two or three years to develop a new approach and constant attention to sustain improved performance.
- **Focused and integrated measurement** This means giving a high importance to measurement and the deployment of data. Employee engagement surveys are an obvious and available source of relevant information on perceptions of their employer and particularly on views on the delivery of the deal. For example, RBS surveys staff in order to gather employee engagement data, which can be examined by geography, function and business unit. Siemens has recently launched one survey to 430,000 employees to signal that it operates as a single company; branding the

survey in this way reinforces the message. But some organizations go further. Vestas has created a loyalty index and Invensys has switched its recruitment metrics away from process measures to brand related ones. It also looks at why staff choose to stay with them rather than move to competitors. RBS stresses the need to integrate data sources, such that attraction and retention information is combined, especially for those populations of particular interest (e.g. new recruits). These types of deeper, more comprehensive measures also provide a check on the all too common problem of enthusiastic central promises and local delivery that falls short.

Measurement should follow the logic of the brand:

number and quality of hires

- values alignment
- reputation in employer market

attrition rates

- early leavers
- reason for leaving

employee engagement – values in action

- company affiliation
- connection to purpose
- fair treatment/management performance

delivery of promises

- learning and development delivery
- competitive reward, etc.

THE ROLE OF HR (IN PARTNERSHIP)

It is all too easy for the employee brand to be regarded as the preserve of the marketing, public relations or communications teams with HR and line managers excluded. In a UK survey in less than half of organizations did HR have any involvement in branding (Reilly et al., 2007). The function needs to get involved in the analysis, design and execution of the brand. Development of the EVP concept helps in that regard because it is more easily seen as 'owned' by HR. And this is not just a question of asserting functional 'rights'; it is a matter of HR offering its distinctive perspective on external fit (through knowledge of the external labour market) and internal resonance (through interrogation of employee surveys and the like).

However, there is also the risk that line managers are not engaged in the process. This is critical as the brand is lived through them to a very large degree, at least as far as employees are concerned.

Our argument would then be for strong partnerships to be developed between PR, marketing, HR and line functions. Such partnerships avoid the criticism and reality that each is 'off doing its own thing'. Thus HR in its EVP development might be acting in contravention of marketing's brand policies. Marketing/communication may create a corporate brand with little value in the employment market. Managers may be critical of the brand message they are asked to convey through the organization. A series of situations organizations would wish to avoid.

Partnerships are therefore beneficial in creating brand alignment and avoiding brand confusion. Moreover, it provides the only way to *actually* deliver the corporate brand promise on the ground.

In RBS there is a challenge and opportunity for the HR function to respond to the threat to the brand. In their case by supporting the new leadership with all the tools it needs to win back the hearts and minds of all internal and external stakeholders. This is being done by rebuilding trust through greater transparency of decision processes and their outcomes; emphasizing values in practice as much as in theory; stating its operating principles and abiding by them.

DEVELOPMENT OF AN EMPLOYER BRAND AT MCDONALD'S

McDonald's is a global company operating in 119 countries and employing approximately 1.9 million associates worldwide. Its business model is decentralized mainly because a large percentage of its operations (70 per cent) are run through franchising. There was concern about how well aligned HR practices were within McDonald's and how internally consistent they were. It was felt that the company's employment image needed to be defined more precisely. This is in the context of an organization that prides itself on the consistency of its products and service delivery, such that their outcome is expected to meet the same standards everywhere in the world. Thus, it was agreed that a global framework would help to better align efforts.

As a result, four years ago at an internal global HR conference in Lisbon it was decided that the company could better leverage its EVP to its benefit. It was recognized that in different locations McDonald's had done well in Great Place to Work or similar ranking lists. Moreover, internal surveys were showing 80 per cent plus commitment scores among crew members, suggesting that the company was doing well by its employees in many ways, but not so well from the customer perception. Customer surveys suggested that they did not believe that the employment experience was as good as employees believed.

The consequences of this disconnect were that attraction and retention of employees could be hindered (especially where the customer base is similar to the employees). The company has a high turnover – up to 70–100 per cent – especially for part-time employees. Negative customer perception affects morale, which causes employee disengagement and results in lower retention. So better retention would save costs (recruitment, hiring, orientation and training) and more importantly, provide better customer service through having more experienced crew members.

The McDonald's initiative on a global EVP also needs to be seen within the context of the 'Plan to Win' that has operated over the last 10 years to turn the company around from a once poor trading position and weak share price. The Plan to Win involved five themes – People, Place, Product, Promotion and Price. Its aim was to concentrate on getting back to basics and delivering consistent performance. Within the last five years, the People element has spawned the Restaurant Strategy, which has looked at how to optimize people practices. This has generated the eight Proven People Practices that restaurants are strongly encouraged to observe in their management of employees. For instance, competitive market pay and benefits for part-time employees (flexible work schedules, development opportunities, and bonuses based on restaurant performance) are offered.

In September 2008, Cesar Martinez (VP HR Latin America) was asked to lead a global EVP Project. Governance was provided by a People Board with cross-functional representation. This was one of four key initiatives recognizing a principal market differentiator of McDonald's: it is a people company serving hamburgers, instead of a hamburger company serving people. The EVP was correlated with McDonald's' Principles and Values as well as the eight Proven People Practices, which are all linked to the Plan to Win.

Cesar started by finding out what the leading countries – e.g. Canada, Singapore and the UK – were already doing in this area on both EVP and employment branding. He then launched a global employee survey in 55 countries covering all continents, representing the cultural diversity that exists within the McDonald's system. This project was conducted in three phases. The first phase involved McDonald's markets large and small: USA, UK, France, Germany, Canada, China, Japan, Australia, Russia, Brazil, Argentina, Singapore, and UAE. From Phase 1 to 3, a total of 10,000 restaurant employees were asked two simple questions: 'What do you like most about working for McDonald's?' and 'What do you like least about working for McDonald's?' Deliberately kept short to boost the response rate, a 95 per cent return was achieved. There were no additional biographical questions, to avoid any concerns about confidentiality. The results were analysed and 33 themes emerged. In order of importance, these were then grouped into three core elements known as the 3 F's: Family and Friends, Flexibility, and Future:

- Family and Friends: enjoying the people I work with, a company culture of teamwork.
- Flexibility: variable working hours, more shift opportunities, job variety.
- Future: skills development, learning and career advancement.

So this could be said to be McDonald's' EVP.

The three aspects of working for McDonald's that the respondents liked the least were:

- Compensation: employees aspire to earn higher wages.
- Among crew: pressure from rude customers for faster service.
- Among restaurant managers: the business pressures and the effects these have on their working hours and hence on the quality of work/life balance.

As would be expected, McDonald's' strategy is to enhance the positives and deal with the negatives when possible. It was clear that the company could not 'deny the voice of employees'. Even if the content sounds disagreeable at times, it did send a powerful message.

These global results were generally consistent with employee attitude surveys within the participating countries. The 33 global themes were analysed regionally and globally.

Although there were slight differences – perhaps in the ranking of the top three – there were no discrepancies as to the top 10 themes.

Across the world, there were good matches with individual country prior experiences with an EVP. For example:

- In the UK there was an excellent fit between the global and locally developed EVP, even when the descriptions were differently expressed.
- Canada's EVP was in full alignment with the work culture and business needs in the country.
- Singapore's EVP also closely matched the global framework.

A key success factor for the EVP was strong support from senior management. The Heads of HR from the 13 countries in Phase 1 were given the raw data without categorization and then asked to group answers. They came up with the same results. At another global meeting with the People Board (HR, Operations and Training leads from around the world), they too endorsed the survey results and committed to embracing the EVP. Since it was introduced, the EVP has aligned people practices with the 3 F's throughout McDonald's global system.

To facilitate this, an EVP Toolkit reflecting the 3 F's was created to guide implementation around the world. The Toolkit is divided into three main areas, which contain tools related to its Communication, Planning and Activation. Among the activation resources, the Alignment Matrix and the Restaurant Assessment Guide include metric capabilities. The Alignment Matrix is used to arrange current and planned people programmes and measure their alignment with the EVP core elements. The Restaurant Assessment Tool enables restaurant managers to assess and measure people practices.

In April 2010, the McDonald's Employment Value Proposition (EVP) and its Toolkit were introduced to the system franchisees during the McDonald's Worldwide Convention. Besides the compelling message resulting from the comprehensive research that was conducted, the business case used to convey the importance of the EVP was that higher employee satisfaction leads to better customer service, which in turn produces higher sales and profitability.

A global action plan was launched within the company's own restaurants (to be followed by the franchisees). This includes:

- mapping current people practices against the EVP 3 F's
- judging how well the restaurants/countries perform against the EVP
- where the results are positive, maintaining or building on this position
- where the results are unfavourable, altering practices or mitigating their negative effects.

Restaurants were asked to look at their own people practices to see how they matched against the company's recommendations. McDonald's is looking for ideas for positive change that are 'actionable within restaurants'. This might include growing skills, better work scheduling, greater teamwork, better communications, and energizing crew and managers through programmes such as Voice of McDonald's (a global singing contest among restaurant employees). McDonald's believes that improving the experience for employees ultimately improves customer experience.

Globally, McDonald's has to deliver what it promises to employees through the EVP, but implementation may vary based on market needs and cultural differences. Franchisees are strongly encouraged to embrace the EVP, and in fact the global Plan to Win was modified to reflect the EVP and its principles.

So far, McDonald's EVP process implementation has shown that a global company with vast cultural differences can articulate a valid, aligned employee value proposition for its associates around the world.

6 *International Talent Management*

> *The talent shock is coming. It will arrive in years, not decades, regardless of the current economic crisis. It is now time for all involved stakeholders to ally forces and prepare for the era of extreme labour scarcity, significant talent mobility and a truly global workforce. (World Economic Forum in Davos, 2010)*

Many surveys point out the importance of talent management to both HR and senior executives. For example, a Mercers survey in Europe (2010) and a survey from The Boston Consulting Group (2010) put acquiring/retaining talent or talent management as their number one people issue. Moreover, 60 per cent of European respondents to a Hewitt's questionnaire (2009a) rated talent management as the HR issue with the highest positive impact on organizational performance.

Despite this evidence, there are several issues with talent management to be considered. What does it mean? To whom does it apply? How is it enacted? For global companies there is a question about how is talent managed differently in a truly global organization or whether there are simply pockets of internationally deployed staff in certain businesses. The tensions we raised at the outset of the book apply just as they did in the previous chapters on culture (Chapter 3) and brand (Chapter 5) and will also do so for governance (Chapter 7) and the service delivery model (Chapter 8). What does global talent management mean in a way that distinguishes it from national talent management? How to strike the balance between local and global talent identification and development? What is to be standardized and consistent across the company and what can be different and tailor-made?

So in this section of the book we will start with a definition of talent management and a review of the principal choices in talent management strategy, before moving on to look at how global organizations have tackled the subject, and as before, we will consider the challenges in delivering talent management before suggesting some actions to mitigate problems and maximize the chances of success.

The Definition of Talent

So talent management is important, yet it is a tricky subject to cover because the term lacks a clear definition. As a result, there is always the risk of hyperbole, as in McKinsey's title of the War for Talent (Michaels et al., 2001) or of vacuousness, as in many conference programmes. However, though probably disliked by some academics precisely because of its imprecise nature, it resonates with managers. It may have gone beyond being a fad because the term 'talent' has such a positive ring to it and it seems to offer the potential for high performance such that organizations want to 'manage' it. Its popularity reached such an extent that has been used by some to mean the whole of HR activity, in the same way some people abused the term 'human capital'.

If we look at various definitions, each has their own problems:

- **Peter Cappelli** (2008) has defined talent management as 'simply a matter of anticipating the need for human talent and then setting out a plan to meet it'. This description has the merit of simplicity but lacks insight as to whether the term *talent* has any meaning beyond a description of those employed. This could just as easily be a definition of resourcing or workforce planning.
- **Dave Ulrich et al.** (2009b) include three dimensions, 'Competence', 'Commitment' and 'Contribution', in their *Talent Formula*. This has the advantage of combining performance and employee engagement, but misses out on potential in the sense of future capability as opposed to present.
- **Boudreau and Ramstad** (2007) have suggested that talent is 'the resource that includes the potential and realized capacities of individuals and groups and how they are organized, including within the organization and those who might join the organization'. This is a good, broad account of talent management because it offers both the corporate and employee perspectives, and covers potential, but has the danger of being no more than traditional staff resourcing.
- **Stahl et al.** (2007) definition given in the Introduction helpfully sets out the talent management processes, and, perhaps inevitably given the global context, concentrates on the 'key' talent.

An important aspect of academic definitions is whether they emphasize individual development or the organizational perspective. Lewis and Heckman (2006), for example, critique approaches to talent management that focus on individuals' development and overlook the 'architecture' of organizations. They proposed a talent management 'hierarchy' that first devises organizational strategy and its implication for 'talent pools' where varied proportions of talent are required. The HR function should then introduce systems and practices that support talent development. Similarly, Boudreau and Ramstad (2007) argue that 'talentship' is the 'decision science' or core knowledge required for HRM practitioners. This means deciding upon the 'pivot points' where talent and organizational performance will most 'enhance sustainable strategic success'.

Whilst these developments are helpful in reaffirming the organizational context of decision making, we are still left with questions about interpreting the nature of talent.

If we move from the textbook to the workplace, this definitional ambiguity is replicated. At one extreme talent management is seen to refer only to those already in senior positions in the organization. At the other end of the spectrum, we have organizations that include the whole workforce when they talk of talent. Somewhere in the middle, though closer to the first view, is a process that manages candidates for fast-track development to senior positions, and a model that seeks to emphasize those employees who are critical to its success.

So we have to varying degrees an exclusive talent management model that gives the impression that it is uninterested in those without 'talent' or more positively wants to channel development resources to where they are most needed and to secure the right opportunities for the right people. These organizations no doubt believe the route to success is acquiring, retaining and motivating these few 'game changers'. Alternatively, the inclusive approach believes performance is driven from the engine room of the organization, not just from the bridge or from a small number of talented crew. We have post versus people differences: do we organize talent management around the key jobs to be filled or on the key people to develop? And, overlapping with the last distinction, we have a talent management focused on pay grades, individual potential or organizational value. Moreover, some of the definitions of talent include attraction, deployment and development; others concentrate on planning and talent identification. Finally, the academic debate on organizational or individual focus is replicated at the workplace.

Moreover, the very concept of having 'talent' is perhaps situated in a particular view of the world to be found in Anglo-Saxon countries. In egalitarian societies the idea of elevating some people to a pedestal above others is an anathema. Those countries that put the collective above the individual will struggle to see the ethical justification for exclusive talent management, as will societies that emphasize other personal characteristics like age or seniority.

So these differences in talent management perspective may be practical – a need to focus on top talent – or philosophical – performance is driven by the few or the many, but it should be obvious that these conceptual differences have important consequences in talent management in practice.

Talent Management Models

The various actual forms of talent management flow from these distinctions in perspective. Taking this point further what are the implications of the various talent management approaches? We will look at four 'ideal types' of talent management:

- inclusive talent management (Model 1)
- exclusive talent management based on grade, really executive (Model 2)
- exclusive talent management based on high potentials (Model 3)
- exclusive talent management based on skills (Model 4).

Apart from Model 1, all the other talent approaches require a segmentation of the workforce, a categorization by grade, potential, performance or skill. They want to send the right message to the right group about their value to the organization and the organization's positive response. These organizations apply what Graeme Martin (2011) calls the 'traditional' shareholder value model (or as described on p. 207 as the 'agency' model). They follow the exclusive talent approach because they believe this is how they will gain maximum organizational benefit (or are pushed towards this method by the markets, as we will hear later that Davis (2009) contends).

As Graeme Martin has argued, by comparison, the inclusive model may be associated with an 'enlightened' shareholder value and stewardship (governance) mindset, as we will describe later (p. 207).

INCLUSIVE TALENT MANAGEMENT (MODEL 1)

The sort of development and deployment processes your organization employs will have a profoundly different shape if you believe talent is ubiquitous (Model 1) rather than exclusive. Development will be open to all, with a strong sense of a learning culture. So acquiring qualifications will be supported. Selection processes will naturally exist to promote individuals, but will not be used to restrict personal growth. And job rotation or job enrichment will be encouraged. The contribution of teams will be valued along with individuals, and following Richard Sennett (2008) there will be more of an emphasis on 'craftmanship' – skills built up over an extended period.

EXCLUSIVE TALENT MANAGEMENT FOR EXECUTIVE GRADES (MODEL 2)

A talent management system that focuses on certain grades is likely to put the spotlight on executives (Model 2). This is because it is imperative for internal functioning and external credibility to have the right leadership in place. In practical terms, organizations with this emphasis in talent management would concentrate on succession planning. They would ensure that there is a sufficient number of capable people to move to these senior positions and that each has a named successor (or three) in case the metaphorical bus comes along and runs them over. Performance management is likely to be tough, with little tolerance of those who fail to deliver. Development may have a much stronger personal coaching focus, with much less attention to training. Career management will be active in ensuring that all posts are filled with the right people, with limited scope for individual experimentation.

EXCLUSIVE TALENT MANAGEMENT BASED ON HIGH POTENTIALS (MODEL 3)

Our third model – the high-potential one – is all about having the right pipeline in place to supply the top team. It follows the GE principle that you need to focus on your 'A' stars, following the 'power law' principle that 80 per cent of the value comes from 20 per cent of the workforce (Martin et al., 2009). This means its centre of attention is on selection – how do you choose these 'highpos'? What is it about them that marks them out? Is it, as Dyer and Ericksen (2007) have argued, those who are prepared to enter zones of their incompetence? Whereas 'competent' employees are 'an inch wide and a mile deep', competent at their job but resisting change that threatens their identity, 'serial incompetents' regularly choose periods of incompetence in order to 'stay one step ahead in an ever changing world'. 'Dynamic' organizations encourage these 'serial incompetents' to innovate.

There are a variety of methods used. Some organizations put all the stress on performance. Others try to identify those with potential, using assessment centres early in people's career. Some infer the necessary attributes by understanding what successful people have by way of competencies. And another group combine performance and potential. There is a further distinction between considering short-term, next job, or long-term, ultimate, potential. The former method sees selection as a one-step-at-a-time process; the latter believes that you can identify enduring attributes in people such that you can try to plan to exploit their capability.

The selected individuals are then closely monitored and given development opportunities both in a learning and a career experience sense. There is frequently a promotion and relegation system, though perhaps more of the former than the latter (as it is harder to remove people given the demotivating effects). Through periodic, gateway, assessment centres (also known somewhat erroneously as development centres) those who do not have the necessary competencies of sufficiently high order are weeded out. Those who survive may indeed be given development help via coaching, mentoring or experiential learning (on projects, new work assignments, etc.). Promotion may come from those once described in Shell as 'late bloomers', often very effective performers whose contribution to organizational success demands their inclusion.

EXCLUSIVE TALENT MANAGEMENT BASED ON SKILLS (MODEL 4)

Those deemed talented because their performance is critical to organizational success (Model 4) may overlap with the high potential described above, but this group is broader in that it is not potential that determines inclusion. There is of course a decent standard of performance required, but it is the special skills or knowledge that they bring that is the defining element. So research scientists, development engineers, 'noses' (in the perfume industry), charity fund-raisers, operational research planners and so on might be included. They are the highly skilled specialists of the organization. In some organizations they are called 'high professionals', which may indicate the offer of a separate, parallel career path or nothing more than a placatory label with little practical meaning intended to reassure individuals about the importance of their group.

Development for them is probably largely in post trying to hone their skills, also to retain them by giving them broader autonomy in their roles, building a team around them (whilst minimizing 'bureaucratic' tasks), offering opportunities to speak at conferences, publish papers or whatever turns them on.

There may be some succession planning to build capability for the future and offer organizational resilience. This may be led by a skill champion, functional grandparent or head of profession. The focus in this form of talent management tends to be very individual and protective.

The Business Context for Talent Strategies

Having laid out four theoretical talent management models, we will next discuss the basis on which organizations can make their strategic talent decisions. In the following section we describe the global context for this decision making before focusing on the various strategic options and targets for talent management.

When considering the adoption of something like these 'ideal types' in an organizational setting, clearly the choice should be determined by the business strategy of the organization, e.g. to innovate, to deliver quality or lead on cost-competitiveness. This in turn will be affected by the size, sector and business situation of the organization.

Nevertheless, in the UK at least, it seems developing high-potential employees or growing future senior managers/leaders are the main objectives of talent management. According to a CIPD survey (2010a), organizations are twice as likely to have these goals as they are to meet the future skills requirements of the organization.

So firstly why is there this emphasis on top talent? According to Gerald F Davis (2009), one of the drivers has been the need to satisfy shareholders, especially in financial services. The pressure to deliver shareholder value has put a premium on short-term performance. Acquiring talent is essential, but as it is a marketable commodity you have to ensure that it is retained and developed. You have to demonstrate to the stock market that you have this talent capability and select talent that maximizes shareholder value by fully using its contribution.

Another externally driven reason for talent management from a business perspective is to satisfy regulators that your organization has in place succession plans for the top posts and – to some extent – high-quality leadership development for a broader senior management population. This sort of requirement is to be found in financial services and other regulated industries. It is also features in descriptions of good corporate governance, where corporate boards are expected to discharge a responsibility for overseeing top talent – a task they may not have (visibly) discharged well in the past.

However, there are other business influences. Some organizations favour resourcing strategies that are responding to future focused business challenges and/or where returns on investment are realized over years not months. Here, talent strategies are aimed at growing talent to meet these long-term requirements. One thinks of energy companies and those working in other extractive industries.

Through the people the company chooses to advance, talent management can be used to send signals to rest of the organization about the sort of characteristics it is seeking (and not seeking) in its leadership population. Organizations have used talent management to push workforce diversity or ethical standards. It has been deployed to indicate 'the sort of people we want round here', as well as those they would rather do without.

The labour market can also have an effect on talent strategies especially for the organizations that rely on specific skills. Persistent labour market shortages will cause organizations to hoard talent. It will reinforce any disposition to acquire people early and retain them for as long as possible. This is especially where firm-specific knowledge is a source of competitive advantage, but requires time to build.

By contrast, where knowledge of organizational culture, products, internal networks, etc. is less important to effective performance and where the labour market is relatively well supplied with competent people, organizations can afford to hire as required. This might apply to FMCG companies that are more likely to be preoccupied by shorter-term considerations of profit maximization where the resourcing issues are less about planning and more about current delivery.

Then there are professional service type firms, where expertise can be very specific. There is progression towards partner level but the development route may be narrower than in some other major organizations. You cannot ask lawyers or accountants to work outside their area of jurisdiction. It makes little business sense to ask an expert in one aspect of management consultancy to broaden into another unless there is an overriding market reason.

Whilst, generally, talent strategies will be driven by specific business needs, there may be times where the prevailing situation regarding talent at an international level may drive business strategy. Availability of talent is not static. Where are the best engineers, scientists or programmers likely to be found in five or 10 years time? What impact will that have on business strategies? The demographic pressures are already making the move of R&D from Europe to South East Asia to tap the best talent available a serious proposition. Offshoring has played a key role in cost improvement, but moving the work to the people may have wider application but perhaps with more serious implications. An organization used to trying to recruit in Sweden, for example, may have to adjust to operating from a new base in say in Korea, especially if that is where future talent resides and/or where the centre of business activity has become.

TALENT MANAGEMENT DURING TOUGH TIMES

Against this background, how have talent programmes survived, or are surviving, recessionary times? They seemed to have fared quite well, thus far, despite widespread workforce reduction, as evidenced by another survey from The Boston Consulting Group (2009) that found that in almost every country participating, talent management remains their most important topic (and one where they struggled to be effective). Indeed, it seems characteristic of dealing with this recession, unlike previous ones, that organizations have, wherever possible, been protecting skills and talent. This finding is noteworthy given, as Sparrow et al. (2004) have observed, talent management programmes are at risk from operating in an 'environment of volatility'. These authors were concerned primarily with maintaining 'focus' against internal change, but external impact can be equally destructive.

However, the sense of the continuing importance given to talent management, even in the face of recessionary threat, is not surprising given the business drivers of talent management that we have identified. Shareholder and regulatory pressures will not disappear, and nor will the need to invest in the future or deal with talent shortages against intense competition and/or demographic shortfalls. As Firmenich's senior management team agreed, one of their most critical challenges to overcome is 'having the right leaders in critical places'.

Indeed, though the recession was widespread internationally, it has not hit all parts of the world equally. Some countries were relatively unscathed, especially in the Asia Pacific region, like Singapore or Australia. Here, the competitive pressures to acquire and retain talent have proceeded without much of a blip. Even those countries with large populations, like China and India, have struggled with supply, both because of their rate of growth, but also because of the absence of talent that can operate in a global business context. This is what a Dubai bank found when it wanted to expand outside the Gulf region. The biggest impediment to success is the difficulty of either using existing resources or recruiting extra resources to fulfil its ambitions.

Especially in tough times, there has been a strong desire to connect talent management to business strategy. This sends the message that talent identification and development is not a discretionary task, even in a business downturn, but one central to business success. SAP made just this point in saying, 'Investing in talent management is like investing in R&D – you can't grow, be profitable and adapt without it.' At Grundfos the strap line 'Be, think, innovate' applies worldwide and according to Professor Henrik Holt Larsen (Institute for Organisation at Copenhagen Business School) 'goes like a laser beam from brand to HR strategy to talent management'.

For those organizations more affected by the recession there is a sense in which organizations that have fought hard in the war for talent to acquire the employees, leaders, stars or specialists they want do not wish to lose them. There is little fat left to cut or poor quality to remove. Moreover, at least in the west, there is also a recognition that the demographic profile means that the flow of young people onto the labour market will be shrinking over the next decades. So, especially in the knowledge parts of the economy, talent is being hoarded during the difficult times so that it can be deployed as we move out of recession (Chubb et al., 2010).

Consistent with this strategy, the recession has caused organizations to identify the people who are vital to survival and needed to make the most of the upturn. In a blurring of our Models 3 and 4, matrices with performance and potential in nine box models (pictured later on p. 156) are being used to identify who needs to be kept and who can be disposed of. There is a sense in which some companies have used the downturn to sift out some of the lower performers, but in many there is a realization that good people are having to be made redundant if there are no alternative ways of quickly saving money. One organization we met chose to protect graduates as the seed corn for the future at the expense of more experienced and perfectly capable staff. This was a decision taken with the expectation that it would benefit organizational capability in the long run. In other companies there has been an emphasis on a more immediate improvement in organizational performance for the core workforce – 'shifting the bell curve to the right' as one business leader put it. This again suggests a difference in organizational perspective between long and short-term considerations.

Moreover, in a needs must way, organizations have had to make the best use of the resources they still have at their disposal. This means putting people in stretching roles, broadening their existing portfolio, taking risks with some appointments and so on. These pragmatic decisions may have the unintended benefit of building talent capability, so long as the people concerned are able to deliver.

What has clearly come through our interviewees, partly as a reflection of current circumstances, is more acknowledgement than before that there are not unlimited opportunities and that candidate expectations have to be managed. Thus the requirement for particular posts (be they senior, challenging or developmental) is restricted and the supply to these jobs has to be controlled.

GOING FOR GLOBAL

The talent management challenges of organizations that are global or are aspiring to expand their operations internationally are likely to be driven by some of the same business imperatives as would be true for national companies. Namely, they must respond to shareholder and regulatory pressures, respond to labour market and short-term business challenges and build people capability for the future. The principal difference relates to context. In particular, people management pressures are felt across the world, not just in a known and seemingly more controllable environment. This broadening of scope means that a successful global organization has to able to:

- understand and respond to shortages of skills and talent anywhere in its operations from general management to specialist expertise
- divert resources not just to labour hot spots but to meet business requirements, be it in the Gulf of Mexico or in Cape Town. This might relate to crises or to business start-ups.
- build organizational human capital to be able to run an international business and be able to respond to global events
- have people capable of concluding trans-national takeovers, deals with national governments, international suppliers, etc.
- ensure the probity of all its activities and that all parts of its operations are meeting stated organizational values and business principles.

In extremis, there should be a recognition that the absence of talent can be a restraint on business performance, especially for those companies trying to grow internationally, where, until the recession stalled the momentum, growing global business activity led to increased competition for the people who could deliver in this environment.

So how are companies meeting these requirements?

Firstly, there is a need to systematize their talent management approach. Many organizations, especially those that are expanding internationally, have been on a journey firstly to get their talent management processes in satisfactory order and then scale them up for global use. The boxed examples of Oxfam, Deutsche Post World Net (DPWN) and Firmenich are illustrative.

In 2000 Oxfam had no career development or succession planning, limited and ad hoc management development and unsophisticated recruitment processes, advertising mainly through *The Guardian Weekly*.

Now, the seven regional organizations, all locations and functional teams espouse a global talent concept. There are 'occasional blips' in not supporting concept, but the need for a global pipeline is well understood and largely delivered. Indeed, a higher proportion of junior/ middle and senior management appointments come from internal candidates, 46 per cent and 54 per cent respectively. The Country Director talent pipeline has a better percentage coming from developing countries.

Similarly, Deutsche Post World Net has gone from being a state owned German post office in 1990 to a global logistics company operating in 270 countries. Over the last five or so years it has built up its performance evaluation capability, moved onto tackling data quality and then launched its 'talent brokerage' role to find the best global talent within the Group.

At Firmenich there was intellectual recognition that it was necessary to refresh the organization (given the ageing population) and respond to the needs of a new generation of employees. It was understood that there is high competition for the industry specialists. But it was the messages from an employee survey that caused the top team to focus on organizational leadership. Progress has since been incremental, with talent management practices spreading by osmosis but with clear goals as to the business benefits.

Secondly, some organizations are responding to a new business climate, of changed or new global opportunities or new business pressures; and globalizing talent management has to be seen in this context. IT companies in particular have to think of knowledge diffusion strategies that keep innovation in the firm rather than leaking out through social media to local or global competitors. This makes for cultural and behavioural challenges, especially in emphasizing the importance of knowledge sharing. Similarly, global pharma companies have to respond to greater regulation, competition and pressure on price that lead to having a more productive and responsive culture. Some financial services companies have had to change business strategy post Crash, especially by focusing on their core activities, as RBS has done.

ANZ is an example of a company trying to grow and take advantage of new possibilities. Thus it aims to double its income within five years. Especially with a declining supply in its Australian home base and the opportunities being in Asia, talent acquisition, deployment and retention becomes critical to business success.

Natura, a Brazilian cosmetics manufacturing company, also said that it was not possible to sustain business growth without developing its own talent, 'that's because we need leaders who breathe and retransmit our vision, values, culture and beliefs' (The Boston Consulting Group, 2010).

Next, organizations are trying to create international talent pools drawing upon a wide range of nationalities, which for global organizations has even more meaning than national ones (see Chapter 4 for more on the question of diversity).

More so in some organizations than others, there is also a desire to exploit talent management processes to achieve other goals in terms of consistent delivery of the organization's policies and practices. This might be in terms of business ethics, standing operating procedures or global processes in financial management as much as people management.

Aitken Spence firmly stated that its overseas operations are controlled from Colombo. This is achieved by, wherever possible, having Sri Lankans in all the key posts abroad. Naturally, local employment practices are applied in line with local employment laws, but the management style and supporting training and development is very much of a Sri Lankan hue.

Finally, organizations have to answer the same questions about make or buy, plan or respond, post or person centred, how to direct talent management, but again in a different context from other national organizations. It is these strategic choices that we will now consider.

Strategic Options

In this section we will review the sort of important decisions to be made on what sort of talent management approach the organization will use. It should be said that whilst there are sectoral pointers to how organizations will behave in their talent management practices, not all organizations within a sector follow the same business strategies, and considerations of organizational culture can also be important in shaping the approach to talent management. Thus the philosophical differences in talent management thinking can cut across organizations' business activities. We will examine these choices in turn, emphasizing the specifics that relate to an international context.

Whilst talent management may be a key business imperative, it should not be assumed that all organizations will have a talent management strategy. A recent CIPD survey (2010a) claims that though more and more UK organizations are engaged in talent management activities, especially those larger companies in the private sector, these may well be ad hoc in nature. It is probably still true that many organizations are developing policy and practices to a more systematic level and explicitly linking them to business strategies.

THE TARGET OF TALENT MANAGEMENT

As expected, there was not unanimity in our case study organizations on whether the attention on talent is focused on the top 100 in the company, those with the potential to reach that position, on employees throughout the organization that contribute to its success or the smaller critical group who are the most vital to organizational performance.

Some of the differences between organizations are simply terminological or the consequence of the way programmes have been branded. Some difference relates to how to use limited resources, but also reflects organizational pressure points – difficult groups to hire or retain. So, for example:

- The Allianz insurance group is especially interested in 'top talent' with potential for leadership roles.
- Similarly, EDF Energy focused on succession planning to build a cadre of 'world class, global leaders'.
- Schlumberger has a 'top tier' for highest potential staff (0.5 per cent of the population) capable of moving into leadership positions and a 'high value' group (15 per cent of the population) who are highly regarded contributors.
- ANZ concentrates on 'stand out' potential. Their focus is on those with high leadership competencies.
- Audi is currently putting in place a development programme for shop floor workers as a response to the demography of the external labour market (fewer people coming through).
- Tesco makes the 'people promise' to all employees that the company offers the 'opportunity to get on'.
- Aviva is reported to emphasize the need to develop the 'vital many' as opposed to the vital few (Guthridge et al., 2008) giving attention not just to the 'A' players.
- These days, Wallenius Wilhelmsen Logistics (WWL) focuses much less on the concept that everyone has talent and has moved towards creating acceptance of differential development. The emphasis is now on the actual evaluation and development of the top leadership talent.
- SAP uses broad definitions of talent, but in practice concentrates development efforts on particular groups – emphasizing that actions may be targeted even if there is an inclusive philosophy. It 'is moving from an exclusive focus on top talent' to talking about an 'inclusive focus on the universe of talents'. Whilst it is investing in all the staff, it is aiming to 'grow great leaders', which means specific programmes are required for the high potentials so identified.
- Similarly, PWC declares everyone is talented and states that everyone has the opportunity to develop 'as far and as fast as they can and want to go', but in reality specific attention is given to those with leadership potential (Hirsh, 2010).

- Firmenich also supports a wide definition of talent but the focus is on 'high impact' talent that drives competitive advantage (the technical specialists, leaders and promising people).

MAKE OR BUY TALENT?

The grow-your-own-timber approach is likely to be found in companies with a long-term business perspective, reinforced by operating in a very competitive labour market for key staff. These organizations that choose to 'make' rather than 'buy' may emphasize Sennet's craftsmanship and slowly acquired depth of thinking and/or they want to build a common culture, an esprit de corps. They may be aware that a high proportion of external hires to senior positions fail.

By contrast, some organizations favour buying in talent because it offers greater resourcing flexibility and keeps up the pressure to perform. These companies may be distinguished by the fact they prefer 'mentally mobile' people who bring in fresh ideas and challenge stagnation and insular thinking.

A third group, perhaps the most pragmatic, might generally prefer to grow their own but want it leavened by those with outside experience and the guts to challenge the status quo. Or they may look at the cost–benefits of the two approaches and choose different strategies for different groups. The aim might be to 'make' your own talent building internal capability in specialist areas, whilst supporting it with external recruitment 'bought' in for general management positions.

The model below, associated with David Lepak, but much used by consultancies and practitioners, attempts to structure this debate by looking also at labour market availability as well as a value/impact dimension.

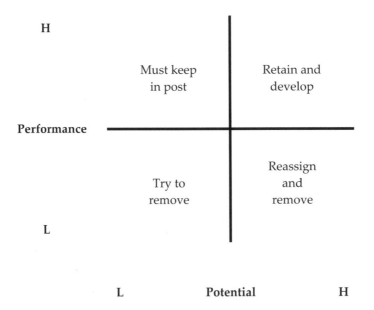

Figure 6.1 Who should stay and who should go?

International company examples

In our research, we met more organizations that were from the grow-your-own-timber school. Shell has had a tradition of so doing, though it moved away from this approach for roughly 10 years after its 1995 restructuring to reflect what it saw as a more flexible labour market, both for employers and employees. The company has come to the conclusion that this was a mistake: that building a coherent culture necessary for business success requires continuity in employment, especially for the more technical or specialist professions.

SAP has come to a similar conclusion. It now has a preference for internal talent development. The company recruits first-degree graduates and MBAs and then develops them. It has found that it is not so easy to recruit from competitors as cultures are often very different and SAP wants people to do things its way, not the way of the opposition.

Tesco approaches talent management by building capability more than buying it, such that Sir Terry Leahy after 14 years as CEO was replaced in 2010 by Philip Clarke who has worked at Tesco throughout his career. Marks and Spencer also believes that growing talent is both more efficient (it costs less to develop than to buy if you take account of the full recruitment, induction and training cost) and more effective (not least in cultural fit). It has a target of resourcing three quarters of its leadership positions from within.

> Oxfam wants 'all rounders' who can cover all the Oxfam fields well and also the deep specialists. Given how hard it is to recruit these latter skills or develop the former generalist group, the organization feels it needs to grow its own. As evidence of its success in doing this, Oxfam in 2007 could point to 65 per cent of senior manager and 44 per cent junior/middle manager vacancies filled by internal recruits.

Novartis, when advertising jobs internally, also posts the jobs on an external recruitment website, thereby testing the market. This must offer an excellent calibration of internal talent against external capability.

Besides company differences we also saw differences that reflect geography – the labour market challenges vary across the world.

In the Middle East and Asia the focus is on recruitment to acquire people. Especially in an Asian context, companies have been recruiting ahead of the demand curve to ensure they have people ready for later growth. Developing those who you have recruited to meet gaps and deal with expansion is important, not least because it might also aid retention. Nonetheless, such is the competitive position that this may be a vain hope, and the organization is on a constant treadmill recruiting all the time to fill holes as people leave.

> A bank in the UAE wants to expand beyond its borders, but is aware that internally it does not have the multicultural skills to operate successfully outside the Gulf. It may have the technical but doubts it has the management capability. Whilst its workforce is diverse there is a particular relationship between UAE nationals and immigrant workers that might not apply in other settings. It is also concerned that such knowledge, skills and experience are not present in any volume in the external labour market.

So even if the global resourcing strategy is to develop internal talent this may have to be adjusted to suit the volatility of the local labour market in general or for specific employment groups. A Boston Consulting Group survey (2010) found that around half their respondent companies were buying in top executives, senior and middle managers due to talent shortages not because of a preference for external recruitment. Similarly, those organizations whose preferred method is to hire and fire may emphasize retention to protect assets that have been obtained with some difficulty. For global organizations this means even more variety of approach since the business situation is not the same the world over.

> Tesco has a wish to build 80 per cent of its talent and buy in just 20 per cent. However, whilst it might achieve those proportions in the UK, in overseas markets it is not there yet. It has to build capability. Benefiting from business growth, it can recruit ahead of the demand and ensure proper induction into the company.

In more mature economies the emphasis may well be on the bringing on of talent. Investment in existing resources may be more cost-effective than constant hiring, and employee loyalty to the firm sufficiently strong to make that outlay worthwhile. However, the recent business situation has affected hiring behaviour. In the recession hit west some companies have selectively hired in those with high potential or specific skills, even as they make others redundant. This might be partly driven by trying to improve the organizational 'batting average' – another means of shifting the bell curve. Thus Canon Europe took its own recruitment ban with 'a pinch of salt', according to HR director Massimo Macarti, because the company wanted to add skills as well as lose some people. It is also affected by the desire to get in resources before the market heats up and makes talent acquisition so difficult again.

IDENTIFY TALENT EARLY OR LATE?

Organizations trying to identify talent early do so to give their talented people a chance to get the necessary development such that they are ripe for appointment to senior (usually general management) positions at an appropriate age. The right sort of preparation is likely to include both breadth (by function and, especially in international firms, by geography) and depth (especially in very technical companies). Those companies are likely to be the same ones that want to grow their own timber precisely for this reason.

The question of identification of talent early or late is therefore really about whether the organization believes in having a high-potential development programme or is simply concerned with filling the top team and those a tier or two below. So 'late' in many organizations may really mean 'just in time' as the need arises.

There may also be a retention purpose in early identification because you can signal corporate approbation to those who will be in high market demand. It may be that promoting them at a young age also allows some unconventional thinking into the firm (the facility to challenge that other companies buy in).

The differences with those that identify talent late are obvious. The development need is much reduced. The preparedness to cover gaps through external recruitment is much higher. The focus is on selection decisions, which you cannot afford to get wrong. Making a mistake on high-potential identification can be rectified at some later point. There is no such scope when choosing a senior leader.

International company examples

In discussions with organizations we found some with more of a planning orientation than others, but also that responding to labour market pressures tends push organizations towards a long-term retention strategy.

Thus Shell still looks at where an individual might finally reach in grade terms, whereas DPWN looks at potential over next 12 months. In recognition of the fact that the next year might be too short a time horizon to plan career development for the especially talented, DPWN closely monitors those 'regarded as especially promising'.

Similarly, Firmenich sees talent management as a 'longer-term strategic framework to identify talent priorities, identify potential talent, and then assess, develop, and retain'. It is currently focusing on the leadership capabilities needed to meet business challenges five years ahead and is very mindful that one of its two largest competitors has its corporate headquarters just four kilometres from its Geneva headquarters.

ORGANIZATIONAL OR INDIVIDUAL FOCUS

Whatever the talent model, there is the question of how much talent management is organization or people-centric. An organization-centric approach is about securing and maintaining the right resources in the right place to improve organizational performance. A people-centric system does not, of course, discount the business driver, but also has a developmental dimension, seeking to ensure positive experiences for the individual, not least to motivate and retain them.

Those with a ubiquitous view of talent are likely be more person centred in their thinking, and this may reflect greater emphasis on human capital in their business strategy. Conversely, cost-efficient companies may be more organization-centric in their talent management, focusing on those that deliver the biggest bang for the corporate buck.

But many organizations would probably opt for a balance between these two perspectives. Talent management has to satisfy organizational resourcing requirements, but it must do so in a way that carries talented people with them. The mutual benefit talent management should provide is an offer to the talented employee of having interesting work that meets individual needs, and productive activity and skill enhancement to meet organizational requirements. This might mean designing jobs around people's strengths especially where there is a shortage of ideally trained people in the market place.

A practical distinction here is whether development is done unto the employee by the organization or whether the talented are the agents of their own development.

Looking at these questions but with a twist: is the purpose of the talent management exercise to control resources or to gain their commitment? Controlling resources centres talent management on deployment of people to meet business necessities. A commitment focus sees the aim of the exercise as generating employee engagement through growing personal capability. It recognizes that development activity can be a form of reward and recognition in itself. This control versus commitment distinction is related to 'careers as resourcing' and 'careers as learning' (Hirsh, 2010). In the former, careers are seen as a series of jobs completed, whilst the latter recognizes the developmental purpose of careers.

A challenge for organizations is to both get the mechanics of talent identification and resourcing right with the softer side of nurturing talent, especially if opportunities are constrained. This has been something of a neglected area, especially in discovering what the talented feel about the processes and programmes designed for them. They can leave, and send a signal, but prior to that they are often not properly consulted on their talent management experiences.

International company examples

We have seen differences in our case studies in how much development is person-driven ('all employees are responsible for their own development' according to WWL) or organizational driven (in EDF Energy the leadership programme was 'owned by core leadership team'). Usually there is a balance between the two perspectives and it often relates to the mode of development. So some companies give a lot of emphasis to on-the-job learning and growth, whereas others rely more on formal programmes with strict entry criteria (like EDF Energy did). These positions are also not static. WWL continues to emphasize that all employees are responsible for their own development, but has lately been focusing more on making sure the company really enables and incentivizes this. (This point is further elaborated on p. 151)

Some organizations do conduct 'diagnostic' exercises to check on both management and staff perceptions of talent management, especially the unfulfilled expectations described above. These audits are useful to galvanize change when you get messages from staff like *'opportunities for development are restricted'* or *'there's no hierarchy to progress through the organization and no career map'* or from Management messages such as *'there is no consistent assessment or understanding of skills across the organization'* or *'there is a lack of drive/commitment to manage talent within the organization'*. Clearly the HR team in the organization from which these comments were drawn had got the 'burning platform' to justify the introduction of a new or improved talent management process.

It is explicitly part of DPWN HR's brokerage role to understand employee motivations. This is helped having a career aspirations part of the performance management process. This has a form to be filled in, signed and forwarded to HR by the reviewee that offers a chance for the individual to take responsibility for and actively influence the development of their own career. It offers a simple pair of options – to stay in the current job or change position. If the latter is chosen, there is the opportunity for the employee to suggest preferences in organizational units and roles. There is space, too, to identify development needs and objectives, suggest development activities such as deputizing or job rotation. The individual is also expected to state their mobility position, from immobile to fully mobile – information that is used sensitively.

POST OR PERSON CENTRED?

This overlaps with the previous question: employers that are post centred (i.e. worry about resourcing above all else) are likely to be organization centred, whereas those that are person centred (i.e. want to ensure a good talent supply) will have more of an individual focus.

However, the distinction is not as neat and tidy as this. The individual focus is about satisfying the needs of employees. Here we are more talking about supply in an aggregate sense. Crudely put, post centred wants to fill vacancies; person centred wants to find suitable homes for its talent supply.

There are practical implications of this choice. The high-potential model is person centred: we will find sufficient jobs for the talented. The top team focus with an emphasis on succession planning is post centred: we need to fill these jobs with the right people. So the planning orientation is different. If the focus is on jobs, the organization is more likely to operate over the short term with a high degree of precision. If the attention is on the supply, ensuring a flow of talented people into the organization, then the focus will be long term and about getting the supply number roughly right.

Future and supply oriented talent management is concerned with broad thinking on developing organizational capability. This approach is associated with skills planning: what are likely to be our upcoming needs in terms of skills and what capability do we have in these areas. Depending upon the answer, we may have to find ways of filling the gaps.

The post centred talent management method is less concerned with these general resource questions, and is more concerned with recruiting good people for specific posts. This will open up the option of external recruitment as an alternative to internal promotion and development, and may be focused on hiring people with specific mandates in mind.

Again, there is a distinction between an orientation to meet the activity requirements of the organization against the benefits of having good people at your disposal.

International company examples

A key issue for Oxfam is to identify good people in the sector, as there is a general shortage of talent there. The organization finds that it is tough to obtain quality people and, if you do get them, you want to hang on to them.

John Hourican, Chief Executive of the RBS global banking and markets (GBM) business, realized immediately after taking over a devastated business in late 2008 that in order to drive a more sustainable talent pipeline for the future, he would have to significantly increase the graduate programme for the investment bank. Whilst others in the market reduced their graduate intake, GBM trebled theirs and set out an objective by 2012 of having 10 per cent of its total workforce as a product of its graduate entry scheme. A target it will now achieve. This is a good example of a supply rather than demand led strategy. Like Shell, it is not so concerned about today's business needs but about tomorrow's, but without being able to specify the exact number and nature of resources it will need, it is recruiting to ensure that there will be quality staff available.

Vetsas has articulated this point even more overtly. The company has a philosophy like the Danish Special Forces of not being limited by posts but by people. You can't be too talent-full.

Swiss Re identifies those with the most potential, but this is not just an abstract term but discussed in relation to the specific jobs these individuals can do. This reflects the specialist nature of much of the company's work. People need leadership talent, but also technical skills to be effective.

OPEN OR CLOSED PROCESS?

The past tendency towards closed career management systems is generally being replaced by open ones. There are several reasons for this. In some countries data protection laws require disclosure of personal data held electronically to be made available to the data subject. So information on career plans, estimated potential or assessment centre results would have to be disclosed. The positive reasons for the general move for greater openness relates to the employee. If the aim of talent management is partly to encourage self-responsibility and self-development then it would be contrary to hold back information that would enable these goals to be met. Moreover, if another point of the exercise is to retain talented people they need to know that they are regarded as such by their employers. Finally, open job advertising permits much faster decision processes. Codetermined placement can be slow in the same way that chains of house moves can be slow: you have to know if candidate A will go to job B, before the individual at job B can be put up for job C, etc. This process can be cumbersome in big change programmes.

The closed approach is still tolerated or even encouraged in some societies. The advantage of avoiding disclosure is that it makes resource planning easier for the planners. They can plot careers, engineer transfers and hold detailed material without fear of challenge. Even in open systems, it might well be there are views about individuals that are not disclosed: they are too sensitive. In open systems, telling people that their career has plateaued can be very demotivating to the individual. Because this is easier to manage in closed systems, decision making managers may be more robust in their assessments. Those favouring (or able to use) closed approaches can place this data in their HR information system (HRIS) and not have to risk holding undocumented discussions.

International company examples

The key international issues relate to personal planning data and job selection systems. We have observed that there has been a move towards more transparent processes. This has been to build organizational confidence in talent management. For example, when Boeing opened up its high-potential list in the late 1990s it found that doing so increased employee respect for the system (Cope, 1998).

> At Siemens the talent management process is entirely transparent – the individual knows what has been discussed about them and the plans being made for them. Everything is documented and put on file, available for the employee to see.

Open job advertising permits much faster decision processes, as Shell found in comparing the speed of transformation of their 1995 reorganization (with a company appointment system) with 2009 (and a open job advertising method).

There are companies that do still continue with closed systems, such as Firmenich among those we interviewed. This can reflect corporate culture or the predominance of the countries in which the company operates. And it is not just what you might regard as the secretive organizations that operate closed processes, but also ones where talent selection is a sensitive matter, and this includes those that highly value equity in their people management approach. Selecting people out for special attention is countercultural.

And certain processes are more likely to be closed than others. Thus succession planning may well be more secretive compared with high-potential programmes because in the latter participation in development activities tends to reveal who is favoured and who is not, whereas in succession planning there is a benefit in keeping the results private: those who are not lined up for the job they want might well leave.

ORGANIZED LOCALLY OR GLOBALLY?

The locus of control question relates to the population covered in talent management, and is necessarily more important in global firms.

Talent management can follow a centralized or decentralized approach. The centralized approach may give greater emphasis to succession planning for senior positions; the decentralized may allow a broader development of people. In the top down mode the corporate centre gathers information to feed its plans, so locations and business units have to meet corporate data/nomination/selection requirements against a common process. Following the bottom up strategy, locations or business units use their own processes available to them to grow their talent as they see fit or meet their needs. In something of a halfway house between these positions, the corporate centre facilitates, integrates and monitors talent management without directing it. Or it may take a role model stance and champion a talent management approach, e.g. with respect to diversity, cross functional movement or fast track development, without either controlling operating company behaviour or completely devolving responsibility. This use of 'soft' power offers some organizations a good balance between centralization and decentralization.

Whatever the global/local balance, the corporate centre is likely to execute talent management for the executive group and there is always activity at local level in managing and developing staff. Both become more formalized in high-potential (and high-professional) talent schemes. The local business is frequently the first tier in identifying those marked for special development. This would be within a framework, where the 'how' is left to local discretion, or against specific rules set by the corporate centre – whether framework or rules depends upon the degree of process standardization. In some organizations the development of the real high fliers might then be taken over by the corporate centre or by a regional body acting on its behalf. Regional structures may also do mid-level career management, i.e. for those who might move outside the home country but are not (yet) of interest to HQ, or act as a second talent selection tier. In some companies the corporate centre then acts as the top tier in a selection process.

In companies with a very strong commitment to high-potential development, the corporate centre may directly be involved in recruitment (especially graduate entry), earlyish career development for the most talented and at mid career to spot potential executives and develop them across the business units or countries. Those organizations with more modest development aspirations might simply do the last of these interventions.

An alternative model, depending upon how power is distributed in the organization, is to rely on the business functions or business units to manage the talent process – at least to some point in the hierarchy when the corporate centre would take over (i.e. to fill top team posts). The functions or units themselves may act as agents of HQ or be quite independent. They may well have a similar global outlook, but may be more concerned with high professionals and technical leaders. Often led by a functional godparent, the functions in particular may well create broad talent pools within the specific area of expertise (e.g. marketing, manufacturing, sales, etc.). Development would then be within the function. They allow a good match to take place between people and posts, being particularly useful in dealing with unpredictable business circumstances where staff can be drafted in at relatively short notice. Cross-functional development will almost certainly be reserved only for those deemed to have the greatest potential – a group which might well be seen as the preserve of the corporate centre again. It should be noted that some organizations operate a mixed model: a number of functions operate a more centralized global model, whereas others devolve responsibility to locations.

International company examples

We came across a variety of different approaches in terms of geographic levels of talent management as described below:

- In IBM, marketing talent is spatially organized, moving from unit to country to region to global, with the latter the focus for senior positions. By contrast, R&D is a global function with its talent managed globally within the function across its locations.
- In a similar way many pharmaceutical companies manage R&D globally, with the business function in control. By contrast, in Novartis talent management is managed at corporate level and, in large functions (like manufacturing or development), by country.
- Panasonic has developed common global criteria on the meaning of high potential, but the corporate centre in advising subsidiary companies on identification in their own setting recognize that 'life is different in Thailand compared to Australia, and what's going on in the Czech Republic is not the same as what's happening in America'

(Grapevine, 2010a). So the corporate centre develops common 'themes' and 'issues', but acknowledges that their application will rightly vary.

- There is no central direction of talent at Siemens. It is examined on a cluster/large country basis. This approach reflects the different country needs. For example, China is different in size, profile and opportunity than the other parts of Asia Pacific region like Taiwan, Hong Kong or Korea. So its approach to recruitment is different – more activities and on a larger scale in China than in Korea and Taiwan, where keeping in touch with the market is the goal. There is also a clear focus on international/global requirements. Therefore the global Sector Headquarters play a major role in talent development together with the regional clusters.
- At Sun there was no coordination of talent, apart from corporate interest in senior executives. Nor did the Region act as a forum for managing cross-region resourcing. The talent management activity was purely country based.
- By contrast, in Schneider Electric the regional organization facilitates talent exchange especially filling gaps, but also developing people. Those who are mobile and with talent who are suitable for overseas appointments are facilitated in their transfer at county and regional level.
- Oxfam's main talent selection and development approaches are corporately led, but, according to Jane Cotton, the centre could not and would not want to do it all. The countries and regions need their own L&D strategies especially so that they can develop locally the relatively junior staff who are further back up the pipeline.
- SAP provides a corporate framework but business units operate their own processes for upward nominations and they propose who to include (or not). The HR business partner, who reports to the corporate centre, facilitates these discussions ensuring a wider perspective is brought to bear.
- Nestlé has Development Cells where managers review and decide on the career and skill development of employees. The meetings cover succession planning, the assessment of high potential and identification of career moves across businesses or functions (Hirsh, 2010).
- There are discussions in WWL at local, regional or global level in a hierarchical progression, with a smaller and smaller number of higher and higher potential staff being discussed.
- RBS is a company that has functional differences in talent management: for example, a more centralised approach in HR and more devolved in Finance.

TO WHAT EXTENT DO YOU USE EXPATRIATES?

Organizations operating outside their home country are always going to resource the bulk of their positions with local staff. However, despite the additional costs, they may use expatriates for a number of reasons:

- To deploy resources to locations where such capability/capacity are missing/in short supply, often with the explicit intention of reducing dependence on expatriates over time. This is especially found in companies in growth mode or geographical expansion.
- To respond to a crisis or specific one-off need, again of specific expertise or general resources.

- To develop high-potential individuals so that they have the knowledge, skills and experience to operate in a global organization at a high level.
- To transfer specialist expertise from HQ (or another more developed part of the company) to a less mature part of the business. This may overlap with the first objective, but applies more in steady state mode.
- To keep an eye on what is going on within an operating company. This may be a normal approach (as in some Japanese companies) or a one-off after an incident (e.g. an operational failure, health and safety incident or significant malpractice).
- To ensure standards of operation fit corporate requirements. This may overlap with the above objective. This is especially true of greenfield sites to establish standards, say, in HSE, financial systems or in employment practices.
- To reassure investors that (new) investments are properly supported. (This is on the assumption that the expatriates are better trained and more reliable than their local equivalents, or at least felt to be by the investment community.)
- To achieve better corporate integration. This may focus on communicating corporate values or instilling company culture and be felt to be especially necessary after an acquisition, but it also works to break down silo or parochial thinking in other circumstances.
- As a form of employee attraction, especially for graduates. This may be a source of competitive advantage in a tight labour market that the organization can offer young people what is perceived to be travel and challenge through expatriate postings.

So expatriates may be home country staff moving to operations in other countries; those from subsidiaries/operating companies coming into HQ; or individuals moving between subsidiaries/operating companies. Each of these will have its own logic.

Research by Sibson Consulting (www.sibson.com) found that in a survey of US global companies the operations function was the one with most expatriate deployment, suggesting that it is the technical expertise that is the principal driver for expatriation.

The organization has a number of options in how to fulfil the above organizational aims:

- the traditional three or four year expatriate assignment, i.e. a temporary transfer to another country
- a shorter-term assignment that may still involve the individual moving abroad – this may well be project based
- a commuter assignment where the person works four or five days a week in another location but keeps a home base where they live at weekends.

The full assignment may have higher pay (to compensate for additional expenditure and to offer an incentive) as well as a range of expensive benefits relating to housing and education. The short-term assignment is more likely to be on a bachelor basis, thereby cutting down on benefits provision. The third option may be cheaper than the other two, but hotel bills can still mount up.

Easier and cheaper air travel should make commuting arrangements more viable both for the organization and the individual. There are, however, reasons to be careful; not just the cost but other issues that will described in the challenges section below.

Another potential substitute for expatriation is making one-off visits from HQ to other locations. Of course this can have benefits in surveillance, transfer of skills, information and standards. It can give learning benefits to the individual business traveller. Naturally, though, all these advantages are rather skin deep because there is only so much you can do a few days at a time.

There are other ways of developing a global mindset – study teams, shorter-term job rotation, etc., but the critical question here is whether these are adequate substitutes to expatriates and the answer depends on why the expatriates are being employed in the first place, what business need are they satisfying.

International company examples

In our research for this book we saw a number of examples of theory in practice as seen below:

- Singapore Airlines has an expatriate manager in each location to ensure that operations meet the company standards. The fact that the individual is beholden to the corporate centre for their career means that they are less likely to 'go native' and promote the local needs above the corporate.
- In theory expatriation is encouraged in Vestas and it currently has about 250 expatriates, but in practice financial constraints make it hard for managers to accept the higher costs, especially a full expatriate assignment. Currently business results come before the global ambition. Global mobility is not mandatory but is necessary for career progress. It is not a question of 'two refusals and you are out', but persistent refusals would indicate the individual does not have the necessary ambition to progress.
- The opportunity for overseas placement was used by Aitken Spence as a strategic tool to attract and retain staff. It was a way during 'the troubles' (war with the Tamil Tigers) to stop the 'brain drain' of good people deserting Sri Lankan companies.
- A combination of the above approaches to overseas management may also be helpful. One US company we know, faced with difficulties in recruiting expatriates to hard-to-fill locations, combined a shortish assignment on a bachelor basis with remote support from HQ and the occasional visit.
- Oxfam manages its response to a business necessity to be able to shift resources rapidly to meet sudden requirements (e.g. earthquake, tsunami, flood, etc.) anywhere in the world by creating a mobile staff group. The organization needs to have people ready trained, technically competent and imbued with the Oxfam ethos. These staff are used locally in their own environment when not internationally deployed or to cover chronic staff shortages in some locations where local recruitment has failed.

Shell has 8,500 expatriates. This is a big increase compared with 15 years ago and is the product of the operational environment in which the company works. The Shell expatriate number once represented three times that of BP and Exxon combined; now it is twice, but still indicates a somewhat different resourcing model. Half of the expatriates are British, which is a large proportion given the by now small UK employment base. To further your career you may have to move if your country base is not one of the big locations, but equally people do not necessarily have to globetrot.

There are large concentrations in some places such as Qatar, Kazakhstan and Nigeria. There are fewer expatriates in the downstream business because of cost challenges and, as the operating company skill base has risen, the need for foreign expertise is less. Moreover, the colonial approach to sending people into non-western countries ('white men with blue eyes' to quote Angela Merkel) is no longer tenable. So the company now only puts in expatriates where 'brains or experience' are required, although there is also a personal development benefit too. The latter is supplemented more than in the past through in-role development (the job itself, task force membership, virtual networking, etc.).

Mobility is less of an issue than the company anticipated it might be. Decisions on expatriation are lifestyle related so that staff tend to be mobile when young and older (without dependents), but not during peak family periods (as there is a need to protect dual incomes and a reluctance by some, especially the Dutch, to use school boarding).

Shell has offered the very best of its best graduate recruits a first posting abroad on the basis that this would tempt some people to join the company in preference to more conservative employers.

SUMMARY

We can draw some of the strands of this discussion into the options set out in Figure 6.2. The options are presented as alternatives on each line and on either side of the page they also line up as opposite choices. But this latter distinction is not so clear cut. Some combinations of options do easily fit: a universal talent approach goes with an individual focus and an open resourcing system. Other options, like selective versus universal, could be in either column. However, very broadly, the left-hand side represents the typical global talent management philosophy.

Combining some of these key options with their consequences in talent management activity is shown in Figure 6.3.

Inherently, there is nothing fundamentally that requires a global organization to operate in this future oriented, resource supply and development manner more than a national organization, but it was striking that most of the organizations we met tended towards developing over the long term rather than buying in over the short term. It is not so surprising that the corporate centre or business function HQ is in the driving seat in these circumstances, being more concerned than an individual location with the future vitality of the organization. It does suggest that going hand in hand with other aspects of global business development that we have already covered (culture and brand) and will cover (HR governance and service delivery), the corporate centre in international organizations is driving talent management against a particular sort of notion of what it should look like.

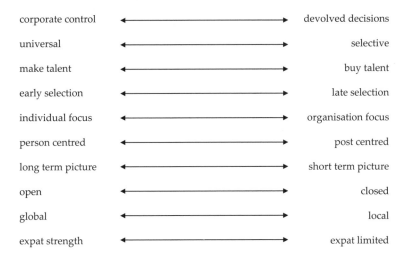

Figure 6.2 Talent management strategic choices

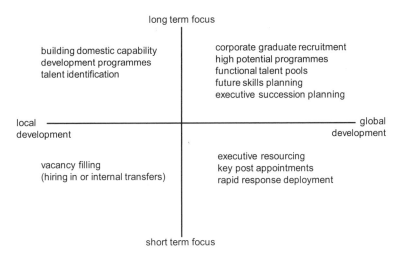

Figure 6.3 Implementation of talent management strategic choices

Strategic Implementation

Putting into practice talent management strategies requires the implementation of a number of policies and practices that relate to planning requirements, filling jobs, managing careers, selecting and developing leaders, high potentials or high professionals and growing skills (the relative balance between them depending upon the talent management focus). In an ideal world, there would also be the measurement of these processes and an evaluation of their efficacy.

Figure 6.4 shows how strategy and implementation connect.

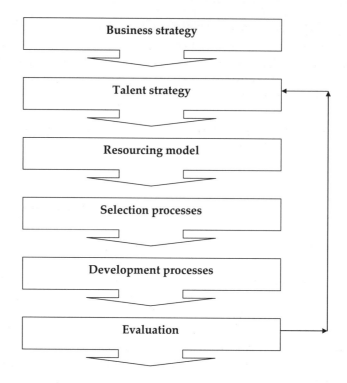

Figure 6.4   Stages in talent management delivery

The variation in talent management definition we have seen between organizations will not matter if there is generally sufficient agreement within an organization on the approach. This seems to be achieved in most organizations, assuming talent management is mature enough – a point we will return to later. Moreover, the delivery of talent management has to constantly align with the business strategy and people management philosophy. The options chosen in terms of talent management methods must be consistent with these goals.

In addition to these underlying differences, the way HR is organized, and its governance policies, will affect how strategies are enacted (see Chapter 7 for more on HR governance). However, despite the philosophical and governance differences, it is important to emphasize that when it comes to enacting talent strategies, most activity tends to relate to key groups and not the whole workforce. Those with an inclusive talent mindset might invest more in lifelong learning or in non-work related development, but the attention of time and resources will be focused on these key groups.

So, ironically, those with an inclusive talent mindset do not necessarily follow through with their vision, as it is impractical to do so. Why is it impractical? It is impractical because if we now think about talent management in action, unless the organization is without hierarchy, you have to acquire, identify and develop those that will fill the more senior jobs. Moreover, with a limited development budget and restricted time, organizations have to concentrate their efforts where the rewards are likely to be greatest. This is especially true in global organizations because the cost of talent programmes is higher than in domestic firms.

Putting this point even more clearly, Professor Adrian Furnham argues that to say that all are talented renders the term 'meaningless'. It is just like saying 'everyone is human'.

Indeed, it is the implementation aspect of talent management that practitioners often find challenging. However good the strategic intent might be, if the implementation of the policies, practices, programmes, etc. are poor then talent management will fail. And it is through poor implementation that much people management fails to deliver. This is partly because organizations focus on design and rush the putting good ideas into practice. As Martin and Hetrick (2006) have argued, 'talent matters, but, more importantly it is managing talent that matters'. This view is supported by Mark Jankelson from ANZ, who argued, 'The problem with talent management is not the definition, it is the execution.'

To try to improve strategic implementation of 'people planning', Oxfam has built a model (Figure 6.5) that seeks to link together its different processes. Talent management (seen as high potential identification and development) is integrated, as shown in the figure below, with 'career pathing' and succession planning. The important facilitators to this process – performance management and learning and development – are also shown as contributors.

Other organizations may use different terminology but the same principles apply in trying to get the right people selected for the right posts in the short term but developed to fulfil careers to benefit themselves and the organization. For example, Figure 6.6 shows how EDF conceptualized the talent management processes.

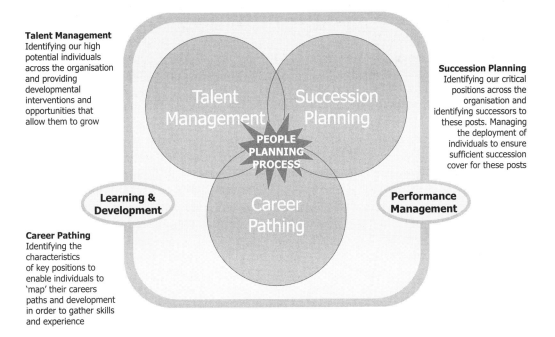

Talent Management
Identifying our high potential individuals across the organisation and providing developmental interventions and opportunities that allow them to grow

Succession Planning
Identifying our critical positions across the organisation and identifying successors to these posts. Managing the deployment of individuals to ensure sufficient succession cover for these posts

Learning & Development

Performance Management

Career Pathing
Identifying the characteristics of key positions to enable individuals to 'map' their careers paths and development in order to gather skills and experience

Figure 6.5   People planning in Oxfam 2008

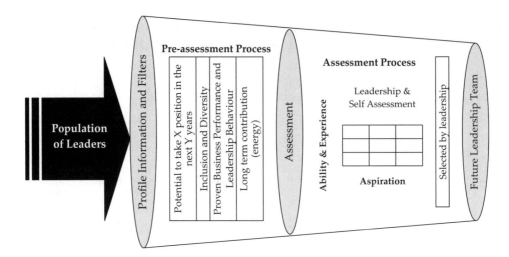

Figure 6.6   Succession planning at EDF Energy

TALENT PLANNING AND DEPLOYMENT

Backing up talent management are a range of HR initiatives that encompass four interrelated processes that we will cover here – workforce planning, resourcing, succession planning and career management.

Workforce planning

Though workforce planning may not have featured so strongly in the boom years, we described earlier that organizations in the west are now more concerned about the supply/demand balance. The 'war for talent' gave emphasis to the necessity of securing a supply of talented people; the war for survival focuses on making sure that the supply does not exceed the demand for jobs. This more realistic understanding of the internal labour market places greater importance on anticipating how the job demand picture will change and estimating what sort of numbers and types of talent will be required. Before the feeling was that you could not have too much talent – Enron being the extreme example of that philosophy where talent was let loose without ensuring proper performance management or organizational alignment (Gladwell, 2002). Though not to the same extent, organizations like Vestas have not developed mature workforce planning processes because sustained growth has provided plenty of opportunities, producing the attitude we described earlier, that you cannot have too many good people, and a short-term business focus – not looking ahead to future needs.

The recession has moderated this sort of thinking. Now talent has to earn its own way. Effort will be expended on retaining the really good people but the talent bar may be raised higher; some pretty good people will be allowed to leave or, indeed, be pushed out.

As the Unilever example illustrates, workforce planning is important in periods of growth as well as during more testing economic times. In some developed economies there is a declining demographic position (reductions in the proportion of young people mean a near 1:1 ratio of workers to retired in western societies by 2050). Then there are the supply shortages in parts of the developing world. In this context, the emphasis is not just on securing the necessary resources, but on deciding where they should be deployed to maximum effect.

Unilever's vision was launched in November 2009 and one of the requirements was that business strategies include a plan to 'ensure talent, organization and culture are aligned to deliver the growth ambition'. The Skin business was the first 'category' to execute this approach globally. It began with projected gaps in the talent demand and supply balance and in capability needs to address business goals. Levers to close the gap were identified to enhance talent management, organization and cultural effectiveness with a prioritization of initiatives to improve talent, organization and culture readiness.

There were three phases:

- **Diagnostic**: focus on sizing capability gaps, evaluating talent management systems and assessing organizational effectiveness to achieve business goals.
- **Synthesis**: prioritize actions and test diagnostic results.
- **Mobilization**: develop implementation plan and track results.

Everything was executed quickly with the plan completed in eight weeks.

There is evidence from the Boston Consulting Group (2010) on the lack of workforce planning simulations conducted by organizations and our own experience is that organizations can suffer from a lack of understanding of the dynamics of demand (assuming too easily that tomorrow will be the same as yesterday), a failure to carry out a proper stocktake of supply (where are the upcoming pressure points?) and an inability to put this into a plan that will lead to appropriate resourcing actions. Despite this rather disappointing account, we identified a number of organizations that do combine information on supply and demand that is reviewed at talent management meetings, be they business unit led or undertaken at local, regional or global level. These meetings can both discuss individual issues and the collective workforce planning situation. For example, SAP uses its matrix grid at talent review meetings to judge whether people are appropriately placed or need more job challenge. Similarly, at a general level talent reviews at DPWN bring together candidate information with current anticipated vacancies. The aim is to build up an informed picture for each job family. At the specific level, they match individuals to jobs.

By 2008 Allianz had 58 Career Development Committees across the world, which covered various countries/businesses. The CDCs looked at the talent situation for some 3,000 leaders and at business driven strategic workforce plans for the future. Now the figures are much higher, both the number of committees and the coverage of leaders across the three management levels. There are now also CDCs for the different functions (e.g. Finance and IT).

On the basis of this analysis, management determines suitable actions to close any talent gaps.

One important aspect of workforce planning in a global organization is to determine the number of expatriates the organization needs and where they will be deployed. This might cover both those being assigned primarily for development reasons (usually the high potentials) and those whose functional expertise is required outside their home country. This may be a very systematic process – setting out where and when expatriates are needed – or, more often, a rather ad hoc approach. And the systematic methods vary depending on the style of talent management from carefully tiered from bottom to top (moving through local, national, regional and global) to concentration only on the senior leaders and the development of the immediate level below.

HSBC exemplifies a combined approach, with corporate banking a significant locus of expatriate development both for development purposes as a pipeline to senior positions and specific assignments to meet particular expertise needs. This is not to say that high potentials cannot come via other functions, nor that they ignore the costs of expatriation.

Nestlé is another company that considers international experience as very important to those wishing to hold senior positions. It corporately manages the top 400 or so people in relation to the top 100 or so jobs. Lower down the hierarchy most development is within functions and they, together with the regional structures, facilitate cross-national development for the 'emerging talent' (Hirsh, 2010).

Succession planning

Traditional succession planning required names to be identified as successors for all key posts for both short term and long term. The number of names recorded varied, partly to reflect the degree of flexibility required both in terms of people and jobs. You judged whether you had the right level of capability by the strength of your *pipeline* coming through and whether you had confidence in your organizational *resilience* by the extent to which you had good coverage for your key roles. Especially where regulations require it, this gives internal and external assurance that the company can manage a sudden resignation, long-term illness or death.

The instability of organizational structures and with it the volatility in jobs structure led some organizations to consider, especially in the professional groups, *pools* of people for clusters of jobs rather than a one-to-one match. This allowed for changes in views on the potential of colleagues and the facts of attrition. It also offered a response to job instability.

Different organizations give greater precedence to continuing coverage for jobs whilst others are less concerned about this and more interested in the talent pool. The planning concern is then more about *bench strength* and less about job filling which becomes more responsive to circumstances, more a just-in-time approach than a planned activity.

Schlumberger believes having a sustainable talent pool is the key source for successful long-term succession planning. It has three succession planning streams – managerial, functional and technical.

Canon Europe's talent management system is based on high-potential identification, follow-up and management of the pool. The Executive Development Programme aims at emphasizing task delivery, personal development and change. It looks at a range of competencies to see where collectively and individually the group is weak or strong.

Rolls-Royce has four talent pools for high-potential staff whose careers are of interest to the corporate centre. These pools cover early and mid career, as well as two at executive level. Moreover, there is a specialist pool to meet a business requirement need to develop excellent technical specialists, what in other organizations might be called high professionals (Hirsh, 2010).

In relation to talent pools, for international organizations there is a choice between having a series of national/local groups or an international pool only, or a combination of the two. Those companies that deploy large numbers of expatriates might favour an international pool because an important criterion for entry is likely to be high mobility and this allows the management to deploy people to meet needs around the world, particularly for high professionals. National pools are more likely to be used where assignments outside the home country are infrequent or unplanned. An alternative model is to have identifiable staff who can be transferred as required, but they not form a 'pool' where there is a defined entry process. Instead, these 'Martini' types (go anywhere, anytime) are flexible to reflect different business requirements, including the crises referred to above.

As we discussed earlier, the method favoured aligns to the talent management focus. Those organizations that concentrate on the long-term potential of the 'best and the brightest' are concerned to ensure that they have sufficiently filled pools. Those organizations where the emphasis is on top talent in grade terms are more job oriented and use more traditional succession planning techniques.

Some companies use a RAGs system to highlight any gaps between the resource status for each post and the labour pool. There is then a periodic review (usually annually but it can be more frequent in fast moving businesses) to check current status and initiate action – both with respect to people development and job filling.

British American Tobacco in its 2009 Sustainability Report sets out its 'local succession coverage'. For each of its regions, for all its senior posts it aims to have one local successor in place for the short term and two in position for the long term. This shows the Americas achieving three quarters of these matches compared with western Europe with only 38 per cent of short-term posts covered – well behind Africa/Middle East and Asia Pacific. The Report also looks at local representation on senior management teams in the regions.

In a different approach, at least for a number of their roles, some organizations centred their talent management on talented teams rather than individual jobs or people. This moved away from formal succession planning or workforce planning, to a more ad hoc but very business focused strategy. As we described in our previous book (Reilly and Williams, 2006), in the knowledge economy and especially in financial services, teams are developed and retained, or acquired from competitors. This might mean entering new geographic markets on the back of having new expertise or, conversely, withdrawing if the capability is lost.

Resourcing

If resourcing is about getting the right person in the right place to do the right job with the right skills then naturally it has an important place in talent management. This is especially true where the focus is more on filling posts than developing people. This orientation is to be found where talent management concentrates on executive and possibly technical posts, besides the usual gap filling. Decisions include whether to recruit to fill the vacancy or make an internal appointment. In an international context that produces further questions on whether the posts should be filled by locals or expatriates (and whether the latter come from HQ or from other subsidiaries/operating companies), and again are these internal moves or the deployment of external hires.

Another dimension to resourcing is whether the appointment is a planned move or a response to an unexpected event either relating to the person (i.e. a resignation, illness or even death) or to the post (e.g. a new job to respond to business growth). In some cases there may need to be the swift assignment of staff to cover a crisis of some sort.

By and large those globalizing their talent management seem to incline towards a planned approach to resourcing. There is generally an aspiration towards developing international careers for specific groups, especially the high-quality graduate intake and identified high potentials. This may not always be possible because of a business crisis (as the Oxfam example showed earlier) or where planning seems impossible to do due to changing business demand.

Most of this activity is directed from the centre, be it the corporate HQ, global business unit or corporate function, though the development action may be organized through regional bodies and take place at the individual's home location, region or beyond that in the world. Here the region may be an agent of the corporate centre or a facilitator of local management teams seeking the development of their best staff.

Career management

Career management connects to both planning and resourcing. If planning is about ensuring you have the right numbers and types of employee coming through and resourcing is about filling specific jobs with the right staff, career management is usually centred on ensuring that individuals identified for development have the right preparation in terms of skill and competence, experience and exposure.

Before the early or mid-1990s the predominant model in career management was one of paternalistic control. The organization knew what was right for individual development and what was best for the corporation. So, like a chess grand master, the resource planning manager would move the human pieces around the organizational chess board. And being a grand master, the resource planning manager would be plotting several moves ahead to ensure that everyone was in the right place at the end.

Obviously, employees participated in this process and conspired to make it work. If they did not like the paternalistic management style, they could always leave. If they were not prepared to accept some of the nominated placements, they would have to accept a slide down the pecking order, or even out of the talent pool.

In a world where greater transparency is required and has led to the creation of open job advertising, the resource planning manager's capacity to manage the chess board has been much curtailed. Individuals have become increasingly awkward about being despatched without proper input, thereby making the resourcer's role more difficult to discharge. This has been especially true of international (and even national) mobility. Spousal, or even more challengingly partner, employment has handicapped individuals' mobility, making it more complex or simply impossible to transfer. Growing reluctance to put children into boarding schools and the sheer expense of providing for/paying for local education has further complicated mobility.

Then to cap it all along came the war for talent, making it impossible to be so insouciant about the movement of people. With talented people at a premium, the organization has had to protect its assets. It has had to listen to their career demands and fulfil them to the extent possible or they would leave for an employer that would meet their requirements.

By then, as Hirsh and Jackson (1996) have described, the pendulum had well and truly swung away from centralized career management towards the notion of individual self-development. Companies felt that they were no longer able to offer careers. Indeed, in the mid-1990s the notion that careers were 'dead' was much expounded in boardrooms, as our Shell quotation illustrated. It was now up to the individual to grow themselves, it was their responsibility. The organization would offer tools and possibly maps to guide them, but the employee, through applying for jobs and asking for training, would build the necessary experience base for further progression if the appointing managers approved of what they saw on offer.

As Robert Waterman et al. (1994) described it: 'It is the employee's responsibility to manage his/her career. It is the company's responsibility to provide the tools, the open environment, and the opportunities for assessing and developing their skills.'

It is a matter of great irony that at a time when the term 'talent management' was coined, those in HR responsible for its activities were having their wings clipped. Job title inflation has been accompanied by role decline.

Now there was the application of the free market, a world of buyers and sellers trading their wares in the jobs bazaar, a fair way from the great chess game. However, employers soon realized that the operation of the market was not perfect, and employees themselves did not find it completely congenial. Staff often lacked the full information to make judgements, a frequent problem with markets. They did not always trust the process – apparently open, yet with a suspicion that the job selection process was often a charade. For management, they could not always ensure that the right people were in the right place. This could damage performance but also deleteriously affect individual careers and endanger the retention of good staff.

So the fully open market was replaced in some organizations by the regulated market, the degree of regulation naturally varying between firms. An approach has been to identify some key jobs (senior ones, naturally, but also important development slots) and exclude them from open job advertising to ensure that the right people are appointed.

In addition, in some firms the most talented are helped to find the right positions. Here the resource planner is back, but in a much curtailed way. The point is that the corporate centre is willing again to interfere or intervene with the normal, formal process to require local managers to take certain individuals.

Thus we have a situation where there is segmented career management (Hirsh, 2010) – active for the most talented, passive for the generality of staff, and a partnership for a third group of either lower potential and/or specialist important skills. It should be emphasized that this career management is presented from an organizational perspective: it is the means it uses to build talent. This is not to ignore either that the organization might wish to build personal career resilience, to adapt and learn, nor that individuals might wish to build their own careers, which at times may coincide with the organizational interest.

However, the development of career paths by organizations can be an important aspect of greater transparency and employee engagement in career management, especially in global talent management. As the Firmenich example (Figure 6.7) shows, career paths describe the possible development routes for employees. These may be purely functional paths, allow cross-functional movement or general management ones. One reason why organizations have used them is to explain important career choices employees have, in particular relating to staying within a specialist area or branching out into functional or general management. These career paths inform readers of the grades or career points (in terms of time or experience) when decisions have to be made, as well as the knowledge, skills and experience and/or competencies they require to move to a particular role. This helps employees plot with their managers their route forward in terms of training and job development.

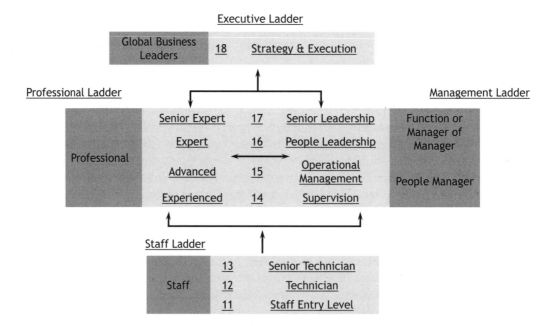

Figure 6.7   Career paths at Firmenich

Schlumberger particularly values technical careers and it has set out career paths for staff whose career trajectory will be in a technical rather than a managerial capacity. It moves people through several stages of greater technical leadership beyond the training phase until, for a very few, they are appointed a company Fellow.

The important point for global organizations is that greater transparency in these options can both flag up the sort of international opportunities that arise (for individuals keen to develop themselves) and indicate where international exposure is a prerequisite.

IDENTIFICATION AND SELECTION

In the view of Adrian Furnham, picking the right people is the key aspect of talent management. It is more important than development because there is a limit to how far organizations can accentuate the gifts the talented have because you have to have the raw talent in the first place (Furnham, 2010). We need to consider both process questions and ones concerning selection criteria. We will deal with the latter first precisely because the selection of the talented is so important.

Selection in the context we are applying it in concerns the identification of those who require extra or special development either (and usually) because they are deemed to have 'potential' or because of their particular skill-set. As we said earlier, some organizations worry only about short-term potential, others long-term. Either way, the organization is trying to see, at the very least, whether a person can rise to the next level. So, to use a sporting analogy: is the person able to move from being a local club football player to a paid professional, through the divisions especially to the Premier League (Seria A or La Liga), or even to representing their country.

Selection criteria

What governs the selection of the talented, what criteria are used, clearly relates to the definitional question we began with on what constitutes 'talent'. So in this section we look at whether the sort of criteria used are different for the global workforce or the same generic ones used throughout the organization.

But before turning to this question we will describe the six sets of criteria we came across in our research, or seven if one includes those that use a combination of factors. These are:

- **Behavioural competencies** Competencies are one of the commonest criteria (at least as one of the factors) used in talent management processes. Most of our case study organizations followed suit in selecting people for further development. However, which competencies organizations select and how they describe them is not always the same, and indeed academics would probably not label as a competency some things that are measured under this heading.

EDF Energy's description of competencies was 'a combination of learned and inherent skills or abilities, experience and knowledge, and behavioural characteristics'. So this approach had reference to 'inherent skills or abilities' as well as the usual behavioural element.

- **Business and technical skills** Although skills are sometimes used interchangeably with competencies (as in interpersonal skills), in this criterion organizations are more interested in job related skills, their expertise in their particular function. For those organizations that set a particular store by specialist knowledge, skills and experience, especially those that define talent in relation to critical roles, they assess these qualities in any talent management selection process.
- **Personal 'attributes' or traits** Personal attributes has a sense of something innate, something that at least an adult has as a settled characteristic. The key point is that innate qualities, as understood here, are not trainable, though they may be enhanced. The traditional view has been that people have them or they do not. This contrasts with competencies or skills that can be developed. Cognitive ability is a good example of an attribute. However, more recent neuroscience suggests that our brains are more plastic than previously thought. So we can, to a degree at least, develop our minds.

PwC uses learning agility as indicator of potential based on behaviours and motivators (Hirsh, 2010). This might also be described as a 'growth' as opposed to 'fixed' mindset (ideas associated with Carol Dweck at Stanford – Gladwell, 2002). The belief that you can change yourself is very important to success.

This is an approach Adrian Furnham supports: 'Maybe leadership potential and talent should be defined as the ability to learn from experience' (Furnham, 2010).

- **Performance** Performance always has to be an element in any selection process. Indeed, some would claim it is the central criterion. Assessed performance may involve delivery against targets and the way the targets have been met (which overlaps with behavioural competencies).

WWL is not unusual in combining these two elements ('what you do' and 'how you do it') in its performance appraisal process. Similarly, DPWN's performance evaluation is based on feedback on target achievement and assessment against a number of competencies.

- **Attitudes, disposition** These do not feature of their own, but usually in combination with the other factors. At Swiss Re potential is, following the Corporate Leadership Council's (2005) definition, described as 'ability, aspiration and engagement'. A key principle of this sort of definition is that potential 'is something you have and something you do'. In other words, even if you are assessed to have a high potential, you will need to constantly work on your development to release this potential. If you do not engage or develop you may be taken out of the high-potential pool.

So people's attitudes to their own development, the extent to which they want to further their career (i.e. their ambition), their preference for controlled risk taking – those prepared to push themselves into unknown areas ('zones of incompetence') – are all illustrations of the attitudes and dispositions some organizations are seeking.

- **Values** The concept of living the organizational values might be said to putting into practice these attitudes and as such is sometimes included with behaviours. However, it is picked out for particular attention because of its importance to some organizations in determining selection for further development. This concept has always been central to charities and those mission led organizations, but in recent years it has become more important in commercial firms, especially in those sectors where there have been scandals precisely because organizational values have been violated (e.g. through the misuse of funds, misrepresentation of the business situation, sexual misadventures, etc.). Emphasis on values that are not related to ethics may be used to shift organizational behaviour either because of these problems or because an organization wants a reorientation towards, say, customer service or quality of delivery. Increasingly, values are playing a key role in reinforcing the organization's overall culture. The 'values' approach to providing organizational glue is a common feature in today's global organizations (see Chapter 3 for more on culture).

GE, for example, assesses staff on their performance against the corporate values. It has taken more seriously failure to demonstrate the values, to be a corporate citizen, than simply not performing as well as expected.

WWL applies its Values and Leadership Principles (e.g. 'stewardship' and 'empowerment') to define expected behaviours.

Invensys has created five values – agility, innovation, meritocracy, integrity and courage – and uses them to choose recruits and more recently in their 'capability review' (Johnson, 2008).

After the scandal over the misrepresentation of oil reserves that cost the CEO of Shell his job, the company revised its leadership selection and development programme: besides emphasizing the positive attributes sought, it also stressed those behaviours it saw as unacceptable.

- **Combined characteristics** Many of our case study organizations combined these criteria in their selection process. For example, Invensys has a talent assessment matrix where results are on one matrix and behaviours on the other. For the latter there are lists of positive characteristics of doing the job the right way (e.g. appreciation of their strengths and weaknesses in specific environments) and negative (e.g. driven by personal status rather than the need to meet organizational goals) (Larson, 2008).

One of the most common combinations is a performance assessment on one axis with potential assessment on the other to construct a nine box grid, or 25 box grid at Swiss Re, as the RBS example (Figure 6.8) demonstrates.

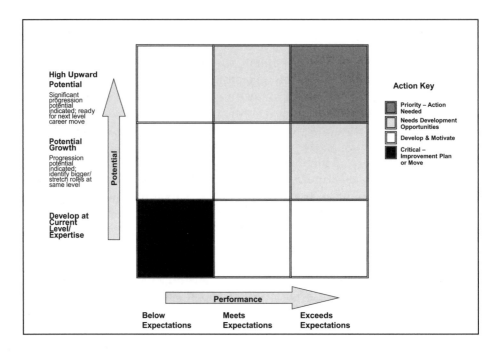

Figure 6.8   RBS's nine box performance/potential matrix

Criticism of this approach has concerned whether performance and potential are sufficiently clear in the model, and whether their definitions are sufficiently separated from each other.

As with the Swiss Re case, the potential part of the model is itself often an amalgam of the other, different criteria we have described. For example, together with a consistent performance rating, at SAP there has to be achievement against six other 'potential indicators' (e.g. change agility, proactive self-development, innovative thinking, problem solving). ANZ describes the competencies it looks at as 'growth factors', where an individual shows potential to develop. These include such areas as 'learning agility', 'breadth of perspective' and 'understanding of others'. Tesco uses Adrian Furnham's model of high potential, assessing cognitive ability, stability, conscientiousness, emotional intelligence and motivation. Marks and Spencer has applied a variation of assessment on 'head, heart and guts'.

So to what extent are these potential assessment criteria generic or tailored to a global workforce and/or to a leadership group given that there are particular issues to be faced in a global setting? This question is especially pertinent given the challenge laid down by Collings and Scullion (2006). They suggest that most selection for international posts is risk free and job centred, put off from selecting on the basis of the relevant interpersonal and cross-cultural skills necessary to be successful in an international context by the difficulty of identifying and measuring these skills.

We came across a degree of acknowledgement of the global dimension in the companies we studied. For example, the high-potential version of the assessment model at Invensys is to a global standard whereas the high-professional one allows more local variation. DPWN uses eight leadership competencies that include 'cross-border thinking' (along with such factors as 'shaping direction' and 'customer orientation') that are applicable throughout the group with detailed behavioural indicators. Swift had, when the research was undertaken, an 'international mindset competency' which was a specific additional criterion to select for those who would work well in cross-national collaborative activities or who aspired to executive positions (IPD, 1999).

So in these cases particular assessment factors that relate to the international dimension are included but only in certain circumstances that relate to grade, level of potential or type of role.

Besides DPWN, other organizations have specific assessment criteria for the leadership group or those who aspire to this position, and the Vestas boxed gives an example of specific action with respect to the leadership population. Firmenich has a tiered approach. It has competencies that:

- relate to all jobs (e.g. customer focus)
- ones that apply to distinct different types of job
    - managerial – facilitating change
    - professional – planning and organizing
    - 'staff' jobs – continuous improvement.

When measuring leadership potential, Firmenich recognizes that the competencies needed shift from supervisory team leadership through to strategic leadership with its focus on vision, etc.

It was becoming apparent to the CEO in Vestas that certain management styles that achieved short-term results were not appropriate for the longer term, because they did not bring people with them. This manifested itself in employee surveys and in resignation rates – as well as in our customer loyalty survey. Their customers were challenging their ability to work well together. So, in March 2009 Vestas introduced a new, clear leadership model based on three principles:

- 'getting ahead
- getting along (i.e. easy to work with)
- getting things done'.

Selection processes

Over the years the process by which talent is selected has become more formal, and more sophisticated. Gone are the days where one international food and drinks company we know allowed its marketing director to hire people he met on his travels, even agreeing their remuneration package on the plane. Nonetheless, some approaches are less formal than others. One organization we came across was happy to allow executives to make judgements on their gut feel of who should be developed and who not. Some seem to rely simply on the high visibility of candidates to promote themselves: what has been cynically described as selection by presentation. The majority of the organizations we interviewed use the much more structured approaches, as described below.

What sort of structured processes might these be? Firstly, do organizations have specific and separate talent assessment processes or do they rely on their usual performance appraisal methods (including second line as well as first line manager assessment) to identify those selected for special treatment in a global setting?

There are a number of possible approaches to selecting staff, including:

- interviews with nominated candidates for talent programmes
- the use of psychometric testing to assess individuals' psychological characteristics so as to predict their behaviour in business situations
- skill or ability tests where specialist aptitude is needed. This might overlap with psychometric testing especially with respect to cognitive ability testing
- review of performance data, 360 degree feedback, self-perception material
- assessment centres that combine the above information and try to replicate business activity through mechanisms such as:
  - in-tray exercises
  - job sampling
  - team-building exercises
  - structured discussions
- relative ranking exercises.

Those organizations that prefer to use standard evaluation methods are more likely to emphasize performance or short-term potential; in a sense talent development is considered incrementally. Those that use assessment centres are, on balance, more interested in identifying special talent features, especially those that will play out over the longer term. They have become a common method for talent identification where it is difficult to identify talent or where an 'objective' method of assessment is required. They may be used at initial graduate recruitment or as gateways into first level management or leadership levels.

We saw several examples of assessment centres in our interviews with practitioners. Take Audi, for instance: it has an assessment centre to select from a talent pool those with 'management potential' to get into the 'management development group'. Vestas had a three day assessment where candidates were put into a stressful, non-business related but teamwork-intensive environment, to identify the ones with the personal competencies for a fast track career.

Some companies have tried to manage this process globally through virtual interaction using modern technological methods.

We also came across examples of ranking staff against each other to produce an order of their assessed potential, based on generalized or specific criteria. Forced ranking first gained attention at General Electric in the 1980s creating A/B/C players based on a percentage distribution of 20/70/10. This approach was underpinned by a notion of talent identification but focused on performance (especially corporate citizenship) with future potential implicit rather than explicit. Potential can of course be given more emphasis by adding it as a criterion in the ranking exercise or even addressing it within a separate exercise, as Shell still does as a stand-alone exercise bi-annually.

Swiss Re tried the GE ranking model to assess performance. Though not without its problems, including managerial ability to communicate the results of the exercise, a clear benefit of the introduction of this system has been a better discussion among the line managers of the specific meaning of performance of their employees.

Where something separate to manager assessment is applied, some organizations use talent boards (or 'people' boards) to review data that might come from performance appraisal but also 360 degree feedback or from personality tests. Originally, such review boards (as part of a succession planning process) considered development as well as assessment, with the advantage of obtaining joint commitment to action, but now selection may dominate. This suggests that the corporate centre does not entirely trust the manager referrals or, put more positively, requires consistent judgement across the global firm.

DPWN uses an annual Global Talent Review Board to determine who should be given special development. These are based on feeds from Regional boards which in turn are based on those identified through performance 'dialogue'. In Siemens information on talent comes through the global performance appraisal process – known as 'open dialogue' – and that includes looking at potential. Confirmation of the level of potential is through a 'round table' evaluation using 360 degree or upward/broad manager feedback so it is not just the view of a single manager that is represented.

Using these assessment tools, the 'system' then has to decide whether the employee is talented in the way important to the organization against the criteria we looked at in the previous subsection. The boxed examples show how organizations take forward their assessment decisions, especially in choosing who has special development.

At DPWN there is a line manager process that describes the reviewee's possible development during the next 12 months. This process considers performance evaluation, career aspirations and the needs of the group. The manager can choose one of four possible ratings:

- stay in job
- review fit with current role
- a lateral move

- promotion.

This provides a starting point for panel discussion of the manager's recommendation.

In ANZ there is a similar but three point assessment scale:

- well placed
- room for development
- stands out.

Panasonic's 'Global Executive Scheme' also has three designations – HP1–3 indicating how close they are to reaching the top position. Regions are asked to identify those with top management potential based on the common selection criteria that recognize potential as well as performance (Grapevine, 2010a).

DEVELOPMENT

The general purpose of development is to build knowledge, skills and experience. This can be from both a technical and from a behavioural perspective. Different development mechanisms grow different aspects that are sought. Job experience can build knowledge and skills including such valued attributes as learning capacity, resilience, optimistic thinking and determination. Development programmes sometimes through internal 'academies' can reinforce some of this learning and add to it in a fresh way.

In this section we will look at two strands of development: on the job related and off the job related. The former will cover all the aspects of career management – finding the right posts, including expatriate, and assigning the talented to jobs. The off the job related will give an overview of building skills through development experiences. In both cases we will naturally emphasize the international dimension to development.

Job related

Adrian Furnham argues that of all development activity, experiential learning is the most powerful (Furnham, 2010). The organizations we spoke to did indeed give singular emphasis to it, but the degree of corporate interest or involvement varied by employment group (i.e. outside the high-potential population). So job development frequently focuses on specific parts of the workforce as shown in the examples given below:

- **Graduates** Giving explicit attention to graduates occurs where the recruitment process is geared to identify some of or the entire intake as high potential. If this is the case, on-the-job development will be partly used as an attraction and retention tool and partly to give these individuals early exposure to the breadth of the business, including its geographic spread. This sort of experience has to be packed into the first years so that the graduates are ready for promotion at an early stage. The Vestas example gives a good illustration of this sort of approach.

In 2006 Vestas launched a two year graduate programme to offer internationally mobile graduate recruits a two year programme with three assignments. Typically, the first is in their own country due to constraints on work permits but the other two are international. Over time this has shifted from more than half the graduates coming from Denmark in 2006 to only 13 per cent for the first 2009 entry. At the last count there were 24 nationalities represented on the programme. There is strong representation from Germany and Sweden but also from Asia (India and China). The target has been to have an intake of about 70 people per year, giving a total of 140–160 ongoing in the programme.

The company is looking for both technical and generalist staff, offering three possible career paths with no specific target numbers or distribution per path:

- people and business leadership
- knowledge and innovation
- project leadership.

It focuses on seeking those who have both the right educational background and high qualifications alongside a personal profile matching what Vestas is looking for. This has covered a wide range of competencies from generic business skills and profiles to very specialised engineering profiles. Over time there has been an attempt to more explicitly link the recruitment to the future business needs: where are the critical areas (by location, function or business units for the longer term); how many need to be hired; where should they be placed, where do they get good management, what roles will they perform, etc.

The economic recession made it more difficult to identify posts. Business unit leaders were hesitant to come forward so that their HR VPs had to emphasize the long-term strategic value of hiring these resources.

There is no explicit management drive towards internationalization, but equally there is a management commitment to not allow a person's passport to affect the hiring decision – if they are sufficiently talented they should be recruited.

- **Leadership candidates in difficult supply locations** Here there is a very specific problem to solve: growing talent to meet labour market shortages. Oxfam is committed to try to build internal resource and is working hard to move away from a 'white expatriate' leadership in countries and regions, but in some parts of the world, e.g. in Africa, it is finding that this is not easy due to shortages of educated staff who want to remain in country. Similarly, along with many companies, Firmenich is seeking to reduce its reliance on expatriates and grow the number of local leaders in Asia.
- **Senior company positions, defined by grade/salary level** By the nature of their position, special attention is given to the preparation of people already in these roles. The Aegon example is typical.

Aegon's new approach to talent management involves succession planning for the top 50 positions where the Management Board will take a greater interest in the appointment to these positions and the development towards them of talented individuals, as well as the size and quality of the supply. There will also be more opportunities for talent to move around the organization across locations and business units. This helps attract and retain talent as global opportunities are these days necessary to obtain and keep hold of the best. It also helps build a more integrated company with knowledge and experience moving across the firm.

As for the content of talent management job development for high potentials, there are again a variety of methods, besides expatriation. The aim as we said earlier is to accelerate development and broaden it. Organizations try to achieve this goal by either by proper work opportunities or by more short-term, ad hoc approaches. The list below moves from the former to the latter:

- **Stretch assignments** are the most obvious form of job development, putting a high potential in a different role that will challenge their capabilities. The difference may be in the function (e.g. a cross-posting from production to marketing), in the location (an expatriate assignment) or in a higher grade. As a former HR director at Shell Research believed, asking even the best to do all three is probably too risky.
- **Putting a high potential into a new role** that will give contact with senior management is chosen partly to build the individual's network and partly to give a chance for leaders to make a closer inspection of the talented person. This approach is especially helpful for those who normally work outside HQ and from another country.
- **Corporate office** Overlapping with the above, organizations give someone from outside the corporate centre a role that gives the chance to do some strategy work – to look outwards and forward. This is particularly used for those high performers who have delivered well, but whose cognitive skills in a more rarefied atmosphere are yet to be tested.
- **Preparatory experience** Used especially for those working in operating companies that are about to assume a more senior position, it gives the individual a chance to learn about a particular aspect of their new job (e.g. through a project), extend their network by making connections that will be useful to them or, in complex organizations, find out how things get done. Again this can be very powerful for those whose work experience to date has been limited to one country, far from HQ.
- **Role shadowing programmes** These give the individual a taste of what a different role might be like. This is especially helpful for cross-functional assignments where employee knowledge may be limited. It is naturally more expensive for this to be done cross-nationally, though the learning benefits might equally be greater.
- **Exposure to customers may also be useful** especially in companies with strong sales and marketing requirements, but even in more technical companies being able to understand customers' needs, communicate product specifications and relate to this supplier/client interface can be a vital skill.
- **Simple meeting of senior people visiting locations** where there is the chance to informally interact or through presentations have the chance to make a bigger impression.

There was no formal career management process at Sun outside of senior executive, but all jobs were offered worldwide through an open, internal job advertising system. However, there was no company tradition of expatriation, and cost pressures inhibited their development. There was, however, job rotation for short periods – Americans to China or Chinese to the USA for six months to 'teach and learn', to 'bridge understanding'.

Within China there were somewhat longer two year assignments for broadening purposes, and some regional activity that included mainland China and Hong Kong and Taiwan. The aim of both programmes was to test out whether technically able employees would make good managers.

Senior executives were put on a leadership development programme and this included job rotation.

The company did not want geography to get in the way of developing talent, but equally, in some eyes, it did not do much to facilitate it either.

Off the job

Development outside the job context can be delivered in a number of ways often through formal programmes (especially for high potentials) or via more ad hoc events. It can be delivered in house or externally. If job related, development is to give practical experience to the talented or senior staff, off-the-job attempts to offer help in areas such as:

- technical job related skills
- cross-cultural awareness
- social learning – working together especially for diverse teams
- behavioural skills
- the nature of leadership and management.

The methods used, particularly with an international flavour, will be described below.

- **Management skills training** How do you build global knowledge, skills and experience such that managers can operate in a cross-national setting? The McGill programme gives a very good example of how this might be done.

In Henry Mintzberg's *International Masters in Practicing Management* executives spend a 16-month period at leading business schools around the world to gain cross-cultural experience. They learn individually and as a group, while remaining in work so that they apply what they learn. Participants continue to work while they earn a Masters Degree through modules given all over the world. Participants travel to a different campus for each of the five, nine-day modules, spending time immersed in the culture of the host country. While there, they go on field studies to local companies, observe different managerial practices and learn from the diverse insights and perceptions of fellow participants – especially those from the host country.

For example, two senior managers, one from Coca-Cola based in India, the other a senior adviser with the International Federation of the Red Cross and Red Crescent, partnered to meet their own business objectives. The former wished to develop his company's brand in India, building its commitment to social responsibility. The latter wanted to show her colleagues how partnering with corporations could help achieve humanitarian objectives more efficiently. Coca-Cola pledged to place its logistical facilities at the service of the Red Cross/Red Crescent in the event of natural disaster. It also agreed to provide safe drinking water to rural villages near its plants. The Red Cross/Red Crescent provided expert advice on these arrangements and publicly certified their quality and value (edited from http://www.impm.org).

- **Leadership development** This has a range of objectives, including understanding the theory of leadership – what is its aims – and how to practise it more effectively, by building skills, developing personal awareness (strengths and weaknesses), emphasizing positive and negative behaviours, by demonstration of how it works in specific situations, including outside the home country. Marks and Spencer has 'leading internationally' as one of its five modules in its leadership development programme. This is increasingly important as the company sees much of its future growth coming from outside the UK and so needs leaders who are aware of global business issues and of the nature of different cultures. International companies frequently use international business schools to deliver programmes to a cross-national group of participants. Shell's HR development programmes have inputs from Cornell, INSEAD and IMD. Tesco also uses business school programmes at INSEAD and Harvard.

At Vestas the whole top management (the top 200) participated in a Vestas leadership programme, conducted by IMD during 2008 and 2009. This was arranged by the Vestas Business Academy. The top 200 group have also met as an executive forum to bring more of a sense of a management cadre and align everybody to the business objectives.

Canon's Executive Development Program is aimed at:

- accelerated task delivery (projects essential for Canon in the particular year)
- accelerated personal development
- ambassadorship on the changes foreseen.

- **Work related experiential learning** As an illustration, a group from PWC spent four weeks on a rubbish dump in Peru to learn about how businesses grow in emerging markets. At Shell as part of their development graduate entrants are encouraged to go to schools and colleges and talk about oil and the environment, alternative energy sources and Shell's view/practice. Starbucks encourages baristas to visit coffee growing areas, which is important given their open knowledge sharing and fluid international career paths.
- **Non-work related experiential learning,** such as the sort of corporate social responsibility activities where people round the world help on local improvement projects or through participation in non-work bodies like the Prince's Trust, builds more generic skills. For example, Shell in the UK has staff working in projects in east London. Such is their desire to embody CSR, at JSW Steel 5 per cent of the performance assessment depends on time spent in the community. Other organizations allow staff to spend a proportion of their working time in charitable activities, which has CSR, learning and employee engagement benefits.

Under the leadership of John Hourican, RBS' GBM operation has given a lot of attention in 2011 to getting people out into their communities and emphasising the role sponsorship can play. Team based community projects are usually successful and do a lot to build morale. This can have business benefits in showing the company in a different light, but is also valuable to staff in giving insight into other worlds and helping personal development. Community projects are a core part of the company's early graduate programme – a good fit with the new generation's thinking.

- **Action learning processes** (i.e. learning comes from a training process that is derived from real world situations usually practised in a group who develop together through challenge and support). As an example of the global use of this method, IATA (Jonsen and Bryant, 2008) has developed an Intercultural Leadership Engagement and Development programme whereby 20 change agents (half from East Asia and half from 'mature' regions) were paid to lead cross-national high potentials and to teach communication skills and cross-cultural awareness to other employees. Vestas has used 'action learning', based on the Reg Revans method, with its global graduate intake. An action set might meet periodically, less frequently with the whole community, whilst otherwise it might communicate remotely. Some executives were initially sceptical of the value of such exercises, but were persuaded of the value by the positive feedback from participants.
- **Where the emphasis is on learning** rather than selection, development centres can be a diagnostic exercise (through feedback) and allow the setting of future improvement goals, but also directly act as the means to put ideas straight into use (see McCauley, 2008).
- **Participation in talent management selection processes** can be used as a development tool in itself. A small group from round the world of the top 200 managers in Vestas participated as talent assessors in 2008. Following their experiences in the assessment centre they have initiated and continued discussions on the nature

of good leadership behaviour in their own parts of the organization. In 2009 another group of top managers was added to the assessor list to broaden out this experience.

- **Coaching** has grown enormously as a development tool for middle and senior managers. In some approaches it is a mutual method whereby coach and coachee address agreed goals (e.g. means of career development, improved managerial effectiveness, tackling a specific performance shortfall). In other approaches, the coach facilities the coachee's self-exploration and determinedly does not try to impose their own perspective. SAP uses both, whilst Oxfam used to have two full-time roving coaches, training national internal coaches and the effective use of external coaches in many parts of world.
- **Mentoring**, as a means of transferring knowledge, skills and experience, tends to be used more for junior or aspiring managers or for professionals who need some oversight or support in their skills development. Mentoring is used more than coaching for high-potential staff. It is not just about growing skills but about visibility, networking and relationship building with senior players. Again this is particularly important in an international company where there is cultural awareness and skills to develop.
- **Cross-cultural learning**, which can be specific to those preparing for expatriation or, like Swift reported earlier, be for those in cross-national activities. It also can be an explicit activity or undertaken covertly by bringing together a variety of nationalities for another purpose, but with the expectation that they will share views and experiences as they network.
- **Or combinations of the above**

Oxfam has a basic management training programme that is run in many different countries in the world with a corporate and a local facilitator. Its Management & Learning Programme brings together over 30 high-potential leaders from around the world to an innovative programme based on action learning and skills master classes with much cross-cultural learning included.

SAP offers a range of development opportunities through, amongst other things, job rotation, coaching and mentoring for all staff, more formal training (such as in project management) for the less experienced and another range of activities designed for the more experienced (like shadowing and innovation workshops).

Hindustan Unilever (HUL) operates a global policy capability framework against which it decides its local training approach contextualized by business requirements. The global capability framework, as understood by the authors, is that training is made up of three elements across the Unilever Group: on the job, mentoring and training events (or calendars). Local adaptation allows variation in the way the three components are split. In HUL's case it is 70 per cent on the job training, 20 per cent of time spent on mentoring and 10 per cent on taught training. This allows the 'how' to be managed locally whilst meeting global principles of blended learning.

There is a variation between organizations that operate with an explicit high-potential group, where there is almost a club membership with special events put on just for the members, and those that behave in a more fluid manner, where attendance at development activities is less rigidly determined.

The organizations illustrated here tend to the former approach, with global events applying to the most senior and sometimes highest potential. Many have tiers of development with local, regional and global programmes, like Oxfam and SAP. This may be based on grade, potential or need (in the more open programmes).

Many organizations of course combine job/career development with other learning possibilities in what they seek to be an integrated manner. Schneider Electric's focus on the 3 'Es' – education, experience and exposure – captures this very well.

> WWL's Global and Regional leadership development programmes continue to be run as a central offer for selected candidates. Additionally, with their new partner for the Global Leadership Development Programme, Thunderbird Global School of Management, the company is working towards a consolidated and integrated perspective on corporate learning through the external programme channel. That said, Tom Solberg, VP HR, regards hands-on experience and cross-functional exposure as still the strongest platforms for career development in WWL.

MEASUREMENT

And finally, what of measurement? Given that corporate investors, and particularly large fund managers, are looking for tangible results that make sense to them when making investment decisions, they want to know how the company's initiatives and processes will *actually* increase the share price. This should reinforce the incentive to find ways of demonstrating the benefits of talent management. There is an even greater imperative when cost reduction is being sought to justify such expenditure.

As we have seen, harnessing it to the business strategy is part of the solution, but the specific processes being used should be validated in effectiveness as well as efficiency terms. However, this can be a struggle for some organizations, not least to measure talent management activities across the world. Indeed, Hewitt's EU Barometer survey (2009b) found only half their respondents used talent measures globally.

Perhaps this is because, as Jim Davis, Director HR Business Processes of Firmenich, says, the task is not easy. He observed that there is an abundance of KPI's to measure the inputs to or the processes of what they are doing (such as proportion of leadership positions filled from talent pool, retention, fulfilment of development plans, engagement), but the real measurement will be whether the company has the leaders it needs, or thinks it needs, and whether that drives continued success. Put it another way: how well do organizations know what is their return on what is often a major investment? The inhibition here seems to be both defining objectives (is it simply ensuring succession to the Board? Having key posts filled with talented people? Or, having the right range of skills to meet future demands?) and having the data to see whether these objectives have been met, especially, as Davis points out, the return may not be obvious for a while.

The problem, as with much HR analysis, is that the input measures are better defined than the outcome – we have data on the numbers entering the talent programme but do we know what proportion meet expectations, fulfil potential, deliver performance? We can see very clearly the cost of failure in the absence of good talent, but, as Enron showed, you can have a surfeit of it, too. These challenges seem particularly acute when looking to validate leadership programmes, selection methodologies and development interventions. How many are assessed for value?

For companies like EDF Energy the measurement challenge became easier by virtue of the recognition that getting talent management right delivered better organizational performance through higher productivity. The argument here is that if you engage employees in their development, offer them opportunities, give them career direction, they will respond in their committed contribution to the firm. But also in a negative sense: if you do not have the right skills in the right place, trained and clear as to their responsibilities (both to meet their own needs for personal challenge and autonomy and to deliver the business results), then organizational performance will suffer.

These insights, and similar ones on knowledge management and talent as a competitive differentiator, allow SAP to measure the impact of talent management, through employee engagement, trained deployment, succession planning, attraction quality, etc., on measures of organizational success. We do not have to spell out the link between employee engagement and organizational performance – reams and reams have already been written about it (e.g. the Department for Innovation and Skills, 2009), but there is also evidence that a specific focus on talent can be beneficial. In a comprehensive review of the impact of talent (albeit on a small sample of 60 from the 'Global 1000' list), The Hackett Group (2010), for example, found higher earnings and return on investment in those with 'mature' talent management processes. Tamkin et al. (2008) in a UK survey found that succession planning was one of the key HR measures associated with superior performance.

The Human Capital Institute offers a strong case for the benefits of talent management:

- Value of top performers: *Two to four times the performance of average employees.*
- Cost of losing talent: *1 ½ times burdened salary.*
- Cost of poor hire: *A $300,000 impact.*
- Labour cost: *On average about 60 per cent of a company's costs.*
- Engagement levels: *Employees who are most committed perform 20 per cent better and are 87 per cent less likely to leave the organization*
- Breakeven point: *It takes 6.2 months for a manager to become productive in a new job.*
- Management focus: *20 per cent of a manager's time is spent on poor performers.*
- Performance expectations: *Less than 50 per cent of employees know what is expected of them at work.*

(Source: Human Capital Institute Talent Library)

So a better definition of the desired outcomes and better tracking of performance against these objectives, would help target spending and move away from running on faith to demonstrable return on investment.

This is what SAP has done. The company presented us with some powerful evidence on the business benefits of talent management through the value of top performers and the cost of losing them, or alternatively the cost of a poor hire and the management of poor performance. As a consequence, at SAP talent management is 'quickly moving up the corporate agenda – taking a front-row seat at board tables across the globe'. The company measures whether the quantity of top talent is achieved and whether it delivers via surveys and data analysis (e.g. turnover/talent 'richness').

Unilever has very impressive graphics to track talent management performance via turnover (by grade and reason for leaving), PDP compliance (by function), distribution of performance pay (for top performers by function) and supply/demand balance analysis (by function and region). This enables the company to identify talent gaps, the internal bench strength and relationship to need for external hires.

Allianz has also identified the financial opportunities that come from improving talent management both in terms of the substantive benefits it delivers and the efficiency in the way this is done, as Figure 6.9 suggests.

Objectives	Impact
Optimized Staffing	⬆ Quality
	⬆ Demand-Supply Balance
	⬆ Ability to compete in international markets
Reduced Succession Risk	⬆ Quality
	⬆ Rating Agency Upgrade
Increased Pipeline Strength	⬆ Quality
	⬆ Workforce Planning
	⬆ Enhance internal motivation
Reduced Complexity	⬆ Resources
	⬇ Systems Cost

Figure 6.9 Talent management and the bottom line at Allianz

Plan International has a range of success factors for its new talent management approach, including whether the workforce planning and performance appraisal links to talent management are working and the quantity and quality of bench strength. It also has specific talent metrics relating to:

- increased leadership diversity
- retention of critical talent
- promotion pipeline sufficient
- employee engagement rising
- ratio of external to internal hires for critical roles.

According to a CIPD survey, the three most common ways to evaluate talent management activities in the UK are to obtain feedback from line managers (42 per cent), to measure the retention of high potentials (35 per cent), and the anecdotal observation of change (35 per cent) (CIPD, 2010b).

The Role of HR in Talent Management

It should be obvious from the preceding sections that HR has a vital role in successful talent management and we regret the retreat by HR from active involvement in talent management in some organizations, especially the personal aspects of the role.

'HR serves only the top layers,' complained one global HR director recently. 'My head of HR in North America works only with the CEO—nobody knows her, and she doesn't know where the talent lies in the business' (Guthridge et al., 2008). This is a frank description of HR's failure to engage with the talented. In an interview with a line manager in another organization we heard that HR seems to play only the role of corporate enforcer because it seems primarily to deal with non-compliance by subsidiaries. It is both spatially and emotionally too far away from individual staff to have a trusting relationship with them: it is not easy to confide in the organizational police.

This illustrates the risks of HR retreating into its corporate bunker, satisfying itself with the statistics of talent management without realizing that it is an intensely personal process. People who deal closely with the leaders of organizations realize that many of them harbour doubts about themselves and, especially for those striving for the top jobs, worry about organizational perceptions and their place on the ladder to the summit.

Instead, HR should be at the heart of this business critical task to design the architecture of talent management in line with the business strategy and lead the execution of the processes that deliver the design intention.

When it was realized in one of the organizations we interviewed that not all of the current incumbents fitted well against a new leadership model, HR was able to offer tools and processes to effect successful change towards the new situation. The company's 'people review process', involving the leadership team, identified a number of performance or behavioural deficiencies. Action plans were made and followed up by HR.

Management must have the central place in the decision making, but managers themselves do not have the time or skills to create effective talent management processes. Moreover, whilst the individual development of employees is a daily task for line managers and formalized through performance appraisal processes, the corporate management of talent needs to be facilitated centrally and HR is the obvious function to do this. Its tasks include among other things:

- ensuring recruitment processes deliver the right sort of intake
- using the induction process to harness raw talent to corporate behavioural requirements
- proposing selection criteria
- creating decision making bodies/processes
- facilitating the selection processes themselves
- planning resource requirements and strategies
- supporting managers to use the talent management tools it has designed

At SAP, the business partners are challenged 'to get into the nuts and bolts of business strategy'. It is not just the annual headcount that is required, but the connection made with the business strategy, market, geography and labour force. This is especially important to the company because of the changing skills profile of the business.

- helping manage the careers of key staff
- acting as a personal adviser, coach and confidante to the most talented staff and to senior executives
- seeking out talent by meeting colleagues in formal and informal settings
- constructing databases to track vacancies and staff moves/needs
- designing development/coaching/mentoring programmes
- monitoring talent management performance, including successful placement, diversity, business impact, etc.

So the HR director should be insisting both that talent should be part of HR's role, and not hived off to another department, but also that it is connected to the other parts of functional activity: it must be integrated to be successful. Yet HR still has to ensure that 'talent' is not seen as an HR thing but a business activity.

In a global setting HR should be uncovering talent, getting it circulating round the organization; having bright ideas on assignments and project working to test people out and get them exposed to senior management; obtaining labour market data and interrogating it to show hot spots and, by linking it with internal job information, revealing upcoming shortages, etc.

'The role of People and Culture should be to support the Country Director by providing a technical contribution to talent management; helping identify/spot talent; ensuring follow through of decisions made; assisting in coaching of staff and working to effect a cross-fertilization of the talented across the organization's regional and global structures,' says Mariella Greco, Country Director, Peru, at Plan International.

HR can model this approach in its own backyard, setting an example to other functions on how to identify and develop talent on a global scale. It can be one of the early adopters of any new talent method to test out ideas before wider exposure.

In summary, HR's role in the better run, more people-centric, organizations is to identify and grow talent, emphasize its value to the organization and run a career management process that delivers benefit for the organization and its employees

Located in Corporate Executive Staffing, the talent brokerage role in DPWN is performed by HR. Its key objectives are to 'increase the quality and quantity of internal staffing' and to 'better match talent supply and demand across regions and divisions'. They do this by brokering a solution between the line manager, the employee and HR business partner. Two years after its launch it was managing 200 vacancies per year; managing the talent pipeline for specific jobs/job families; 'fostering exchange within the HR(D) community on vacancies and talent' via, for example, calls to regional HR for a talent update and building up knowledge of the candidates and promoting their wares.

Challenges

A key message that emerged from our discussions with organizations, and our brief review of the academic research in this area, is that the design of talent management is generally no different for global operations than for national ones, though some processes have to be adjusted to suit. The questions that need to be answered in selection, planning and resourcing and career management, etc. are largely the same, but the context does present some more options and challenges in delivering these policies.

In a critique of talent management, Sally Hulks (2009) complained that 'talent management systems can be dangerously static, bound by complicated decision making processes, generic competency frameworks and leadership criteria, applied across all functions and divisions, regardless of context – all of which can serve to identify high potential clones'.

Thus, if there are arguments that some of the talent management processes are underpinned by flawed assumptions about talent – exaggerating the best, denying opportunities to those who otherwise would be able and ignoring context in establishing the right talent for the right circumstances – it would be fair to say that they are even more problematic in an international context because operational execution is even harder to get right.

THE COST OF TALENT MANAGEMENT

There is an underlying challenge that cuts across many of the other challenges described below, namely the cost of global talent management. It is an expensive business at least in a couple of ways shown below.

- **Expatriation is clearly costly**, but so are assessment (bring in selectors together from around the globe) and development processes (the necessary face-to-face contact of those on international programmes). The risk is always there that under a greater efficiency banner, these expenditures are cut back with the consequence that the truly global nature of talent management is compromised. If, for example, selectors are drawn from the home country only and assessment and development activities only take place there, the result will quickly be that non-home country staff will be excluded, especially when travel budgets are also reduced. It takes a confident and assertive HR department or a committed CEO/leadership team to continue to spend money in this area when expenditure is closely scrutinized, as it has been during the last recession.

- **Expensive management and leadership development programmes** Firstly, are they worth the investment, especially given their expense? The difficulty is that many development initiatives have not been properly evaluated and so no kind of return on the investment has been established. So, according to Martin Classen, the 'tree hugging' programmes are the first to get axed when the business conditions deteriorate because there is no hard evidence of their efficacy (Classen and Reilly, 2007). You can only run on faith so far. Secondly, do they keep up with change in business or organizational conditions? Some interviewees were sceptical of the value of leadership programmes because they appear to produce few discernible results. Money seems to be constantly pumped in but they do not deliver as intended. There always seem gaps to fill: skills are missing and people are unprepared. Thirdly, there has been the criticism that the design of management programmes neglects how people learn. It is important to remember what really works in terms of learning and development, and that only around 20 per cent of learning actually comes from formal learning (classroom style and e-learning delivery of content) yet this has typically been where 80 per cent or more of the budget has gone.

ASSESSMENT METHODS

Research suggests that having a common set of selection criteria and processes is problematic in an international environment because embedded social customs and assumptions make it extremely hard to find common ground. The consequence is that organizations tend to override these differences on the basis that the organization wishes to recruit those people who are prepared to accept the company definition of merit and the company approach to its identification.

- **Overly complex frameworks** Competency frameworks may be misleading organizations. The mental model is to create something stable and enduring against which to judge people when we know that circumstances change and the work environment is shifting. This puts new demands on people that should be addressed. Competency framework designers respond to this challenge by offering more and more competencies for organizations to choose from. However, offering over 100 different competencies produces another problem, that of complexity. Managers get put off by what they see as a bureaucratic nightmare that gets in the way of a proper discussion with their appraisees. Furthermore, we create standard competency frameworks but know different cultures value different leadership traits. Do we simply ignore this as an inconvenient fact or try to acknowledge it in some way?
- **Search for a star** This tendency overlaps with another problematic characteristic of talent management as recently practised. These systems tend towards assuming a super-person syndrome, someone expected to be good at a long list of qualities. This leads to the search for and investment in a charismatic form of leadership – the hero who can transform an organization through the power of his or her personality. It is associated with a star system that might or might not be appropriate to sport (depending upon your point of view), but is dangerous in business. As the Chief Executive of the Finance Reporting Council, Stephen Haddrill, said in a speech in

2010, against the background of a collapse in parts of the financial services industry, there is a need for a change in behaviours that would allow more challenge to the executive by company boards. The same applies within the executive and lower down the organization. Leaders, as with everyone else, have their deficiencies as well as their strengths ('spiky' leadership), but that may not impede organizational performance if there is complementary capability elsewhere in the management team. Building individual competency does not lead automatically to improved organizational performance.

- **Over-reliance on managers' assessments** Relying on managers to select the talented for development may be understandable, but it is not without problems. Especially in some societies managers often find talent discrimination difficult, not least because they may value virtues (good attendance, hard work, task efficiency) and that may be necessary, but not sufficient to identify talent. They may find it easier to separate people on the basis of performance, but find potential assessment harder. This might have a number of causes. They might be inadequately trained for or committed to the task. There might be a cultural inhibition to assessment or a lack of experience. They might be just not really up to the job such that if they themselves were subject to this sort of (new) selection process they might not be successful. Once again it could be said that the selection process says more about the assessors than the assessed.

- **Poor assessment design** As we have seen, assessment centre style selection is an important means to choose talent, but, although it can work well, research indicates you have to think very carefully about design. Firstly, how well do the exercises replicate real business situations or are they too artificial? Secondly, do they tend to focus on things that are easier to measure, like communication, and ignore important characteristics, e.g. courage, that are hard to rate? Thirdly, do the exercises properly sort out the sheep from the goats, i.e. do they accurately discriminate between levels of performance? Finally, do they equally suit all types of senior roles and all potential sources of staff? For example, they have been shown to disadvantage technical people in relation to those coming from commercial or operational functions. Likewise, using leadership competence frameworks in a very restrictive way may omit other vital skill requirements or strengths of a person which are 'not on the list'. The rigid profiling and scoring of individuals has been very popular, but may not provide a good holistic overview of a person or their potential.

- **Cultural assumptions** Assessment centres need adaptation to work effectively cross-nationally. There is apparently 'quite strong' difference on the introversion/extroversion spectrum between Europeans and Asians or Africans (McCrae and Terraciano, 2005). Thus making assumptions about candidate behaviour from different backgrounds is dangerous. For example, Japanese candidates in assessment centres seem to find it hard to take the lead or personalize their contribution. This is because they tend to present themselves in more self-critical manner than, say, Americans. Even East Europeans may not be used to vocalizing their opinions. This questions whether you compare all nationalities against a global norm or whether it is better to do this against fellow citizens. Similarly, assessment is more difficult in a global context where there are culturally based differences in how people represent themselves, not just in person but on paper via CVs and such like. In some countries, the norm is to produce a long list of activities; in others it is a broad-brush selling job. Indian managers, for example, stress knowledge over managerial skills, especially interpersonal skills. The risk is that good people from, say, Africa or parts of Asia 'fail' these assessments and that damages their career but also deters others from putting themselves forward.

- **Feedback accuracy** Some feedback mechanisms (like 360 degree) are not easily accepted in certain cultures and, as a consequence, they cannot always be relied upon to be accurate. Problems relate to the giving and receiving of feedback in some societies. There are also question marks about the reliability of cross-national benchmarking of multi-source results (McCauley, 2008).

- **Personality tests** have to be properly validated for international use and, according to Collings and Scullion (2006), a minority of tests have been tested for their suitability across cultures. Straight translation from English (or from any other language) into the user's native tongue is fraught with difficulty to get the right contextual meaning. Reasoning tests seem to be less prone to bias than personality tests. Moreover, the status (and indeed legality) of testing varies from country to country.

- **Bias in competency frameworks** may favour some cultures more than others. The choice of many competencies is likely to be uncontroversial, but there are a few that are more problematic. For example, humility is seen as a virtue in Japan (and is said to be a key characteristic of many executives and, as earlier reported, it is used in Fairbairn Private Bank), but it may be seen as a sign of weakness in more macho cultures. Some candidates are better schooled in responding to assessment methods because their cultural background is aligned with the system. Kock and Burke (2008), for example, report mixed results for competency based talent management in South Africa because of this bias in competency selection programmes. White middle-aged males tend to perform well on skills assessments because they are like the HR professionals who design the tools and make the judgements. And note that this problem has occurred within the same, albeit racially divided, country. The challenge is scaled up when considering cross-national operation of competency frameworks.

- **Flawed execution** Even if the design is not an issue, the execution of competency based assessment may be flawed. This may be due to outright bias, but is more likely to be due to deeper seated cultural differences that assessors are unaware of. As an example of what we mean, see the box.

We can relate one of the authors' own experience in observing a multicultural assessment panel. Participants came from across the world and were assessing students from the UK and Far East as part of a training exercise. The differences in assessment of potential crystallized in two cases: one was a Briton and the other was from Hong Kong. The westerners in the group rated the former higher than the latter; those from Asia marked them the other way round. This was not the result of racial bias. It was because the westerners understood the self-depreciatory style of the Briton and looked beyond it to his achievements. The Asian assessors preferred the full frontal assertion of his abilities by the student from Hong Kong. The westerners found the Hong Kong student too boastful. The Asians found the Briton too unassertive.

- **Language and communication** Problems may relate to language (if you are not interviewing in their native language, are you testing their linguistic skills rather than their competencies/attributes?), differences in ways of communicating orally and in writing, and in what is considered important to them in their cultures (e.g. deference to elders). This happens in all selection processes but outsiders (e.g. from the corporate centre) might not pick up negative cues that fellow nationals might be alert to. It means that sometimes the job does not go to the best candidate, but to the better English speaker or more culturally sophisticated.

NOMINATION PROCESSES

- **Poor feeder systems** Even if the assessment centre system is working well, there can be problems with the feeder system to it. Indeed, the old adage that you have to be one to spot one applies to talent nomination processes: 'It is talent that knows talent,' according to Anne Krogh Nielsen former Director, Talent Development at Vestas. Country based managers do not always have the conceptual capability to identify raw talent. This may start as far back as the initial employment decisions. Local managers may favour short-term doers over long-term potential. They may not value talent as a source of growing business capability. Managers might not really understand what is required to nominate staff for special development. They might forward their best people, even if these are not good enough. Or they might mark down, not up, the highest potential staff who may be very determined, really pushy and in some environments this would not be a prized attribute. While this problem exists in a national context, getting full comprehension of the talent model across the globe is necessarily harder. It needs a particular sort of insightful local manager who can see that an individual might prosper in another setting where their abilities will be recognized for what they are. Moreover, they are not always good career counsellors to give sensible advice to staff interested in further development. As described in SAP, most companies' people were only developed within their work location to the level of the posts available. This notion of global talent identification and development is rather foreign to them.

When Vestas introduced a talent management approach in 2007 it was felt by Anne Krogh Nielsen that not enough managers had a sufficiently 'long-term organization perspective', rather they had a much more short-term (and local) focus. There were also a variety of management styles: some reflecting local subcultures, others the personal preferences of the particular managers. Moreover, the management philosophy was interpreted in different ways by the various business units. The CEO and CFO at that time had an aim of 'breaking down this silo thinking', but despite the clarity of their objectives, they found it hard to unify the leadership team around their views.

At its first attempt at high-potential identification, nominations were made by the Vestas business unit management teams, but it was quickly apparent when the nominees were compared against each other that their quality varied considerably because assumptions about what 'high potential' differed across the group. In particular, some of those in the scheme lacked the ambition to be high potential and queried why they were there.

Some leaders, whilst acknowledging the theory of the new nomination process, found it hard to put into practice. They had not internalized what the talent system meant – it was just words on a piece of paper.

In 2008 Vestas introduced a defined nomination process against set criteria for high-potential identification with two 'gates' to pass through. Going through Gate 1 involved the business unit management considering the nominations from their business unit to decide which individuals they wished to propose for global assessment at Gate 2.

A lot of Danes and Americans were successfully nominated through the Gate 1 business unit nomination process. There were also a few successful Indians, some southern Europeans, but no Chinese. Two were nominated but did not get through the sift. This exemplified the challenge of achieving what was being sought – not great Chinese managers or managers in China, but global managers. The goal was to find:

- people who could 'bridge cultural divides across the Vestas world'
- people with a global mindset
- people who could make global teams work together.

The difficulties of getting these appeared to be:

- uneven selection processes
- variable understanding of what was involved
- different levels of engagement/commitment
- difficulties in the Vestas group communicating what was needed.

In some societies the 'variable understanding' was exacerbated by cultural norms, especially ones of 'face'. The best candidates from the operating company had to be put forward, otherwise it would be disrespectful to them. The Company selection criteria were less important. Of course, their rejection through the assessment process arguably produced an even bigger loss of face that had to be managed.

- **Not playing the game** These problems are compounded by managers who do not even try to support the system. Once employed, managers have a vested interest in keeping their best people. They may play games by appearing to support talent systems whilst simultaneously subverting them. They may hoard talent to meet their business unit/location targets rather than make it available for the common good. They even may not tolerate pushing people forward ahead of themselves, blocking those who appear to be a threat in taking over their job. Worse, they may even offload unsatisfactory people as a means of 'solving' a problem. More benignly they may not have enough awareness of future opportunities, especially those outside their immediate purview. Individual failings may sit alongside a cultural inability to make the process work as it should. Managers may just not be as tuned into the process as they should be.

Nimal Perera (MD of Spence Shipping in Colombo) told us that some years ago he was blocked from moving out of the Shipping business into the Power business by his boss who did not want to lose him. It was not as if he was indispensable in his current role. It was just that his manager kept the talent within his business unit and was not interested in resource optimization for the company as a whole.

- **Specific talent release** If it is difficult for the corporate centre to get locations to release their best people for the greater good (theirs and the corporation), it can also be difficult the other way round to suggest non-standard candidates. The nationality of candidates can be a problem particularly where there is historical enmity (placing a Greek in Turkey) or more recent negative assumptions about certain nationalities in certain locations (e.g. 20 years ago a Dutch colleague being discouraged by his father from accepting an assignment in Germany).
- **Limited managerial freedom** It might be understandable given the above that the corporate centre is reluctant to give business units/locations complete freedom to nominate candidates without some form of check. Indeed, there are organizations that do not trust the performance appraisals they receive, fearing abuse through favouritism or social control ('if you support me, I'll ensure you get a good rating'), causing them to try to second guess the nominations from the business units. However, this corporate oversight is resented by the more sophisticated business units/locations, which believe they should be allowed to nominate whoever they would like.
- **Technologically induced inflexibility** Technological 'improvement' may also hinder successful implementation. The use of e-performance management mechanisms may standardize assessment processes to the corporate norm. This might bring benefits in terms of internal consistency, but is a handicap if the managers have variable views on how the assessment purpose should be fulfilled. It pushes people towards a regimented way of conducting performance appraisal that may work in one environment but not in another. It reduces the flexibility to adjust the method to fit different cultures.
- **Exclusivity** Some nomination processes do not follow good practice. There is the risk of creating in groups/out groups. Some people may be excluded from talent management programmes, not because of a lack of talent, but because they fail to compete effectively against the preferred internal competition. There are those who prosper because they went to school or university with a senior patron or they developed close bonds during an (expatriate) assignment. In other words, those in the old boys' network may be favoured in who is nominated. There may be functional snobbery that believes talent may be found in say finance or marketing, but not in HR or production. Women or ethnic groups may be deliberately or inadvertently excluded. This risk is greater in a global firm trying to pull together the nomination decisions of a disparate set of managers with their varied conceptions of what is good practice.
- **Charisma** Then there are those who are seen as better only because they project themselves better, either because they are indeed good presenters or because they put themselves in situations where they get noticed. This is something that some

nationalities find easier to do than others. They may pass the 'elevator test' in convincing leaders of their worth (in the time it takes for the lift to reach the top floor). These characteristics may be valued but may also cover up more important weaknesses.

- **Cultural rejection** Succession planning and very selective talent management processes may be resisted in some societies or types of company because it is seen as anti-equality, thereby potentially inhibiting the nomination process as managers hesitate before suggesting names. This can be an issue in parts of continental Europe and other countries that favour collectivism over individualism. For example, in a Danish centred company like Vestas, trying to start a high-potential scheme is harder than in some other places (like the USA or UK) because of the strong streak of egalitarianism in that country, as evidence by the boxed illustration. For Anne Krogh Nielsen it usefully began a debate about 'is someone better than someone else'? This same issue has also had to be faced in a voluntary sector organization like Oxfam where again equality is an important value because it underpins much of its campaigning work.

To illustrate the strength of feeling in Danish society on equality, when building flats adjacent to the Copenhagen harbour, there was a possibility that some would have harbour views. Many would not. It was decided that it would be fairer if none of the flats would have views rather than discriminate against the majority by allowing some to have a better aspect.

EXPATRIATE CONCERNS

- **The inability to attract people to expatriate assignments** People in some countries seem happier to move abroad (e.g. Indians) than others. Where there are problems of expatriate supply the reasons vary from country to country. For example, there have been suggestions made to us that Americans in particular are loath to move out of the corporate spotlight for fear of being inadvertently marginalized. We also heard that Middle East nationals are concerned with the culture shock of moving. There are reported worries about leaving the wider family network behind and about living in the cold weather climates of North America or northern Europe. In Asian communities there is often immobility in early/mid career because there is a responsibility to pay back to parents by helping with their eldercare because the parents sacrificed to facilitate the children's education. By their forties, in countries such as Korea staff are reluctant to leave a long list of clients and relationships behind. In the west there are the problems of second careers and education of children that inhibit expatriation in the middle years. Some suitably skilled and experienced staff are just not suitable for expatriation. One American confided to one of our interviewees: 'I don't want to go to Europe. It's too scary. They speak foreign languages and drive on the wrong side of the road.' Then there are those reluctant to go on expatriate assignments because of their fear that they will lose out on job opportunities at home (out of sight, out of mind) or will not have a (satisfactory) job to return to. Finally, some locations are difficult to find suitable expatriates for because they are seen as unpleasant more due to security issues, crime or corruption problems than climate or distance these days.

There is also an increasing problem with getting work permits/visas for incoming expatriates. We were told of this difficulty in Sri Lanka, whilst it is getting more of an issue in the UK with changes to immigration, and the recession has meant that other countries are sensitive to protecting local employment against incomers.

- **The fact of expatriate failure** Even if you successfully identify talent from outside the home base and manage to transfer it to other parts of the world, including to the HQ, there is no guarantee of success. There can be status shocks when the position in the local firm is not the same as at home – a problem Japanese staff apparently often find hard to manage. There can be language and cultural barriers to contend with at work, not to mention problems of dislocation and readjustment at home. This might mean for some westerners getting used to gated housing in Beijing and Johannesburg, or working in alcohol free states in the Gulf. Think of the stories of footballers' wives complaining of being transplanted from southern Europe or South America to cool, wet Manchester. One of the authors remembers vividly how a well-regarded Spanish manager cut a sorry figure in the Netherlands, unable to bridge the geographic divide, or of an expatriate lasting only a week in West Africa when his partner came face to face with the reality of domestic life there. Or a sales person might be brilliant in one work environment but incapable of adjusting to be excellent in another setting. As one advertising executive we know discovered to his cost, selling business in New York is not the same as in London – the techniques are not quite the same. The greatest challenges for expatriates are to be found in China, Russia and India but these are also important destinations for expatriate assignments (Brookfield Global Relocation Services, 2010).
- **Difficulties with repatriation** There is a serious risk that expatriates on their return are vulnerable either to resignation or to diminished effectiveness. The retention challenge may come from the expatriate always seeing the overseas assignment as an opportunity for career building outside their current employer or that their additional experiences make them extremely marketable. Alternatively, their repatriation is so badly handled they leave in frustration that their self-perception of improved worth to their employer does not seem to be matched by the organization's perception. If these dispirited managers do not leave, they may mope around the organization waiting until a 'proper' job is found for them. Part of the problem is that some organizations are just not aware or, if aware, are not geared up to deal with the issue. Nobody takes responsibility for returners. Another part of the problem is that the returning expatriate may have an over-inflated view of themselves following their job abroad. They may simply be suffering a reaction from being a big fish in a small pond to a minnow in the teaming (with piranhas?) HQ ocean.
- **Retention problems** Surveys of companies using expatriates report organizations finding retention to be extremely difficult as expatriates are much more likely to leave their jobs, during or after an international assignment, than other employees. In the Brookfield Global Relocation Trends 2010 survey, it is reported that 17 per cent of expatriates left the organization during an assignment, 38 per cent within one year of returning, 23 per cent between the first and second year, and 22 per cent after two years. This compares with a per annum attrition rate of 13 per cent for all employees.

- **Does mobile mean mobile?** This question becomes a situation in some companies (usually those where expatriation is common) when employees are asked about their mobility status they are often less than frank in their answers. This can occur where being mobile is the corporate expectation which employees embrace in theory, but hope in practice to negotiate when it might become real. As we said earlier, there may be many reasons (childcare, eldercare, spousal employment) why at any one moment an individual is immobile and they would want to convince their employer that they want to be mobile, it is just due to specific circumstances at this time that they are not free to move. Or employees are mobile it is just not to that job or place. For example, Indians may be mobile to North America and some parts of Europe much more easily than being mobile inside India. (They may find supportive networks in the international diaspora that are not so available in another region of their home country.) Some organizations are relatively tolerant of this kind of reaction, whilst others take a hard line – one rejection of an expatriate assignment and you are never asked again, with implications for your career. If tolerant organizations are not careful, they get into a games playing loop where nobody is up front and honest. This makes effective resource planning incredibly difficult because your mobility data are unreliable. Hard line companies risk employees playing a very cautious game, not offering themselves for overseas assignments because they are writing the company a blank cheque. This restricts the supply of expatriate candidates. This difficulty can be eased by the open advertising of jobs because people can self-select. Nonetheless, there will be times even where open resourcing operates that the organization will want to intervene to appoint to a senior, important or hard-to-fill role, and it does not have the data to do so with confidence.
- **Lack of good knowledge on expatriate supply** The organization does not surface those outside the home country (or possibly other big labour pools) who are able and willing to move. For the best and brightest of that country this may be a necessity if they want to make career progress in the company because of few opportunities in their country. By neglecting this source of talent, the organization may impede meeting its diversity, as well as numerical supply objectives.
- **Disturbance to local staff** This comes in a number of forms. One is the knock-on effect of expatriate pay on local basic pay. A Eurasian bank, for example, has found that local wages have been pulled up by the international nature of their operations. Internal auditors have complained that the company pays above market rates in the financial services sector in some of its locations, but management feels it has to do this in order to attract staff to, say, Mongolia and this has a consequential uplift to the pay of local staff (who anyway expect a premium for working for an international company).

  Simply parachuting in managers from the home base only to deal with local shortage may create as many problems as it solves. Not only are expatriates expensive, they may lack cultural awareness or sensitivity. If so, they can generate resentment and irritation, not least because they are better paid than locals. This situation can be exacerbated if the manner of the expatriates is haughty and condescending to the local staff.

  In one voluntary organization we know, local staff objected to the attention (and money) showered on the graduate high-potential group. These were largely privileged westerners who were sent on expatriate assignments whilst still wet behind the ears, and it was the locals that had to train and support them.

A related problem is where there is an over-emphasis on individual development, building long-term capability by moving staff around. This can equal a lack of continuity in the receiving location as expatriates cycle through.

- **The responsibility–knowledge gap** Expatriates often but not always hold positions of authority in the countries they work in. Moreover, in certain types of location they are afforded even more status especially if they come from the HQ. Although they have these advantages, they have a significant disadvantage: they do not know their place of employment. This is less of a worry for very technical roles because the expatriate's expertise may be superior, but in jobs that require knowledge of local markets, of government, rules, practices, they are dependent on local staff. Most of the time this is not a problem, but in some places the expatriates are given the information they expect to hear, rather than what they need to hear. Deference has real drawbacks.

So there is a need to recognize that expatriates may not be the most appropriate to represent the company in a national setting. There are language and cultural differences to overcome, with the risk of being seen as 'neo colonials' as Garmt Louw of Shell puts it, as well as local business ignorance. Conversely, there can be a benefit in using expatriates to demonstrate the face of a global company, especially if such outsiders are held in high esteem. There may not yet be confidence in local capability and/or there is a desire in an acquisition to convert staff to new ways of working. As with many global companies, which approach has the more positive effect depends on the current standing of multinational companies in that country.

PROBLEMS WITH ALTERNATIVE EXPATRIATE OPTIONS

The traditional assignment has reduced in popularity, because, whilst there may be good reasons to use expatriates, it is undoubtedly expensive. Commuting type assignments are, as we said earlier, another option and are being particularly used within Europe because of the short journey times and relatively cheap transport costs. However, there are not just transport costs to be faced, but the wear and tear on the employee's health and on their domestic arrangements. One individual known to the authors claimed a split UK/continental European job literally nearly killed him because of physical damage done. Extended business travel can also raise tax and immigration issues that are not easy to administer.

Technological developments mean that, in theory at least, work can more easily be moved to the people rather than the traditional other way round. So, one sees virtual teams in operation, especially in IT companies, where, rather than being co-located, individuals stay in their home location, keeping in touch via video conferencing and the occasional face-to-face meeting. However, despite its attractions, this approach has not grown as much as one would expect. This is because:

- At its most basic level people like to meet and whilst teleconferencing can be effective, it tends to work best where the individuals are well known to each other and relatively culturally homogeneous.
- This makes knowledge/skill transfer particularly difficult in a remote working context

- Some countries do not readily accept the break up of the office concept. Japanese firms rely so much on the office as the social and business hub that moving staff away damages the building up/sustaining of the corporate ethos.
- Some jobs in manufacturing, retail, primary industrial extraction, etc. are by definition not done away from the factory, shop or site.

SUPPLY SHORTAGES

- **Supply shortfall** Another big problem in global talent management is an insufficient number of talented people coming from all the organization's locations to build the desired diverse international cadre. This supply shortage may apply specifically to top management positions, top specialist roles or indeed to fill the senior local posts. The Boston Consulting Group survey (2010) reported that over half its respondents faced talent gaps for senior positions 'in part because their internal talent pools are too shallow'. Again, this has happened within SAP and has been a difficulty at HPH.

SAP's preference is to develop local talent, but in some countries (especially in Asia) there is insufficient even to appoint local managers, yet alone export some to elsewhere, and so expatriates need to be transferred in from Europe. Part of the difficulty has been the speed of the company's development, which has made it hard to build internal expertise, and the relative suddenness by which it has become a global company with all the expectations that brings.

Francis Wong said his biggest challenge at HPH was the development of its leadership, as there has been little capacity for succession planning and a stretched team has had limited scope for learning in the company, especially given the consequences of its acquisitive growth path. This problem has been eased by lack of competition in its key markets, but made worse by the concomitant absence of a market from which to hire. The economic slow down, however, gave HPH time to reflect and consolidate, not only its business plans, but also for its leadership cadre.

- **Global competition** Then there is the matter of competition for global talent. We hear a lot about UK executives needing to be well paid so their employers are able to compete in the international labour market. In fact, if anything, the situation is more difficult in securing and holding on to talent outside of North America and western Europe. In some geographies good people are especially in short supply. For example, we spoke to Indian and Chinese companies that believed that their current bench was not broad enough nor deep enough to cope with their companies' strategic (global) growth plans. The management stretch of its limited talent capability was already apparent, eased only by the recent economic slow down. Moreover, in terms of management style and mindset in China experienced managers tend to have a more government approach – top down and directive, rather than inclusive and participatory – that does not always fit western notions of good management.

A number of McKinsey studies have pointed to talent shortages in China and to the supply/demand imbalance there. And this was reported to us in all our Chinese interviews with Shell, Siemens, HPH, Sun, Plan International and Schneider Electric. Parts of Africa have been ravaged by civil war and natural disasters thereby disrupting the education system, limiting still further the available supply of trained resources. In other places, as we described earlier with Brazil, there may not be these handicaps, but the education system for whatever reason leaves employers with a lot to do to compensate for its failings.

Manpower (2009) reported that although the recession had reduced shortages and hiring had declined, still 30 per cent of organizations were having difficulty recruiting globally. Skilled trades, technicians and engineers were in the top five most difficult groups to get, along with sales representatives and managers. As to location, there was an interesting mixture of locations where recruitment was hardest including Taiwan, Romania, Peru and Japan, where over half the organizations surveyed were having problems.

- **Skills gaps** This is not only (or even) a question of absent technical skills, but a lack of language and social skills. Thus China and India may be different from Brazil in having a functioning education system in place but the numbers with the social skills to work in global companies is much more limited. As Rao and Varghese put it: in India there is 'not a labour but a talent shortage' (CIPD, 2010a). In South America, we heard of the lack of English training holding back their nationals in the internal competition for jobs in an organization where everyone at management levels needs to speak English.
- **Experience gaps** The other restriction is that staff have not got the years of experience under their belt as they would have in Europe or North America. Capabilities at first and mid management levels may be lacking. As a result, companies have to make a heavy investment in leadership and skills (e.g. in change management, coaching others to perform and meet business targets). In some societies there is a lack of initiative, of a drive to change (Entreprise&Personnel, 2006). In others a certain parochialism means that there is little conception of what becoming world class entails.
- **The ambitious won't wait** As a consequence of a shortage of those with potential to succeed in global firms, the educated are in high demand with opportunities in their country and abroad. A wide variety of organizations, both national and international, are looking for talent, particularly entrepreneurial firms, leaving these people very sought after. Moreover, though you can invest in them through training and development, especially by means of expatriate assignments, they are very vulnerable to being poached, especially where there is apparently less loyalty to their employer. This may be because they treat firms as simply places that offer stepping stones on their career ladder, not as ends in themselves. Apart from those who choose the fun and rewards of leaving to set up their own business, it is clear that some locals will not stay with global companies because they believe that they will always be denied the top job. These people will not always wait around for corporate preferment. This

is especially true of those with ambition and often those with entrepreneurial flair. The boxed examples give illustrations of the problem.

SAP finds it difficult to get local people into the more challenging roles in the developing countries, not least because 'you have to compete with home grown companies playing to other rules'. Money plays a part in some circumstances like the over-heated South African economy in the run up to the football World Cup, driving up wages which international companies have to respond to. But it is not always so much to do with pay: it can be to do with competing opportunities.

Our interviewee at Schneider Electric pointed to the absence of Chinese resources for critical jobs (e.g. design and solution experts) certainly against planned expansion. She also observed that especially young Chinese needed a mindset change. She complained that they are currently too eager to jump to different jobs for extra money without thinking of a career and how to build one.

According to Wilfried Meyer at Siemens, if you do manage to get talent to move abroad and train them in global business processes with international responsibility, then they are extremely marketable when they come back. There is always money to tempt them and perhaps there is less corporate loyalty than there used to be, certainly compared with the Germany of old. Moreover, do you have the positions to compete with offers on the global market?

- **Conservatism at the top** Some organizations struggle to push their best local staff through to the next level up (e.g. regional management positions). This may be because they lack the experience, they do not project themselves as well as those from a western HQ or their language skills may not be sufficiently developed to operate in a global sphere. However, organizations have also reported to us that the HQ may prefer a known expatriate whom they trust rather than take the risk with someone less well known from another culture.
- **The job gets harder** Finally, there is the challenge of the work itself that puts a strain on the supply/demand balance. For example, the model of delegated authority in retail is a good principle but tests the skills of managers. The skill demands are also high for those who work in global matrix organizations. This is especially tricky for those new to the global game. By way of illustration, one organization explained that it is hard for local managers to satisfy corporate requirements whilst meeting the need for Asian growth. They find it a challenge for managers to deal with this tug of war.
- **Talent on tap** The effects of the boom years on views on talent supply, described earlier, are compounded by a executive perspective that might charitably be described as seeing them as 'elastic'. Less charitably some managers share the allegedly Russian attitude to workforce planning (and no doubt born of its history) that the labour supply is 'infinite'. These managers believe that trained and capable staff can be whistled up at short notice to be deployed anywhere in the world. Of course these

same managers would not tolerate expensive resources sitting on the proverbial bench waiting for the call, but also they do not seem to understand that, apart from an elite group that might be ready to switch roles, most people are embedded in their local societies and are not easily extricated on a just-in-time basis.

MANAGEMENT OF THE TALENT RESOURCE

- **Only focus on the best** The focus on the retention of the top 10 per cent, because they give the most value to the company and they are vulnerable to poaching, is understandable. However, you may be investing in a leaky pipeline, as the most able people are the most likely to move on to further their careers. They are after all the get-up-and-go types. And it is a rational decision, as research suggests that these individuals make more money through organizational mobility than by staying put (Martin et al., 2009).
- **The importance of social capital** Moreover, the organizational stars need a conducive environment within which to perform. This means they have to have support from the body of the kirk. This will not be obtained if they believe the talent management process is flawed, delivering the wrong sort of people to the top because, say, of the way they obtain results or promote their own cause. The 'talented' may prosper but the rest may be demoralized. To put it in more formal academic terms: intellectual capital depends for its creation on social capital. It can be as dangerous in performance terms for the stars as for the rest of the team, if their capabilities are really very context dependent. McKinsey research also argues that 'strong networks help retain fickle young Gen Y professionals' (Guthridge, et al., 2008).
- **Talent is not everlasting** There is a tendency for talent management selection processes to assume that talent is 'forever': it doesn't wilt and die; it may only retire. But we know that this is not true. The HR director of a large manufacturing company told one of the authors in the mid-1990s that managers who had succeeded in slash-and-burn strategies during the recession struggled with building for growth. The reverse problem has probably been evident over the last couple of years. As Paul Sparrow (2009) so elegantly put it: 'Even the highest talent can be "in the groove" at one point in their career, but can soon be out of it again, simply because the business context has changed.' Leadership, we should therefore know, is situational, but yet we design particularly competency based approaches that ignore this fact.
- **Halos and horns** One of the dangers of talent selection and development is that it can easily lead to self-fulfilling prophecies of failure as well as success due the tendency of managers (especially senior managers), in a form of cognitive dissonance, to adjust evidence to reinforce their positive or negative opinions about people. This produces a 'halo' or 'horns' effect that is particularly evident in global companies with exclusive talent processes. This leads to a risk of believing the weaknesses of the less talented as enduring just as much as treating the strengths of the talented as everlasting. Those who are marked out as exceptional get the opportunities and development to reinforce their capabilities. They gain in confidence from the organizational approbation. The converse is of course equally true: people find it hard to shine if they have been marked down as 'ordinary'. This sort of distinction may be justifiable if the selection process is based on identifying innate qualities, but firstly is the selection infallible and secondly is there no scope for improvement? Moreover,

there is the danger that over-promoted 'high potentials' do not get 'found out' until too late, especially when they may move quickly from role to role with different managers overseeing their work.

- **The talented are not easy to manage** Especially the most gifted staff can be difficult – demanding and unusual in particular ways. Some are extreme perfectionists; others may suffer from surprising self-doubt. By definition they are not 'average'. This puts pressure on their line managers to cope and inevitably some will flounder. They may be too accommodating of the eccentricities or requiring unnecessary conformity.

- **Need for status** Staff in countries with high status needs want to hold positions that demonstrate to their family that they are being successful. This puts pressure on management that, at the very least, leads to job title inflation, at worst to them making unsatisfactory appointments.

- **Performance uncertainties** Sometimes the organization has to take calculated gambles with assignments, either because of uncertainty over the candidate or over the receiving location (e.g. right sort of job, quality of managerial support, etc.). Concerns may also apply in international appointments – is the candidate up to it or going to be sufficiently stretched? Oxfam, for example, has appointed local staff into senior roles and has seen a few of them really struggle. If organizations do not identify a problem early or do not act fast enough then there can be problems in the performance of the role or, as Oxfam found, excellent staff are lost from their teams.

- **Talent demand varies** The management of talent is affected by the state of the business, which may vary widely by location (growth in one part of the world, contraction in another). It is therefore difficult to operate 'a one size doesn't fit all' model says Wilfried Meyer of Siemens. As he points out, one has to acknowledge that flatter structures and restructuring, especially in mature economies, have tended to lead towards fewer opportunities being available, and that causes the organization to look to growth markets to provide the new positions to develop the talented – which either worsens the supply situation or leads to the use of more expatriates.

- **Too much change** Business change has handicapped the process in other ways – one spends 15 years preparing people for a position, only for the configuration of jobs to alter. The new structure has bigger more complex global senior roles than before. Conversely, the country CEO jobs have become less attractive because you do not have a full portfolio of responsibility; they have become more specialized. As Birkinshaw et al. (2006) argue on the basis of their cross-national research, 'managers running the subsidiary are highly constrained in their ability to shape their own strategy.' Yet in some organizations these country CEO roles, as we remarked earlier, still have their own complexities, especially in matrix organizations. Whilst they may not have the breadth of the past, in a company like Siemens, neither are they simple 'puppet on a string jobs where all the decisions are made at Headquarters'. The job holder has to manage ambiguity which takes some skill. In those companies with a more centralrized decision making process, role specialization has a more profound adverse effect.

- **Short-termism** Yet a long-term view is necessary for talent planning. As Vestas has found some cultures are not conducive to forward planning. According to Anne Krogh Nielsen, the company has a culture of learning through doing not thinking. Managers prefer to get into the 'meat and potatoes' of daily work rather than 'hearing a professor talking about the theory'. So they supported the talent management programme whilst they were participating, but back in their business teams, they might return to type. Their contribution at business unit performance reviews was handicapped by a preoccupation with short-term issues:

Would I lose face if I identified a poor performer?

If I support the release of an individual, how will I replace them?

Identifying performance issues reflects badly on me as a manager.

- **Poor delivery** The formal systems do not always deliver. As one international financial company found, those on the succession plan do not always get appointed as intended and those not recognized leapfrog those who are. This may be because the planning is flawed or that managers are not disciplined. And it should be noted that whatever the formal system is, in the field of talent management managers have always used informal means to circumvent the system. As Nimal Perera told us, 'If I have a good person to develop I ring up one of my fellow managers in Aitken Spence and try to see if I can place him there. I will keep the HR director informed of my actions.' Similar tactics are used in the other direction: to test out whether 'the system' is offering a good addition to the team or trying to offload someone hard to place. Even in open job advertising, the formal processes and informal often run in parallel.
- **Local restrictions** Bypassing internal job advertising to place selected candidates is harder in countries where works council oversight is designed to prevent (or restrict) this happening

THE EMPLOYEE PERSPECTIVE

- **Unclear organization** The jobs pecking order is not always easy for employees to fathom and may shift from reorganization to reorganization. At Siemens some business unit jobs are better graded and are more attractive than the country ones, e.g. the wind power head based in Denmark with a global role has a bigger job than the Country CEO. In Shell, there are some country HR representative roles that are bigger than business unit business partners and in others, like Siemens, it is the reverse.
- **Frustrated expectations** As we have already seen from a corporate perspective, talent retention can be a problem. From an employee point of view, their grouses may relate to frustrated expatriate ambitions, denial of promotion within the country, insufficient development training or exclusion from the top talent list. We learned of one Chinese manager working in an international bank who resigned precisely because he thought he would not progress to the top given his nationality. He resigned to join a Chinese firm, where he subsequently became the MD. These are particular challenges in the parts of the world where talent is in short supply (they can easily get an alternative job) but also where face considerations are important. For example, one Danish CEO wanted talent management to apply only to the top 5 per cent of people. In a country like China, many of those left in the 95 per cent of the non-high-potential population would simply leave if the names become public knowledge.

- **Managing the benefits balance** For the organization it is difficult to get the balance right between organization and employee centred talent management. For the employee it may well be a case of take what you can get. In what is a frequently made observation, Mark Jankelson at ANZ complained that the company's talent management programmes seemed to convey more status than substance. Individuals saw it as an important badging exercise – the key question is whether you have attended it or not – rather than having an organizational development purpose. Indeed, some nationalities acquire training qualifications as mainly a CV enhancing exercise rather than a learning one. This questions whether if this is the outcome, it is worth the cost.
- **Cultural norms** Talent development that requires individuals to push themselves forward for jobs and/or training programmes might work well in those cultures where self-promotion is accepted as a desirable trait, but it has to be recognized that in other cultures it is not the done thing. How do organizations respond to the problems faced by some people, who may have all the necessary high-potential characteristics – including ambition – but who are inhibited in their progress by the social or cultural characteristics of a western designed system?
- **Making connections** The same sort of cultural mores may also limit another aspect of talent development that of networking. There is a requirement in global organizations to connect with different people around the world and across businesses and functions. Again, networking in this way comes seemingly naturally to those who grow up in certain societies, especially if they have had privileged educational experiences. Those who have studied abroad have confidence in languages and are aware of the different ways places work. Those with more sheltered upbringings may find it hard to compete with the more polished performers. The organization needs to identify underlying talent and help overcome any disadvantages from childhood or from nationality.
- **Unknown motivators** Do organizations know what 'cosmopolitan talent' wants by way of reward? Leave aside the expatriate group whose needs should be well researched, what about the international and mobile talent pool of high performers? Do we know what attracts them to organizations and keeps them there? Do we know what turns them on (or off) and how do we collect this information? Without it surely organizations are in the dark on setting appropriate reward and recognition policies.

Success Factors

Although we have grouped the success factors under a number of headings, they are not distinct categories; they overlap. This emphasizes that to make your talent management practice successful, you need an integrated approach.

BUSINESS ALIGNMENT AND INTEGRATION

- **Alignment with business strategy** The talent management strategy must first and foremost align with the business strategy. Whether you have an exclusive or inclusive model, a centrally or a locally driven model relates to the sort of organization you are, the conditions under which you operate and where you want to position yourself for the future. Indeed, Tesco uses a definition of talent management that it is the 'capability to deliver the business strategy'. The boxed example from SAP illustrates the point.

SAP's talent management processes have to address the following questions that deliver changing business strategies:

- Talent pipeline: requirement for different sorts of sales people and account managers. The former have to have many more leads and are to be found more in the mid market.
- Development and other tasks: got to get faster cycle times of products to market reporting a different, more flexible mindset. Also legal/contract administration is so much less bureaucratic in a 'Business Objects' world.
- Cultural challenge – have had to retain or let go people not able to operate in these market conditions and the geographic focus is switching to the Middle East, Brazil and China in markets with higher growth potential.

Without this business alignment, it is impossible to design appropriate talent management policies and processes that will meet the organizational requirements in terms of the number and nature of the talent flow and how that is managed. The development model, for instance, should conform to what the business demands by way of staff prepared to fill senior or specific roles. Moreover, business fit means that the talent selection criteria are decided not on the basis of best HR practice, but in line with what will deliver the sort of capabilities the organization needs. As another example, the decisions made on staff resourcing ought to meet the business requirements especially those relating to expatriation, as shown in Figure 6.10. This means choosing the right assignment vehicle to fulfil the organizational need.

	3 year assign.	short assign.	commuter	project/ placement	'fly drive'
supplying resources	X		X	X	
offering expertise	X	X	X	X	
crisis response		X		X	?
talent development	X	X	X	X	
corporate oversight	X	X	X		X
company integration	X				
talent attraction	X	X	?	X	

Figure 6.10 Mapping expatriate purpose against method

- **Evidence based approach** Despite our emphasis on a contingent approach, organizations should look at the evidence of what appears to work in talent management and what does not. For example:
  - Growing a team seems to be more successful than buying one in. This seems to have been demonstrated in football if you compare Barcelona with the short-term success of Real Madrid's Galacticos. The same may apply between Manchester United and City. This is certainly the view of Chelsea winger Salamon Kalou regarding Manchester City: 'You can have 10 new players and it doesn't guarantee you anything. It's good to have the same team' (Hytner, 2010). (Though by the time this is published, Real Madrid and Manchester City may have disproved this point!) Evidence has been found in financial services (US stock analysts) where performance has dipped both for the transferees and the teams they have joined. As Groysberg et al. (2004) found:

    When a company hires a star, the star's performance plunges, there is a sharp decline in the functioning of the group or team the person works with, and the company's market value falls. Moreover, stars don't stay with organizations for long, despite the astronomical salaries firms pay to lure them away from rivals.

- Do not simply rely on performance assessment to judge potential. High-potential staff will be high performers, but it does not work the other way round. Indeed, Corporate Leadership Council research (2005) found that nearly three quarters of high performers were not rated as having high potential both because of personal attributes and capability.
- It may be better to focus, especially for roles with an international component, on the ability and motivation to learn, including from experience, and adapt to changing circumstances, rather than having particular knowledge and skills at the time of assessment. (This is the essence of the PWC 'learning agility' method referred to earlier.) Stahl et al. (2007) found it was better to look at cultural fit with the organization than job related skills and experience or formal qualifications. This supports the adage 'recruit on values, train on skills'. Moreover, The Korn Ferry Institute has presented research (De Meuse, et al., 2009) that demonstrates that at least one tool to test for learning agility is reliable in different parts of the world. Interestingly, though, the similarity is greatest with respect to 'results' and 'mental' agility (the highest learning agility factors) and relatively less so for 'people' and 'change' agility.
- Seeing that the key to organizational performance is through people and that the task of the leader is to harness and integrate individual and team contribution is what constitutes outstanding leadership capability (Tamkin et al., 2010), organizations should apply this insight into leadership selection and development, especially in understanding how this plays out in a global context.
- Related to this point, interpersonal skills are vital in global companies, especially in reconciling the quite legitimate but different stakeholder views of countries, regions, business units, functions, corporate centre, etc. This means having networks that span geography and, in some corporate roles, business functions, and building relationships in this environment. Similarly, the ability, sometimes described as having a 'global mindset' to balance the tension of standardization and control on the one hand with flexibility and responsiveness on the other.

- Specifically concerning expatriates, it appears (IPD, 1999) that certain personality traits (like finding it hard to deal with ambiguity or being highly judgemental of people and situations) leave some people more prone to finding assignments abroad difficult. These individuals ideally should be screened out. It is particularly noteworthy that some personal attributes that are very successful in one environment, the goal getting, very driven individuals that make it in the USA or UK, may be very unsuitable for assignments to certain other countries. Instead, it is those with good coping mechanisms, who are empathetic and open to ideas who are the people who are the more likely to succeed. Managers need the skills to collaborate, build support and achieve through others.

> Research (Lievens, et al. 2003) has suggested that with respect to expatriates, both careful selection of assignees and pre-departure cross-cultural awareness training leads to more successful outcomes. Cognitive ability tests predict the ability to learn a language. Both personality tests of openness and assessment centre tests on communication, adaptability and teamwork predict performance in cross-cultural training events and subsequently expatriate performance.

- According to Wendy Hirsh there is a consensus that has emerged on leadership potential criteria. It involves some combination of:
    - strategic business thinking – taking a wider and longer view of the organizational needs, high-quality decision making, identifying innovative solutions
    - working with and leading others – high-level interpersonal skills, developing others, motivating and leading during periods of change
    - drive for performance – having the energy and resilience to achieve improved organizational performance, often with a strong customer orientation, but able to prioritize as circumstances change
    - values orientation – especially necessary to balance with results
    - self-awareness and desire to develop.
- **Consistency with other policies** It is vitally important that your talent management approach is consistent with your other HR policies and practices, not just in the obvious areas of career management and learning and development. If talent management helps reinforce the culture you want to retain or change, then its focus should be consistent with these goals. Take an exclusive approach to the identification of talent, is that because you want to emphasize excellence? Is it supported by an approach to remuneration that especially favours rewarding the highly talented via long term compensation grants or shorter term variable pay systems? Conversely, if you believe the organization achieves better performance through the contribution of widespread talent, then you would expect to see greater equity in pay, more use of team based pay, etc. Integration of people management processes should also be found in job design. If you expected to retain the talented then roles should be stretching with plenty of space for autonomy. Clever people quickly twig the disconnect between hearing that you wish to 'unleash talent' and seeing that the jobs on offer allow little scope to shine.

- **Laying down your talent management principles** is both a good way to communicate an important message about what talent means to the organization and how it will deliver this, and how it will achieve the effective people management and business management integration described above.

Plan International's principles are recorded thus:

'In order to remain in line with Plan's organisational philosophy and culture the Talent Management Programme will be guided by five core principles:

Transparency

Providing a transparent process built around a strong evidence basis and fairness which is clear and understood by all employees.

Inclusiveness

Recruitment, promotion, development and retention practices are based primarily on merit, potential and performance and on diversity that reflects, across the workforce, the global nature of Plan and its work.

Accountability

Shared responsibility for development and succession between Talent review forums, line manager and the individual.

Commitment

Positive career and development discussions will be available to all employees.

Cost-effectiveness

Talent management will be used to increase Plan's cost-effectiveness in delivering effective programmes.'

- **Effective targeting** Especially in straitened times it is more than ever necessary to target investment in talent on those who will repay the most in business terms over both the long and the short term. This means nurturing existing talent and not stopping recruiting talent, especially graduate, even if the organization is not doing so well. A particular focus on the future skills that the organization will need must fall to the corporate centre, or global business units, as the operating companies may be too oriented to the here and now. Nonetheless, however you define talent or operate your system, care should be exercised over creating undue exclusivity and narrowness in sources. This is because it is vital not to switch off key personnel whom you rely on for success. Critical, specialist resources may feel overly excluded from development processes, as may well-respected local staff. Labelling the former 'high professional' may not be sufficient to overcome a sense that they are regarded as second class citizens.

Swiss Re has three categories of especially valued staff – *top talent, key talent* and *key contributors* (high performers suited to their current role). The intensity of development varies by group with naturally the top talent receiving the most.

Marks and Spencer has a 'vanilla' development programme for all its leaders but a 'platinum service' for those with the highest potential within this population, offering a more personalized (and hence more expensive) programme.

EMBEDDING THE TALENT MANAGEMENT PHILOSOPHY: STAKEHOLDERS

Many talent programmes fail because they are not embedded in the institutions and culture of the organization. There are various steps organizations can take which relate to stakeholder engagement and process development.

- **Shareholder alignment** For listed companies it might be helpful to find out more about investor priorities in talent development and executive appointments. An early conversation with your corporate investor relations team, therefore, will help shape the talent measurement criteria in a way that meets shareholder interests.
- **Executive endorsement** In stakeholder engagement it is particularly important to get the commitment of senior management to the talent approach at the outset so that it is not seen as another bureaucratic imposition dreamed up by HR. If the leadership does not endorse the exercise the process will not be meaningful. One way to do this is to roll out your talent approach in stages rather than as a big bang. This has three advantages: it can prove the concept first before over commitment (especially helpful if there is a sceptical management); it can produce a demand to be included from locations or business units (exploiting the competitive spirit in some firms); and it does not over stretch HR resources to support implementation. Another good idea is to obtain senior management participation in selection decisions. Their support should also inhibit games playing by business units/locations and stamp it out if it does occur. For example, WWL achieves ownership of talent management by the Global Management Team through their involvement in the annual Global Talent Review Boards, which include both a discussion on inclusion in the global top talent pool and individual evaluation and identification of development needs. Firmenich sees business engagement as critical to the extent that it has as one of its 'value indicators', i.e. a measure of its success. The HR team believes there has been a 'radical change in attitude of business leadership to the topic of talent management' that augurs well for its future. SAP wants a 'mindset' where talent management is 'championed by leadership and jointly developed with HR'.
- **Professional delivery** The business leadership has to be backed up by well-trained and committed selectors, coaches, mentors, facilitators. They all have their different contributions to make, and they need to execute them professionally. HR, as we suggested earlier, should be supporting this activity by defining roles and helping to build skills.
- **Managers' acceptance is key** For these contributors to the talent management process to be able to do their job, middle (line) managers have to be on board. It

is vital for managers to see the point of talent management in driving the business forward. The aim is to 'get line managers to talk as passionately about talent as they do about organizational results' (Kock and Burke, 2008) or for talent management to be an 'integral part of line managers' routine' (Dr. Daniel Dirks, former EVP and Head of Group HR, Allianz). Managerial engagement can be grown in a number of ways:

- By getting them more purposely involved in the talent processes through describing their role and its importance to the process.
- By ensuring that this role gets proper attention through making clear a line manager's accountability for their staff's development. This is being done in DPWN by making managers responsible for executive development in their own business units. At another company 'having a talent mindset' was seen as a key leadership performance indicator and the fostering of talent a critical part of the role.
- By designing credible processes. This is especially important outside head office where some managers feel they take part in pointless processes (succession planning comes in for special criticism) and ones that do little to drive their business results.
- By investing in the people capability of managers. As we know from other work (Purcell and Hutchinson, 2007 and Purcell et al., 2003), the people management skills of managers are not always their strongest suit. Organizations can deepen the commitment to talent management through the way they select managers. You put your money where your mouth is by choosing managers that promote talent development and do not accept as managers those failing to live up to your leadership model.
- By developing a corporate mindset in your management cadre so that they positively support the talent management processes. This is especially important where managers are dispersed around the world and it is hard to track their behaviour. One company tried to overcome parochial thinking by insisting that managers should always think what is best for the firm.
- By encouraging leaders visiting operations in different countries to talk about talent (e.g. high-potential possibilities, supply issues, pipeline strength) to the local management team as much as technical business issues.
- By creating a common global language around talent management. This is especially necessary either if it is an under-developed concept in your organization or where you propose changes in the way you conceptualize it. Having in managers' heads the definition of talent, on what criteria it is selected and how it is developed aids decision making processes no end.

The creation of the leadership model at Vestas and its implementation in graduate selection, offered a reference point and a common language to the organization. Rather than being born out of a theory or philosophy reflected in formal policies, it was built through doing. This had the benefit of getting the managers involved such that, once convinced through participation, they became ambassadors of the model 'because it works'. Says Anne Krogh Nielsen: 'It was like building an aeroplane whilst flying.'

- **Then set them to work** Firstly, managers must encourage employees to engage in their own development and upskilling, managing their hopes and fears. They need to coach and mentor, as well as driving for better performance. Next, managers also ensure the first feed into any talent pipeline is with the right quality of talent. They have to not just identify the talented but develop them – in their role and by releasing them for learning and development activities and for career enhancing assignments. As corporate citizens, they will be expected to receive colleagues who are developing, but who are not yet the complete package in terms of knowledge, skills and experience.
- **Wider employee involvement** One stakeholder group that is easy to ignore is the employees themselves – as one interviewee put it, 'We do not want to have individuals who are bystanders in the talent management process' and another said, 'We do want not just a management process but a staff process.' Whilst accepting there may be some cultural sensitivities over ostentatious acknowledgement of success, staff can still be encouraged to support an environment where continuous improvement is understood and acted upon, where celebrating achievement is not an embarrassment, where talent is allowed to flourish. It is easy to see the converse in a situation where employees are suspicious of talent processes because they do not trust the integrity and competence of management, or do not have faith in the integrity in the talent management approach chosen. This will hinder any truly successful talent management activity. So organizations need to a degree to go with the grain of the prevailing culture, but also to try and shape it so that the talent model is endorsed.

EMBEDDING THE TALENT MANAGEMENT PHILOSOPHY: PROCESSES

There are a number of core processes that need to work well if talent management is to operate smoothly.

- **Keep it simple** Keeping the talent management system as simple as possible has a number of advantages. Complex processes put off managers as well as adding time and cost. The first point is evidenced in a survey by the New Talent Management Network, which found, according to co-author Marc Effron, that 'business leaders want the simplest way to get the job done' (http://www.businessweek.com/managing/content/mar2010/ca2010035_970348.htm). Driven by notions of best practice, the charge is that HR frequently over-complicates things. However, sometimes this is for justifiable reasons – seeking fairness of process and outcome, ensuring diversity goals are met and such like. In talent management system design these desirable aims do need to be balanced with the objective of having a user friendly method.
- **Effective skills building** Good workforce planning is a prerequisite of any talent management system in that it is vital to get the supply/demand balance right. Use the workforce plan to estimate the size of the supply that requires building up and then take necessary action. But, an all too common failing of HR is to ignore demand, or at least not understand it sufficiently. In many global companies resource requirements are shifting from west to east, and HR must understand this process and be able to respond to it. It should also recognize any alteration in skill demands, just as much number against location requirements.

- There is a specific decision to be made about whether to allow an over-supply of staff to be developed as talented in the knowledge that a good proportion will not find jobs. This is costly to the organization but also to the frustrated ambitions of good employees. However, it has two advantages: 1) it helps grow capability in the organization through the training and experiential learning offered and 2) it means that you avoid tough decisions in assessment centres where an uncomfortably large number of people might be rejected. The alternative is naturally to fit the supply of talent to the demand, yet this can be inflexible and inappropriate to a growing organization or one that needs to retain flexibility to respond to changing circumstances, as well as putting quite a strain on the nomination and assessment systems to make good judgements.

Plan International's talent boards combine reviewing information about talented individuals – their selection and development – with broader questions on whether supply will meet demand, including the bench strength depth for each critical role. They also review important talent risks:

- Vacancy risk: there are no critical roles left vacant.
- Readiness risk: nobody is appointed into positions without having the requisite capabilities.
- Reputation risk: inappropriate individuals are not placed in jobs.
- Diversity risk: diversity targets are met.

- **Build supply** With supply shortages in certain parts of the world, it is even more imperative to be aware of where there may be supply gaps and consider the best way to fill them. The 'war for talent' should not be seen as a global battle but rather as a series of specific engagements where talent really is in short supply. Look at cross-business unit/location transfer, internal promotion/transfer or external recruitment. Introduce training courses or more extended educational facilities to grow skills in countries where there is a clear supply shortage. There are arguments either way for doing this in house (better alignment with corporate needs) or shared with others in a third party venture (cheaper). Moreover, this skills building could be designed solely for the current internal employment base (where it is more a skills than numbers issue) and/or focused on the external population (to develop capability in the country). The latter can be achieved through various means, as described earlier under building the brand, including education scholarships, making available educational facilities or resources. The leadership of the organization should be encouraging recruitment ahead of the curve where necessary to anticipate wastage and build capability. The aim should be 'liberating talent trapped in national silos' (Guthridge and Lawson, 2008). Awareness of resource constraints means you should avoid agreeing to business plans that cannot be delivered due to a lack of resources.

As noted earlier, HPH has put its own people into the top of company acquisitions. To reduce the management stretch it is not only developing international Chinese managers, it is trying to build broader leadership skills and stronger functional capacity.

- **Effective execution** Having got your overall plan it is important to execute it such that talented people find themselves in the right jobs, at the right time, properly prepared and inducted into them. Some organizations have a commitment to this process. Oxfam wants to share talented people around internally for both organizational and individual benefit. Shell has had a long track record in effective career management. In our view, organizations should err on the side of greater rather than less intervention in making the right placements happen. Schlumberger's wish for 'dynamic career management' is the correct objective. Plan International believes in the 'cross-fertilization' of talent across the world and wants to take active steps to achieve that goal. One approach may be move opportunities to the people, rather than always requiring the reverse. This is a way of accessing talent from around the organization by having roles that were traditionally performed at HQ moved out to other locations where there is available talent.
- **Ensure process integrity** Where there are formal talent management schemes that have a selected membership, relegation from them should be seen as important as promotion to them, and in all cases there should be appropriate feedback to those nominated, both to the successful (who may still have development gaps) and unsuccessful (who deserve an explanation and advice for the future). This is to ensure that schemes retain their integrity, reinforce the feeling that selection and retention happens on merit and help prevent the inevitable rise of those who are not as talented as they think they are and who may end up in jobs beyond their capability, with unfortunate consequences for themselves and their organization. It is true that the organization may fear resignation from those so demoted, but perhaps this is not such a bad thing as it opens up space for others who may be more talented. A word of caution should be given on how this approach is managed in societies where face is very important. Ideally, great care should be exercised over who is nominated to avoid later disappointments, but there will be pressure to accept on schemes individuals pushed forward from certain countries. If excessive preferential treatment is given those candidates, other people will complain that their company has become like a trans-national body (like the UN or EU) where a balance between nationalities can be given more weight than pure merit. Some organizations deal with this dilemma by not overtly telling staff that they are in or out of the high-potential group.

Richemont, one of the world's leading luxury goods groups, believes strongly that everyone is talented in their own capacity. Whilst everyone has an inherent talent to be developed, individuals must earn their 'talented' tag and must work to turn this it into a real strength for the business.

This is backed by an approach to performance management that trains managers to identify individual talent alongside assessing effectiveness on the job and developing common core competencies.

- **Manage with sensitivity** You should sensitively manage the question of open/closed selection systems. In many countries there is pressure towards openness that may prove irresistible. In other parts of the world expectations may be quite the contrary – it is not appropriate to disclose such plans. It is possible to manage a segmented approach in this way. What we would not advise is to operate a mixed model within the same geography. We have heard of some organizations that leave it to managers' discretion what to inform and what to keep to themselves. Previous personal experience is that this approach leads to discord and employee irritation.
- **Look out for bias** To deal with a diversity shortfall, a review of your talent management selection processes might identify biases. In this regard, having a more open process is undoubtedly helpful, especially if there is a suspicion that the closed model only provides 'jobs for the boys'. In addition, research into gender differences in self-assessment and appraisal indicates that use of 360 degree feedback in supplementing other methods for identifying talent may well overcome the bias against women inherent in other types of assessment (Millmore et al., 2007; Lombardo and Eichinger, 2002). What is more, 360 degree feedback is also more likely to reveal whether people who are delivering good results are doing so at the expense of those around them. Some American companies have been more proactive still, using talent spotting as a lever for achieving a more diverse management population.

Schlumberger actively strives for a more diverse management population from top to bottom. Through recruiting where it operates, the company's nationality headcount matches its operational profile geographically. As it is a long-standing practice it is now part of the corporate culture, but it is backed by a presence in over 300 universities worldwide.

- **Bring leaders with you** Whilst it is easy to be critical of development programmes, especially in more recessionary times, there is a counter-argument that well-designed programmes can be an important means to inculcate in the leadership population the behaviours that the organization wants to see that will drive better performance and help prevent unfortunate managerial actions that might damage the business (e.g. excessive risk taking or inappropriate behaviours). Moreover, development events are important as a means of building social capital, particularly in a global organization. So an evaluation of development activity should conceive of what they offer in this context.
- **Consider what adaptation is necessary** to operate talent management globally. You cannot assume that attraction, selection and development will work the same way in every geography. We have already discussed that the brand projection may send unintended signals, but selection methods and content may need adjustment to pick out the sort of people you are looking for because they may present themselves in a way you are not used to. Western development programmes might also need some adjustment to fit the cultural mores of certain nationalities.

Marks and Spencer has found that its leadership development programme has 'translated' reasonably well when delivered through its regional hubs across the world. This might well be because the people working at senior level in global companies are comfortable with western ways of doing things. Nevertheless, there has to be some adaptation, specifically in mode of delivery – greater clarity of message, more reference to spirituality in Asia.

- **Encourage skill development** Activities such as embedding social learning, action learning groups, coaching and mentoring and, importantly, building the capability of line managers to support their team's development are where much focus of development should be, whilst recognizing that there is still some need for formal learning for people to be introduced to new concepts and practise behavioural skills, as well as in the socialization process.
- **Encourage personal growth** Relatively recent behavioural science (especially represented in positive psychology) challenges the view that talent is immutable, arguing that training and experience can make a significant difference to performance and potential. One factor that is picked out is 'confidence'. Apparently (Stajkovic and Luthans, 1998) confidence to achieve in specific situations has a bigger impact on success than other factors (e.g. goal setting, feedback, behaviour training). You can build confidence through 'mastery experiences', role modelling, positive feedback and 'managing the mental state'. Similarly, attributes like resilience, optimistic thinking and determination can be developed.
- **Support local HR** Give extra support to managers and HR colleagues in (developing) countries that struggle to meet the talent requirements of the organization through faulty attraction methods, a poor selection track record, weak endorsement of the development programmes, etc. This is an acknowledgement that some corporately designed processes simply do not work so well in some settings, or take time to develop.
- **Check out what is happening on the ground** HR should get out more and meet the talented across the organization and form their own personal links so that they can give appropriate support. This is especially important in a global company because it is necessary for all the talented to feel that corporate interest is being taken in them. It also allows, say, the head of talent management to form their own, independent view of these individuals, which can be helpful in career management – judging the right moves for people, the speed of progress, the line of direction, etc.
- **Effective expatriate process management** Actively manage the expatriate process better to avoid the problems reported on pp. 179–182. This means:
  - **Correct proportions** Making sure the proportion of expatriates is right from a cost and performance perspective whilst looking at the benefits, not just the short-term getting the job done ones, but also those relating to growing internal capability that can be drawn upon as the need arises. This suggests that expatriation is a necessary (even if expensive) route to building capability rather than a series of short trips. However, organizations should balance this objective by not compromising operational local performance. The nature and frequency of expatriate assignments should bear this in mind.

- **Develop an international cadre** Having a cadre of internationally experienced staff can be vital if crises develop or business suddenly booms. To achieve this, you want your staff to immerse themselves in the countries and cultures they go to, rather than having a quick dip in and out. In this context build a cadre of internationally capable managers who are comfortable working abroad. Having such a group also has the benefits of offering an international career instead of the occasional one-off assignment, which leaves the individual more at the vagaries of the internal appointment system. Such uncertainty does not make for easy recruitment to expatriation or successful outcomes. Companies like Shell and Schlumberger are well practised in this art. But those with global ambitions will have to do the same. HPH, for example, is developing a group of international Chinese managers, joining the more common Australian and British expatriates.
- **and local capability** whilst ensuring that the work gets done to an acceptable standard, act on the longer-term imperative of developing local talent to take the expatriate's place. You have to ensure that able, local staff believe there are opportunities to grow and that promotion will not always be blocked by foreigners. Where possible we would quickly withdraw expatriates after an acquisition because in the long run a dependency culture will be less effective than an empowered one. And the local staff must be selected on merit. There must not be any sense that they are 'Uncle Toms' chosen for their compliance rather than their competence, or those with the social graces and western qualifications that might look talented, but may not be as talented as those without these superficial attractions.

Practice varies in how long home country expatriates remain after an acquisition. It seems that Japanese companies are keen to ensure that those companies they buy are inculcated with corporate methods and business practices through keeping their representatives in situ for a while (e.g. Nomura keeps Japanese expatriates in place for two years after a company purchase).

Over more recent years, HPH has tried to limit its imposition of new Chinese leadership on its foreign acquisitions. It might still take the key roles of CEO, CFO and COO, but it is trying to maintain some element of local leadership representation in other roles. HPH has also expanded through joint ventures, leading to having a more blended leadership team in place. In its bigger foreign interests, HPH has also taken the commercial/marketing roles, though this is adjusted to the local needs of specific countries where local contacts and knowledge are key, such as in Korea and Indonesia. Indeed some of these staff are also now becoming part of HPH's global leadership cadre.

By contrast, Tata and JSW are more likely to withdraw their expatriates at an early stage on the principle that you should trust the local staff to run their own operation.

- **Bridge gaps** Considering the use of 'bi-cultural' intermediaries to bridge the gap between home and host countries (Jonsen and Bryant, 2008). These are people who through education or family background are aware of both the home and host country cultures. For example, a Chinese having studied in the USA who is given a role by an American firm in China may be more a more effective 'bridge' back to the corporate centre than someone who has never left China.

One of the authors while at Shell undertook a project on those studying in higher education outside their own country as a possible source of high-potential recruitment.

In line with this approach, Tesco has been recruiting Chinese graduates in the UK who are destined to go back to work for the company back home.

- **Right face, right place** Consider how best to undertake the reputational duties in a country: when is the face from the global corporation better than the face of the location?
- **Select expatriates more carefully** Assessment centres, well designed and adapted for international use, can be helpful to identify those who will prosper outside their home country. However, you need to be clear what characteristics you are looking for and follow the research evidence described earlier. Instead, you could select those with the ability to adapt, rather than somebody who meets predefined criteria, and choose a tool like the Kaisen cultural adaptability assessment (IPD, 1999) to perform this task because it looks at the psychology of coping in strange situations and the individual's fitness to achieve this. Du Pont uses an external company to test through the application of a 'Cross Cultural Adaptability Assessment' both the putative expatriate and their spouse, if they have one, on their cultural adaptability. ConocoPhillips uses the same tool. In their case it is positioned as part of an Employee Assistance Programme. Others use the Cross-Cultural Adaptability Inventory developed in the 1980s as a self-assessment tool for assessing cross-cultural effectiveness as part of a battery of interviews and testing. Alternatively, you may not be convinced that you can effectively test and predict performance because you take the view that expatriate circumstances vary too much: some people will work better in some settings than others. This suggests that you do not ignore selection but fine tune it to specific needs. There are other organizations where this academic debate is all very well but you have no choice in candidates. This obviously more true where the need is for specialist expertise than general management. This leads to a conclusion that realistic but well thought through (and validated) selection processes are probably the most sensible way to proceed.
- **Offer pre-assignment training** in cultural, social and business differences between the expatriating national and the receiving location. This means providing information, learning appropriate skills (over and above their normal set) and, if possible, giving the potential expatriate a sense of what the assignment might be like (through simulation or real exposure to the location). For example,

in many societies the expatriate has to be accepted by the receiving team before they can move on to completing the task. This knowledge and appreciation would help the potential expatriate enormously before they leave.

According to the 2011 Interdean Mobility Survey Report, language training is offered to assignees by 62 per cent of organizations compared with 38 per cent that offer cultural training. Given that we know that cultural adaptation is a key feature of expatriate success, you might have thought that those organizations that are prepared to help with language adjustment would also help with cultural.

- **Ensure a proper induction process** Failure to bed in newly arrived staff can be a serious problem both for the expatriate's and for organizational performance. So organizations need to think through how best to prepare individuals both before they arrive (as above) and during the settling in phase. There should be a proper induction process at the receiving end, not just about the job and office practicalities, but on cultural aspects (the local dos and don'ts). This helps with acclimatization to the new location and to the work environment. Buddying the expatriate with another transferee and/or local member of staff is one helpful method, but so is the simple business of the HR team making sure that accommodation, transport and domestic arrangements are working satisfactorily.
- **Manage any downsides** If the business need requires the assignment of an individual because of the technical skills who would otherwise be seen as unsuitable for expatriation, then consider how best to ameliorate the downsides by briefing the receiving manager, giving more long-distance support, arranging for a host based mentor, etc.
- **Take risks with talent** by 'giving people bigger coats' to see if they fit. But accept that in any assignment, especially an expatriate one, there is always the possibility of failure and this needs to be managed before as well as during the posting. Organizations need to think through their attitude to these sorts of risk as the boxed examples show. But this is about risk management, not avoidance.

The HR director at Oxfam recently discussed levels of risk with their Trustees and agreed that one can take them with developmental postings at relatively junior levels, but for Country and Regional Directors, selection must use their competence frameworks and take much less risk – for the sake of the staff they lead.

One of the authors was struck by the apparently more open talent process in ABN AMRO at the point RBS acquired its part of that organization, where more people seemed to have moved between disciplines or indeed from front to back office and vice versa, than had been the case historically in RBS which was much more siloed in its thinking.

- **Develop a comprehensive set of expatriate policies and practices** In particular, be very clear on both the financial terms and conditions of expatriation and on the living circumstances, partner work possibilities (unpaid only in some locations), education provision, etc. This is especially necessary for shorter-term assignments, where often less attention is given to terms and conditions to aid flexibility, but risks inconsistency and, in the end, extra effort. Indeed, Deloitte suggests that having a global mobility function that manages such processes clearly leads to more effective expatriate processes (Deloitte Consulting, 2009). And the 2011 Interdean Mobility Survey Report suggests that whilst organizations give a lot of practical support to budding assignees, less than half help with accompanying partner assistance. Perhaps this is because of a progressive move towards shorter commuter based assignments, driven by the need to control costs: a central finding of the survey.
- **Provide personal support** Give proper personal support to those expatriating or expatriated to minimize the risk of failure. Organizations must be very mindful of domestic issues in making expatriate appointments (pre-assignment marital problems might be 'solved' overseas or could be a serious headache to the receiving organization); what happens during life abroad (often it is the domestic settling in that makes or breaks assignments); and challenges that occur on return (facilitate good advice in housing, education, etc.). This means investing in pre-assignment visits or videos (where the former is impractical); having counselling/advisory support attuned to expatriate issues; and internal awareness and support for issues on return.
- **Track performance carefully** And intervene quickly if things are going awry, recognizing that 'fault' for any problems may be difficult to apportion – understandable difficulties in adjustment for the expatriate, unreasonable demands from a local manager, personality (cultural) clashes, real performance failures; different expectations about role autonomy/deference to authority/responsibility for goal setting, etc.
- **Keep the expatriate in the corporate loop** by visits, calls and e-mails so that they are aware of broad corporate developments but also issues that affect them personally. Consider appointing a home based mentor.
- **Give reintegration training** so that somebody who has been away, especially for a long time is helped to acclimatize. This offering suits situations where there is a lot of change in the home country (post war, recession, boom, etc.)
- **Decide on personal tax policy** Some organizations have chosen a tax equalization policy whereby all expatriates pay the same personal tax irrespective of location and fiscal regime. This reinforces a sense of fairness among the expatriates themselves and facilitates staff movement since net pay is less liable to fluctuation. The alternative of net pay being determined by geography and national tax policy risks those in low tax regimes being reluctant to move and those in high tax regimes agitating for a transfer.
- **Evaluate effectiveness** Review the various aspects of your talent management approach – selection, development, planning, etc. – to ensure you are recruiting and retaining the people and skills you need for now and the future. This should include assessment of the different methods of knowledge and expertise transfer via expatriates and other methods of dissemination, for example through experts delivering master classes or via virtual learning groups. The aim should be to measure and report results, but also to take action.

7 *HR Governance*

HR governance may not be sexy but it's important! (Susan O'Donnell, Head of CAO Business Support at RBS)

Introduction and Definitions

Indeed, as Susan O'Donnell says, HR governance may not be the most interesting, or well understood, concept in the management lexicon, but it goes to the heart of how you manage the organization and the debate on how to do it is as old as management itself. The broad choice is whether you manage through tight or loose control, and history has examples of both forms. One can go back, for example, to 221 BC and the Chinese emperor Oin Shi-huangdi to see a perfect case of tight control (Sun, 2007). He brought unity to the Empire through a concerted standardization drive to the extent that dissenting scholars had their books burnt and were buried alive if they did not conform: an approach some HR directors might want to reintroduce! As an illustration of his view on the benefits of harmonization he had all arrows made the same length with standard, replaceable arrow heads.

By contrast, even earlier, in the fifth century BC, the Persian Empire was run on a different principle. Rather than 'might being right', the Persian form of occupation was like 'a light morning mist settling over the contours of their empire; you were aware of it but it was never obtrusive' (BBC, 2010). Unlike, say, the later Roman Empire where subjects were encouraged to identify with and see themselves as Roman, Cirus, the Persian king who founded the Empire, wanted a confederation of allied states that allowed a lot of autonomy to individual kingdoms. So long as they accepted the principle of Persian rule, he encouraged local elites to collaborate between them and with the centre.

So, there is a unitarist view of the world where the headquarters' view is the one that has to predominate because of its superiority, and as a reflection of its relative power. As the historian Tony Judt (1997) put it in relation to the eighteenth-century enlightened despotism of Prussia and Austria, they had an 'ideal of efficient, universal administration, shorn of particularisms and driven by rational calculation and the rule of law'. In opposition to this view is a pluralist vision that sacrifices efficiency for fit with different cultures and replaces pure rationality with more acknowledgement of the importance of affective relationships. Whilst, by no means a perfect example, the Ottoman Empire followed the Persian approach in absorbing conquered peoples and adapting its way of doing things to local customs and culture, especially in respecting 'personal law' of religious groups/nations through separate judicial systems for each.

However, some management theorists want to address and, if possible, resolve this dichotomy. Thompson more than 40 years ago was describing the trade-off between efficiency and flexibility as a central 'paradox of administration' (cited in Raisch and Birkinshaw, 2008). It still remains one of the biggest challenges facing the HR function. On the one hand, it has to drive down cost and find ways to deliver services more cheaply than ever before. On the other hand, it has to contribute to organizational performance, now and in the future.

More recently, Raisch and Birkinshaw (2008) describe the requirement for an 'ambidextrous' organization, where this tension between the efficiency aim to meet demands of today's business (through standardization and centralization) and the flexibility requirement (through autonomy and exploration) to adapt to future needs is addressed.

In trying to answer this same question Roberts (2004) uses the economic concept of 'complementarity' to deal with the limitations of being forced to decide between 'tight and loose coupling'. Complementarity is used to describe how managers need to make the right choices in the light of the internal and external environment. If they choose correctly they can achieve benefits to both the aims of flexibility and commonality.

These academic observations may correctly diagnose the problem and offer a theoretical solution, but, as often is the case, the translation from theory into practice is problematic.

In this context, HR governance is becoming a hot topic among global companies. Encouraged by management consultants it is being discovered as an important issue destined to be high on the list of functional priorities. Moreover, academic, regulator and practitioner insights on the causes of the banking crisis have brought into sharp relief the need for improved corporate and HR governance. However, it appears not to have an agreed definition, or, perhaps more accurately, the definition has not entered management language (at least in the UK) with a shared and known understanding.

A Mercer report in 2003 considered HR governance to be an 'emerging organizational practice' and as a term that 'may have been conceived in the mid-1990s' as part of HR transformation. Their paper describes HR governance as 'the act of leading the HR function and managing related investments'. It seeks, in their view, to optimize human capital performance; fulfil fiduciary and financial responsibilities; mitigate enterprise HR risk; obtain HR and business alignment; and enable functional decision making. Hewitt (2009a) has a similar view on the importance and content of HR governance. Thus it states that 'effectively managing the complexities of a global HR organization requires a concerted focus on governance'. As to its definition, the firm talks of 'best-in-class governance' being 'tied to business outcomes and focuses on making critical decisions regarding fiscal discipline, risk management, and policy creation'.

Control Objectives for HR ('What is HR Governance about?' 28 May 2009, http://www. hrgovernance.co.za/00/)) describes HR governance as 'senior management's ability to direct, control and evaluate the use of an enterprise's human resources in support of the achievement of the organization's strategic goals'. From this perspective the focus is on leadership, organizational structure and processes as the means to 'leverage HR resources to produce the information required and drive the alignment, delivery of value, management of risk, optimized use of resources, sustainability and the management of performance'.

So HR governance appears to be about functional management (including defining structure, roles and processes, and allocating and managing resources, especially relating to organization-wide programmes or projects) with a clear business aim and in such a way as to account for and manage risk. Governance of whatever variety includes clarifying accountabilities and providing assurance.

CORPORATE AND HR GOVERNANCE COMPARED

It is interesting that the term governance is being defined in this HR context without apparent reference to the well-developed corporate governance discourse. There are also different theories of corporate governance as it applies in the private sector. 'Agency' theory gives precedence to owners' interests, and governance is about controlling the executive who is likely to pursue 'self-interested opportunism' in his or her own agenda. As the Chinese proverb says, 'When you are far from the Emperor the sky is higher': so owners wish to limit this tendency towards independence. 'Stewardship' theory sees a convergence of interest between owners and managers, with the shared objective of wealth creation. 'Stakeholder' theory widens the interest base to those outside the organization as well as inside it. This is where CSR connects to business objectives – what has been described as 'corporate altruism' (http://www.bethkanter.org/sncr-1/).

Dow Jones has an index that measures sustainability. It defines 'corporate sustainability' thus: '[A] business approach that creates long-term shareholder value by embracing opportunities and managing risks deriving from economic, environmental and social developments. Corporate sustainability leaders achieve long-term shareholder value by gearing their strategies and management to harness the market's potential for sustainability products and services while at the same time successfully reducing and avoiding sustainability costs and risks.'

Corporate governance, therefore, can concern both wealth creation and protection (See Martin and McGoldrick, 2010 for a discussion.). Sir Adrian Cadbury described the stakeholder view: 'Corporate governance is concerned with holding the balance between economic and social goals and between individual and communal goals ... the aim is to align as nearly as possible the interests of individuals, corporations and society' (World Bank, 1999). Jim Wolfensohn when at the World Bank seemed to combine all these strands when he said, 'The key challenge for good corporate governance is to seek an appropriate balance between enterprise (performance) and constraints (conformance) which takes into account the expectations of stakeholders for reasonable capital growth/ service provision and the responsibility concerning the interests of other stakeholders of the organization' (www.worldbank.org).

As *Control Objectives for HR* (op cit) points out, this means corporate governance concerns among other things risk management, internal controls, reporting, value delivery and compliance. HR governance can take just these things from corporate governance and the balancing of stakeholder interests, described by Cadbury and Wolfensohn, and apply them in the narrower sphere of HR functional organization and decision making. Including, therefore, the corporate governance viewpoint, widens the concept of HR governance beyond merely functional management for business ends to take in more of a corporate social responsibility perspective.

This is the approach taken by Swiss consultant Marcel Oertig (2009). His objectives of HR governance are:

- the alignment of HR with the normative and strategic objectives of the company
- the maintenance of social and ethical principles (ethical compliance)
- compliance with legal and financial requirements (regulatory compliance)
- the reduction of HR risks (e.g. of vacancies, of lack of skills, reputational)
- the provision of effective support in decision making in HR related issues to all management levels
- the clarification of roles and responsibilities of the HR functions at all levels
- the strategic control and measurement of the value added contribution of the HR function.

Why is it Important?

So there are number of different perspectives on HR governance that lead to a variety of definitions, but it cannot really be said that it is a new concept, certainly in the sense of managing the function. Organizations have always had processes on how to structure decision making, often reflected in formal documents on accountabilities and sign-off rights. This may not have been necessary in simple organizations, but even within one company once there are multiple locations or business streams then procedures of this sort would have become necessary. In the context of an international business the challenge of decision making structures grows significantly.

It is certainly likely that attention given by multinational companies to accountabilities and the development of decision protocols has grown for a number of reasons. Firstly, the demand for quality assurance has highlighted these issues. Secondly, external regulation, most notably in the Sarbanes-Oxley Act, but also by the international banking standard known as the Basel II (now III, the conditions laid down to borrow money, bid for contracts or supply goods) has affected organizational behaviour. Moreover, accountancy standards and market expectations also push companies to behave in particular ways. Thirdly, there has been a CSR desire to abide by voluntary codes such as issued by the ILO. Finally, there has been the direct impact of the organizational crises – economic and/or reputational – with a desire to avoid future system failure.

We will look at these sources of pressure to consider governance structures in turn.

The drive towards quality assurance and the adoption of standards like ISO 9001 and lean processes like six sigma has touched a wide variety of organizations from manufacturing, with the need to ensure safety and continuity of production, through IT companies, needing formally to document processes, to service suppliers getting admittance to procurement frameworks. These sorts of QA procedures in the HR domain try to establish well-defined policies and procedures and remove ambiguity over how they can be changed and by whom.

As to regulation, it arose originally because with the move away from the 'my word is my bond' way of doing business to open markets it was obvious that some controls were required to manage behaviour or define responsibilities of business executives. Various scandals led to legislation such as the Sarbanes-Oxley Act of 2002. Known colloquially as SOX, it applies to all US public companies and requires among other things that senior executives take individual personal and legal responsibility for the accuracy and completeness of corporate financial reports, which were themselves extended to a wider range of financial transactions. The Act further requires internal controls to be established to ensure the accuracy of financial reports and disclosures and timely reporting of material changes in financial circumstances. Thus, there is a greater need than before for firms operating in the USA at least to develop standard mechanisms for data management and reporting. SOX regulation has caused some companies to hardwire their financial control function such that it now reports directly to the centre, and not via local business unit leaders as before. In finance and accounting circles, 'control' has become very much the order of the day. Whilst the effect might at first sight not be so dramatic in HR, there is in fact a growing need for oversight of SOX compliance from the people perspective.

Another source of influence on global organization behaviour is the International Labour Organization. It maintains and develops a system of international labour standards 'aimed at promoting opportunities for women and men to obtain decent and productive work, in conditions of freedom, equity, security and dignity' (ILO Website). The standards are legal instruments that set out basic principles and rights at work. They appear either as *conventions*, which are legally binding international treaties when ratified by member states, or *recommendations*, which act as non-binding guidelines. Through these means there are also requirements that organizations have to meet in some countries that have embraced the ILO standards, regarding the treatment of labour (relating to wages, work conditions and discrimination), collective bargaining, 'freedom of association', training, employment security, etc.

Not surprisingly, these sorts of standards are especially relevant in developing countries, but also apply in some first world locations to firms supplying goods and services to the public sector or to other companies with firm ethical principles.

Corporate governance has again moved to centre stage with the financial services collapse of 2008. In some companies this process has happened earlier due to a business crisis, the origin of which has varied but with a common characteristic of impacting on organizational reputation. It is a salutary thought that currently (early 2011) there are 42 former CEOs in prison in the USA incarcerated for corporate crimes. Governance is an important issue when questions are being asked about how companies put themselves in such exposed positions.

In the UK a revised Corporate Governance code was introduced by the Financial Reporting Council for quoted companies in mid-2010. The code set out principles relating to the role and effectiveness of boards; it encouraged chairs to report personally in annual reports how these principles have been applied, and advised that 'the board should undertake a formal and rigorous annual evaluation of its own performance and that of its committee and of individual directors', setting out how this has been done in the annual report. The code also includes a new provision that 'evaluation of the board of FTSE 350 companies should be externally facilitated at least every three years'. It stresses that achieving a high-performing board is 'a challenge that should not be underrated' as 'to run a corporate board successfully is extremely demanding', depending on factors such as good leadership by the chair and 'the frankness and openness of mind with which issues are discussed'.

Interest in HR governance also seems to stem from the consequences of the recession (especially given its length and depth) with the failures in risk management that preceded it in some companies. Organizations are now trying to put right what they saw as having gone wrong in the build-up to the Crash or the crisis. For some, there was insufficient challenge both to leaders or experts that, if it did not lead to the collapse, then certainly made it worse. In others, the finger is pointed at leadership development: how did we produce executives who created such cultures? This mirrors a similar response to past business scandals and safety or environmental disasters. The requirement is therefore seen to be to ensure the possibility of challenge in governance processes. This may be done informally by the insistent reference to values or by a structural change to facilitate a more open debate about options.

> A UK manufacturing company is addressing this question by starting a project which would improve the level and quality of challenge within the company. It already has a process that outlines an opportunity for challenge, which could include testing assumptions, testing what data had been used, testing what inferences had been drawn from that data and testing what conclusions and decisions had been based on those inferences.

Some organizations are of the opinion that there was over-control by the centre in organizational decision making; that the CEO or the board was too powerful in the way the firm was run. So governance has to reflect a more devolved business model, where risk is not concentrated in a single person or a small group but is more widely distributed. This has the benefit that managers retake responsibility for their decisions but in a context of clearer accountability.

By contrast there are those organizations that take opposite view that there needs to be more control not less, especially in the context of global HR management. The organization feels it needs to avoid over-exposure to risks in what people are doing in its name across the globe. This is especially true in societies where nepotism and patronage are still practised, where policies are applied individually on the basis of position in the hierarchy or affected by personal connections.

Either way, organizations may in these circumstances be deliberately challenging the prevailing culture and using governance as the vehicle for so doing. However, as the new governance model emerges there may be real tensions over where in any particular case control sits and how much it needs to be specified in full. In organisations where the corporate centre is trying to (re)assert control there may be legitimate suspicions that HR is 'gold plating' external regulatory guidelines or accruing more central power than is actually required, perhaps in good faith, but also perhaps to fulfil functional ambitions.

Another effect of the Crash has been to push organizations to be more transparent in their decision making and, in some cases, in the outcomes. Thus institutional processes like remuneration committees and succession planning bodies are being reviewed to check that they are fit for purpose. The pressure for openness is leading to even greater disclosure of remuneration levels and awards. This is a challenging issue for international companies because the western world's reaction to the recession, following the lead of the public sector, is to put more information into the public domain: an approach that would not necessarily find favour in other parts of the world.

Shell's recent interest in governance comes from the reserves crisis of 2004 that led to the resignation of the Chief Executive. The fall-out from this led to a restructuring of the company and a rebalancing between operating company powers and that of the corporate centre. Greater central power and the new business organization streamlined decision making, but there was investment, too, in developing a different sort of culture. People had to be accountable for their actions within their responsibility. It was no longer possible 'to hide behind the matrix' as an excuse for failure. These events acted as a catalyst for a revamp of HR.

Siemens, too, had a scandal that entered the news pages in late 2006 over the use of bribes to win business. It, too, changed its Chief Executive and simplified its organizational structure by concentrating power in fewer hands. At the same time, it changed its business proposition emphasizing the 'one company' message and a single brand.

To deal with these challenges, HR governance can appear in a number of forms:

- decision making governance – concerning authority to make decisions
- process management governance – determining who owns the process
- internal stakeholder governance – the use of institutional arrangements to demonstrate due process and ensure that rules are adhered to
- response to external governance requirements – that could be in relation to regulatory bodies, especially in the financial services sector the need to demonstrate competence and good management processes, or to satisfying the needs of wider interest groups.

What Does it Seek to Achieve?

Against this background of definitions and causes, what are the objectives that HR governance is seeking to meet? Again there are a number of strands to these goals that relate to either internal or external pressure, or both.

- **Controlling against risk** – this can have a number of dimensions:
  - complying with external regulation – organizations do not want to fall foul of regulators: it can be expensive in fines and in any consequential business loss
  - protecting organizational reputation – especially where news travels fast, organizations need to be diligent in stopping incidents escalating
  - limiting exposure to ill-considered decision making – this might involve preventing devolved power bases exercising their freedom in a way that is damaging to the whole
  - making the decision process more explicit such that accountabilities are more transparent and better defined.
  - 'stress testing' the organization against extreme business scenarios to decide how much power can be safely delegated to protect against these extreme circumstances if they ever came about.
- **Promoting values** – this can also be to limit non-compliance but also positively to drive the organization on a particular dimension.

- **Ensuring consistency** – as David Cushen (VP HR Planning, Process and Integration at Shell) puts it: 'We want internal equity in the way people are treated in the organization. We want to remove unnecessary and unjustified variation in people management.'
- **Pulling the organization together** – especially if there are fissiparous tendencies, governance may be important to integrate organizational activities and negate the effects of decentralized power.
- **Harmonization** – especially following mergers and acquisitions, organizations want common HR arrangements.
- **Reducing duplication** – one of RBS's governance project aims was to make policy application easier by codifying and simplifying the rules and this also had the effect of de-duplicating material.
- **Prioritizing functional spending** – making decisions about how to use limited funds
- **Reducing functional costs** – especially with the recession, HR has had to find ways of cutting its own expenditure. This can come from standardization and automation.
- **Making the HR structure work** – The three legged HR structure can achieve higher efficiency than a distributed service delivery model through the economies of scale benefits of shared services and centres of expertise, but it will not work without
  - direction and then management of the change to structures, systems and processes needs
  - making sure shared services, centres of expertise and business partners work effectively in harness
  - deciding how to standardize processes, policies and practices. As Andre Lamberty of ABB says: 'The change only works if you have full harmonization of processes.'

It feels to us that to achieve these aims, global organizations (and those aspiring to be global) have for these reasons chosen, in Raisch and Birkenshaw's terms, the efficiency over the flexibility aim. The current organizational emphasis is on how the HR centre controls the activities of HR units distributed round the world and limits the freedom of managers to manage in the way they see fit. This could have been expressed more neutrally than 'control'. We could have said how does the corporate centre 'structure' or 'manage' decision making, or as Oertig puts it, 'the clarification of central and decentralized control' (2009), but in fact most of the organizations we have dealt with are seeking something more than a degree of oversight over what operating companies or business units HR teams are doing.

How this control is exercised and the topics over which it is applied may vary. For example, especially in financial services, HR is intervening in manager decision making on sensitive topics (for example, performance bonuses). This is despite the fact that most HR functions have spent the last 15 years trying to get away from the 'prop and cop' label to describe their relationship to line management. The cost, reputation and regulatory pressures are such that HR has adopted a new stance.

What Does it Cover?

What is covered under the HR governance heading will be determined by its aims. This means that at BASF there is the description of global principles that would add value across the group, say in the manner of variable pay or the handling of international transfers. By contrast, other companies like Shell and SAP would be more detailed in their content. In the box below is Siemens list of principles to give an idea of what might be the scope. However, it is not always clear whether we are seeing the normal HR leadership meetings discussing policies around talent management, succession planning processes, the brand and employee value proposition, etc., as they have always done, or a specifically formed HR governance process. Some content may be new or being considered in a new context (like global employee surveys referred to in Chapter 5), but the emphasis of governance at present seems to be on the management and control of functional change.

Siemens has set a number of 'principles' over what will be determined corporately:

- talent acquisition and branding (not the operational tasks but standards and common processes including IT application)
- global sourcing (only for senior positions) but common succession planning process
- HR and people strategy development
- performance management (and use of common tools – rating, 360 degree, etc.)
- certain aspects of compensation (common for senior managers; same grade structure – values are for the local market; and the variable versus base pay mix including variation for different groups)
- market position for benefits and pension guidelines with change requiring Management Board sign-off
- learning – global programmes (both management and functional)
- HR performance and reporting (definition of KPIs, comparison on cost/quality internally and externally (through Saratoga) to facilitate learning and improvement rather than as a stick to beat people with
- the running of the HR function
    - its strategy, organizational structure, HR talent development
    - role in workforce planning
    - its role in mergers and acquisitions
    - change management tools and structures (for use within HR and outside it).

As we have described earlier, much of the impetus for the recent establishment of HR governance structures is the management of HR transformation, so it is not surprising that each of the main elements of change (automation, standardization and consolidation) feature in the content of HR governance decision making covering design questions through the construction of the HR service delivery model to implementation and operation.

The emerging global HR service delivery model will be considered in the next chapter, but here we note that the key features in governance reflecting the drive for standardization and automation, and the continuous improvement of the service delivery model, include:

- **Harmonization** of people management principles, policies and practices to ensure the whole organization operates consistently and efficiently.
- **Process optimization** to improve quality and speed and to reduce costs, encourages the use of common tools and the wish for common outcomes.
- **The need for quality data globally** to both judge HR functional performance and to identify areas where there are people management problems.
- **The need for data integration** Again most organizations would see benefit in having an integrated data system, but this is much trickier to deliver in the international than local context. Just think of factoring in all the different legal and tax requirements, together with the various pay mechanisms and you get an idea of the obstacles faced. This is why surveys show that global payroll and records systems are not that common. Nevertheless, many multinational companies believe that the extra investment is worth it in being able to provide management information that accurately combines personal and remuneration data across the whole firm.
- **The requirement to reduce the number of transactions** through both business process reengineering, the creative use of intranets and manager/employee self-service. This is essential if a global service delivery model is going to operate successfully. In the old days of paper, a change of address, bank account or marital status would have to go in the internal post to Personnel where staff would enter the data into their computer. Imagine trying to do that in a Shell or SAP where there are just three services centres worldwide. Things being lost in the post would be a constant source of mutual irritation.
- **Using technology as a binding mechanism** Through the intranet, global firms can communicate the brand, the organizational values, the culture, as well as the HR information. This is of course true in a national organization, but for a global firm it helps reach places that the corporate centre might find hard otherwise to reach. It keeps everyone on message in a situation where it is not easy to convey the corporate purpose, theme or instruction.

There also other aspects of people management that of late are being managed in a fresh way because of the changed regulatory and public relations climate. So areas where the organization is exposed to risk will get particular attention, for example:

- **Oversight of the method of determining executive bonuses** and, in some cases, approving the bonus decisions. The Hay Group (2010) reports increasing centralization of broader reward policies to ensure the correct business focus, contain costs and more effectively manage risk.
- **Satisfaction of regulatory requirements** This applies to a surprisingly large number of organizations that have to meet various stipulations that cover a range from health and safety rules, through training and succession activities, to employment law.
- **Leadership values** This aims to get leadership behaviour in line with corporate values to minimize the risk of deviant behaviour that might have deleterious consequences for the organization, as the previous Shell example showed.

These governance objectives may, as we saw earlier, sit alongside global talent management programmes that may need the articulation of shared principles and the definition of common processes, or alongside the development of the brand or EVP.

In considering the development of talent management at Plan International, Jean-Pierre Djokpe, Regional People and Culture Partner in the West African Regional Office in Senegal, suggested: 'We should review all policies and procedures in Plan and choose the best ones to apply across the organization. Harmonization of talent polices will facilitate the movement of people from one country to another which will enhance organizational diversity and enhance individual career experience.'

Implementing HR Governance

In implementing HR governance, firstly, organizations have to think through by what process it will be organized: will formal structures be used? Next, when and how does the organization create the HR governance decision making process? This can be done at the outset so that it can run the sort of process it wants for the future; or the HR governance body can be designed after the organization has made the key HR transformation decisions. There is also the implicit question of what model, or style, of decision making is used.

Thirdly, there is the question of how these bodies operate once the style of management is established and how change is managed. Is it a top down push with the corporate centre imposing its vision, or a more collaborative, bottom up creation?

Next, who is going to implement governance decisions: who are the agents of any formal structures created?

Finally, how is the control and governance framework going to be monitored, assured and tested?

HOW IS IT ORGANIZED?

The theory

Mercer's 2003 paper on HR governance talks approvingly of 'creating an explicit structure for HR governance is a way to enhance decision making using the diverse insights and talents of the organization's most experienced professionals to think, decide, and respond'. The clearly preferred model is a 'council' with a 'charter' that 'articulates the council's areas of focus based on strategic, operational, and functional accountabilities. The charter may also address roles, meeting structures, and protocols'.

The question of content for the decision making bodies is naturally of significance to their operation. They could be limited to an advisory role with decisions taken elsewhere. They could be institutions with oversight and performance monitoring responsibilities, which might be a low-key affair except when problems or risks are identified. The approach may vary with the content. Alternatively, these could be bodies that are actively involved in running the function, making decisions about the allocation of resources, prioritizing activities, supporting the integration of HR's work or dealing with differences of focus between the various players. Which approach is chosen says a lot about how the HR Director wants to run the function or, in some cases, is able to run the function.

Decision making processes can be organized to reflect:

- HR roles, and here the question is whether this is organized around business partners and/or experts
- business unit responsibilities
- geographic responsibilities
- work area within HR (e.g. Mergers and Acquisitions or HR IT systems).

Which form of grouping is chosen again reveals where the power lies, though many organizations may try to balance different interests. So if the decision making body is dominated by subject matter expertise then it can be assumed that the corporate centre has control over policy formulation. Conversely, if the business units or locations are predominant, one might assume that power is more widely distributed but more in the hands of the operating units.

In line with their conception of how HR governance should operate, Mercer (2003) has produced a neat illustration of how the allocation of processes can be done based on an example from a pharmaceutical company (Figure 7.1).

The main message for us is in a) the distinction between global, regional and local and b) whether we are talking about principles, processes or procedures. However, we would add systems to the latter list and would make the definition of 'processes' much more open since saying they should be 'common' answers the question before it is posed.

Balancing global (G), regional (R), and local (L) objectives to design and operate a global performance management program

Employee development	Succession planning		Leadership development	
	Principle	Process	Policy	Procedure
Leadership development	G	G		
Management development			L	L
Management behavioral evaluations/assessments	G L		R L	L
Non management training and development design		L	L	L
Performance management process	G	G	L	
Individual coaching of management	L	L		

Principles: Central beliefs that articulate boundaries for global practices

Processes: Activities done in a common way with a standard set of tools

Policies: Descriptions of measurable boundaries with consequences for noncompliance

Procedures: Detailed, task-level descriptions of expected work processes

Source: Mercer, 2003

Figure 7.1   Mercer's allocation of governance processes

The activities will also have to be more granular than in Figure 7.1 to be successfully allocated to the point of decision making. Performance management, for example, needs to be broken down into subcategories. Thus, there can a principle of all staff having a performance appraisal, before one considers the policy of having a reward led appraisal (i.e. to drive a pay increase or bonus) or development led (e.g. response to competency shortfalls) and a decision has to be made on whether there is one mechanism combining both elements or separate mechanisms. Then the process has to be considered. Which of its numerous elements – objective setting, assessing performance, giving feedback on performance, assessing skills and competencies, assessing potential, identifying training needs, etc. – need to be common? Similarly, there are a number of dimensions to the procedures around the forms, data management, sign-offs, etc. and organizations have to decide what level of granularity is necessary to make the right decisions in the right places. This will especially apply to policies and processes. There are likely to be few principles and many detailed procedures.

The practice

What research that has been done suggests that though a majority of organizations have some form of governance body, a minority of international organizations have governance bodies that cover operations across the world. In a Hewitt survey (of what are probably the more 'progressive' companies) 39 per cent had such global bodies compared with 80 per cent applying to narrower geographies. Where they did have governance bodies, they tended to be in the form of Councils (Hewitt, 2009).

In our more selective research there was variation in how governance was exercised. The different models that emerged from our interviews comprised normal executive decision making through to more explicit governance structures. They reflect the different ways in which power is distributed within the organizations concerned and this is shown in terms of decision making body membership, role, authority and content and how much they recognize various stakeholder interests. All the examples of governance structures we came across had some form of representation of business units or functions (usually via the HR business partner) and some included a specific geographic component.

A number of decision making bodies have a single tier structure; others operate two tiers. The latter generally allow the tighter group to make the key decisions – easier when there is a smaller number of participants – with consultation of a wider population.

- SAP has a fairly tight oversight group comprising the business partners responsible for main business units, the heads of the centres of expertise (learning and development and total rewards) and the Chief Operating Officer, along with the HR Director.
- BASF has a global council as a decision body for global topics, with the corporate HR function, HR heads of the four regions (North America, South America, Asia Pacific and Europe) and the head of HR governance plus representatives of the HR business partners who are assigned to the operating divisions.
- Siemens has an HR board that is formed of eight people plus the Executive Vice President HR (who is also a member of the Managing Board of Siemens AG globally) – the three meta cluster heads (Americas, Asia/Pacific and Germany/EMEA), three industry sector HR heads (Industry, Energy and Healthcare), as well as the head of HR

for the globally organized Cross Sector Businesses and Services and the head of HR strategic development and leadership.

- Shell has an HR executive that operates as its governance authority. It comprises the five representatives of the business and corporate functions, the three functional process executives (Remuneration and Benefits; Learning, Organizational Effectiveness and Diversity and Inclusiveness; and Talent and Development) and the head of HR Strategy and Internal Communications. (The shared services operation reports in through the EVP Remuneration & Benefits.)

Most of the governance bodies meet regularly but not necessarily frequently. Contrast this with Henkel that has an HR IT 'control board' that meets twice per week to respond to change requirement requests from business units and locations.

Then there is the question of whether the governance is carried out at a global level, as in SAP or Shell, or at a regional level. Take Canon: its HR decision making is increasingly carried out at regional level, having moved from being very largely country based. There seems to be no current appetite to move to a global model. And within the regional model, there are differences in practice: the USA dominates the Americas region, China and India dominate Asia Pacific (excluding Japan), whereas Europe has a much wider distribution of power.

As we said earlier, there are companies that do not have specific HR governance bodies that oversee the service delivery model or standardization. This seems to be especially true of the Asian owned companies that we spoke to. They appear to be run on more decentralized lines. Canon Europe relies on the normal HR directors' forum to discuss any issues that arise in managing cross-national issues, but in the context of the extent of harmonization having been decided. HPH and JWS Steel both operate with very devolved HR responsibilities and there is no global forum pulling them together.

Governance bodies are obviously also absent from organizations that do not see governance as something new and different. Their existing fora seem to them to be sufficient. They achieve something of the same objectives, arguably in a less transparent and purposeful manner, in another way. One HR leader reflecting upon this point said that one of his colleagues in HR Operations plays this role in an informal style, using his personality and experience to bring people together and seek further performance improvement. The counter-argument given by another HR leader was that whilst there is still complexity to manage, at least his organization had created structures to help manage that complexity. The position he advanced was that, without some form of governance body, how do you resolve the tensions between the parts of function, especially in the Ulrich model? A Canadian company we spoke to, for example, told us of early conflicts in its HR transformation between centres of expertise and business partners over power and status. The position had improved, but who has the responsibility in any given situation has to be resolved by discussion between the parties on a case-by-case basis.

ESTABLISHING GOVERNANCE BODIES

Having decided whether or not to have a formal governance body, there are then questions for organizations about how governance processes are formed. In other words, how have organizations gone about determining the most suitable decision making process such as the ones we described above and what sort of operating philosophy has it instigated?

Obviously there is a degree of variation especially between very limited, if any, consultation that the corporate centre undertook to a form of negotiation between stakeholders, but where it is obvious where the power sits (centrally, at business unit/function, location), through to situations where the model evolved through discussion without pre-set ideas.

It might be helpful at the outset, therefore, to plot the way we have seen HR governance formed along a spectrum thus:

Dirigiste centrally driven	Negotiated openly but with power at the centre	Negotiated openly but with power at the business unit/function/location	Emergent, exploratory and implicit

Reading the likes of Mercer or applying a client based Hewitt definition (the 'act of effectively managing the HR function based on *jointly agreed rules and norms* to enable the function to meet its objectives'), you would assume that the decision making model for making these choices would be inclusive and consensual – very much to the right of the spectrum. The consultants' preference for inclusivity is exemplified by emphasis on the architecture of decision making through formal joint bodies. The expectation would be that these would be set up through a process of stakeholder involvement.

The continuum in practice

It may be that our perspective reflects the choice of organizations we spoke to, but in the construction and indeed operation of governance models, we saw a stronger pull towards the left end of our spectrum. Whilst there is nothing wrong at all proposing having formal decision making processes that draw in views from across the organization, nor that decentralizing tendencies would push organizations in this direction, but what we have in fact more often seen is the corporate centre being quite dirigiste in its centralizing of decision making. There may have been the form of consultation or even negotiation but without the substance. This has applied to the terms of HR transformation (the service delivery model, standardization and automation), employment and reward policies, the brand and employee value proposition, and, perhaps in fewer cases, the identification and development of talent.

This bold statement has to be tempered somewhat. As Figure 7.2 indicates, there are a number of factors influencing the form of governance. Certainly, it is affected by sector and business positioning, reflected in the nature of the brand – whether a single, unvarying proposition or a more variegated one. The cultural heritage of the firm may play a part, although business pressures may erode this. Although it should not be overemphasized, the governance approach may be a consequence of country of origin. For example, US companies have had a long tradition of managing their global operations from their HQ and therefore governance structures, if they are acknowledged at all, will be based on central power. What might also be true, and is more interesting, is that as organizations become more global they tend in their choice of running their organization towards a centralizing mode of operation. We will look at the evidence from a number of the organizations we have researched.

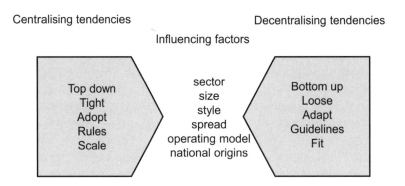

Figure 7.2 Factors influencing the governance model

Continental European companies tend to be more participative, to the right of the continuum, i.e. more inclusive and consensual in setting up (and indeed running) these bodies. This reflects an organizational culture the origins of which lie in attitudes to corporate ownership and management that come from national preferences based on the 'stakeholder' governance theory. In Germany and many other European countries there is a tradition of consensual decision making and a political infrastructure that balances interests – the relationship between the Länder and the Bundestaag is a government example and the supervisory board and the executive board is a corporate illustration.

However, even in continental European companies decision making is moving in the centralizing direction, though sometimes slowly and in tune once again with their organizational culture and business model. Some multinational companies have successfully moved away from the consensual approach to the Anglo-Saxon manner, but others have tried to adjust and failed. This may be because the power balance is such that the executive's sway does not hold, or that locations/business units still exercise a veto, or the institutional arrangements (especially the nature of the legal structure, often post merger) prevent radical change. This might mean rather than face head-on any opposition from locations or business units to a process of centralization, the corporate centre proceeds slowly, testing reaction to its ideas as it goes along. It gets agreement to any joint or common processes on a case-by-case basis. This may be either an explicit or 'emergent' strategy, depending upon how clear the corporate centre is in its goals and how covert it feels it has to be to meet them.

For example, at Evonik, an industrial group operating in over 100 countries with over 41,000 employees, there is a real debate between the corporate centre and operating units. Evonik faces a number of challenges in determining the optimal form of HR governance. The company was formed out of a merger of several firms operating in the fields of energy, property and chemicals. The merger has not resulted in the creation of a single company: instead, a number of legal entities remain. Moreover, power is widely distributed, with site, business unit, regions and legal entities each having their own power base. Reporting lines are consequently complex, including for HR; its shared services operation reporting not to the HR director but into a Services GmbH. Traditional ways of doing things are well established and hard to change. The management style within the HR community is collaborative and decision making consensual.

Against this background, decision making has to be participative recognizing the interests of the different stakeholders. This affects the speed at which restructuring function, process mapping and standardization can be achieved. All these inter-linked decisions have to be agreed by the key parties. The aim is to build a trustful culture and a common HR philosophy, but to date success in harmonization has been achieved less through the exercise of formal authority and more by exploiting personal relationships.

The Metro Group is a German based retailer with 2,100 outlets in 33 countries in Europe, Africa and Asia employing around 300,000 employees. Its business philosophy, as articulated in its SHAPE programme announced in January 2009 and applying to its new business structure, is 'as decentrally as possible, as centrally as necessary'. The aim is to 'give employees more freedom to conduct operational business and will enable the sales divisions to address the ever-changing needs of their customers in a flexible, fast and autonomous way. The areas that are critical to the financial management and the controlling of the Group will be increasingly centralised'. In this context, because the company sees the benefits to be obtained from economies of scale and the negative performance consequences of inconsistency and, moreover, because it faced pressure from its auditors for data alignment, in the biggest part of the company (Metro Cash and Carry) the HR function is trying to exercise greater functional leadership. Through its governance processes, it is aiming to effect some degree of standardization, particularly in HR IT systems, as we will describe in greater detail in Chapter 8.

Siemens is an example of a company that has moved further along the governance spectrum. Nevertheless, it is explicitly seeking a 'middle way' between the two polar opposites on the centralized/decentralized continuum – the American central HQ model where HR is the same around the world, and the former Siemens model where each country was different in the way things were done. Given its historical background this still represents a shift towards greater corporately determined standardization and control. It was recognized, however, that 190 organizations doing things differently was expensive and time consuming, especially because much of the variation was unnecessary.

Shell, with its strong Dutch heritage and previously decentralized power structure, still does not believe it is as centralized as its US competitors, but over the last six years it has moved closer to them in terms of cost control and a common global approach to people management. Whilst there will continue to be flexibilities in the model – given that the company will increasingly operate in a world of complex JV operations –the flexibilities will be set against a core of increasingly standardized processes delivered with efficiency and effectiveness via the service centre model and leveraging the Shell People (SAP Human Capital Management software) infrastructure. The way it set up its decision making structure and the manner in which it will function, is based on a clear vision on the form of coordinated central control, even if it might have arrived at this decision through a collective choice by the HR top team.

The reason for the change is that HR is following the business imperative since 2004 of pulling power back to the centre. The fact is that corporate direction and standardization suit companies like Shell, with a long record of integration of HR policies and practices, more than a Unilever or Philips, partly because the management of its substantial expatriate population requires significant policy harmonization. Moreover, Garmt Louw argues that this approach was simpler to introduce in Shell because the capital intensive not labour intensive nature of its activities allows more investment in HR; the 'sense of national identity is relatively low'; and it is no longer run by functional/business 'barons' or by county big shots.

SAP built its previous HR governance model over the period 2009–2011 in a consensual manner, as befits its German origins and the aim to ensure support from the HR community, to grow a sense of 'ownership'. In particular, together with business representatives, a cross-section of HR leaders defined the current status of the 'HR Guiding Principles' on a series of continua (tight vs loose, risk tolerant or averse, highly or loosely coordinated) and to the 'to be' aims. This enabled agreement to be reached on the future decision making model. However, the direction of travel was to pull power from the locations towards the global centre and then manage the function from the HR leadership team.

ABB was also a very decentralized company, but because its wish to globalize was hindered by this devolved approach, it had to change. For example, in Switzerland alone there were eight different SAP Human Capital Management systems. Moreover, the need to obtain sustainable cost savings in overheads necessitated the reduction of the current complexity and duplication of processes and systems in the corporate functions. It now has a single HRIS per country and has classified its processes into a) local b) optionally common and c) mandatory and global.

Whilst a more dirigiste approach to establishing governance is the commoner in our experience, there are examples to the contrary. The way Vodafone set up its HR architecture is at the centre of the spectrum shown. As the boxed example illustrates, it managed the allocation of activities by setting up an involving process bringing together HR stakeholders from across the company but steered from the centre.

Vodafone moved towards common systems, common processes and a similar operating model as part of an approach to deliver a consistent HR service globally. The advantage from a Vodafone corporate perspective was that management information systems and terminology became the same company-wide. This allowed a more effective internal benchmarking to take place from which the performance of people management can be judged.

Vodafone had a vision of a 'Global HR Process Architecture'. This took seven work areas (such as learning and development or reward and recognition) and broke them down into a number of sub-processes. Through a joint process between corporate HR and operating company HR managers it was then defined whether the process was to be standardized across the Group (such as managing international assignments) or wholly locally designed (such as recognition schemes) (Reilly et al., 2007).

RBS's review of policies under a governance banner was more modest but it deliberately involved corporate and local HR representatives in its working party and this group agreed the harmonized policy set that would apply company-wide. In its review of governance RBS acknowledged that it is a collection of different businesses, each with its own needs. The corporate centre may have expertise but it values sectoral knowledge. It will require consistency within a business unit but does not require it across business units.

If we move outside Europe there are other examples of more consensual decision making.

Indian multinational companies also have a tendency towards decentralization and allowing a lot of local freedom to act. This is seen in the way for example Tata behaves within its original structure but also to its acquired businesses like Jaguar Rover or Tetley Tea. Satish Pradhan, Executive Vice President in Group HR, says that the centre's role has been described as 'minimalist' and he agrees that it is 'not intrusive'. He believes that the HR operating model is 'persuasive, inclusive and enabling. It's about unifying, not uniformity. It's about frameworks, not specifics' (Chubb, 2008).

HPH and JSW Steel are companies that through their devolved approach to corporate management recognize their multi function/product nature and varied presence of the firm. The key word used in conversations with them was to 'empower' the local HR teams and to accept the very different cultural norms of the local populations. HPH has a more varied profile of business locations than JSW's large manufacturing sites, but its ports operate within broad policy principles and frameworks rather than detailed rules. There is little or no control of the country HR teams at large ports such as Felixstowe, Rotterdam and Busan in Korea. However, it should be noted that even in as decentralized a company as HPH the potential financial savings from rationalizing certain activities on a global basis has started to appear as a business imperative, as a response to economic recession in certain parts of the world. For example, the company is in the process of developing a global HRIS to help connect information (subject to data protection issues) and capture key information on top talent.

Japanese companies tend to approach their HQ/operating company relationships in a different way to the Anglo-American model. They take a balanced view of subsidiary performance with attention given more to their future potential for growth than their past performance, as Canon Europe, for example, told us. It is not under instruction from the Japanese HQ to follow this route or that, especially not to apply a common approach to HR service delivery: as Massimo Macarti says, 'I don't receive such e-mails from Japan'. There are Japanese advisers from the corporate centre to be found in London, but these operate in a low-key manner, certainly not a dictatorial one. They listen rather than talk. According to Macarti they are not 'corporate evangelists'. So he was able to choose to achieve standardization through consensus. The aim was to balance, on the one hand, business alignment and consistency in the context of regional management's pressure to harmonize with, on the other hand, responsiveness to local conditions, thereby allowing the 'special things a country [operation] must do' to meet its needs. Rather like Siemens, Massimo Macarti is all too aware that there are 'risks in going too far in either direction'. He felt that he and his fellow country based HR directors managed an open and honest debate about what to harmonize, leading to a well-constructed conclusion. Learning and development proved to be the trickiest subject to gain agreement on, with a tension between local attachment to their own programmes and Massimo Macarti's doubts about their ROI.

Besides differences in the governance model and nature of control that come from organizations' national origins, there are differences by sector and stage of development.

Fast moving consumer goods companies are more likely to emphasize the flexibility hand of Raisch and Birkinshaw's ambidextrous organization (2008). They need the speed to adjust to changing circumstances more than manufacturing or those operating in the primary sector of the economy. In the latter, where the corporate centre acts to set HR standards and requires business units and locations to abide by them, it is likely to be in tune with the way the business is generally run.

As to the stage of company development, the argument is similar. Once organizations reach a certain level of maturity they may be prepared to put in place a proper HR governance structure. It will create processes and procedures that aim to surface risks and liabilities. It will introduce formal risk registers and mechanisms to authorize change or investment (e.g. in pension funds). These sorts of controls would be an anathema for those in their entrepreneurial growth phase. Like FMCG companies they want speed and flexibility but in their case the primary driver may be the requirement for creativity and innovation.

For organizations going global there is even more pressure for systemization so that 'we are all on the same page' unless, like Tata or other holding company structures, this makes little sense. Sitting in the corporate centre of an integrated company it seems only natural to minimize risk of maverick behaviour by introducing a corporate set of operating principles and a shared culture, and to save money through having common systems, processes and then service delivery models. As the HR director of a global UK organization told us: 'We are one company. We have one set of customers. We have only one set of competitors. So why wouldn't we operate in exactly the same way across the whole firm?'

THE MANAGEMENT OF HR GOVERNANCE

The next question is how decisions are taken within these structures, which of necessity overlaps with their formation, and to the absence or presence of formal bodies, but even where the latter are in place there are still choices to be made in the way decisions are implemented. Here the role of the corporate centre is critical. It could see itself as an enabling body, providing frameworks and guidelines to assist operational units settle their affairs. Its approach could be to determine the 'what' the organization should be doing but leave business units and locations free to determine the 'how' they implement. More actively, the corporate centre could facilitate operational units' choices in deciding how to operate the HR model – e.g. how far and how fast to drive towards a global service delivery model or a common talent management approach. Finally, it could dictate to business units and locations how they operate.

So there is a continuum on how decisions are made, which goes like this:

The corporate centre determines both the nature of the policy or practice and how it will be implemented	Specified requirements on policies and practices, with the corporate centre helping their implementation	Statements of requirements made by the corporate centre in broad terms but allowing scope for operating companies to decide on how they implement	Enabling frameworks and principles, with operating companies free to choose their approach

One can illustrate this range of options through considering the subject of performance management.

The corporate centre determines the format of the performance management policy and ensures that it is implemented to a common standard and timetable across the world	A corporate requirement that operating companies must have a performance management practice, with the corporate centre helping their choice of process (with the inevitable consequence that there is convergence towards a single system)	A corporate requirement that operating companies must have a performance management practice but its nature is left to operating companies to decide	A corporate statement that performance management is a good idea which operating companies might wish to adopt

This is not likely to produce a black and white answer because different policies/practices may elicit different organizational responses, and the way decisions are made is also affected by the question of to whom they apply.

The continuum in practice

Given that the main driver for a new HR service delivery model (with its associated standardization, automation and consolidation) is to reduce cost by the de-duplication of systems, processes and policies, it is not surprising that the main approach we have seen is to set a standard method and then require compliance to it. As Joe Plavetic at Unilever explained it, the corporate centre has had to practise 'tough love' in resisting special pleading and assert the harmonizing demands of the centre in the areas in which global common processes are non-negotiable. Companies in this environment see it as a weakness to have multiple performance appraisal processes, a plethora of recruitment suppliers or various different IT solutions. So the aim is to reduce variety in policy and practice as much as possible and to choose suppliers, models and so on that can apply globally.

Likewise, at National Grid (Withers et al., 2010) there is a strategy of standardizing processes wherever possible and creating a global approach to policy, whilst allowing only some discretion in regional execution.

Although at Siemens decision making at the HR board is collegiate, with geography and business unit interests taken into account, its operating principle is that any issue within scope (content coverage is described on p. 213) will be decided at corporate and/ or meta cluster level and only if that is not possible will it move down to cluster level – smaller geographic configurations (e.g. North West Europe) – or country level.

According to Garmt Louw, the decision making process at Shell tends to be led by the (HR) functional EVPs. It is they who drive the agenda, leaving the HR business representatives to judge the impact of the proposed initiative or policy variation on their business or function. As Dave Cushen puts it, on HR policies and processes 'HR business partners now get their marching orders from the corporate process owners'.

In most of the organizations we looked at, processes involved movement of information both upwards and downwards. Typically, decision making was initiated at the corporate centre passed through the decision making body and out to the business units or locations. So a new HR policy or process would flow in this downward direction.

Sometimes this could be a draft document where feedback is sought from the locations or business units. Issues can be raised by locations or business units for consideration by the decision making body. These may be interpretations of policy, a wish to develop new services or, one of the key processes, requests to deviate from the standard policy or practice.

To formalize the assignment of roles, some organizations use the 'RACI' decision process categorization for the involved parties, thus:

- **Responsible** for the action or implementation of an activity
- **Accountable** for successful delivery
- **Consulted** prior to decision being taken or action made
- **Informed** of action or decision but no influence over either.

Figure 7.3 shows an example of how this might look.

SAP, for example, has applied this approach to defining the responsibilities for the main decision parties and key activities.

A different challenge occurs if in the more open and participatory decision making structures, conclusions are not reached. Or, if from the corporate centre's perspective progress is not being made because there is no consensus to move forward. In these situations, too, we have heard senior HR leaders having to exploit personal relationships to cause some movement to happen. However, relying on favours leaves the corporate centre very vulnerable to a change of mind or circumstances.

You might ask whether there cannot be an appeal to a higher authority to make decisions to unfreeze the logjam. This may be possible but the essence of the dilemma is precisely that the way the organization is structured or managed prevents, or limits, decisive decision making. So where leaders can cut through disagreement, probably there

Activity	HR Director	HR Executive team	Centre of expertise	Operational HR
business needs assessment				
HR budget planning				
HR budget management				
work prioritization				
policy design				
policy implementation				
service delivery				
risk/compliance management				
HR communications				
HR staff mgt. & development				
HR resource deployment				
HR IT strategy				

Responsible: for action/ implementation of activity. Consulted: to be consulted prior decision/ action. Accountable: ultimately accountable for success. Informed: one-way communication

Figure 7.3   A RACI process

are already effective decision making processes in place. It is where leaders can only work through consensus or where there are separate lines of authority, where the stasis is most likely to occur.

But one also see leaders in organizations become so exasperated by objection or fear the possibility of being interminably delayed by argument that they drive through change even where it is not the usual habit. For example, Siemens management decided that they would push through a new approach to performance management even without investing in training in its use and would require everybody to rigidly adhere to the rules. And this was done with a recognition that the solution was only 80 per cent right. Abbey National took a similar approach to changing its service delivery model. The latter company took the view that it was best to drop managers in at the deep end; in other words, not to spend much time preparing them for their new responsibilities but to find out the consequences afterwards. Training could then be targeted on real needs, not based on anticipated fears (Reilly, 1999).

Those wishing to make certain that the decisions of the governance bodies are carried out can exercise control through ensuring that all parts of HR report through to the corporate centre. This is especially important with respect to business partners who have the greatest opportunity to experiment and are the most exposed to going 'native' in upholding local interests against the centre. So, for example, in SAP all HR business partners wherever they sit in the world report into the centre. Similarly, at Shell, Siemens and HP country HR organizations and business partners report to the global HR organization. Unlike these companies, but in line with their governance approach, at each of JSW's plants there is a key HR head who very much holds the functional power in the company. A variation of this approach is to devolve HR governance responsibility to the business partners without requiring them to report to the HR director. In conjunction with the business unit director, they are then required to ensure proper control and compliance. This is the approach that RBS has chosen. It has the added advantage of making explicit the business unit's role in governance, rather it being something done unto it by the corporate centre.

Another related control mechanism is to retain corporate management of budgets and spending. Moreover, to avoid 'unnecessary' work generation, a resource allocation model is created that allocates money and people based on some form of prioritization mechanism. This can allow greater control over what goes on locally and ensure there is no conflict with global programmes. This means that only those projects, initiatives or changes to standard policies/processes that deliver real value to the organization will have resources committed to them. We reported in our last book the example of Coca-Cola's prioritization process.

Coca-Cola Enterprises uses a 'sieve' that selects out HR projects that satisfy five criteria:

1. contributes to business performance
2. promotes early delivery of business benefits
3. maximizes employee engagement
4. improves or simplifies people management activities
5. supports legal or regulatory compliance

(Brocket, 2004). Reproduced with permission (www.melcrum.com info@melcrum.com).

In researching this book, we have seen more explicit use of these prioritization models as a means of retaining corporate control not just over expenditure but also over divergence from corporate standards.

Thus, in SAP the HR leadership team manages a 'portfolio process' whereby it determines how many projects the company can afford to do per year given its people and financial resources. Those which are prioritized are those with a high level of value delivered to the organization and those where there is a compliance issue. So the HR Leadership Team divides projects into those that are mandatory, those with a 'hard' commitment, those with a 'soft' commitment and 'nice to have' (which will not happen in the current climate). Whilst the focus is naturally on global initiatives, attention is also given to proposed local ideas because they consume resources as well, or have important regulatory consequences.

Other organizations may have a less formal, more reactive, method of intervening in business decisions. They may 'call in' proposed business unit projects to check their cost–benefit.

Managing exceptions to the standard

As most people recognize, there are inevitable tensions between the various players representing different interest groups such as geography, business units and the corporate centre. Many of these stem from the different reporting lines, organizational challenges and goals. Perhaps the key question is whether these tensions are formally acknowledged and openly dealt with. One interviewee believes in his organization that there is 'open and transparent' discussion of any conflicts between interest groups. One demonstration of this approach is how exceptions are handled.

In Shell at least there is a formal process for dealing with requests for exceptions to the defined policies and processes: they come before the HR Executive meeting. If an operating company wants to take an initiative on an employee relations or other policy area (i.e. something broadly within their competence area) they would check with a regional person or process owner first. If a policy is already in place they would adopt that. If not, there would be confirmation that they could go ahead and develop a new one. This then might be used by other operating companies. Similarly, RBS operates its model on the principle that if the policy is agreed as common, local HR (including the business partner) must abide by it. If there is no defined approach, the business partner is free to decide on what best suits local circumstances.

Viewed from the perspective of operating companies in other companies, the formal processes can, instead, be seen as opaque or obstructive. Interviewees in this situation described how they have had to use informal channels to oil the wheels and obtain effective resolution of their problems. Indeed, one manager explained that, once again, it was necessary to develop personal relationships precisely to anticipate this need.

Of course, it may not be the process that is the hindrance from the business unit or location perspective. It can also simply be the outcome that is a problem. The process may be transparent but the decision in business units/locations eyes is flawed. We spoke to Irish subsidiaries of UK and US companies who felt constrained by the corporate straightjacket imposed upon them and how it made it hard to respond to local needs. This is most likely to happen where the HR leadership takes a very narrow view of the circumstances in which deviation from corporate standards, rules or norms is permitted.

Those that believe standardization is the right approach firstly suspect the intentions of business units/locations and secondly doubt the validity of the arguments. They are only really persuaded that legal or tax requirements are justifiable reasons for exceptions to be made. The Henkel approach, for example, states that business units 'meet local legal requirements in the context of global standards'. Sometimes this is stretched to include employee relations circumstances but again this may be really to do with regulatory context, such as the handling the works council – the ondernemingsraad – in the Netherlands. As an HR executive of a US IT company put it, 'The organization is not sympathetic to reasons other than legal ones.' To build a case for exception you have to give a lot of information, stress the role of local competitors and explain (as, say, in share plans) how the legal and taxation position is different to the USA.

The logic of the standardization approach is, to quote Andre Lamberty of ABB, 'every exception has a price tag'. Shell has accepted over 1,000 exceptions within its 29 processes. According to Dave Cushen this has a cost multiplier effect. Resource can be consumed locally and globally. For example, 10 staff in the USA are required to manage a gym offering. As a consequence, HR is not simply responding to every customer need, but challenging whether the need is justified against the expense. Why, for example, are the rules for 'acting up' in a senior position different within the same business unit, in the same country?

Where exceptions are more tolerated is in circumstances where the organization operates in a very different business and labour market. So applying standard rules, especially relating to reward, to an emergent market like China does not really work. In particular, there appears to be less loyalty to the employer such that labour moves swiftly to the highest paying organization. In a volatile economic environment and where fundamentally there is a supply shortfall against the demands of the multinational companies there is plenty of opportunity for employees to chase the money. So recruitment and retention processes or remuneration structures designed for steady-state western situations do not operate so well. A classic remuneration architecture works in a mature market but not in a new market. Top talent can out-earn a receptionist by 10 or 20 times, and an executive 100 times, just on base pay. This simply reflects the market demand for good people and the opportunities they have. So in following the classical model, you either overpay at the bottom or underpay at the top – add costs or fail to recruit good people. You need adaptation of the global model and flexibilities until maturity is reached. So, for example, Shell has had to modify its standard 80/120 pay architecture to allow Shell China to hire and retain talent successfully.

Another example is where the different HR practices of an acquired company have to be dealt with. The response of the acquirer will depend upon how centralized or decentralized the company is run and the nature of the variation. Companies seek to remove what they perceive to be an aberration immediately, wait until a suitable moment for assimilation to take place, or accept or tolerate the variation. Take reward 'inconsistencies' or differences. We heard earlier that RBS quickly imposed its remuneration model on ABN AMRO, whereas BASF has integrated HR instruments of acquired companies, such as sales incentive plans, into the corporate toolbox because it was necessary to meet market expectations.

THE AGENTS OF HR GOVERNANCE

Who are the agents that deliver the decisions made? Here we should separate out the intent or purpose from the execution. This is because centralization of decision making, however, does not mean centralized implementation, so there is a varying degree to which the locations, subsidiary or operating companies can choose the 'how', if not the 'what', of people management activity.

We came across two principal vehicles for governance implementation, namely the centres of expertise and an operations management role.

Shell is a good example of the centres of expertise playing the leadership role in governance delivery. The company uses its subject matter 'process owners' in reward, talent and development to take the lead in specifying what is appropriate in their area of influence. They are accountable at global level for common processes. As such, they have decided on what and how to standardize, in consultation with the global business partners. Development of the policies is managed through expertise networks, such as 'paynet' where all those embedded policy staff within business units globally discuss the future requirements of their subject area. However, in the latest HR model, the cluster HR vice presidents are expected to challenge local policy variations to establish they are necessary for good business reasons.

Unilever's centres of expertise also design the global solutions, but they too work with others to formulate policies, in their case with operating companies. For example, as HUL is one Unilever's largest operations (and strategic centres), it gets early involvement in many of the global policy frameworks or process standards to ensure that the fit is right at the design stage.

At RBS the new Chief Administrative Officer (CAO) has responsibilities to look after:

- HR strategy
- IT and change
- business information
- risk management
- functional finance
- functional communication
- (The HR shared services is also managed from this division.)

Its purpose is to drive accountabilities by describing who is accountable for what part of a particular process and in what way, and then ensure managers discharge their duties.

Although its remit was broadened in early 2011, à la RBS, to include the shared service centre and other activities, the Chief Operating Office (COO) team at SAP is also a key party in making HR governance work. Its expertise in this area is in process not content. As such, it is staffed by people from a variety of backgrounds, not just HR people. This teams aims are to enable effective operation of the function through:

- facilitation of the development of the HR strategy
- portfolio management with key stakeholders from HR and the business
- the management of centralized HR management processes (e.g. budget process, compliance processes, etc.)
- ensuring a link between the HR strategy and project delivery and process optimization

- the monitoring and performance tracking of HR activities (e.g. strategic projects) and human capital processes
- driving collaboration within HR and between HR and the business.

The SAP COO offers an interesting role combination: it acts as the corporate 'glue', but also audits and drives HR performance. Lean methodologies are used to push continuous improvement to streamline common processes, as they are at Shell where the strategy/communications unit has similar responsibilities to SAP's COO. Shell employs 'lean architects' to improve processes. Vestas also has a 'lean' team and a business performance group (internal project management and IT tools development/implementation).

There is a similar business management process at AstraZeneca where the roles of people analytics and measurement were combined with HR strategy, planning, governance and portfolio management.

Naturally, there are variations to these two patterns. For example, at BASF the HR regional heads are members of the Global HR Council and act as principal agents of driving the governance decisions into the regions. They have the job of convincing the business partners of regional business units that the corporate approach is right.

MONITORING OF GOVERNANCE EFFECTIVENESS

How do you judge whether your HR governance approach is working? We described earlier that Marcel Oertig saw added value measurement as a key ojective of HR governance. Similarly, Hewitt (2009b) argues that it is clearly linked to metrics. Based on their EU Barometer survey, their evidence is that its measurement is still an underdeveloped activity: 43 per cent were still looking for quantitative measures and only 19 per cent of organizations were using the same metrics for all regions.

Yet it is not clear to us at least what form this measurement of HR governance should take. Different organizations have different approaches and these may relate to the tight or loose decision making option chosen. So in a tight management context, an organization might monitor performance through both prescriptive rules and/or more diligent oversight. Those that opt for lighter touch governance via frameworks and principles might be more concerned with outcomes than how the results are achieved.

The Hewitt EU Barometer survey (2009b) found that customer surveys were the most common form of governance measure, but this leaves open the matter of what sort of questions customers are being asked that relate to governance as opposed to the usual service satisfaction. Then there are the standard human capital metrics (relating to, say, attrition, attraction, productivity per head, etc.). But again their relevance to governance specifically is unclear. Many organizations use benchmarking in assessing performance, involving both internal and external comparison, and building the case for change. Internal benchmarking can be used as a standardization lever to challenge idiosyncrasy in process adoption, especially where the cost of deviations is revealed. Similarly, transparency on costs by business unit can highlight differential expense that might be the consequence of deviating from or keeping to standard processes. External benchmarking can test the cost and quality of processes against other similar organizations to highlight areas ripe for improvement. Our Canadian interviewee used the Hackett model to plot the efficiency and effectiveness of the company's processes so that they could see where to focus their improvement drive.

Shell uses benchmarking to identify how close it is to top quartile performance in a range of HR content areas (e.g. onboarding or managing data). It considers both efficiency and effectiveness. JSW prides itself as a learning company and is indeed looking at other industries to see what it can learn. It benchmarks with new sectors such as telecoms and other service economies.

Whilst one might have concerns that of course the choice of elements to benchmark and the quality of data similarity is critical to the outcome, and risks being manipulated to deliver the 'right' answer, nonetheless, it can offer an impressive analysis. This is especially true if the quantitative benchmarking can be combined with qualitative customer and HR function opinion. So one company we looked at was able to offer the following picture (Figure 7.4) of its HR performance across its business departments (the detail has been adjusted somewhat to preserve anonymity).

Increasingly organizations can (and sometimes do) use their technology to check whether operating companies/units are abiding by the rules of the corporate game. Despite Shell acknowledging that there is good management information emerging, the company is not yet using the full potential of it and there is a reluctance to operate as an internal policeman to improve data quality.

Internal audit can also point to weaknesses in the achievement of HR governance goals as the third line of defence after the function's judgement (or the line management's when it is a people management question) and an operational risk assessment. Audit can look at outcomes as well as processes. Tracking of project performance is another element of performance management that can be applied.

Process	**Structure**
• no standardisation within or between departments • potential for core processes to be aligned for specific work areas • limited use of outsouring such that cost saving opportunities missed	• poor HR/FTE ratios compared with industry benchmarks • no consolidation of administrative support. It is duplicated across divisions • payroll is still decentralised by division
Technology	**Service delivery**
• no single platform across departments • within departments single platform not implemented • paper processing still exists • MI not available in some units • opportunities missed for e-enabling training, recruitment	• limited use of contact centres • multiple access points to HR, depending upon topic • customers confused over access routes • some ignorance in HR too • inconsistency of service performance

Figure 7.4   An assessment of HR performance

SAP seems to combine features of its existing performance monitoring with new aspects. So the conventional monitoring includes integrating and enhancing the existing HR scorecard that contains Key Performance Indicators (KPIs) with defined business outcomes. Responsibility is assigned to appropriate process owners for meeting these KPIs. SAP also has a project management tracking facility to see that projects are kept within scope and deliver to time and budget. What may be innovative is regular internal auditing to ensure compliance (e.g. with SOX) and appropriate risk management within HR. The monitoring process can also check how well the RACI 'rules' are applied – whether accountability and responsibility, in particular, are being accepted.

Unilever also uses KPIs to judge HR process performance. All KPIs are agreed both at the business level and centrally. The specific measures of course depend on whether they are managed locally or globally. Staff engagement measurement is a good example of how the HR community has a common KPI across Unilever. Scores of employees in the staff survey are benchmarked year on year against global comparisons and a target increase for each business. Companies like Shell and Siemens similarly apply global employee surveys, and of course RBS is famous for its cross-national benchmarking. This might now be considered an aspect of 'people' governance rather than HR governance.

Challenges

In this section we will concentrate on the governance challenges facing those organizations engaged in trying to set up and run a global service delivery model, but we will also include wider control questions where appropriate. The core problem is one of achieving alignment with the rest of the organization and gaining sufficient control to effectively deliver change. Though not clearly separated these alignment and control challenges appear variously in relation to organizational structures/direction and culture and harmonization.

MISALIGNED WITH BUSINESS MODEL

- **Organization functioning** In an issue we will return to in Chapter 8, the function can easily find itself in a 'bad place' if it is going against the business model. As Shell experienced, being in front of the way the business is organized causes difficulty. Your line colleagues do not understand or accept the model you are developing, which is especially difficult if it is in any way contentious. Trying to drive standardization or exercise central control when the organization is not ready for it is high risk to say the least. Trickier still is when the mode of decision making is in flux. What were once simple processes become difficult because of tugs of war between different stakeholder groups – those in the centre trying to get more control (perhaps to meet external regulation, say about the payment of bonuses) and those in operating roles who want to retain freedom to act. HR can become an unhappy piggy in the middle, especially if the requirement for oversight is not explained or explicit. Decision making may become highly politicized. New undefined ways of managing are shoehorned into existing formal processes. If they fail, HR gets a bad name for poor execution. Similarly, there can be a tension between the business units wanting vertical integration, so that harmonization occurs within the business unit but not between the units, and the corporate centre wanting horizontal standardization to drive down the costs that business unit differences bring.

- **Redundant structures** There is a danger in some approaches to dealing with competing power bases to assign responsibilities to all organizational geographic levels – global, regional, country and local – and to business unit/functional structures. This may become quite confusing and ultimately bureaucratic. Instead of speeding up decision making, it might actually slow it down with turf wars occurring over the interpretation of 'agreed' rules. There may be a lot of second guessing. Indeed, some of these 'levels' may in fact add little value. One interviewee for the book, when asked about the role of their region in HR governance, responded: 'Well that's a good question!' Another interviewee talked of the region as an extension of the corporate centre, which poses the question of whether that structure offers more than simply being a conduit through which messages are passed. Removing redundant decision structures may, however, be easier said than done given the likely power dynamics. Think of the problems that the European Union has had in deciding the respective rights and responsibilities of the various players (national governments, the European Parliament, Council of Ministers, European Commission and new roles like the European President) and the confusion over who does what, complicated by different views on the role of the EU.
- **Incomplete ownership of HR** If the corporate centre does not manage all the parts of the HR operation it makes it all the harder to get decisions made. This is not just a question of reconciling potentially different views but also of managing the different power bases referred to above. A common challenge is that the HR shared services work is organizationally part of a separate company (at Evonik) or has a separate reporting line (e.g. Siemens).
- **Powerless centre** How does the corporate centre in these circumstances keep locations or business units to the standards it has set where there is no benefit to them and the centre has no carrots to offer or sticks to persuade?
- **Limited central resources** There are resource implications to create and govern a common set of policies, systems and processes that the corporate centre needs to face, especially in the more complex, matrix organizations. Many organizations have slimmed down support functions to avoid 'excessive' staffing of the corporate centre. This has driven HR directors in the past to minimize central resources and push them out into the business as much as possible (Reilly and Williams, 2003). Yet you need people (with specific skills) not just during implementation of the model – these may be easier to justify as part of the project – but to monitor business unit/location behaviour and, if necessary, intervene to prevent non-compliance. However, build up resources for the control function too much and the operating companies will object to the financial burden being placed upon them.
- **Good governance is never recognized** but bad governance is all too apparent. HR is not thanked for all the hard work it does in holding the ring between competing interests, especially between HQ and business units/locations. As one CEO privately admits, HR takes the flak for his insistence on oversight. However, if controls fail for whatever reason and problems occur, HR can be quickly blamed either for poor design

or execution. This might be not identifying a 'bad apple', allowing a succession gap to appear or permitting an excessive bonus.

- **Fit with broader people objectives** It is perhaps surprising that on the one hand, through its approach to governance, HR is frequently emphasizing consistency and commonality, whilst on the other hand, at the same time the function is arguing for the segmentation of the workforce and denying that one size fits all. Thus there is an apparent disconnect between the strategy that HR is adopting for people management in the business and the one it applies to itself as a function.
- **Too top down** The assumption behind the governance model is that strategy is top down and determinist, whereas we know that in reality much strategy making is emergent and comes from reacting to changing events. It is a 'living strategy' to quote Stefan Stern (2009). Experience during the recent economic problems has emphasized that point, especially as tensions arise in cost and resource allocation during tough times.

PEOPLE POWER AND CULTURAL CONUNDRUMS

- **Challenging the line's status quo** There is likely to be resistance to overcome from the line in changing the HR governance model. As one interviewee put it: 'Managers have to be convinced of the value of this change. They like the cost reduction opportunity but equally they are very comfortable with the individual, tailor-made support.' The HR manager from the corporate centre observed that 'this was a luxury the company could not afford'. But it is still a difficult message to get across. Indeed, if there is a very consensual decision making process where continuity with the past is prized, and the HR director is either unwilling or unable successfully to challenge that consensus in the face of line management opposition, the status quo may continue to operate.
- **Limiting devolved HR power** There are also likely to be objections from HR managers and staff who feel 'confined' by a more assertive corporate centre. Business partners in particular may side with their business unit or location in opposing corporate control. Those in country leadership roles may be particularly reluctant to cede authority to the centre. This may be because they do not believe the new governance arrangements will work or simply that they do not like having their wings clipped. They wish to return to a time when they had the power to exercise their own decisions as they wished.
- **Underground resistance** Some of this resistance may be covert rather than overt non-compliance. Games playing starts with apparent acceptance in public and subversion in private. Managers, including within HR, may give the impression of supporting the change towards commonality but in practice they follow their own path. It may not be apparent directly, especially in a dispersed global operation, but it appears through the proliferation of parallel systems and hidden resources. One US company we know of found that non-compliance, especially in Europe, was such that it moved away from detailed procedures to one of flexibility within a framework.
- **Lack of honesty** An important implication of covert resistance is that the corporate centre hears neither about the philosophical objections nor about genuine implementation difficulties. Learning is buried rather than shared. If colleagues are not honest with each other then they will not develop better policies and practices.

- **Us versus them** The opposition may be personal, or at least emotional. One organization described the risk that operating units see the corporate centre as inhabited by 'control freaks'. We were told of this happening in another company where there was both a whiff of choosing to ignore HQ as a matter of principle and because of the nationality of those who were asking.
- **The world is not the same** Whilst there are strong globalizing trends, there are real geographic differences still present, which we described in Chapter 3, that organizations ignore at their peril. The labour market, the business climate, legal and political systems vary widely. National cultural differences may be masked by a strong organizational culture, but this does not remove all attitudinal variation. The challenge is how much space does local HR have to adjust to suit its peculiar circumstances? Some organizations do not allow that much.
- **False assumptions** In particular in the governance process, organizations have to be particularly careful about ethnocentric views of the world. As we described earlier, decision makers in one geography may misunderstand how others in another geography may receive their message or it may be that a decision that looks sensible through one lens does not look quite so sensible from another vantage point. Take a simple example of privileges relating to flying time (e.g. class of travel). Europeans might see a four-hour flight as quite a distance as it takes you from one end of the continent to the other. This is appreciated differently through US or Chinese eyes when it is simply an internal journey. At best this may be due to a lack of cultural sensitivity or knowledge, easily repaired through greater exposure to other cultures. At worst, this may be a form of cultural imperialism, forcing one view of the world onto others. As an example of ignorance, one American company tried insisting that all locations should institute an employee vetting programme because of regulations it was acting under in the USA. These requirements would, if implemented, have been illegal in some countries. Anticipating this risk might have saved the HR team some embarrassment and the operating companies from irritation. During our interviews we heard other tales of cultural myopia.
- **Communication failures** This lack of cultural and institutional, or even legal, awareness is exacerbated where the corporate centre has poor communication with its operating companies, yet seeks to exercise global control. This may be due to the poor quality of management/HR staff at the local level. Expatriates may not know enough and national managers may care less to satisfy their distant masters. There is the simple fact that leadership over an extended distance is problematic, however well wired the organization might be. In a less obvious problem, there may be apparent support for the corporate approach but in fact it is really only superficial agreement. Unlike the earlier point, it is not that there is opposition, but that the understanding of what is required and why is missing. This is especially risky in cross-national operations where there are large language and cultural differences. The meaning associated with a decision may be quite different from one group to another. A lack of deeper shared purpose can reveal itself at times of pressure.
- **People will talk** Moreover, can the corporate centre control the communication flows as it might want to? There is an increasing desire for everybody to be 'on message' and if you don't like the message you should leave. Nonetheless, social networking and the like allow employees to circumvent the corporate communication channels. They can go off message on Facebook. This parallel universe may challenge the

company orthodoxy or even be subversive. The use of social media to mobilize strike action in 2008 in a textile workers' strike in Egypt and in 2009 at Total's Lindsey oil refinery is instructive in this regard.

- **Non-aligned rewards** Be especially careful with reward systems: they signal what is important. If you get rewarded for getting the process right, it will produce different behaviours/mindset from one where the outcome in terms of value/profit generation is the goal.

THE STEAMROLLER OF STANDARDIZATION

- **Too stifling of improvement** Excessive central control can limit organizational learning and stunt innovation. In decentralized structures, although there is a cost of inefficiency and repetition, there is the benefit of encouraging dispersed HR teams to develop their own ideas to meet their own circumstances. In the past companies have drawn upon the best ideas from wherever they have come – Australia, Singapore, Mexico. In a standardized approach with policies, processes and systems development only flowing from the centre, if the organization is not careful there is not enough diversity to spark creativity.
- **Too rule bound** A 'learning company' allows people to make mistakes through experimentation, and leaders have to accept that this is the price to pay for ultimately better performance. Standardization sends a different message that it is better not to be too imaginative and best to follow the rules of the corporate game. One might have a concern here about the quality of staff who would be happy with this limited discretion. Good people would leave. Those who remain may not be suitable for the jobs in the corporate centre that do require creativity. At worst this may become a Taylorist management method that denies colleagues any hope of self-actualization. The result may be that the cost saving obtained through standardization is negated by the loss of employee engagement and the discretionary effort that it brings.
- **Too impractical** Moreover, centres of expertise have been criticized (Reilly and Williams, 2006) from being too remote from the business, coming up with grandiose schemes that are expensive or unsuitable; driven more by a notion of HR best practice than by the need to solve organizational problems. So if the centres of expertise are the sole authors of organizational policies and practices, the corporate centre must ensure they are informed by the locations and business units, and be receptive to ideas from within and outwith the organization. And this challenge is not just at the outset in the design phase, but throughout the process – organizations need to be able to adapt and evolve policy: so is there that capacity within the system? Oxfam faced this dilemma, as Jane Cotton explained, in developing the HR centres of expertise the leadership team had to accept more 'centralized control'. She had a concern that growing HR 'professionalism' would 'stifle passion and innovation' elsewhere in the organization.
- **One size doesn't fit all circumstances** The Du Pont example below is a salutary tale of pushing the standardization concept too far in applying a common approach to different types of business unit. The same point may apply to occupational or grade groups. There is also the likelihood, as one interviewee put it, that standardized process can deliver 'stupid decisions in individual cases'. The harmonized model might not have been constructed with a particular set of circumstances in mind. To

use one of the author's own personal experiences, a standard recruitment advertising format might work well for most locations but be damaging to the business in a particular case. As one interviewee put it, those at the top are 'smart enough to realize it's not right'. The problem is not with their good intentions but with the execution through others who follow the letter but not the spirit of what was intended.

When Du Pont acquired a 1,500 employee German company it was obvious that it should give the new operation the opportunity to benefit from its low-cost service delivery approach. There was a strong business case for harmonization of HR policies and practices and the transfer of HR administration to Spain. It was not long before the former owner of the acquired company complained 'you are destroying my business'. What Du Pont had unwittingly done was ignore the existing employment model and brand proposition, thinking their solution necessarily would be superior.

This experience has led to a re-evaluation that simply 'harmonizing a low-cost model' was too facile. It was recognized that segmentation was required to adjust the service delivery approach to take account of market, location, size and growth rate. You cannot have the same recruitment mechanism for Switzerland as China with 1,500 hires per annum.

- **Too ignorant** The implication behind standardization is that there is one right way to do things. This might be a fair reflection of the HQ view of the world, but a scan of HR practices across the globe would show up significant variation. Take selection methods: western firms may be committed to structured interviewing, psychometric testing and job testing, but in other parts of the world graphology and phrenology (including to a degree in parts of Europe still), family background and even blood group are used to recruit staff. This is not an argument for these methods, but rather that ignorance of the underlying assumptions behind them prevents proper debate about the introduction of corporate standards.

Success Factors

The factors that make for the successful governance of a global service delivery model reflect in part dealing with the aforementioned challenges, but there are other principles of good change management we would like to emphasize.

SET THE RIGHT DIRECTION

- **Increase model alignment** As far as is possible align your HR governance model with the business model. You can see from other examples quoted here of previously 'federated' or 'decentralized' organizations (e.g. British American Tobacco, Aegon, Canon or ANZ, see overleaf) moving towards greater corporate direction and organization, but at a speed consistent with wider organizational repositioning. SAP may be moving faster in consolidation and standardization but that is because it aligns with a general business direction of 'organizing for scale'. Siemens may be accelerating its change programme because the downturn has given a cost imperative that, if the intellectual capital of the business is to be protected, the support functions have to slim more quickly through greater standardization/automation driven from the corporate centre.

When Shell shifted towards global businesses, HR shared services had to be reinvented and then had to catch up. The incoming HR director, Hugh Mitchell, when he arrived, took responsibility for delivering the project and made sure it happened. He simplified and strengthened the governance processes, but the business change also gave a mandate where there was not one before. The introduction of process ownership, and the accountability that went with it, gave corporate leadership the sense that the structural changes enabled the standardization, rather than the other way round.

ANZ was a federated, even 'fragmented' company. HR's approach matched the 'atomized' business where something like 30 P&L units were free to operate as they chose so long as they delivered the financial results. There seemed to be no requirement for central oversight. The business model has now changed: the aim is to leverage the power of the whole firm and benefit from cross-selling. The 'one ANZ' approach has led to a re-evaluation of the role of HR.

Novartis has now reached a clear understanding on what should be organized on a 'cross-divisional' basis (the company would not use the term 'centralized'). Essentially, in the support functions, like HR, Finance and IT, it is felt that synergies can be found through commonality. By comparison, the company recognizes that its business divisions operate in different markets and with different customers, with whom they need close alignment.

- **Destiny in your own hands** Wherever possible HR should seize any opportunity to define its own destiny, rather than being dictated to by other forces. It may act as a motivating factor if you have control of the change process. It also means if things go wrong, there is nobody to blame but yourself! However, you do need top team support, not just to endorse the change but give backing when the inevitable opposition arises. This reinforces the point that HR's actions have to be consistent with the direction of organizational change, not in contradiction to it.
- **Goal first, design second** Define the goal you want to get to and then work your way towards it. As we noted earlier, SAP, for example, has defined at a level of principle where it wants to be in terms of delegation, risk, level of coordination and information sharing in the context of an overall decision making architecture. The important point here is to realize that there is no single 'best practice' in HR governance. Your size, sector, geographical footprint (especially distribution of sites), degree of business internationalization and management method/structure, all should shape your decisions.
- **Get the language right** To ensure that HR governance is seen as a true business activity use the concepts of risk management that are applied elsewhere in the

organization. HR should be 'assuring' that key processes are compliant and ensuring that control is being applied to key policies. For example, in financial services HR has to assure that the business has been appropriately undertaking performance management reviews for 'code staff' (as defined in agreement with the Financial Services Authority – FSA). In RBS HR's role is increasingly seen as one of organizational 'stewardship', as referred to on p. 207, and this forms part of their recently refreshed functional mission statement.

AND DESIGN THE MODEL TO FIT

- **Set the scope of governance** At a high level you should decide on what terrain HR governance covers. RBS in its recent review of the subject made a clear distinction between people governance, which is the responsibility of line management, though nonetheless operating to company standards, and functional governance. The latter concerns how HR discharges its role in supporting the line, providing services to customers, facilitating people management improvements and enforcing corporate requirements.
- **Map what's loose and what's tight** The next step may be to look at the activities you want to consolidate or standardize, and manage under a global governance structure, and which remain locally determined. As Jane Cotton of Oxfam put it, 'Be clear what must be managed tightly (the non-negotiables) and where you can be more flexible.' Do not simply require a whole complex organization to adhere to a single set of processes where they might damage the business. As Wilfried Meyer explains, 'You have to ensure that common processes don't stop the need to meet business needs – especially upscaling and downscaling.' Similarly, Joe Platevic at Unilever has said, 'With HR, one size doesn't fit all. You need a different approach for different problems and geographies.' So the company has standardized policy through principles and standards rather than detail; thus allowing local regulatory differences to be managed sensibly – an approach well received in India (see box). At Rolls Royce, though, the company expects only 10 per cent of corporate processes to be tailored. Yet even where the process is the same, the content can be different.

Unilever launched its 'one HR function' initiative in 2005, balancing local and global needs using policy frameworks. Leena Nair (Executive Director for HR in India) was very positive about the country impact of the global process model adopted across Unilever: she felt 'it was fantastic that we have one company way of doing things' but allowing the right amount of empowerment to local countries or regions.

- **Agree who's in and who's out** This governance approach does not have cover all geographies. Such a decision making is all the more necessary if you have some aspects of your business delivered globally and some locally. Even if this is not the case, some organizations take the view that it is not worth the effort to migrate the policies, practices and processes (and sometimes even systems) onto a common template for particular business units/locations because the divergence is too great and/or the employee numbers involved are too small. The Canadian company we met, for example, excludes 15 operating countries from its HR IT solution because together they represent only 3.8 per cent of the workforce compared with 18 countries that cover the rest.

- **Evidence based decision making** To make these decisions on governance coverage, which may well be contentious, it is probably better to be evidence rather than assertion based. You could use a model developed by Marcel Oertig (2009) and adjusted slightly here. This sort of model is already used in marketing. Unilever has, for example, mapped its brands on a graph with consumer behaviour on one axis (global to local) and scale benefits (global to local) on the other axis. The advantage of using a tool such as this is that it forces you to identify the benefits of HR governance (through standardization but also through a common service delivery model and central automation drive) and to examine the same question from an efficiency perspective. The drive to standardization can cost money before it saves cash. Harmonization of systems particularly can be expensive. So you have to examine the cost–benefit of any change.

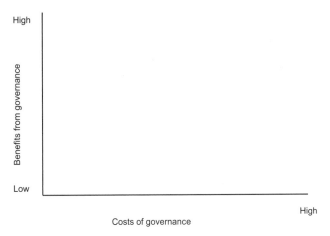

Figure 7.5   An analytical approach to governance decisions

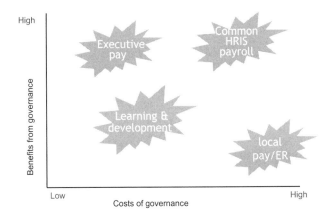

Figure 7.6   Application of analytical process to governance decisions

- **Take situation number 1**, for example, the introduction of a single integrated HRIS/payroll: the advantages are obvious in improved data management and quality of management information, but the cost of rolling out the system worldwide, replacing numerous local systems, is high.
- **Situation number 2**, for example, shows implementing the same global executive incentive scheme. Here the benefits of greater central control are clear to ensure not only consistency but also to avoid potential exposure to negative public relations. The cost of harmonization under corporate oversight is low as the population is known and small, and implementation is merely the despatch of policy documents. Auditing compliance is straightforward.
- **Situation number 3**, for example, is the least straightforward, as on the one hand there are benefits to a single learning and development activity, certainly in design and commissioning, but also in using (or purchasing) a single, integrated delivery arm. These both save you money. On the other hand, this decision can stunt organizational innovation if you are not careful. Where will the new thinking on learning and development come from – only from the corporate centre of expertise?
- **Situation 4** is clear: there is little corporate benefit to having a common approach to local (e.g. manufacturing sites or retail outlets) employee relations given the diverse nature of legal regulations and a high cost in harmonizing terms and conditions, as the pressure will be to average up not down. There are perhaps convincing arguments about having a common philosophy or strategy (for a shared direction), and in standardizing HR administration (for efficiency reasons). There are more arguments for and against operational standardization where cost versus quality of service is more balanced. In the end, though, it should be the organizational context and business drivers that answer these questions.

ANZ has learned not to try to standardize everything. It is become clear that two criteria should guide standardization decisions: replicability and scale. Processes that can safely be copied and used to operate cross-nationally would be subject to standardization. Compensation, resourcing and learning and development policies and practices are more likely to fulfil these criteria than others where local/business unit customization is more necessary.

- **Adopt the best processes** Choose the outstanding HR processes from anywhere in the company (or imported from elsewhere) on which to base the standard approach. Do not see excellence as only to be found in the corporate centre or in a particular geography.
- **Define levels of granularity** Then decide which processes should be described in rigorous detail so that there is no ambiguity and those where there is only a set of common guiding principles and hold the organization to them. Using process scales it is probably not sensible to get down to the lowest level of granularity on any topic nor to be as broad as the highest level, but you need to decide where in between the extremes it makes sense in relation to a specific activity. So, bonus decisions may be

covered carefully; learning and development interventions may be less precise. This relates to the decisions made using Figure 7.5 and to the nature of the topic, but also it may relate to the corporate centre's judgement on risk and where it is safe to trust operating companies/subsidiaries and where it assesses high or low capability in operating with more flexibility.

Oxfam it has opted for the minimum necessary convergence and has not gone to the nth degree in standardization. It has not rewritten policies that were working acceptably well. For example, its performance appraisal system is 'light on process'. This is because the organization employs 'passionate' people, who tend to be anti-bureaucratic and are not good at filling in forms. So there is just one form to complete, a guidance booklet and some pointers are given on assessing performance, attitudes and behaviours.

- **Agree process owners** Define who owns which process, being clear between corporate and operating businesses, but also within each business unit. But it has to be recognized that standardization drives towards aggregation at the highest geographical level. So to avoid duplication, work (and responsibility for those activities) has to be pulled from countries to regions and from regions to global entities. With respect to risk management you can helpfully create a centre of expertise on controls and governance, which could be linked to a COO structure or in place of it. This can oversee not just emergent people and operational HR risks but also develop control and governance methods and protocols.

ATTENTION TO IMPLEMENTATION

- **Control does not just come from doing it yourself** As we suggested earlier, there is a tendency towards centralization of decision making that is represented in the corporate centre designing policies and then driving them through. It may be that this actually gives apparent more than real control. Your corporate centre might be better advised to limit the number of areas where it is essential to have commonality and then devolve responsibility for the implementation to the business units, holding them accountable for their actions.

RBS has found it hard to differentiate between central and standardized and uses the two phrases interchangeably. Shell clearly differentiates between them. Standardization is the what, a corporate imperative on generating synergies. But how it is delivered is not necessarily the responsibility of the centre.

- **Agree process variations** Discover how processes are used and whether they are working well. If there is evidence of non-compliance, discover the cause of the variance. Through listening to colleagues, distinguish between unnecessary bells and whistles added to suit HR local predilections from those adjustments to meet genuine business needs.

- **Unforeseen needs** It is also right to acknowledge that locations/business units may have to introduce policies and practices to address their specific issues, not properly covered by corporate approaches. So they must be given 'permission' to develop their own solution, if one does not exist within the company. This learning can then be used elsewhere in the organization. RBS uses an 'exception to policy' approach to deal with unexpected events. This can be applied as a stop gap whilst the company works out whether the control is relevant in a certain country; the decision can be made that, because of business circumstances, the control should be dropped for now or a permanent change can be proposed by the operating division HR head to the global policy owner for discussion and potentially approval.

- **Recognize your limitations** The corporate centre should recognize that there are limits to driving through standardization in an entirely top down manner. It should understand that it is necessary also to build trust both in its competence and in its integrity if operating companies/business units are going to accept and work with the new way of governing the function. For genuine working together to common norms, as the Tetra Pak example will show in the next chapter, you need the wholehearted understanding and support of the HR people involved. The corporate centre has to build positive relationships with business units and locations rather than be seen purely as the corporate police. As the Metro Group put it, to have 'supporting partners' elsewhere in the organization. And these 'partners' have also got to trust each other in the representation of joint interests to the corporate centre, but also the adult acceptance that legitimate differences do exist between them and should be respected.

- **Own up to mistakes** It is important to building trust that if corporate centre realizes it has made an error of judgement in pressing standardization too far, whether in an individual case or concerning a whole policy, the centre corrects it. Garmt Louw says in Shell that executive team discussions work because the participants face up to their issues and an acceptance that company can 'overdose' on corporate initiatives. It helps to that many of the main players who are now gamekeepers were once poachers (i.e. in business unit roles before their current corporate ones) so they know the score from both perspectives. But it is still important that there is mutual respect, professionalism, honesty over mistakes and decisions being data not prejudice/ill informed driven. Honesty and greater internal transparency also come from the requirement to meet investors and be clear and frank with them. So performance/results should be internally challenged to ensure they are right, certainly before external exposure. Whilst encouraging a blame free culture helps learning through owning up to mistakes, there has to be some consideration of the penalties for serious control failures.

- **Gradually loosen a tight approach** The judgement in the extent of local flexibility to allow may change as the culture becomes more 'corporate' oriented or as management capability grows. Oxfam did this; after tightening up on discretion more than was strictly desirable in the first instance, it gradually let the pendulum swing back on the tight/loose axis towards greater managerial freedom. If you have developed stronger and more capable managers that understand the inevitable tension between consistency across the world and discretion to meet local circumstances, then this makes sense. As Oxfam found, you can move from rules to guidelines and frameworks based on the confidence you have that managers will not abuse their responsibilities and can be trusted to make sound decisions that acknowledge corporate imperatives and yet meet local operational demands. Managers are in greater control now of the implementation of policies, but they also know when to refer.

So some 'grown-up' global companies either do not centralize specific policies, requiring instead operation to common principles that can be tailored to local legislation or circumstances so that implementation can fit local/business unit needs, or they move to this position. This seems to be accepted practice in employee relations, where the role of the centre is to prevent locations acting in a way that could harm other parts of the company. It can do this by signing off mandates in the light of the principles it has laid down. This approach could be extended to other areas of HR work: set out the goals and principles and allow the business units discretion in how they enact them.

In ANZ in 2008/9 there was a move away from very tight corporate control, a 'shift in the dial' towards giving people in the business units responsibility and telling people not to abuse it. Unnecessary corporate activities that were unaligned with business requirements were stopped. Mark Jankelson observes that the corporate centre naturally finds it easier to trust individuals it has a positive relationship with and is more doubtful about those business units that have past 'form' in what they would see as deviations from corporate standards.

- **Encourage fresh ideas** Experimentation should be permitted and the movement of ideas from the bottom up and not just from the top down should be encouraged. The boxed examples illustrate approaches that clearly put a premium on knowledge sharing across the company. These accept that these flows can go horizontally as well as vertically around the world.

British American Tobacco, for example, has specifically allowed South Africa to develop well being policies on Aids. It is clear to Rudi Kindts, the HR director, that there are no-go areas (e.g. in developing a new bonus plan) where operating companies cannot be allowed to trial new practices, but outside these topics he is happy to see good ideas flourish – so long as he is kept in the loop.

Oxfam also encourages experimentation – try things out and see how they go – believing that the tension between the two poles of an efficient and well-functioning organization on the one hand, and the need for innovation, on the other, should be addressed in a pragmatic way. The tiller may be pushed in one direction or another, depending upon results of its pilots.

- **Network solutions** One way to help generate ideas is to allow knowledge sharing. So rather than seeing networking mechanisms as an unnecessary cost, they should be encouraged to gain greater commitment to the organizational approach, to surface doubts or problems and to resolve them. Shell, for example, uses 'Nets HR' where senior practitioners debate issues with process owners to ensure policies are sensibly and successfully implemented by ensuring that the corporate centre is aware of local or business unit specific sensitivities or circumstances. This sort of discussion is increasingly undertaken via on line collaborative tools.
- **Develop comfort with complexity** In order to make these matrix arrangements work and to handle effectively situations where there is flexibility on some things and constraints on others, you need managers who can handle complexity. This requires a cultural change, a shift in mindset. Massimo Macarti from Canon Europe, for example, positively comments on how he has observed his fellow HR directors in the region moving towards a more collegiate approach. Instead of emphasizing difference, the team has a focus on the common regional good.
- **Build centre-local trust** But it also has to work the other way: those in the corporate centre have to trust those in the locations and make sure there is plenty of dialogue to develop mutual understanding. Yasmin Leung when at Sun Microsystems in Beijing explained how she had frequent phone calls with the US HQ to understand corporate requirements but also to explain local needs. And this acknowledgement of real difference has to go beyond the patronizing 'only changing the colour of the screen' but proper recognition that adaptation is acceptable.
- **Promote a global mindset** To help this process you need a mindset that is international in outlook that will see the opportunities that globalization brings. This mindset will have to be aware of the corporate as well as local imperatives – to assert what is necessary to run a business in a specific location, but also to accept corporate priorities as legitimate. As Chris Sullivan (RBS UK corporate bank CEO and a Liverpool FC fan) says rather than there being a club versus country tussle, business functions should adopt a mentality of club AND country. Job rotation, secondments, exchanges, expatriate assignments and opportunities for networking are some of the ways of building managers at ease with global issues, as well as improving language capability and cultural sensitivity. It can also develop important management skills like delegation and ability to take difficult/unpopular decisions (neither of which is easy in some societies).
- **Demonstrable HR leadership** In some cases the centre may not have resource power or even significant positional authority where there is strong local autonomy. But it must at least have expertise power. The centre has a key HR leadership role in setting professional standards, encouraging HR practitioner development through HR networks and monitoring HR's overall global performance. The function should role model good governance without bad bureaucracy, not least because it is itself a 'control function' (as the FSA has now specified alongside legal, finance and risk).
- **Recognize the limits of formal controls** In the end what makes governance systems work is the quality of people you employ, their commitment to the success of the organization (an 'enterprise first' disposition) and their relationships with their colleagues. This is far more important than laid down procedures.

- **Ensure effective measurement** Finally, with respect to measuring and monitoring HR governance performance measurement ought to relate to its aims. So a set of measures might concern itself with:
  - compliance – number of deviations from defined practice
  - risk – incidents of exposure to unnecessary threat
  - degree of synergy obtained – via audit
  - process cost versus value ratios
  - tracking project performance against goals
  - auditing of data quality to reveal deviations from the norm
  - client satisfaction
  - reviewing spans and layers of control to ensure clear accountability
  - number of handoffs (to avoid having chekcers checking checkers).

Inevitably, these data may be both qualitative and quantitative. They may be in some cases difficult to collect and be seen as softer than the usual metrics. These are indeed challenges to face, but there is the alternative danger that what can be measured easily gets measured and the result is data that adds no more value than you get from the KPIs of your service delivery model. So we would urge organizations to persevere and accept that some of the output is indicative rather than definitive.

8 *A Global Service Delivery Model*

HR has become fragmented because of the unintended consequences of outsourcing; adopting Ulrich's model too rigidly or simplistically and introducing different work streams to fit the models; and shifting HR activities to low-cost providers, line managers or consultants. (Lynda Gratton, cited in Ashton and Lambert, 2005)

Introduction

HR transformation has preoccupied companies over the last 10 or 15 years, and some have seen globalization of their HR operations as part of their change goals. Others have more gradually and pragmatically moved towards a global approach; whilst a third group is only now embarking on globalizing their HR service delivery model. Dominating the mode of change, certainly in large complex organizations, is the so-called holy trinity of consolidation, standardization and automation. Or, as expressed by Peter Voser, Shell's CEO, the acronym is 'ESSA' – an injunction to eliminate, streamline, standardize and automate.

Surveys reveal the importance of these ways in which HR has sought to achieve transformation. For example, two thirds of respondents picked out standardization as the focus of HR improvement; somewhat more than half identified IT change and somewhat less than half chose restructuring the function (Deloitte Consulting, 2009).

In this chapter we will see how these drivers of HR transformation have been applied in a global context and have helped organizations towards a global service delivery model, whilst recognizing the challenges that Lynda Gratton refers to in the opening quotation to this chapter.

The Change Drivers

Driven largely by the need for cost reduction and partly on improvement in service quality and focus on business critical issues, organizations have used service centres and call/contact centres to bring together information and administration to permit economies of scale and the pulling together of deep technical know how through the creation of centres of expertise (*Consolidation*). Moreover, as we have seen, centres of expertise can be the agents of standardization. They can design policies and processes that should apply across the organization and can also monitor adherence to these 'binding standards' ensuring compliance to them.

Many organizations, especially global companies, have embarked on projects to bring greater consistency and transparency to their HR operations through setting standards in processes, systems and policies to which parts of the organization must comply

(*Standardization*). It is driven by cost reduction and increasing the speed and quality of service delivery.

And through e-systems like manager self service, employee self service, e-recruitment etc costs have also been reduced and service speed and data management improved (*Automation*). It also facilitates standardization because there is only one electronic performance appraisal form, training booking system, etc. It allows the organization to quality control and convey a single brand message, and this is both internally and externally.

What Might a Global Service Delivery Model Look Like?

So what does the usual HR service delivery model look like in global organizations as a result of response to these drivers? It is clear that the default model is the so-called Ulrich or three legged stool structure (i.e. business partners, centres of expertise and shared services). However, it is equally clear that the way this structure manifests itself varies considerably, in part because of the degree of globalization of its operations, but also because of organizational history, type of business and stage of development. As research from the UK (Reilly et al., 2007) and Netherlands (Maatman et al., 2010) has shown, adaptation rather than adoption has been the watchword.

These structural changes are backed by the other components of the trinity, namely standardization and automation.

A GLOBAL HR SHARED SERVICES CENTRE?

Over the last 15 years HR shared services have become an increasingly prevalent feature of the organizational landscape, especially for large and complex organizations. Indeed, according to EquaTerra, by 2008 80 per cent of the 'Global 2000' companies had adopted shared services (http://www.hroassociation.org/file/3962/equaterra-announces-shared-services-value-assessment.html). This appears to have been led by some US owned companies which have moved faster than their European or Asian counterparts (Deloitte Consulting, 2006). Consolidation has been easier to achieve in the USA because of the size of its single market governed under largely one legal system and in one language. Economies of scale obtained at home have allowed investment in technology, facilitated by the presence of a number of innovative IT players in the country. Thus there is a ready made model available for export. However, even though US companies have tended to move faster towards global shared services than European or Asian owned companies, the proportion of truly global operations is still limited, according to Hewitt (2007), even for US firms. This is what we found, too, in our case study organizations.

In the context of this book, we were interested in:

1. What choices are exercised by organizations with international operations between delivering shared services centres locally, nationally, regionally around the world or globally?
2. Is the work done in these locations purely for customers in that geographic area or is it for the wider organization?

3. What content is covered by the common service delivery model, and is this affected by the degree of service aggregation?
4. Does the same service delivery model apply to all locations or are some excluded?
5. Consequently, is there a general move towards global service centres? If not, why not?

1. What choices are exercised by organizations?

As Table 8.1 indicates there are a number of options open to organizations in where shared services centres are located and who their customers might be.

Table 8.1   Geographic basis for HR shared services work

Location/work content	Local	National	Regional	Global
Local				
National				
Regional				
Global				

The shaded areas indicate the possible combinations of work content by location. Thus a global shared services centre can do the work of any local operation but not vice versa.

There are multinational companies that still deliver HR administrative services locally without any form of shared services aggregation. This is because their operations are in small units and widely dispersed by location, and/or their business activities are very heterogonous. So economies of scale cannot easily be obtained by reason of small size or divergent policies/practices. Thus many international professional service firms handle their administration locally. Federated companies, like AS Watson, do not bring together the transactional work of their different subsidiaries into one shared services operation.

At the next level up, there can be a series of national service centres serving national needs. This makes sense where again the country business units are small (such as in a marketing firm), making it too expensive to combine administration at even the regional level or in companies where really one country operation is dominant and the benefits of having its shared services centre extend its coverage to much smaller countries makes no economic sense. Take the Standard Bank of South Africa Ltd: it has a shared services centre that processes payroll and other administrative matters for about 70 per cent of the bank's global total employees who are in South Africa (Business Week Research Services, 2007).

Canon Europe has considered a pan-regional shared services centre but is not sure that the economics justify it. Being a sales and service company in Europe means that its workforce is relatively widely distributed and numbers in any one country relatively small. With only 50–60 HR administrative staff across the continent, if these were aggregated to one place what manpower saving would there be? This is especially true when one considers that the regional team would have to cover 15–20 languages. So, at the moment, administration is done at country level. An interim step towards getting 'critical mass' for the European body might be to consolidate the transactions of the three biggest countries to achieve some economies of scale. What Canon has done is to insist on common systems for payroll, record keeping, recruitment, etc. which are operated locally. This would permit easier outsourcing, if that were ever felt to be desirable.

HR also normally sensibly follows the business model: if it is decentralized then the pressure to consolidate through shared services will be less. Take EDF Energy in the UK: it was under no central directive to follow a French-directed model or band together in a cross-national shared services operation. This is true of how the company is generally run – in a very decentralized manner. We have seen other examples, interestingly from French companies where the management style is relatively laissez-faire. UK operations are left to follow their own path so long as the financial figures are okay. In particular, the French parent companies do not seem to be seeking to operate either a national or regional shared service centre.

Other non French examples of organizations without HR shared services are given below.

The Arup partnership operates through a three sided matrix of regions/practices/markets. It has small global HR team that provides services to businesses around the world in reward, learning and development and international mobility. It has no common shared services centre.

As described in more detail below, Aegon is moving towards a degree more centralization and internationalization. Some subjects, like expatriate services, will, as a consequence, now be managed on a more coordinated basis, with a high level of cooperation between the corporate centre and individual business and country units. However, there is currently no plan to create global (or even regional) service centres.

Regional bodies appear in a variety of guises, efficiency or the business model determining the optimum configuration. There are companies that have a number of shared services centres that in some cases operate for large countries' operations and surrounding area. Philips NV has such an arrangement. It has created six shared services centres based where there are the largest concentrations of employees (e.g. the Netherlands, USA, Singapore, etc.). They carry out work for employees in that country and for the immediate region. Siemens started with shared services centre at national level (like in the Asia Pacific region where there is a shared service centre in India and one in China) with the intention of moving some back office functions or processes to regional hubs.

Nestlé also has regional HR shared service centres. In 2011 it opened a centre in Accra, Ghana to cover its African operations. This sits alongside shared service centres in Brazil (for Latin America), the Philippines (for Asia and Australasia) and Ukraine (for central and eastern Europe).

RBS has three regional HR centres in Rhode Island (serving the US operations), Manchester (covering the UK and Ireland) and Singapore (supporting South East Asia) with smaller satellites operations in Amsterdam, India and Hong Kong serving in country business lines. The company has also started to a limited extent to add activities beyond that customer geography.

SAP or Shell's regional service centres are a distinct move further forward in the direction of global aggregation. As Table 8.2 indicates each of their three service centres delivers for their part of the globe, but, as the Shell Krakow example demonstrates, the global imprint can be deepened by having the centres covering customers in more than one region. A point we will expand on below.

Table 8.2   HR shared service centres at Shell and SAP

SAP	Geographic coverage	Shell	Geographic coverage
Prague	Europe, Middle East, Africa	Krakow	Europe, Africa, Russia, French speaking Canada and Portuguese/Spanish speaking Latin American countries (11 languages supported)
Singapore	Asia/Pacific, Japan	Manila	A night shift to service North America and an extended mid shift to support global Learning and Recruitment administration activities
Philadelphia	USA, Canada, Latin America	Kuala Lumpur	Asia, Australasia, Middle East (5 languages supported)

Regional centres covering different parts of the world is perhaps the limit of the ambition of multinational companies. We have not come across an organization with a single global centre dealing with the administrative work of a number of country operations across the world. There might be one activity which is carried out for all the global business units/ locations, as we will see below, but not one integrated shared services model. Why is this?

Shell, which as a company would in theory have the capability to move to this system, has thus far chosen not to do this and its perspective probably explains the reluctance to introduce a global service centre. Its view is that putting all one's eggs in one basket makes the operation vulnerable to political unrest or natural disasters (floods, earthquakes, volcanoes, etc.). The company recently had this brought home to it when floods in Manila came perilously close to the service centre there.

2. Is the work done in these locations purely for that geographic area or is it for the wider organization?

We have come across relatively few examples where a national or, more likely, regional centre, extends its activities to cover other geographies beyond what is necessary for that country or region. The advantages of such an approach come from concentrating expertise in narrow, specialist subjects in one location or in achieving greater resourcing flexibility. Shell is benefiting from expertise concentration by having all expatriate tax affairs dealt with in Krakow. This centre was chosen due to proximity of key stakeholders, availability of key skills in the centres and the subject matter chosen because of the complexity of European tax arrangements and the number of expatriates to whom they would apply. Other global activities, such as learning administration and recruitment operations, are handled centrally from Manila.

Resource flexibility may not be built into the model as a matter of course, but may be exploited on an ad hoc basis. We have seen this happen when one regional centre goes down (due to a power outage, for example, or the Manila problem described above) and another steps in and takes over its work.

As organizations increasingly take a global perspective for their service delivery operations we could see interchangeability and expertise concentration both becoming more common, as they offer a more reliable way of achieving at least some of the efficiency of having a single global service centre.

3. What content is covered by the common service delivery model, and is this affected by the degree of service aggregation?

For all the options there is the further decision about what is the content covered by the shared services centre. What areas of activity are included in service delivery models is, as we have already hinted, in fact closely related to their geographic span. What is evident is that some organizations struggle to offer the full range of services across national boundaries. The deciding factor on whether cross-national aggregation works is whether the principal activity to which the administration applies is delivered locally, regionally or globally. So a Shell can support job evaluation globally because their job evaluation system is run in the same way across the world. By contrast, in many organizations pensions and other employee benefits, employee relations related services and payroll are the activities most likely to be retained locally because specific local employment regulations have to be dealt with. Similarly, some administrative activity may be undertaken locally to support site based or nationally run activities, like training courses or junior level recruitment.

For some activities or processes there is a debate about the benefits of cross-national operations. Contact centres are one such topic. Nobody doubts that non-personal contact processing work, such as data entry, can be done anywhere in the world. However, people like Wilfried Meyer of Siemens take the philosophical view that personal interaction via a contact centre or even e-mail should be country based so that it takes place in one's own language and with people with the same cultural perspective. By comparison, companies like Shell or SAP are happy enough to have regional contact centres.

IBM originally set up an EMEA contact centre in Portsmouth and by 2001 it was covering 17 counties. It was able to deal with the various countries with their differences in usage (in call duration and content) by employing a variety of different nationalities (Industrial Relations Services, 1999). The firm in 2004 nearshored the operation to Hungary.

There are other topics where aggregation makes clear and indubitable sense. Data processing and management may well be one of the most vital activities to integrate worldwide. Yet it is not the easiest task to coordinate internationally. Monsanto does it by having HR IT staff in its St. Louis HQ maintaining a single global HR information platform with other team members responsible for regional HR data centres in Antwerp, Singapore and São Paulo. Interestingly, the overall international lead sits in Antwerp (Business Week Research Services, 2007). Tetra Pak has one global HR information system coordinator based in Italy who deals with 100 queries per quarter. She works with the HR directors across the world, convincing them of the need for good data and with 80 data supervisors distributed similarly to ensure the master data in their SAP system are in good shape. Metro has a global data coordinator based in Germany who is called the 'HR process owner'. He works with country HR teams to migrate them to the common SAP framework and centres of expertise to get the right IT infrastructure.

> Eva Akesson coordinates the HR Transformation portfolio of Tetra Pak, where the main purpose is to implement their 'Develop & Manage People' and reward processes, in parallel with launching common tools for HR, managers and employees to enable the execution of the respective processes. Contemporaneously, she is establishing a project methodology within HR, following the basic principles of the company's overall project management framework.

4. Does the same service delivery model apply to all locations or are some excluded?

As to whether global companies include all their locations worldwide in their shared services structure, it is common practice to exempt certain smaller, or atypical, locations from the main service delivery model. These locations do not necessarily have to use the standard, global IT system (or perhaps as in Shell, with its 'SAP-lite' version, a scaled back functionality is offered primarily on cost versus benefit grounds for smaller units) or apply standardization policies and processes (for example, Unilever does not try to integrate the HR activities of French West Africa into the global model). These companies may apply specific criteria to decide whether to include a location in firstly a shared services operation and secondly a wider service delivery model. Employee numbers is an obvious and simple criterion. Some organizations use a threshold (5,000 or 10,000 employees have been quoted) below which the business case is not strong enough to justify the creation of a shared services operation. This calculation is based on the cost of consolidation set against the benefits that will accrue from investing funds elsewhere. Metro expects all its operating companies' HRIS to be based on SAP at some point, but below 2,500 employees in a country it is just not worth making any migration with respect to payroll.

There are organizations that take a quite opposite approach to managing location size: Standard Chartered Bank introduced its shared service centre on a global basis, despite having a large geographical spread, precisely because the numbers employed in many countries was quite small (Withers et al., 2010).

The other principal criterion used to make these decisions is the degree of difference between a particular location and the main shared services centre. This might concern language used, the terms and conditions employed or the judicial system in place. The point is how much adaptation to, say, a contact centre or payroll system is required to cope with a language spoken by a small population or by distinctive pay and tax arrangements.

5. Is there a general move towards global service centres? If not, why not?

Some commentators argue, and we observed earlier with good reason, that there is an inexorable move for international companies from local administration to global shared services centres. In this view, organizations may introduce interim forms of organization as a stage of development towards a global service delivery model. Shared services can be extended to include a greater number of locations, more business units or the processes they support. A next step might be to extend its sphere of operation to other national business units that are adjacent or similar in nature. It could 'nearshore' the shared services centre as a further move towards globalization, gradually including more and more countries as its competence develops. The final step is then to choose between having a series of regional operations or a single global one.

This progressive attempt to maximize shared services coverage for 'transactional' tasks, based on the adoption of a global platform, applies to many organizations. However, it is not easy to accomplish when attempting the move across country boundaries when language, culture, customs and laws get in the way! As Figure 8.1 shows Shell has this sense of a progressive move towards a wider and deeper shared services operation. Always international, it has become more effective globally through a much clearer requirement on operating companies to participate rather than voluntarily opt in. The company is, moreover, encouraging country based HR to shift as much as it can to the global shared services centre, gradually reducing the locally run processes.

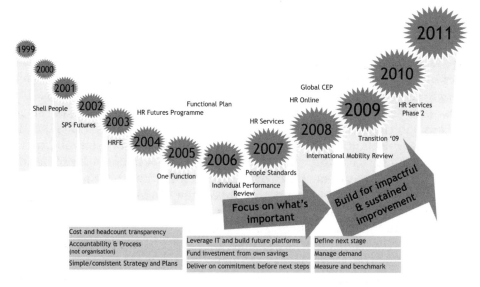

Figure 8.1   Shell's service delivery progression

The boxed example from Bayer is another demonstration of this point.

Bayer AG, a pharmaceutical company based in Leverkusen, near Cologne in Germany, launched shared services in October 2006 for about 20,000 of its German employees. Bayer's main shared services centre is in Leverkusen because the company migrated existing HR staff or other workers to jobs in the centre. A few months later, the company opened a shared services centre in Pittsburgh for 16,000 employees in North America and then progressively extended shared services to all German operations and the rest of Europe thereafter. Bayer was, at the time of this research, studying whether to implement HR shared services in Asia, where it anticipates having a third shared services centre (Business Week Research Services, 2007).

Or at least, what one may see is taking globalization in bite sized pieces by geography or content. For example, Vodafone has (Reilly et al., 2007) an advisory contact centre in the UK, used by employees and line managers for guidance on HR policy and employee relations, as well as administrative support. It has been developing a global shared service centre in Hungary, initially covering international assignments and supporting Vodafone's staff working where there is not a company owned operating entity. Vodafone is currently harmonising its HR systems to enable the further harmonisation of the HR operating model.

One German Bank had a number of regional service centres across Germany with different processes, weak data integrity and poorly specified roles. Generalist HR staff had heavy administrative workloads. The result was a high-cost and poor-quality service. Their solution was to create a single service centre in the country.

Another organization has seen how meeting efficiency requirements pushes change towards greater globalization, describing the move in Figure 8.2.

However, as we have also suggested, this notion of a maturity curve of an inevitable globalization of service delivery has its limits and exceptions. Why might this be so?

As we said at the outset of this section, some organizations do not have the business structure or geographic work profile for global shared services. For example, there are no HR shared services at JSW Steel and Metro Group because HR, following their businesses, is decentralized. The business operational structure may militate against a common global approach.

In other cases, the culture and ambition of the organization is still firmly rooted in their home country, or the preponderance of its operations may be there. Even genuinely global companies may still have their operational centre of gravity at the home base. This is where its shared services centre and centres of expertise are sited, but again they do not operate outside the country, or, even in some cases, the major location.

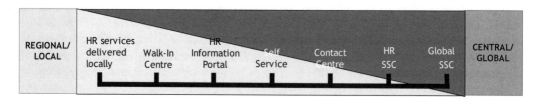

Figure 8.2　Moving towards global efficiency

Besides the cost–benefit reasons cited previously, organizations may be reluctant to globalize all forms of service delivery because of various quality concerns. Some take the view, closely related to a wider business perspective, that national characteristics are important and cultural differences should be respected and are thus disinclined to develop a global or even regional service delivery model.

At a more specific level, we reported earlier the debate on contact centres and problems globalizing processes with a strong national legal or cultural flavour. This leads many organizations to a segmentation of services depending upon their characteristics. They keep as local those services that, though perhaps more costly in delivery, offer a better quality outcome.

The outsourcing option

Another way of course that organizations can secure a global service delivery model is through outsourcing. The big international outsourcers can offer a global approach to HR services that obviates the need for organizations to achieve that goal themselves. For example, in 2003 Procter & Gamble chose to partner with IBM to provide HR services to its 98,000 employees across 80 countries. Unilever outsourced to Accenture to provide its HR administrative services, including payroll administration, reward administration, performance management, workforce reporting and core HR administration. This service is delivered to more than 200,000 Unilever employees in 100 countries in more than 20 languages. Accenture has delivery centres in Bangalore, Manila, Dalian, Bucharest, Prague and Curitiba.

AstraZeneca announced in December 2009 that it was going to outsource HR administration to NorthgateArinso. This decision to outsource, primarily to achieve a greater degree of efficiency and value added, was partly a means to get global consistency and control, a belief that this would not be achievable so easily (or at all) in house. So, the two parties have been defining together standardized end-to-end processes alongside simple and consistent tools to allow line managers to more effectively discharge their roles and make for an efficient and, from an outsourcer's perspective, doable service.

However, as the inevitably anonymized experiences below show, outsourcing is not always a problem free route to having a global service delivery model.

A new HR director decided to globalize a highly efficient HR regional shared services operation to realize its benefits more widely. To do this he decided to outsource it. However, the contract was awarded largely on cost grounds to an inexperienced contractor. The result was a 'disaster' for both parties, such that the work was brought back in house at the earliest opportunity.

A UK subsidiary of another global firm found it hard to get all its business units to combine their activities because of the rather siloed nature of business operations. By outsourcing the recruitment process it hoped both to obtain expertise but also to effect harmonization. As was found by the IT function in the 1990s, outsourcing problems is ultimately self-defeating. After seven years, the company brought the work back in house because it was not well managed, especially because there was no internal capability to handle the supplier appropriately.

An alternative to outsourcing all your transactional activity is to take a blended approach, mixing together an internal shared services provision while outsourcing other parts of the service delivery model or varying the method by geography as illustrated by the Monsanto case. The advantage of this route is that it can allow organizations to reflect localization within the business when appropriate and outsource to achieve globalization when that cannot be easily achieved in house. This blended approach may also be used where either the organization has got a really good level of efficiency and capability on certain processes such that there is no financial gain in outsourcing, or it thinks these processes are core to the firm and where the issue of confidentiality is particularly sensitive – which may be more true in global outsourced arrangements.

Monsanto Co has a shared services centre covering HR administration and payroll for its 8,000 US employees at its corporate headquarters in St. Louis. However, payroll outside the United States is primarily outsourced as is benefits administration (including pensions, stock options and health insurance) in the USA (Business Week Research Services, 2007).

GLOBAL CENTRES OF EXPERTISE?

There are some of the same benefits with global centres of expertise as with shared services, namely that cost efficiency can be gained through economies of scale by consolidating staff in one or a small number of places. Of course, because there are few experts involved the cost driver is weaker than for shared services, though if there is an associated consultancy pool the saving figure grows.

As we will see in the cases of Aegon and Canon Europe later, formal or informal centres of expertise (sometimes then called communities of practice) may be a means towards obtaining global reach. This may or may not be a precursor to the creation of a full global service delivery model and to the launch of international shared service centres. It may simply be the vehicle for the centralization of policy and process. Organizations may not be able (or willing) to obtain economies of scale through consolidation of administrative services, but for reasons, as we reported earlier in Chapter 7, of organizational integration and risk management, and to obtain a higher quality of consistent people management, there is a need to have some corporate resource to develop these policies and practices and drive them through the organization.

As we saw in Chapter 7, where the argument for global centres of expertise comes to the fore is in the role they can play in pushing corporate policy across the world. This means that key processes and key populations can be managed in this way. A Hewitt survey (2009) found that executive reward is the commonest global centre of expertise in North America, followed by leadership development. This is consistent with our earlier point that these are the areas where organizations seem to seek the greatest commonality and where organizations seek the greatest control.

When sited, like Shell, in the corporate office they are well placed to perform this role. Similarly, Vestas has 'Excellence Centres' that are responsible for ensuring optimal processes across the organization. TCS has global 'process' leads in talent management (including performance management and compensation), recruitment, talent deployment (competencies/training) and compliance (local staffing issues). This approach is deployed uniformly across the company. It is keen, wherever possible given legislation/regulatory constraints, on delivering a common 'client' experience and highlighting its professional services proposition (as an outsourcing provider to clients like Citigroup).

By comparison, though Oxfam's centres of expertise (covering reward, ER/HR policies, learning and development, talent, the global HRIS and occupational counselling) sit centrally in Oxford their primary purpose is to advise and support the international division, the UK operation and regional HR managers.

Other centres of expertise are located in the shared service centre with more of an emphasis on fielding level three customer queries from the contact centre. For example, Monsanto has global teams for benefits, compensation and rewards, and staffing operating on a shared services model (Business Week Research Services, 2007). RBS applies a hybrid model. Policy advisory services are provided in the UK as part of the Group centres of expertise; whilst in the USA they operate as an extension to the service centre. According to a Hackett survey, this integration with shared services seems to be particularly true for resourcing and to a lesser extent employee relations and learning. The benchmarking company argues that there is 'a growing level of confidence among HR professionals about SSOs' [shared services organizations] ability to deliver results in these more strategic activities' (The Hackett Group, 2009). Naturally, where centres of expertise are established in this manner, the arguments for global level operations are tied up with those for shared services.

Despite the apparent duplication of effort, this idea of having centres of expertise not just at global level but at regional and even national level is not uncommon. It reflects the fact there is still perceived to be a major role for national policymaking. Obviously the decision relates to extent to which large countries still operate with their own policies and whether regional aggregation makes any sense or, because of the diversity of the region's activities and the power of national institutional arrangements, it offers limited benefit.

Many organizations will of course have a hierarchy of aggregation from local to global. For example, Vodafone has global centres of expertise to cover global policy design, development of standard processes, principles and strategy, whilst also having them at regional level for guidance on implementation and at local level to execute standard processes, design and implement local policies/non-standard processes and manage local employee relations (where these are complex or important; otherwise the shared service centres deal with them). Nike has a set of regional centres of expertise with a hard line reporting into the corporate centre. At the time of writing, the company was thinking of having global ones. Novartis has corporate and divisional centres of expertise, as well as in some big countries centres of expertise for compensation and benefits and talent management. (As we described earlier, talent management is also organized at functional level within major divisions.)

We should also remind ourselves that in more federated business structures, the corporate centre plays a more traditional role in policy advice and development with greater interest in some key processes. There is no intention of globalizing but there is of holding the organization together. Thus the corporate centre at JW Steel is very much focused on leadership and talent acquisition, monitoring of talent programmes, overall organizational structure and OD, and oversight of each business's manpower plan. As with HPH, the corporate HR centre is 15 heads with a further 60 embedded in the various operations of the business. Leadership roles (functional heads and anybody over a certain compensation price point) are managed from the centre.

Economies of scale as well as concentration of expertise have led some companies to have global consultancy teams, with or without having centres of expertise. For example, Oxfam provides an illustration of global consultancy from within the centres of expertise. Canon Europe has a regional project team that is called upon when there is cross-regional change required. It is regarded like an internal consultancy firm in the way in which it supports pan-European projects.

GLOBAL BUSINESS PARTNERS?

Changes to the business partner role are in some senses less pronounced in a global setting than other parts of the HR function; after all they are still aligned to the key business activities. However, there are two broad approaches we have seen with respect to the staff that sit outside shared services, corporate centre and centres of expertise. There are true business partners aligned to the countries, regions, business units or functions who play a strategic role in people management in their business area. How the organization configures itself such that location or business unit is the prime customer base varies, but the point is that the deployment of business partners follows suit. So if business units are globally organized so, too, are business partners.

However, there are also in-country resources retained to undertake the work not transferred to shared services and centres of expertise. This might be employee relations, complex case work (requiring face-to-face engagement), the management of manual workers' terms and conditions and dealing with legal requirements. These are not true business partners in the proper meaning of that term, not least because they are not aligned to a specific business unit, but they may be called so – or something like HR advisers.

Siemens in the UK is aiming to have HR advisers shared across geography and sector, but still retained in the UK. Their work areas include:

- Operational Support
- project implementation
- case management (including individual consultation/industrial relations)
- policy interpretation/advice.

Many international organizations seek to reduce the number of 'HR advisers' as much as possible by transferring work to the shared services centre, whilst at same time ensuring that the business partners shift their operational tasks to the in-country resource. Thus Wilfried Meyer within his AsiaPac cluster urges cost control as a means of capping HR numbers, on the principle of 'idle hands make light work'. Shell's latest HR reorganization had the effect of cutting back the numbers of local advisers. Its aim is to have as few 'HR in country' people as possible, and these are there predominantly for work connected to employment legislation.

HP has taken all the transactional work from the business HR 'leads' to 'make' them business partners and moved it to the global shared service organization. This is a global organization 'because we need to deliver our programs globally, said ' Marcela Perez de Alonso, VP HR, HP (Conference Board, 2007).

However, in-country HR staff often play an important representational role in their locations, which is why you may have to have some senior people retained. So, for example, it is necessary to be seen to have a high-ranking business executive located in each country and with evident organizational clout and who can deal with the national authorities, accompanied by a senior HR representative to handle employment issues. This complicates the relationship with business partners, at least in terms of grading as the in-country staff may be the same or higher than those of the business partner, where the country is complex and important to business success. Moreover, the business partner's strategic role may overlap: one more focused on country, the other on business unit/function needs.

A Canadian company we spoke to gets round this grading problem by having the senior business partner in any country acting as the representative for that company, but like other organizations it finds it hard to position non-business partner HR generalists, who do a useful operational support role, but sit outside shared services. One Belgian manufacturing company deals with this by having 'business support centres' distributed around the world precisely to pick up these local operational matters. One consultancy named these 'solution centres' and pointed to the exemplar of Deutsche Bank (Kates, 2006).

In more federated organizations this distinction between strategic global and local operational is a lot less clear. For example, at JSW and HPH the business partners are generalist HR managers that partner the business in 'localizing' the various tools needed for managing implications of domestic business issues and performance. Issues concerning business capabilities, including local culture and talent, are managed within the region/country. All of this is translated into a clear plan which is confirmed by the corporate centre.

The perennial question of reporting lines also applies in global situations and gives an important clue to their role: do business partners report directly to the business unit leader, to HR or to both in a partnership model? This decision will reflect the balance of power between the corporate centre and business units, and between HR and the business. As we described in the HR governance chapter, the tendency among many global organizations is to have business partners report to the corporate centre so that they are part of the common drive to a globalized service that meets HR's objectives in cost-efficient standardization.

Implementing the Service Delivery Model

COMMON HR POLICIES, PROCESSES AND PRACTICES?

Having common HR policies and practices is an essential prerequisite to successful process automation and for introducing shared services. Variety of process and policy is expensive to manage. So standardization of policy and practice is a key feature of a global service delivery model. There is also a separate quality driver that is often bound up with global efficiency.

Global standardization stems from a belief that there is often little reason for the variety of HR policy and practice across an organization's world. As Wilfried Meyer explained, having worked in five continents, '90 per cent of what was being done had the same content.' He recognizes that there are some genuine cultural differences, but CEOs and HR the world over want to assert difference and to exercise control, but, as we described earlier, Siemens realized that organizations doing things differently was expensive and time consuming, especially because much of the variation was unnecessary.

So there is the belief that the vast majority of policies and practices should be the same irrespective of geography and that the traditional way of doing things, which in some countries is still strong, should be challenged. There is an assumption that local operating companies, business units and the like indulge themselves in creating variations that are not really justified, but come from the exercise of power under the pretence of cultural difference. General managers and heads of HR may work together to fulfil mutually supporting ambitions and resist corporate involvement. Or, as one interviewee put it: the 'clever' people in his company did not want to conform but to invent their own policies/processes, etc., such that there were 25 different HR competence frameworks around the world. In other words, both the line and HR managers want to be creative, to do their own thing and protect their own much loved creations against outside interference. If you appoint capable people to local roles they will want to assert their independence and make their jobs more interesting. Similarly, there is frequently strong local attachment to local suppliers and resistance to using centrally chosen global providers.

So, to be clear, cost and quality benefits of standardization come from:

- **Having just *one* of something** It is particularly true of IT systems – lowering purchase and maintenance costs. For example, Atos Origin has one worldwide data system. This can apply to HR policies. As Siemens in the UK found, trying to support 48 redundancy policies is more expensive than managing one. Similarly, Oxfam have one standardized performance appraisal process to ensure organizational effectiveness and because it is 'far more sensible to invent it once'.
- **Greater consistency of delivery** by getting everyone to follow the same quality standard. For example, using six sigma type process improvement methods means that Shell promises to get an employment offer out within 24 hours of interview anywhere in the world.
- **The need to employ fewer people to manage standard processes** At SAP they can give you the example of having 783 people in non-standardized payroll for its 48,300 employees but only 78 people in Total Rewards that run the standard processes. Or the fact that because their shared services centre can now handle 45 per cent of all tier three problems though using standard processes, the number of business partners can be reduced and those who remain can be relieved of trying to resolve these sort of issues.
- **Simplifying processes allows rebalancing of the HR/line relationship** As advanced by Metro: if you simplify and standardize to the point that any retail manager can operate them, the line can take on data entry tasks from HR, without feeling so 'dumped upon'. Moreover, line managers can take more self-responsibility for their people management decision making, relying much less on HR. Standardization achieves this indirectly through the reduction in the size of the function. Fewer HR people means they have not the time to 'hand hold' managers, thereby 'transforming the function's relationship with the line' (Iain McKendrick Global Head of HR Strategy, Planning and Analytics at AstraZeneca). As we will cover in the conclusion, business partners can also be released to play their more strategic role.
- **Harmonization of procurement** giving quality assurance as well as cost advantage. This is particularly applied to recruitment and learning and development processes. Unilever, for example, found it had 3,000 third party contracts across the world and realized the financial saving that could be made from reducing that number by aggregating buying power.
- **Benchmarking to make performance more transparent** Organizations try to apply best practice (obtained from within the organization or from external sources) as a standard to achieve this raising of the performance bar. Internal and external benchmarking pushes up performance by highlighting those areas that are not complying or falling behind the performance leaders.
- **Using it as a helpful vehicle in post merger or acquisition integration** It permits easier integration if systems, policies and processes are aligned. Similarly, in complex business arrangements, especially separate legal entities standardization is one way to achieve coherence. The same applies to those wishing to reduce the power of divisional baronies and assert the benefits of the whole organization over its parts.
- **Corporately aligned management** Standardized recruitment processes can apply a common method for selection (i.e. assessment centre, structured interviewing technique, etc.) using the same set of corporate competencies to identify suitable

candidates. The result should be a higher alignment between personal and organizational values across the world.

British American Tobacco describes the importance of a single set of corporately assured leadership and management development programmes. The aim is to educate managers in using a single corporate model of how the company wants leaders and managers to do their job. They want the same set of principles and values inculcated. They do not want the variety that would come from the multiplicity of programmes generated by the devolved approach. If, say, a manager does not like the corporate leadership style (more empowering and less command and control) then they are probably not suited to working for British American Tobacco. This point applies to the wider workforce. British American Tobacco is one of many organizations that explicitly recruits on attitudes and trains for skills.

Similarly, recruitment at JSW Steel is very much around finding the different skills required, but a common mindset around performance, growth and entrepreneurialism.

As Oxfam found from being a rather siloed organization and with a 'disobedient culture', having some common HR processes reinforces being part of the one organization across 70 countries and different businesses, and the fact that the process is the same for all helps integration because of the required consistency. Jane Cotton, HR director, has sought to tackle the mavericks that used to exist and she insists on taking a corporate view where there is a knock-on effect around the globe for example in reward (say, paying bonuses) and in change management (e.g. the treatment of redundancy).

- **Resource prioritization** As we said earlier, permitting an easier way of global prioritization of resources ensures that programmes with the most benefit get the lion's share of the funds available.

In the choice of the process on which to standardize global companies are naturally interested in areas that will benefit from cost or quality improvement. They do this by looking out for examples of internal or external good practice – to choose a well-designed case of a common policy or practice – but they are also searching for 'scalability' – can a process/policy operate on a worldwide basis? SAP, for example, reluctantly closed down a leadership development programme in Australia, though it was well regarded by HR and customers alike, because there was recognition that it could not operate on a global scale.

At SAP there are seven process clusters based on the employment lifecycle model from sourcing to exit, each with a smaller number of sub-processes. So in total there are less than 40 global processes. Where possible all processes are global, certainly all the 10 'significant and recurring' ones are. For an example, 'onboarding' might appear local, but in fact take the UK workforce: only two thirds work for a UK operation, the rest for regional or global functions/activities. So a local induction process fails to accommodate the latter.

> At Schneider Electric there are global programmes especially in learning, OD, compensation and benefits (e.g. global grading, incentive scheme and performance management, expatriate policies) and strategies/principles, such as EVP and talent.

So, on the basis of these sorts of criteria, what is the content of standardization? In our discussions we have seen a whole variety of subjects considered as areas ripe for harmonization:

- HR strategy
- job evaluation and grading
- compensation and benefits
- performance management
- workforce planning
- talent management
- learning and development
- mergers and acquisitions.

Reward is often in the van of the standardization drive. Research by a team from Gent Management School found that all the aspects of senior management remuneration in a sample of international companies tended to be centralized, whereas only certain aspects of middle management pay were and 'operational employees' were handled mostly on a local basis (Baeten, 2010). We have heard of centralized practices in relation to common incentives for sales staff at SAP; a global profit sharing scheme at Vestas; globally sourced pay benchmark data (using international firms like Mercer and Aon Hewitt, not local ones) at Schneider Electric; common reward statements at Arup or Firmenich; and a common executive remuneration system in Shell and others. This can be for reasons of organizational integration (profit sharing), common – data – standards (benchmarking, reward statements), business oversight (executive pay) or management simplicity (sales incentives).

Learning and development has been another area where harmonization has been prominent. For example, Unilever uncovered 340 leadership programmes worldwide before it rationalized them. Similarly, SAP shut down 74 development leadership programmes to be found worldwide and created a single global one.

Recruitment processes have also been simplified and in some cases globalized. This has also involved, as with learning and development, an attempt to rationalize suppliers. Shell has decided only to use three global executive search organizations worldwide.

And we have already stressed the interest in standardization of data systems.

To give the reader a flavour of the sort of activities subject to standardization we have come across here is a selection to consider:

- using standardization to facilitate the integration of a series of businesses following a merger (Evonik)
- having an agreed framework for HR IT systems (Metro Group)
- developing a global job catalogue divided into job families (Ericsson)
- a single learning and development model for management levels (SAP)

- creating a single, global master data set based on a single, global HRIS platform (TetraPak)
- having a common global total reward statement (Firmenich)
- using a single annual employee survey across the world with a response rate of around 90 per cent (Ericsson)
- the principle of having an annual performance 'dialogue' between manager and subordinate (Siemens).

Despite the picture painted here the impression should not be given that HR's standardization of processes has now been sorted. Indeed, as one interviewee put it, 'One should not suppose that "declaring victory" in standardization means that tensions between HR in the business and process owners have disappeared'. Various surveys point to the continuing desire for further harmonization. For example, Hewitt (2009b) found that about half the respondent organizations reported being behind target in the drive for greater consistency in HR activities.

INTEGRATED IT SYSTEMS?

Automation of HR processes underpins an effective shared services operation. This is because it reduces the number of transactions that have to be processed, thereby easing the workload of the shared services centre. Without reengineered and simplified processes and extensive manager and employee self-service, shared services staff would either be overwhelmed or resourcing levels would have to be set unacceptably high. Moreover, workflow on automated systems facilitates global activities especially permitting shared service centres in different locations to work on separate aspects of the same case using shared files.

This leads most of the organizations we have dealings with to seek to have a single integrated IT system, if possible both for employee records and payroll. The benefits of 'cloud' technology in facilitating technological integration of diverse IT using the web have yet to be realized, so organizations that are globalizing their operations, organically or by acquisition, face a number of challenges in bringing together dispersed and heterogonous IT kit. These challenges we will describe in a later section, but here we will remark that even a company that prefers to run its business in a decentralized way is prepared to push towards having common employee data globally, as the Metro example below illustrates. This limited model of systems integration and data management only came about because the Board was convinced it was the way forward and overcame any opposition from the Sales lines.

Metro has specified a set of minimum requirements and developed a common HR IT template using SAP HR software that contains the 'master data', payroll and 'organization management'. This applies across the whole Metro Cash and Carry group.

Corporate Metro Group HR has implemented a six step change process:

1. Countries inform HQ about demands for
   - new processes

       –   new functionalities
       –   deployment of Common Template HR core.

2.   HQ validates demand.
3.   HQ authorizes countries to move ahead.
4.   Countries officially register demand with Common Template HR.
5.   Common Template HR evaluates demand.
6.   Common Template HR executes demands together with Metro Systems.

Control rests with the corporate centre but there is a transparent and formal change process. However, as befits a company that is trying to balance centrifugal and centripetal tendencies, the corporate HR has also agreed with the business where different process ownership for 'HR solutions' will apply. This approach replaced an earlier method that divided processes into three: ones where one or other of the principal brands has control (e.g. e-learning); where control is shared between the brands (e.g. travel management) and where Metro Group corporate HR is the process owner (pensions, recruitment and talent management).

The key benefits of having good HR IT in a global context are:

- **Having the requisite quantity and quality of data** is vital to create a complete and accurate workforce picture around the world. This allows those at the corporate centre to use the data to inform the organization on retention rates, supply shortages, skill requirements, diversity performance and so on. Where there is at least an element of global resourcing, it means interventions can be made to deal with supply/demand imbalances either in the short term (by expatriate staff transfer or permitting extra local hiring) or long term (by creating new streams of recruits, e.g. through those corporate universities we described under talent management). The Unilever example of strategic workforce planning relied on this sort of quality data. Similarly, keeping control of bonus decision making is helped by data being supplied in a standard format and preferably into a common system.
- **Standardized operation** The e-enablement of processes like reward and especially performance management allows standardization in how they are undertaken. This gives the corporate centre assurance that defined quality requirements are met (even simply that these processes are undertaken) as well as the data referred to above. As with standardization, automated processes help line manager conformity to the common processes: it drives them to adopt the right solution to problems.

Aviva is reported as using automation to assist standardization. Andy Moffat, European HR Director, explained that the organization has moved from 'a federation of almost independent companies to a structure where we are one business doing things much more consistently'. This process has been assisted by introducing an HR system that 'enables us to manage our pan-European policies and practices with a single tool' (Churchyard, 2010).

- **E-recruitment**, using the same platform, ensures that global selection standards can be applied across the world. It also cuts costs by reducing manual intervention in the process. It gives the corporate centre the chance to publicize the employer brand in a consistent manner. Recruits from anywhere in the world will go onto the same home page and take part in the same hiring exercise. E-recruitment offers the organization the chance to presents a common employee value proposition and begins, even before formal employment starts, the process of enculturalization.
- **Likewise e-learning** draws employees together. At least in a virtual way people have the same development experience and one which is corporately determined. So if you are in Dubai working for a French company and undertaking an e-learning course on lean management, you will be participating in the same experience as someone in Brazil, with the same course material and assessment mechanism.
- **Creating cohesion** Intranets can be used similarly to convey important messages to employees internationally on what is important to the organization (via leadership statements) or announcements of change in personnel, policy, business operations, etc. It is a very helpful binding device for far-flung organizations. In supplying information about HR policy and practice they ease the burden on contact centres providing information in simple formats to customers.
- **Systems can be used for compliance tracking** It is very obvious where locations and business units deviate from standard processes, as they will appear on exception reports.

Conditions for a Global Service Delivery Model

Surely a characteristic of a truly global company is that it delivers its corporate functions, like HR, on an international rather than country basis. We have suggested in this chapter that while this might be definitionally correct, it ignores the variety of change against the background of business and organizational drivers that pull in a different direction.

So, as we have seen, certain organizational configurations relating to size and distribution of operations and the degree of decentralization militate against having cross-national HR shared services, and, to a lesser extent, global centres of expertise. The degree and nature of standardization is also affected by the business context. For example, small, growing companies are not as interested as mature organizations in harmonizing: they are too busy making money. Those firms that emphasize speed and flexibility of response are similarly less inclined to choose to harmonize HR policy and practice. By contrast, standardization may come to the fore in recession hit businesses wanting to take out money now. For example, at ABB the target for HR costs to be only 0.5 per cent of revenue has caused some country operations to collaborate on their HR services. Finally, tight or loose organizational control will, in a similar manner, impact on the degree of global automation. It is also affected by the funds available for investment, which in turn will be determined by the rate of return, i.e. by the size of the prize.

The factors involved in organizational decision making are set out in Tables 8.3 and 8.4. The former looks the way the facets of HR transformation are affected by organizational structure. The latter shows how the work context, i.e. business positioning and labour market, together with environmental constraints relate to where spatially HR does its work.

Table 8.3   HR transformation and business structure

Business structure/HR transformation response	Single business activity	Holding company for diversified business activities	Integrated company with diversified business activities
Consolidation	Largely unnecessary unless company operates from multiple locations	Hard to justify across business units if very different business processes	Key element in developing 'one company' philosophy
Automation	High benefits because should have common processes	Business case may be difficult to win but high e-HR investment costs argues for cross-business unit investments	Strong investment case, part of integration argument
Standardization	No reason not to have common processes	Difficult to achieve across business units but should be achieved within business units	Essential for shared services to be effective, but question of how far to go given business differences

Table 8.4   Context for HR's response by geography

Work context/ HR's geographic alignment	Business alignment	Workforce drivers (labour market)	Integration constraints
National	Limited international business activity or can be dealt with by business trips from base	Locally recruited and deployed	Complex local terms and conditions
Regional	Follows regional business unit structures or too complex to organize globally	Some regional development programmes	Diverse range of languages and small populations in regions
Global	Follows global business units' practice or ambitions	International cadre of staff or large expatriate group and/or international labour market operating	Difficult cultural integration due to workforce diversity and range of country institutional arrangements

We rejected earlier an inevitable move towards global HR shared services as overly simplistic, as Tables 8.3 and 8.4 suggest. Nonetheless, there are pressures towards elements of centralization and standardization without necessarily going the whole hog of a global service delivery model. The Canon and Aegon cases illustrate the point we are making. Recent business conditions, growing regulation, the pressure to reduce HR functional costs and a philosophical shifting of view towards the benefits of process/policy commonality (as opposed to the advantages of diversity) have all pushed in this direction. These examples also show how companies adapt the default service delivery model to suit their particular circumstances, and how change can be incremental rather than revolutionary.

Up until a couple of years ago the financial services company Aegon might well have been an exception to the centralizing and standardizing tendency. Despite employing 29,000 people in 20 countries the company has had a long tradition of decentralized management, both seeing the benefits of countries responding to local business needs and encouraging decision making close to the customer. Even though Aegon as a brand is widely used, consistent with the above approach there has not been insistence upon its use. If it makes better business sense local brands are used, like TransAmerica in the USA.

HR followed suit, with little in the way of corporate control or interference, trusting that country HR heads know their own local situation best.

Change has been coming over the last 10 years driven by:

- Sarbanes-Oxley and other regulatory pressures to demonstrate good governance and risk management across the whole company.
- The fact that regulators see Ageon as a single entity.
- Operating in a global market that means developing at least some global products against global competitors.

The recent financial and economic crisis has accentuated the need for good governance in a holistic manner and the need to pare down costs.

The result of these influences is a move towards some degree of greater business integration and corporate control over business activities. So a number of global products have been developed (e.g. Asset Management and variable annuities), which are managed by global business units to sit alongside local products. The company still insists it has local businesses being run by local management, but it has now more than ever developed 'shared global resources, knowledge and perspective'.

Again HR has followed suit. It is effecting a small but important shift in the balance between local and corporate power in favour of the latter. Yet, as HR Director Peter van Os stresses, there is no intention of creating a 'politburo' in the Hague dictating to business units how to run their affairs. Instead, on reward and talent management there are now frameworks within which locations operate with both more corporate oversight and involvement. The global framework will be an 'add-on' not replacement to local activities, according to Peter van Os. The corporate centre will continue to respect local circumstances, legal frameworks and traditions/cultures, but the business unit or country HR teams must also respect the need for and recognize the benefits that flow from commonality.

Before 2000 Canon was, according to Massimo Macarti, HR Director for Europe, a 'polycentric' organization. The first European HR director was appointed in that year, but it has been only over the last three or four years that there has been a significant move towards regional harmonization. Some common tools have now been created in performance management, salary review, recruitment and workforce planning. Previously, there was a great deal of variation – in, say, whether recruitment was via agencies or networking, and in the time and nature of pay adjustment. Moreover, the number of learning and development activities has been reduced because this added cost but returns were uncertain. The position has developed to the point where processes and associated policies will be moved to the European centres of expertise when it does not 'hinder service quality too much'.

As we described earlier, there are no current plans to reinforce standardization of policies, processes and systems through a consolidation of transactional service delivery. Canon is committed to having a country based HR business partner to ensure that there are people on the ground. Whether one also needs someone at the HR director level is more questionable, certainly for the smaller countries. Nevertheless, whilst there is a country CEO, having an HR director makes sense.

Challenges

There are specific challenges for the various parts of the service delivery model that are necessarily affected by the organizational design:

CONSOLIDATION

- **Doing it on the cheap** As with other areas of HR transformation, if the change process is poorly executed there will be an inevitable consequence in a weak structural outcome. If the change programme is under-resourced or lacking in experience or expertise then this will be visible later and probably in the end cost more money where there are constant reiterations to get the model working right.
- **Pricing and segmentation** Does HR present to business units a set of priced service offers with minimum performance standards allowing customers to pick and mix? Or does it avoid this producer complexity by denying customers any choice and simply passing over to them a general overhead charge? HR may find itself with a Hobson's choice of either sticking to its guns on the benefits of a common approach to systems, policies, processes, etc. and thereby irritating managers who want to adapt the corporate fiat to suit their 'special' circumstances, or caving in to management demands thereby incurring 'unnecessary' cost. Some organizations avoid this dilemma by pricing exceptions and telling the 'offending' business unit to pick up the tab. This response, though, also has its critics. For one thing it incurs extra bureaucracy (and cost) sending internal invoices backwards and forwards. For another, it accepts 'inefficiency' as legitimate, rather than something that should be challenged.
- **Complexity costs** Giving the best possible customer experience is laudable, but, in particular, it is expensive to run a contact centre in multiple languages and to accept contact via multiple methods. Moreover, servicing a diverse customer base (especially if standardization is in its infancy and the use of e-solutions is limited) makes support

costs very high. Changing to e-mail only questions does not suit all locations and may lead to its own efficiencies, as described below.

- **Shared services centres and attrition** A common problem in these centres, turnover has potentially a bigger impact in cross-national ones because the work complexity means that the cost of turnover (recruitment, induction and training) is greater. Using graduates in shared services centres can improve quality of performance (at a cost) but they may have skill use and career demands that may be hard to satisfy, with the inevitable risk of higher employee turnover.
- **Creating cohesion** Overcoming the difficulties of getting a **shared services** centre team to cohere is one way of reducing attrition, and of increasing performance, yet it is especially difficult with the almost inevitably (culturally, linguistically, nationally) diverse workforce.
- **Demand creep and failure** can drive up costs unexpectedly. You think that contact centres should reduce expenditure, but according to critics the economies of scale benefits may be outweighed by:
  - generating traffic that did not exist before (Managers just got on with making decisions without the opportunity to check/confirm that the contact centre offers.)
  - dealing with questions through the intranet, by phone and then by e-mail either because they have not been dealt with properly the first time round or this method is unsuitable for the nature of the issue.
    So it may end up costing more money – if all cost, especially time, factors are included. This is what E.ON discovered (Reilly et al., 2007). And on an international basis given language and cultural diversity, the risk is potentially that much greater.
- **Personal contacts in preference to advertised contacts** Another challenge is whether to 'stream' incoming calls to a **contact centre**. In other words, if there is no differentiation, managers, employees and HR colleagues all come through on the same number with no prioritization on complexity or urgency. Again, people will bypass this arrangement if it does not deliver: they will ring their own personal contacts met at meetings and training courses or hangovers from the old service model.
- **Limited range of global knowledge** We described earlier that **centres of expertise** can be remote, lacking in business focus and pursuing inappropriate policies, but a further problem in an international setting is a lack of staff with sufficient global awareness. For some, say in reward and employee relations, there has to be knowledge and understanding of different systems, of expatriate policy practice, of consultation mechanisms, etc. For those in learning and development or OD there has to be particular sensitivity to culture and diversity. Moreover, there are problems with specialist country knowledge – business, legal, cultural, etc. Nobody in the centre can know everything about everywhere. As with business partners, you cannot easily remedy this situation through recruitment as there is a paucity of such global expertise.
- **Unsupported line managers** Determining how many **business partners** to have and where to locate them is usually a tricky question. It makes sense in a global service delivery model to have business partners assigned to the global business units. Certainly, some subsidiaries are not large enough to offer sufficient challenge

to justify them, especially where the corporate centre determines the key HR policies. So it is hard to recruit good people into those sorts of roles, reinforcing a reluctance by the corporate centre to devolve much responsibility. The consequence, though, of having a few very strategic contributors may leave a bigger than usual hole in your support to managers.

- **Delivering on the role** Getting the **business partner** role working well whatever the environment is proving difficult for many organizations. The challenges of a global business partner are largely the same except writ large: risks of going 'native', remoteness from the employee base, the complexity of dealing with a local 'baron' as well as a global business unit head.

STANDARDIZATION

A lot of the issues to be faced with standardization we described in the last chapter but we will add a few extra points here. They really concern the fact that however well the governance mechanism is established, the standardization element of the service delivery model will not succeed if it not properly attended to.

- **Ineffective design or execution** Standardization will fail where the processes do not work as intended, or are based on a flawed design, say because they do not acknowledge local conditions, institutional and legal requirements. They may also not run optimally because of a poor change process. HR colleagues and line managers will bypass them if they are too clunky or ineffective. We have been told of the problems that arose when an organization chose to standardize complex processes before straightforward ones and to simplify these processes after standardization rather than before. Vestas found that other priorities, in its case to attend to high levels of recruitment, diverted resources away from the design and enforcement of common processes, thereby slowing the thrust towards standardization.
- **Inflexibility to change** If standardization is pushed because of a certain set of circumstances (recession, acquisition, brand damage, etc.), the danger is that the solution is institutionalized though the problem has changed. In fast moving business situations, HR's approach might not keep up. The context (time/circumstances) may have shifted but the organization is stuck with an outmoded approach. Its operating model may be ill suited to the mode of business operation. As Rohan Pandithakorralage, HR Director of Aitken Spence, told us in Colombo: 'Policies should not be set in stone but adjust to their context.' Rohan was thinking about the impact the end of the Sri Lankan civil war would have on recruitment and retention policies to take just two examples. Or, take working in joint ventures: there is a requirement for flexibility in operating the service delivery model to adjust to the fact that the partner's ways are not necessarily the same as yours.
- **Dealing with reconfiguration** Whilst an acquisition might drive standardization in order to integrate diverse HR activities, it also can be a stumbling block. BASF is constantly buying new businesses, but this makes it hard to settle on integration before the next acquisition comes along. Or HR finds itself having to manage a set of legacy terms and conditions that cannot be bought out or integrated with existing rules. In these circumstances, the degree of organizational change might almost persuade the corporate centre to manage HR more on a holding company style basis

– defining high-level principles and agreeing certain reporting requirements – than to strive for harmonization. Moreover, especially in some countries, there is a tendency not to create a single legal entity out of the diverse acquisitions and this makes it even harder to produce a common vision and stick to it.

AUTOMATION

- **Because we can** There is a tendency to believe the application of computer and communications technology necessarily leads to greater efficiency: automation is always good. The risk is that the technology gets applied just because it is there (think of software product upgrades to see the point). The IT argument trumps the business need. It may not be right to automate all your processes from a quality/customer of financial perspective.
- **Too many bespoke systems** In similar way to the problems of structural integration, it can be hard for the corporate centre to operate a common approach if it is confronted by lots of different IT systems not well integrated with each other, or with the local customization of a single allegedly standard system.
- **Patchy cooperation** Even where there is a single technical infrastructure, problems may occur if the corporate centre is dependent upon the cooperation of dispersed HR units. If you take the Metro Group's model described earlier, it is very reliant on data being entered into the common system and entered accurately. Another example is Ericsson where some data are coherent and truly global whereas, for example, compensation data are not a part of the single infrastructure. When needed centrally, compensation data are requested case by case, and thus response and cooperation vary widely.
- **Too many crossed wires** Moreover, it is hard to be held accountable for data and process integrity if you are not responsible for the execution of the systems that generate the data or of the supporting processes. There is a specific risk that if data are entered twice into two systems, one local and one corporate, errors are made and inconsistencies develop.
- **Varying legislation** From a practical point of view, another challenge lies in the collection and transfer of personal data where there is restriction due to confidentiality legislation. Laws on data protection vary. There are constraints on transferring personal data outside the European Economic Area especially to countries that do not have adequate data protection provisions. And even within Europe, some countries, like Germany, have further specific regulations, e.g. unless legally permitted it is a requirement to get employee consent to data transfer outwith the country. Metro writes this into employment contracts so that staff assent to their details being passed elsewhere. There are specific worries about sending employee data offshore to countries that do not have the same level of data protection. There are real fears that the data may be passed to others. The 2010 T Mobile case of celebrity information being sold heightened these concerns, not least because this happened in the UK where there is data protection legislation in force.
- **Huge scale equals huge cost** The very scale and nature of the technological investment for a global service delivery model is off-putting to some organizations. Companies like Centrica did their outsourcing deals partly to acquire technology

they could not afford to develop in house. Working with a single platform also raises issues on data security and system integrity that must be addressed.

- **Not user friendly** Poorly chosen or badly implemented manager self-service/ employee self-service especially can also set back the path towards standardization, as Shell found with its first 'unfriendly' iteration of self-service. Like standardization, if systems (e.g. in self-service) do not work as they should, users bypass them, going back to manual solutions, introducing unapproved system solutions, using their own work-arounds or managers delegating tasks to specially appointed administrators.
- **Loss of 'face time'** Where there are automated processes in areas that were previously conducted face to face, inevitably low touch will replace high touch. So e-recruitment and e-learning will, at least to a degree, be conducted without human intervention. There are lots of good arguments for this, well rehearsed in a national – western – context, but there is a risk that this will not be so well received in all geographies. The drive towards globalization may mean that any objections to automation will be overridden.
- **Technology hype over-promises and under-delivers** Technology is not always as far advanced as supposed (at least in many organizations), which limits the effective operation of self-service and shared services centres. This complaint is nothing new, but again is more serious in a global service delivery model. Take finding answers to questions on the web by the shared services or contact centre: trying to handle a wide range of variation of terms and conditions and policies can be resource intensive. If there is no decent intranet search facility for the customer, it can increase the number of calls and slow the process down for HR and its clients. Self-service failures can also generate unnecessary demand.

Success Factors

GENERAL

- **Achieve customer delight** A good approach to global HR transformation is to delight the customer and offer a new experience. In what Garmt Louw of Shell has described as an 'immaturity phase', before customers see the benefits only the problems of HR transformation, this might seem a forbidding prospect. Yet, if the aim is to appeal to the customer, then the change design should bear this in mind. How much better a remote service will be depends upon previous experience. So it may be faster, more accurate transaction processing; quicker and more helpful contact centre responses; or more control over data entry may be an improvement on the past service. If the common IT system and associated protocols are working well, it sets a positive impression of the benefits harmonization can bring. Such positive impressions also build goodwill for future change. Moreover, standardized policies and processes allow greater consistency of service delivery the world over – which should be attractive to mobile managers or those with geographically dispersed line responsibilities. If these arguments fail, you could also say 'it is the best function we can afford', as Hugh Mitchell, HR Director of Shell, has argued.
- **Choose the right model for your circumstances** Organizations should resist getting the best practice bug and seek a best fit solution. Thus a decentralized

manufacturing company with a small number of big sites may come to a different conclusion about back office aggregation than a company with a widely dispersed management consultancy team. The degree of homogeneity or heterogeneity in the workforce across geographic boundaries will affect the cost of harmonization and constructing a single global service delivery model, because handling variety is expensive. Similarly, operational interdependence lends itself to common solutions in a way that high separation of business activities does not.

- **Engage customers in change** To minimize customer objection engage them in the process of design, consulting as you go. If this is not possible, and it is harder to do in an international context, then at least model change with their participation, checking that revised processes work to their satisfaction. To make this an effective global process, consultation should be with a wide range of stakeholders.
- **Piloting change first?** As we discussed in our book *Best value HR: the shared services option*, rather than implementing a change wholesale, you could pilot it to test out whether it works. This is what HPH does. Francis Tong 'road tests' new policies and processes using both large and small ports to check how HR interventions would fare before a global roll out. He also discovers what issues they will face during any implementation.
- **Ensure effective implementation** Organizations should put a high stress not just on determining the correct design, but also implementing it well. As Figure 8.3 shows, there are arguments in favour of the various ways of sequencing change involving systems, processes and structures. Leading with structural change suits organizations that have to build a body that will drive through HR transformation. So it may be favoured by dispersed companies, like retail firms. Putting systems in the vanguard may be chosen by those committed to an IT investment around which change is delivered. This might be used by merging companies that are both weak in technological terms. A process led revolution may be used where the form of structure depends on the process reengineering. So, great care has to be exercised to choose the sequence that best suits your organization's particular circumstances, and then implementation has to be mindful that there will still be booby traps! An anonymized example from a global company is shown in Figure 8.4.
- **Clean up before standardizing** The unanimous view of our interviewees is always to modernize processes before standardization. Trying to reengineer processes whilst at the same time harmonizing them adds to the complexity of an already difficult implementation. The view was also expressed that leaving unreformed process for a new structure to operate risks early poor performance from a shared services centre from which it may never recover. As Rob Voss of Siemens put it, talking of his UK experience: 'It was tough moving to the new structure because we didn't get the processes right in the first place.' So undertaking process mapping is a very useful precondition of developing HR governance.
- **Keep at it** To sustain the performance you need to keep constantly getting it right. As Garmt Louw says, it means 'boring is the essence of success'. Processes have to be meticulously followed by all those involved, whatever their location. Deviation or process failures need to be eliminated wherever possible.

There are specific success factors that apply to the various parts of the service delivery model.

	PROS	**CONS**
Structure first	- mobilises resources - drives through change	- multiple change waves - unclear structure design
Systems first	- alignment with kit - no wasted design effort	- tail wags dog - unnecessary design
Process first	- gives platform to new organisation - bottom-up change	- no ownership of change - unclear structural fit
Concurrent	- emphasises interdependence - one change	- more complex to deliver - longer to complete

Source: after Booz Allen, 1998

Figure 8.3   Different sequencing options

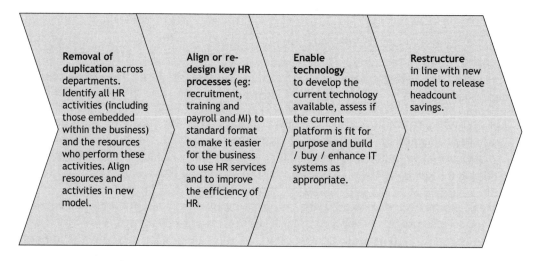

Figure 8.4   Applying change sequence to a global organisation

CONSOLIDATION

- **Shared services are not identical** Avoid being drawn into the proposition that the treatment of HR service delivery through **shared services** should be the same as for IT and Finance. As Hewitt's shared services study (2007) persuasively argues, there are many differences between the functions, some of which we have already alluded to – namely the personal and complex nature of many of the interactions between service users and providers. Hewitt's paper makes the additional point that service volumes are much lower for HR than IT and Finance. This is especially true for contact centres.

Hewitt declares that IT contact centres receive over 10 times the number of calls for the same population. The use of employee self-service and corporate intranets is reducing HR transactions and calls, leaving those that remain even more complex to handle. Indeed, it is the aim of most HR transformation objectives to bring this about. The nature of the interaction and its frequency are important considerations in global service delivery design, especially in determining skill requirements.

- **Get the right resourcing model and address turnover risks** There is a danger that organizations choose their shared services location because of huge early tax breaks, property support and training reimbursement rather than because the labour market offers the right skills base. This can come back and haunt the organization in terms of a threat to service quality if staff recruitment and retention are problematic. The use of graduates to do shared services centre work can address the quality question as Shell has found, but it has meant having a high attrition rate by the company's standards, though half the industry norm. SAP in Prague also illustrates a positive approach to dealing with contact centre turnover.

As a response to the challenge to attract and retain staff where there is a labour shortage of candidates with the right skills, intense market competition, leading to wage inflation, SAP's Prague shared services centre focused on new target recruitment groups. It looked to hire mothers on parental leave, students, handicapped people and older workers. It offered them more flexible work patterns and workplaces, developed an employee referral programme, built an Employer of Choice brand and worked with the government to improve the local supply through cooperating with secondary schools. Retention problems centred on what were perceived to be boring job profiles, limited promotion possibilities and the absence of a clear career path. SAP tackled this by listening to staff, collecting feedback, measuring employee satisfaction and understanding reasons for leaving. Applying the lessons learned meant implementing job enrichment programmes (e.g. project work, job shadowing, job rotation), developing, supporting and monitoring individual development plans, including identifying top talent.

- **Shared not centralized** To make shared services a reality as a 'shared' not centralized service, organizations can offer a range of services that business units or locations can choose to take or not. There is likely to be a minimum harmonized set of services (contact centre, records and payroll) that have to be taken, but it does allow flexibility to meet the varied needs of global business units. Internal charging mechanisms can make these choices more explicit.

Following a report by McKinsey's that found that RBS had too effectively driven down the cost of its service delivery model, the company is taking a somewhat different approach. It is offering business units the chance to decide whether to buy extra services or enhanced performance standards that are paid for by the customer. So, for example, the normal three day turnaround for a recruitment offer letter could be changed to 24 hours on the payment of a fee to cover the extra costs.

- **Provide local support** As we saw earlier, operational support to local line managers is often filled in by having country based (or sometimes regionally or 'cluster' based) staff to carry out either the more operational tasks or those where local knowledge is essential. Naturally, the number of these staff and the nature of their role will depend on the extent of policy and practice standardization, but we would be careful not to pare down too much because we have argued the need to respect genuine national institutional and cultural distinctiveness.
- **Consider having a business management role** Creating a business management team can also help, not just with process improvement but also with performance measurement. The designation of the role as 'business management' may be helpful in securing resources with the promise that it will pay for itself through performance improvement.
- **Get the business partner role working** The standardization of policies and the creation of shared service centres means that business partners have no excuse but to focus on the strategic facilitation of people management in their business units. They should be adding strategic value through their participation as members of the business unit leadership team, pushing the people management agenda, influencing colleagues to get the most from their staff, dealing with people implications of change and so on. It is the global context that is different, and so influencing and balancing local with corporate interests will have to be done transnationally. If this role is well developed, as at say Du Pont, aspiring top executives will see being an HR business partner as a good preparation for the route to the top of the organization.

STANDARDIZATION

- **Get customers onside** How to handle customers and standardization? Do you try to build their support for it first? Or, fearing inevitable objections, do you drive through the change justifying this with an argument on affordability? Unless the organizational situation is desperate we would favour the former option. It might be a slower, more tortuous process, but early customer engagement is likely to yield later commitment to the outcome.
- **Customer empowerment** A vital issue is the extent to which you permit process variation to deal with local circumstances. As we have remarked, some organizations allow little scope for variation. Another approach is to insist that the service delivery model is the same everywhere, but the location is 'empowered' to adjust corporate policies where necessary in implementation. Indeed, British American Tobacco specifically allows market facing businesses to amend the delivery of learning and development programmes to suit the local environment. The extent of variation will naturally depend on the local circumstances and the nature of the subject matter, but, as a general rule, we would err towards more rather than less customization if the extra cost is more than offset by customer support and engagement.

Vestas Asia has a performance rating system that links to a bonus system (because it is the norm there), which is not found elsewhere in the company. Similarly, the Shell Nordic countries operate a 20 per cent variable pay element compared with 40 per cent elsewhere, in recognition of different socio-economic/cultural circumstances. Budhwar (2010) advises that those western companies operating in India should adjust their policies regarding employment termination, career management and reward. He also quotes a Japanese manager reflecting on the hierarchical nature of Indian firms compared with Japanese and how this has meant adjustment to their usual recruitment and development policies.

- **Vary the approach to suit employment group** on the basis that their needs differ. One UK retail company we met uses a standardized, e-enabled recruitment process for branch assistants (because without a consistent method managers might do their own thing, for good or ill). By contrast with this 'high tech' method, pharmacists are dealt with through a more personalized 'high touch' encounter because they have to be drawn towards the company in a very competitive labour market. This notion can of course be extended to geographic differences.

According to Rick Brown, there used to be arguments about the 'rules of football' at Shell (e.g. over whether it is right to have common standards and services). These 'rules' have now been agreed to, but it is still seen as legitimate to argue about the performance of the game, tactics, etc.

- **Vary the approach to suit complexity** Another Belgian international company we met segments its standard 'products' such that those with 'strategic' content are written in English, whereas those of a more practical nature are written in the local language. This gives another option in the dirigiste to enabling spectrum of governance.
- **Remember flexibility** Whilst having a target direction is good and helps organizational alignment, you should be flexible and able to adjust to change. As we have reported, whilst writing this book, some companies we interviewed had altered their governance arrangements and service delivery model quite considerably. This may reflect changed economic circumstances, a new business model, a different leadership team, etc. As Dave Cullen from Shell put it, you should not see getting the governance and service delivery model right as 'a single project, but a continuous journey'.

AUTOMATION

- **Explore the options** The IT HR goal might well be data harmonization, but this does not require full systems integration. The use of the web can successfully and more cheaply achieve the same goal. So according to Carl Bate of Atos Origin:

  A web based IT strategy integrates rather than redevelops existing applications and it frees the data in the organization's current and combined set of IT applications. In a rudimentary sense, it provides a kind of information 'face' for each existing application into the Web world (Bate, 2010).

- **Better data quality improves decisions** What is not really appreciated is that a new HRIS is not really about allowing easy change of address alterations, it facilitates a strategic change in management. It enables the organization through quality data to have a better understanding the talent pool (knowing when you are short of reserves globally); to check remuneration consistency; to monitor diversity; to show up local variations to policies and practices, etc. Thus it allows better planning and managing – surfacing things to tackle.

- **Common systems support further standardization** Having a common HR IT system and the right technological infrastructure in place does facilitate standardization in other areas. The more the organization wants to extend an HR shared services centre reach, the more it has to be able to move data around from location to location. High data quality is essential at any time but especially in trans-national operations. Moreover, the successful introduction of manager self-service and employee self-service reduces the number of transactions thereby making the volume of work to be undertaken more manageable. Thereafter, deal with as many queries as possible via a web interface and, those that do need manual handling, use simple procedures.

- **From transactions to manager advice** The launch of a well-functioning self-service system reduces the number of transactions enormously, such that much of the work of the HR shared services is shifted to giving advice on policy application. Managers become more self-reliant and are happy to take responsibility for their actions rather than pass them over to HR. This offers HR the opportunity for a further role change from simply being a servant to the line answering their questions to one of offering high-level advice and constructive challenge.

- **Bring in the right expertise** One solution to the problems with IT harmonization is create a centre of expertise in HR IT or use a business manager or operations management structure to define procedures, ensure data maintenance and liaise with process owners.

CHAPTER **9** *Conclusion*

As we said at the outset, the aim of this book is to help practitioners to improve the performance of HR in a global setting. We have set out a number of challenges, but also we have offered suggestions to overcome them. In this short concluding chapter we will look at what one might call the meta challenges. For us, there are five of these:

1. In business change, how can HR contribute to organizational success? How dependent is this on the type of the deal or transaction and what impact does a global setting have?
2. To what degree can organizations build a universal brand and EVP around a common culture? But in so doing, is it inevitable that the organization creates a narrow ethnocentric view of the world rather than a pluralist or diverse one?
3. To what extent and in what way can international organizations create and sustain a global talent pool? Does this approach reinforce the common culture, brand and EVP?
4. Is it current practice to create HR governance structures to allow the corporate centre to hold the ring between the various global players within the function and outside of it? Or is the predominant approach a method that controls the behaviour of business units and locations?
5. Can there be a global service delivery model? If so, is this predicated on a high level of standardization and automation that makes it possible, for example, to introduce HR shared service centres that operate on a cross-national basis?

In succeeding paragraphs we will try to summarize the results of our investigations.

And then in the final section we will conclude with some of the implications for the skill requirements of the HR function in the light of these global challenges.

HR's Role in Business Change

The difference between effective HR that really adds value and a function that is 'downstream' of the principal decisions is never more obvious than their role in mergers and acquisitions, though the same point could be made about business change more widely. The former type of HR team is involved in the decision to acquire or merge/form a partnership, as well as attending to the transactional elements of dismissals, aligning benefits or harmonizing payrolls. If the goal is one of organizational collaboration it is helping the organization take a view that there is a cultural fit. If the aim is to obtain human capital then it is leading the assessment of the talent. HR's contribution is less obvious where the company wants to impose its business model on the target organization, but even here HR can help the organization not get too 'macho', as one interviewee put it. HR can try to stop the acquiring organization cutting off its nose to spite its face by losing knowledge, skills and experience from the acquired organization through ill-advised demonstrations of power (by firing the wrong people) and domination (through insensitive gestures like archiving or deleting current or previous project work).

By contrast, the less effective HR team is merely concerned with the people elements of change implementation. There is nothing wrong with ensuring that consultation achieves business objectives, that terms and conditions are combined in a sensible manner or that redundancy selection is fair and defensible. All these things have to be well managed, and the best HR functions do this, too, but they also work truly in partnership with their business colleagues to achieve joint organizational goals.

So what can HR do to get itself ready to play the higher value adding role? It needs to be able to build the team's capability for change management, especially in the mergers and acquisitions area, and focus that effort by creating an expertise hub. This capability will include a deep understanding of how the organization works, and, in commercial firms, where are its principal sources of revenue and cost. This should help ensure that senior management trusts in the function's competence and ability to add helpful inputs. This may well need to be reinforced by demonstrating effectiveness in other areas of HR work (otherwise it is weakened if this effectiveness is not apparent) and during business as usual not just during change.

Having established its credentials, HR can take a lead in facilitating a discussion in senior management circles on the aims of any proposed deal and whether it meets agreed business goals, so that colleagues all work towards a common goal. Too often mergers and acquisitions do not succeed because participants lose sight of the business objectives: most importantly why does this deal make business sense? This should offer the key to the style of merger or acquisition – collaboration or imposition.

This facilitative role can be strengthened by HR developing a sound project planning process and by constructing a suitable toolkit. This needs to be attuned to the global context. One tool might usefully be how to conduct a cultural audit of the other party, especially if it is headquartered in another country, to see where the challenges in integration might arise. Another might be a risk assessment method that guides the organization through the difficult judgements on what to worry about and focus attention on. This might surface the complications in particular locations of complex stakeholder management, onerous legal obligations in post take-over resourcing or the undocumented nature of executive remuneration packages.

HR can also emphasize and prepare the organization for the scale of the challenge, the need to be adaptive to the circumstances, yet rely on well-worked techniques. This means in a collaborative deal especially being aware of cultural sensitivities, areas of difference that cannot easily be glossed over, of the importance of symbols and signs of genuine togetherness rather than fine sounding words not backed by actions. This can be particularly well exemplified if the organization demonstrably learns from the other party, implementing good practice that it has developed. This may come from building quality relationships across the 'divide'. Especially for western companies acquiring those from the developing world, the necessity of avoiding a sense of a neo colonial takeover should be borne in mind.

The change process is not complete when the contract is signed. Indeed, embedding the new ways of doing things is just as vital as making the right call in the first place. Good implementation needs particular attention to be given to the protection of talent, the maintenance of an engaged workforce and the retention of knowledge and skills. Since without these things, the deal will fail. This can be helped by ensuring that the leadership models the behaviours it expects to see from others as a visible manifestation of its organizational values. Bringing the deal through to a successful conclusion will require real leadership capability. Ideally that will already have been developed, but, if not, support should be given to senior and project management through coaching and similar techniques.

It should be emphasized that though we have concentrated on mergers and acquisitions the principles we have outlined here apply to in any type of business change.

Universal Brand and Culture

Our research for this book suggests that organizations with a strong and powerful business brand will be much more able to create a global employer brand or EVP. This is even truer where the business model is to deliver a uniform product or service across the world. In these organizations there must be a strong temptation, or perhaps expectation, that developing a common culture is what is required. This is what one will find in companies like Coca-Cola or McDonald's. It has to be recognized that delivering the uniform product or service necessitates standard operating processes to achieve the desired consistency of outcome. It is not acceptable for staff to go off piste, with their own ideas on how to serve the customer. This same model is not just to be found in parts of retail and manufacturing, but also we saw it in a consultancy firm like TCS, where the business objective is to give the same customer offering the world over. This is driven in large part because their customers are also global companies that buy their services from global suppliers precisely because they know what they are getting in advance (and can maximize their procurement advantage). Where this involves the provision of a global outsourcing service the requirement for uniform delivery is probably even stronger.

To meet this goal, the resourcing model is to select those who will meet this service standard, and performance management and reward will reinforce the expected attitudes and behaviours.

To those who would challenge the inevitable cultural homogenization of recruiting staff to do the same job in the same way anywhere on the globe, a simple answer might be that people know what to expect when they apply. Just as there is no ambiguity about a Big Mac or a Coke, or even a consultancy intervention from a global firm, there is no uncertainty about the employment experience in these firms. So people self-select. They know that there will be cultural features that have more to do with Oak Brook or Atlanta than with Tokyo, Bangkok or Caracas, but that may either be an acceptable price to pay for the job or be part of a positive attraction to the firm.

There are, by contrast, a whole host of organizations that operate under multiple brands that relate both to products and to the EVP. Thus as we saw a Unilever, RBS or an Anheuser-Busch InBev can represent themselves under the main brand, and attract, badge and develop on that basis, or they can operate under a specific brand label. It is important to note, though, that these sub-brands are themselves becoming increasingly global. Nevertheless, in this context employees may think they are joining a Ben & Jerry's rather than a Unilever. This gives the company some flexibility in tailoring the offer to particular locations, especially where the business practices are different. So if you go to the Ben & Jerry's website your application will be managed by a Unilever site but the employment offer includes the benefit of 'three free pints of Vermont's Finest super premium ice cream, frozen yogurt and sorbets every day'!

Having sub-brands can also help when the main brand is damaged. We saw earlier how RBS has benefited from having other names under which it can operate both in the commercial and employment environment.

This brings us to a third category of organizations, those that are more federated or holding company in nature. These organizations, because of the diverse nature of their business activity, do not try either to create a single brand image or a single EVP. They are sometimes called 'polycentric' as they rate highly the importance of differentiation. We have described how companies like Tata allow subsidiaries a great deal of freedom to operate in their own way. Whilst there will be some overarching common principles and some common practices it makes no sense to try to project Jaguar Land Rover as the same as Tetley's Tea.

This account gives a rather mechanistic view of the people proposition as being wholly settled by the business model. Is there no choice in the matter for HR to exercise its judgment?

As we have repeatedly stressed, the HR approach must fit the business requirements: it cannot get too far ahead (or behind) the organization's direction of travel. Yet in the matter of culture more than structure and process, HR has, in theory, somewhat more wriggle room. It can offer distinctive insights into how heterogeneous the culture might be; how much the EVP has to adjust to local circumstances both in terms of recruitment and retention; and what the resourcing model should be to reflect diversity goals.

Yet there are still pressures towards uniformity: the desire not to have managers that might expose the organization to reputational risk through their actions leads to having global selection, induction and development programmes and global delivery methods executed by global agencies (internal or external); ensuring the easy mobility of staff across operating companies and building a global mindset to facilitate that; using global e-recruitment portals to deliver a common message; applying common communication mechanisms, etc. The globalizing process naturally standardizes and homogenizes, all again for good reason.

So maybe we are asking the wrong question: except for the federated companies like Tata why would organizations not want a common culture? The business reasons in favour are as we have seen formidable. There are, however, arguments that we put forward on p. 84 on the business benefits of diversity, especially avoiding the risks associated with the narrow thinking that comes from cloning. So how do organizations deal with what Garry Hamel has called the 'unavoidable trade-offs that have been the unhappy legacy of modern management ... to build organizations where discipline and freedom aren't mutually exclusive'. We quoted Raisch and Birkinshaw (2008) on the desirability of developing an ambidextrous organization that can reconcile the consistency imperative with the flexibility requirement. Yet this still leaves open the question of how this circle of commonality and difference is squared.

We think this is best achieved by being firm on some common principles. You do not have to agree with the cultural convergence thesis or the victory of west argument to accept that these principles might reflect the universal values that are embodied in documents such as the UN Declaration of Human Rights. It is both a matter of practicality and philosophy that inclines organizations to use, say, a meritocratic selection and development method: practical because how else do you pick out the 'best' people for the organization and philosophical because it meets the western liberal definition of 'fairness'. To counter accusations that this ignores other approaches that seem 'fair' to other cultures, organizations can point to the UN research (2005) on government effectiveness that demonstrated that

> A merit-oriented and career based civil service is decisive in explaining cross-country differences in the performance of governments in terms of the quality of services and the absence of corruption. The presence of these factors helps to foster organizational standards, behavioural norms and esprit de corps that promote commitment and integrity among public servants.

Organizations have to build a common culture for their global management cadre that is based on a common set of business ethics, but it should be recognized that a) this clearly does not apply to one and all (so long as they abide by the corporate principles). So a South African miner, Brazilian coffee grower or Chinese rice farmer will reflect the social norms of their environment – and that is quite legitimate. b) That the management cadre is refreshed by people from varied backgrounds who do not simply have to be clones of the ones that they replace. It is tricky to know how many and what type of mavericks you can allow. It depends, as we have suggested, on the business you are in: there are rightly more awkward research scientists than production managers. You may need creative people in marketing and conforming types in manufacturing. And c) you need to respect the institutional influences as well as social customs.

So we are back to what makes business sense. By this means you may approach having an ambidextrous organization – whether you are more right handed as an organization depends upon the business model. Perhaps only a few organizations are equally competent with both hands.

Yet this business alignment should not be construed as meaning that you conform to current perceptions or indeed stereotypes. One of the reasons why CSR has developed some momentum is that organizations now understand that their long-term future depends on their having a license to operate in their communities. This will mean that diversity must go beyond tokenism and that promoting a variety of nationalities does not mean just finding Uncle Toms. If you are, say, the Bahrain government it is just not going to be acceptable that the top commercial jobs are held by expatriates and that the indigenous population is not being sufficiently developed to replace them. The recent social unrest in the Middle East exemplifies how fragile the current social order might be. One wonders how long it will be acceptable for a Malaysian lawyer in a multi-polar world to say to a British journalist, as one did in 1994: 'I am wearing your clothes, I speak your language, I watch your films, and today is whatever date it is because you say so' (Morris, 2010). As Nick Ostler (2010) has pointed out, the use of a foreign language is an evidence of conquest and conversion, as much as commerce, and is not guaranteed to survive if the benefits of using it are reduced.

So rather than risk being ethnocentric, should global organizations not aspire to be geocentric, where, as we said earlier, the organization celebrates the benefits diversity brings and takes good ideas from anywhere in the world? In addressing the question of cultural variation in this way, western international companies may also helpfully protect themselves against the downsides of change. The risk for North American and western European international companies is that the imposition of their business model will not look so clever if growth comes from the east and developing world, out of which local companies will emerge with a different world view, more in tune with their own societies. You can already see how Indian and Chinese global companies operate to a much more federated model and give much more alignment to local conditions, with a real emphasis on corporate social responsibility.

So in answer to our question: yes, global employer brands are indeed possible for some organizations and they might reasonably wish to establish a common culture, but, depending on the type of organization and the part of the population under consideration, there is room to customize and acknowledge that some diversity in staffing and scope for variation in organizational norms is a positively good thing, and necessary for long-term survival.

Global Talent Management

We described in this book that while there are many different definitions of talent and target groups, from executives through high potentials to ubiquity in the organization, in practical terms organizations end up focusing most of their efforts on a special few, however defined, rather than the many whatever their rhetoric or preference might be. All the organizations we met and with which we discussed talent management had aspirations to develop some forms of global talent management. It seems to be understood, correctly, that it is both one of the main facilitators of creating a global enterprise and one of the foundations upon which it is based. Organizations have to have people committed to common goals around the world, reinforcing the shared culture and being shaped by it.

Yet we have come across serious difficulties in achieving this goal, especially creating a management cadre from those diverse backgrounds we were just discussing. The problem starts with sourcing the talented from round the world – getting clear what 'talented' means; getting managers to see good staff and release them for development; producing selection processes that are both fair in the sense that they meet the corporate meritocratic principles, yet recognize local variation in how talent presents itself; and finally making career management work – are staff mobile, will they adapt to new circumstances, will they be retained once they return home? And all this is a costly activity.

Mostly, our organizations were prepared to foot this bill, though at times they were queasy about the lack of evidence of success. The problem is that this is really an investment for the long haul with the return often not being visible for 10 or 15 years and is naturally often taking place in a demand vacuum where the organization does not really know its future requirements.

We would agree with this recognition that talent is an asset worth nurturing. Our concern is that HR as a function is not doing enough to lead this process. And it needs leading because it is corporate and future oriented, not local, operational and short-term. Tasks include deciding on the appropriate resourcing ratio between make and buy, getting the balance right between individual self-development and organizational requirement, ensuring that the organization retains specialist expertise as well as generalist potential, and so on.

These are not easy decisions, so they even more necessitate HR leadership. The function must push the organization towards greater strategic workforce planning – looking at where the gaps are worldwide and seeking the means to fill them in the short term, but also to build capability for the long term (especially in areas of the world where the supply of quality staff and the competition for them remains problematic) and in a way that anticipates, where possible, future business challenges. It must avoid bureaucratic practices in performance appraisal and succession planning, yet ensure that good data is acquired about those who have potential and that key posts are covered for replacements. Simultaneously, HR should be seeking to embed these talent management processes so that they become second nature to managers, a natural part of what they do. Achieving this goal requires growing the people management capability of the line and developing a common language around what talent is, what it looks like, how it can be built and sustained. Institutionalizing talent management practice also requires both senior executive buy in and participation in the creation and running of bodies (talent boards and the like) that will lead and drive the process.

One of the particular challenges in delivering a simple talent management system is the natural tendency to use existing selection criteria and assessment processes for global processes. The problem is that there are specific requirements for working in a global environment, especially for expatriates. We know well enough the pressures that sometimes require a less than ideal appointment ('but he is the only person with the necessary skills who is prepared to go to Neverneverland'), but organizations need to know who is a good fit and who is not, such that it can put in place support mechanisms or even contingency plans. More fundamental for the aspiring geocentric organization is that the normal selection processes must be adjusted so that talent in different forms comes through, otherwise you will simply get clones of the existing management. This may be helpful for convergent thinking but an impediment where creativity or divergence is required.

We also want to emphasize that talent management should be a very personal process since we are talking about the qualities, performance, aspirations, etc. of individuals. The systematization of talent management processes has had benefits in the consistency of their execution, but if this has been accompanied by a dehumanizing of the activity there are penalties to pay. Automation and remote management of process may be more efficient, but the loss of personal contact is a danger. How well now do HR people know their most talented colleagues? Those in global talent management roles may be physically and structurally too far away. Business partners should be ensuring that they not only recognize who the good people are, but have some idea how they tick and what motivates them now and what they aspire to for the future. Corporate talent management staff should insist, despite the cost, on retaining mechanisms for meeting upcoming high potentials and gathering them together in training courses, networking meetings or other fora where there can be personal interaction.

Finally, organizations must be much more prepared than at present to evaluate their talent management processes through the whole activity chain – from attraction through selection to development. What is working well and not so well? To do this organizations need success criteria and an understanding of costs. Concentrating on a narrow financial return, however, will miss the subtler benefits to be found in the sort of development programmes means to build social capital, described above, which are so important to the effective functioning of a global firm, particularly its knowledge sharing aspects.

The Form of HR Governance

We are pretty convinced that organizations have nearly always introduced governance processes to drive HR transformation in order to meet a narrower efficiency imperative or to control behaviour so as to manage risk/limit organizational exposure.

There are of course some differences by sector, especially the regulatory context, and form of company – manufacturing/engineering tends towards the automation/ standardization that is the product of this controlling approach. Fast moving consumer goods (FMCG) have very little margin, move quickly and are very market responsive. Labour costs often form an important part of the total cost base, so there is always pressure to be labour efficient, and sensitivity to the market means that policies/practices are adjusted quickly. Listed companies more than privately owned have to respond to stock market pressures to deliver efficiencies in a particular way and to regulatory demands. Mature companies may well be more concerned with cost pressures than those in the growing phase, and more likely to introduce bureaucratic means of controlling behaviour.

Nevertheless, is a dirigiste form of governance an inevitable part of the route to globalization?

It is certainly interesting that the academic view of, say, 5–10 years ago was that networks would replace hierarchies, 'horizontal commitment' would replace global firms tendency towards 'vertical control' in a more decentralized decision making environment. The role of the centre would then become one of 'stewardship', integrating local initiatives and building a shared mindset through creating 'a climate of trust and collaboration'. Ideas would then not only flow from the HQ outwards, or indeed from operating companies to the centre, but from subsidiary to subsidiary. (See Harvey and Novicevic, 2003, for this point of view.)

Sparrow et al. (2004) recognized the tension between globalism and localism, but thought that HR in the corporate office would similarly become a 'broker' between 'country localization demands and global line of business consistency requirements'; its functional added value coming from managing a 'delicate balance' between these perspectives.

Even earlier, Handy (1992) talked about the benefits of the 'federal' company that in his view would deal effectively with the paradoxes of power and control by 'encouraging power within bounds'. He took the optimistic view that people will act in the common interest if they are well informed and educated. He thought movement in this direction was inevitable because he was critical of the centralizing power of bureaucracy. Indeed, in a position consistent with the Major government's concurrent belief in 'subsidiarity' within the EU, he thought power ought to be exercised at lowest possible point in the hierarchy.

Jing Wang might be right to say, 'no model is perfect' and right to advise that 'you have to be an optimist and believe any model can be made to work if you devote positive energy to deal with any frustrations that arise'. Yet are the governance mechanisms optimizing performance even in their own terms of simple efficiency?

We go back to the question of in how much detail is it right for the corporate centre to lay down how the organization operates. We would not dispute the need for common principles or broad process goals, but surely some freedom should be given to locations and business units in how these requirements are implemented? As we emphasized, centralization of decision making does not mean centralized implementation, so there should be a degree to which the locations, subsidiary or operating companies can choose the 'how', if not the 'what', of people management activity. It is an approach of adaptation not adoption. As Jing Wang says of China, 'It doesn't make sense to force fit to a global model when the situation here is very different.'

Moreover, the corporate centre's desire for control over decision making lower down the organization may have the perverse consequence of increasing risks rather than reducing them! If you disempower managers, they will take no responsibility for what they do. They will simply delegate problems upwards for resolution. This can create a logjam whereby those at the top are faced with either stasis or making decisions under pressure and with inadequate information, especially in relation to remote operations. Unless the leadership is blessed with a global mindset and worldwide experience it may make default decisions based on its narrow understanding of the world.

In the service delivery context there is a real danger that the understandable drive for efficiency will lead to the tail, in the form of satisfying the needs of the HR functional savings, wagging the dog of meeting business needs. Certainly the goal of shared services can be expressed in terms of the cheapest possible service, but there has to more attention paid to business value. This puts cost on one side of the ledger but quality and customer satisfaction on the other side. Achieving business goals is not just about the expense of an activity, but also the impact it has on organizational performance – the value it generates. How one manages Sparrow's 'delicate balance' is evidenced by the treatment of exceptions: are they justifiable responses to local product market strategies and cultural needs or expensive deviations from corporately determined rules? Of course, the answer is in the detail such that some local practice is suboptimal even in meeting their business requirements. But we are really talking about a state of mind. Are those at the centre really prepared to acknowledge the need for balance or do they see their role as the persecutor of heresy? Or to mix our metaphors, is the corporate centre like the Monty Python foot that squashes all in its path!

Naturally, experienced practitioners see that there is perhaps a false dichotomy between establishing a marching band where all are in step and a jazz band where the players are free to improvise. How one plays the tune depends on the music.

So Wilfried Meyer sees the new Siemens HR operating model that we described earlier as finding a middle ground between decentralization and centralization, is confident that the new model will last precisely because it is a compromise. How long it will last, he recognizes, depends on how long the business adopts its current operating model. But we would argue that it also depends upon how sensibly and sensitively HR operates the compromise in practice and how much scope it gives to innovation and learning, including between business units or locations as well as two way traffic from the centre to the subsidiaries. We heard about how some governance models only worked because personal relationships oiled the wheels, but this is hardly the basis for long-term effectiveness. The institutions have to work regardless of whether the job holders get on well together.

Harking back to our earlier debate on cultural uniformity, if you push standardization too hard, it is likely to be on a 'home' country model and you could stand accused of corporate imperialism that might easily have a colonial taint to it. If standardization of policies is pursued in a more collaborative manner, based on good practice from anywhere on the globe, these challenges will be much reduced.

The alternative model, which is to keep standardization to a minimum and insist on commonality on principles or perhaps within a loose policy framework, will cost in terms of efficiency, but perhaps more importantly it might damage organizational coherence. There is a real drive by many organizations to create a single sense of organizational belonging. The question is whether that has to be achieved through standardization of everything possible, or can it work with greater plurality?

In what we think of as a nice analogy, Toby Peyton Jones sees the ideal governance model to be a wheel where the struts are the common principles, integrated systems and key processes. These are inflexible rods of iron that hold the wheel together. But between the rods are the thinner spokes which are more flexible and are adaptable to local or business unit circumstances.

These are not easy matters. Whilst Toby's model is attractive, there are still some tough, detailed questions regarding how the flexible spokes will operate. At the very least, organizations should be debating the issue of what is the optimal approach to suit organizational requirements, avoiding a 'me-too' rush to what the majority seems to be doing, egged on by best practice benchmarking.

A Global Service Delivery Model?

As with national HR transformation, the service delivery model seems to be in the vanguard of the drive towards global HR management; indeed, towards the definition that Bartlett and Ghosal (1989) offered of a global company.

The creation of a global service delivery model is essentially a practical question: there are no philosophical objections, besides some reservations about cross-national contact centres. A service delivery model concentrates on having trans-national shared services, global centres of expertise and, in a rather different way, business partners operating in more than other geography. The principal benefit is cost reduction through economies of scale and thus widening the scope of the service delivery model offers the chance of achieving greater benefit. The practical issues surround the feasibility of aggregating the services. The obstacles stem from the perceived need for technological integration, the resourcing implications of transnational services and the absence of common HR policies and practices.

It is not surprising therefore that standardization and automation are important to the growth of the global service operation since they make it more feasible to aggregate services in general and widen the content delivered. Where there is too much divergence of content or system, the financial benefits disappear. Web based 'cloud computing' claims to offer a solution to IT disaggregation, but there is no real way round the lack of scale advantages where there is a wide diversity of terms and conditions.

The real debate in service delivery operations is the balance between local and global. Companies like Shell are driving for as much as possible to be delivered through their three global shared service centres. Other companies, operating in a more decentralized manner, keep more done locally. There is no argument about remote transaction processing – this can be done anywhere – but there are question marks, in some minds, about distant customer interaction, particularly operational support to managers, and to a lesser extent personal support to employees.

Those who argue for more devolved activities point to the cultural differences between countries. Not all societies are the same, so why have the same service delivery model? Just compare Brazil's high 'sociality' compared with China's more reserved society (Griffiths, 2004). In 'high touch' societies, like Turkey or India, there is an expectation of more face-to-face contact. Conducting business is more personal in nature. Management is more paternalistic as that is their role – to look after their staff. This also reflects the effect of the socio-economic and physical environment. During one of the authors' visit to Sri Lanka serious monsoonal floods prevented large numbers of staff coming to work at MAS. Many employees lost their homes and it was the company (not the State) that gave them help. Similarly, in South Africa visiting Absa, personnel work involves dealing with the consequences of armed bank raids and the devastation wrought by Aids. It is not easy to deal with these sorts of issues through an international contact centre, however well run.

Sensible organizations recognize these needs and create asymmetrical models – more local resource retained in, say, Africa and Asia and less in Europe and North America. What must be avoided is the use of crude benchmarking tools that suggest through external and internal comparison that the HR/employee ratio is too high in some places and should be brought down to the 'norm'. A crude cross-organizational benchmark may ignore the implications for size of function of running, say, a global talent management operation and having to develop their own expatriate remuneration policies and practices, which is presumably what is demanded of the function by business leaders, as well as the diversity of operational support. You then get the tyranny of best practice imposed on the organization, promoted by global consultants. The result is that HR policies and practices are standardized to facilitate this numerical reduction and achieve the best practice goal. As we have already observed, this is a real case of the tail wagging the dog, especially given that the barked objections of line managers and covert non-compliance of some local HR people indicates dissatisfaction. The service offered should follow the customer and business demands, not precede it.

It should be recognized that the pressures to standardize are high at present due to the recession and the consequential drive to take cost out. Not so many organizations can say, as Massimo Macarti did of Canon Europe, that there is 'no big pressure to significantly cut HR costs. Yes, we must be efficient, but the company has bigger fish to fry'. We believe the pressure for efficiency will not ease up any time soon. This led Hackett Research Director Michel Janssen to say in 2007, even before the economic crisis, 'In the next few years, companies with world-class HR organizations are also likely to make greater use of offshore resources, either through captive shared service operations or outsourcers. The labour arbitrage opportunities are simply too great to ignore' (The Hackett Group, 2007).

But there are limits to a truly global service delivery model, both in terms of content (some matters are necessarily local for institutional reasons) and practicality (staffing limitations for some and risk management for others). Whilst we may see some move towards the three global centres that we illustrated at Shell and SAP, there is also a chance that organizations will use developments in technology to go for more virtual units (a more dispersed central operation) that might give economies of scale benefits but also local alignment advantages.

The Role of HR

The transformation of HR has happened in many geographies and in many sectors, all with the aim of making the function leaner and more effective, especially in contributing to organizational success beyond efficient administration. Our last book questioned whether those in HR were up to this challenge and up for the necessary adjustment in their way of working. Credence to this view has been given from within the function itself. A Mercers' survey (2010) of HR executives placed the skills within the function as the second biggest barrier to successful HR transformation (after the people management skills of line managers). An ADP/HROA 2008 report put the skills of HR staff as the greatest hurdle to HR transformation and the survey also raised the challenge of delivering change in a global context. A CIPD survey (Reilly et al., 2007) also highlighted knowledge and skills constraints, especially among experts and business partners.

As this book has described there are further challenges to undertaking functional transformation on a global scale. We have described in particular the specific issues to be faced when business change is cross-national in nature; talent has to be developed internationally to handle global requirements; the positioning of the brand and EVP have to resonate around the world; a global governance structure has to be established that balances consistency with flexibility; and the creation of a service delivery model has to be designed in a way that delivers effectiveness as well as efficiency.

Moreover, there are different starting places, not only are organizations different in the stage of their HR maturity, but also HR's role varies by country. It is seen as simply an administrative function, especially in the former Communist countries of eastern Europe and in China: what Polish consultant Roman Stolarski has called 'its bureaucratic legacy'. We heard of the further difficulty from a Chinese tobacco company that they found the western concept of line management hard to understand as it did not fit into their conception of work organization. In many societies, especially in Africa by contrast, the line manager believes very strongly that they are the sole decision maker in relationship to their own staff and would not tolerate any interference from HR or treats employees simply as a resource to be exploited. Although George Sikulu, Plan International's Regional People and Culture Partner in the Eastern and Southern Africa Regional Office based in Kenya, says that 'HR has changed its face' in having greater ambitions to be more strategic to the business than previously, the past clearly still influences what HR does currently, where it can be successful, and it affects whether (or at least how) HR develops policies in areas like talent management and employee engagement. It has to be recognized that in some parts of the world the employment experience remains a simple transactional one of payment in exchange for effort. There is not yet much sense of the self-actualization opportunities of work whilst basic survival needs have to be satisfied.

Moreover, the number of HR people who both understand the need for sophisticated HR management and have the skills to deliver it is limited and will be so until a new generation, trained in a different context, moves through to senior positions. This explains why there are still many expatriate HR people in post. They bring experience and skills to the role, but also confidence and a gravitas that may help the HR message be received by those managers who might otherwise be sceptical.

Thus it may be unfair to criticize an HR team for failing to be strategic, when it has no permission to be so and asserting itself is culturally unacceptable. The nature of a strategic contribution may be interpreted in various ways, depending upon the location, and surely one definition should not be regarded as superior to another so long as it fulfils business requirements. Moreover, this understanding challenges the notion of having a ubiquitous role conception for HR. As Reg Bull of Crowne Finch (ex Unilever and LG Electronics) put it when constructively criticizing Dave Ulrich's universal formula: 'We live in an international HR community seen through many cultural lenses, not just an American one.'

At various times in earlier chapters we have pointed to the debate within HR as to how best to achieve the optimum result. We have seen that there is no single answer, no best approach, not least because, if as we have rightly argued HR should follow the business model and the circumstances of its delivery, then different outcomes will be needed to fit the different ways organizations manage the running of their affairs. Thus it would not be right to argue in this chapter that there is one, single set of implications for the capability needs of the HR team: it will depend on what they are asked to do and in what context.

Nevertheless, there seems little fundamental departure from the three legged stool model for large, complex global organizations, only adaptation to deal with its limitations in terms of customer complexity and boundary management. We have argued that there is a general move towards consolidation of transactional activity into shared services and specialist know how into centres of expertise and the standardization and automation of processes and systems. Moreover, the standardization thrust across organizations suits HR because it always has a tendency towards encouraging consistency and commonality, and it is often explicitly given that role by CEOs. Even in decentralized companies the HR director is often the one who sees efficiency and risk management gains in harmonization. And the expense of e-HR investment can often only be justified on an enterprise-wide basis.

Assuming we are right, this will have a significant effect on the roles and capabilities of job holders. So for those organizations that have moved or are moving towards this type of service delivery model, the following impact may be seen. (And for those readers in organizations that see themselves continuing to work with another approach, we ask for their forbearance.)

In thinking about the future role of HR, we are attracted to the world described by Toby Peyton Jones of Siemens. He sees that shared services will increasingly be run on business lines requiring all the necessary commercial and contractual competencies. This fits with the increasing interest described earlier in lean management and in the role of a business manager/Chief Operating Officer. The main task of the remaining, and core, HR function will be in helping managers deliver the people strategy for the business, the pipeline of talent and employee engagement in order to improve organizational performance. This HR Business Partnering role requires very different skill-sets from the operational service line management described above. Both will require a keen attention to leadership behaviours and skills. So management development expertise will be at a premium. There will be less investment in policy design because there will only be change where required for legal compliance or change in the business operating environment. There will be less HR fiddling with best practice fads and fashion. Standardized processes will operate automatically wherever possible, and manual intervention will be minimized. Along with other interviewees for this book, he sets a lot of store by the generation of high-quality management data that can be used by business partners as the key intelligence to inform their advice to line managers. The challenge HR has in this area is reinforced by the fact that over 90 per cent of respondents to an InfoHRM survey (www.infohrm.com – 2009 Global workforce planning survey) agreed with the statement: Our abilitiy to interpret and understand information continues to lag behind our capability to collect, store and report data. This reinforces the view expressed in our previous book that analytical skills will have to improve if HR is to make full use of the management information generated. It also suggests the growth in workforce analytical roles that are appearing in some organizations.

With this background in mind the following role and capability issues may have to be considered.

CORPORATELY RUN ROLES

Those working in management roles in the corporate centre, centres of expertise and shared services will clearly need a global outlook, a broad awareness of different cultures and work environments within which their business is operating. This is all the more true if the service delivery model is global in scope. In these circumstances there are particular challenges to balance local pressures with global imperatives that can be seen in the *design* decisions in what and how to standardize, in what to include in a global or regional shared services centre and what to leave to locations to manage through operational or embedded HR.

More testing still to the capability of corporate HR (in its various guises) is the *implementation* of these harmonized systems, policies or processes, and the running of international shared services. We have heard of Sparrow et al.'s (2004) conception of their role as a 'broker' between local demands for bespoke solutions and global insistence on common approaches. The other view is that these corporate agents will be enforcers of the central diktats, ensuring compliance to the corporate standards. A third group, the corporate agents, will run the model so that there is an optimum balance between diversity and commonality. They will need to have the capability to judge how to get the best from the latter, without endangering the former. In this type of organization, interpersonal and facilitation skills, especially in influencing stakeholders, will be vital to ensure that the organization is still knitted together.

Even in centralized organizations, the staff in the corporate centre will have to ensure business units and locations abide by the central imperatives, and that will involve some persuasion as well as insistence with some of the contracting skills that would apply if the service were externalized. In other words, HR still has to have the skills to play a controlling role. Moreover, if you have a highly standardized model and sudden change happens, you still need the flexibility to respond. There is a risk that those used to doing, not thinking, are flummoxed. They will be used to relying on fixed processes – now they will have to improvise and may find it hard to do so unless there is some preparation for this situation.

Networking capabilities will necessary, especially for those organizations that operate under an enabling framework, to help the function cohere. The HR corporate centre has a responsibility to hold the three legged HR structure together. It must also decide on the extent and nature of standardization and secure funds for automation. All this has to be achieved in conjunction with and maintaining adherence to values and mission, to the overarching strategy and to the overall, holistic organizational need.

BUSINESS PARTNER ROLES

As we said earlier, for the business partner the role changes in a global setting are less marked, but the challenge of meaningful contribution is still there. As Guthridge and Lawson (2008) have argued in the same way as our last book, HR has focused too narrowly on systems and processes and not enough on people and culture, so that it is not well enough informed about the goings on in the organization. This limits their influence. It is the business partners who should be filling that gap. They should be adding strategic value through their participation as members of the business unit leadership team, pushing the people management agenda, influencing colleagues to get the most from their staff, dealing with people implications of change and so on, but also they should be taking the temperature of the organization and identifying talented individuals. This is a role description that applies everywhere. It is the global context that is different. Influencing and balancing local with corporate interests will have to be done transnationally in the context of global business units, which adds to the challenge with the extra cultural dimension especially where they are acting as a coach and sounding board to the business leadership.

The standardization of policies means that business partners have no excuse but to focus on the strategic facilitation of people management in their business units. However, the relationship with the line varies between countries. This is not just a matter of capability but, as we said above, of the national historical and social context, as well as the international nature of the organization. A Shell can perhaps more easily drive through a change where managers take responsibility for their actions than in some other companies. Even in Shell the line did not altogether like the change to the function, as they were used to 'co-opting' HR people to do their bidding. Now, business partners are there to challenge. This puts even more pressure on business partner skills.

A mixture of history (the company is long accepted as being an early disciple of Ulrich in its implementation of the business partnership model), confidence, capability and ultimately functional leadership provides RBS with a solid base from which HR business partners can play a key role in the strategic planning of the firm. As with other examples in the book, one of the key reasons for this success has to be the solidity of the HR executive team with, at the time of writing, at least five in their third job within the leadership of the function. They are thus able to see the challenges of each aspect of the HR function from each other's perspective. So much so that to join the HR Executive in future, tenure in both business facing and centre of expertise roles is a must, as is awareness of the markets within which the company operates.

One of the internally accepted strengths of HR in RBS is that in each of the operating divisions, HR is very central to the agenda of change. Colleagues in each of the business functions are playing a key role in supporting their respective CEOs in defining the people agenda within their five year strategies. But more than that; many are also playing a stronger role challenging the very operating models of that division – the footprint that each should retain, the resources deployed in each, the management layers needed to balance cost efficiency with appropriate oversight.

COUNTRY BASED ROLES

Depending upon the degree of a) standardization and b) consolidation, the most affected by HR operating on a global scale are those working in local HR. If much of their traditional work has moved to a call or service centre and what is left is the implementation of standard policies and processes, then there are fewer 'HR in country' people (to use the Shell term) and the scope of their role is much reduced. We are talking here about what Ulrich calls the operational executioners. Transactional activity will have gone to the shared service centre and the strategic contribution will be in the hands of the business partners, the remaining work can cover such things as individual case work (discipline, absence, grievance, etc.), local recruitment, basic training, employee relations including trade union consultation and negotiation. If, however, there is little opportunity to vary the corporately defined process or to create new solutions, then as one HR manager crisply put it, the task is 'not to think but to do'. The skills requirements for the role are even more than before those associated with implementation. They deliver in their location the global performance related pay scheme or performance appraisal process. They conduct recruitment exercises according to the designated corporate selection criteria and help managers identify those for development on international schemes using the common competency model. There is little chance of creativity.

One of the risks of creating this brigade of doers is that they cease to challenge and become simply subservient to the global leadership whatever it suggests. They conform but do not contribute new ideas. As we suggested in Chapter 7, this situation is unhealthy as examples from other institutions in the boxed examples would attest.

Writing not just about the financial crash but about any ecosystem, Andrew Haldane of the Bank of England observed that 'complexity plus homogeneity did not spell stability: it spelt fragility' (2009).

In an example of the dangers of excessive commonality, it has been suggested that Catholic Papacy's actions to enforce doctrinal orthodoxy over the last 40 years has led to 'the promotion of men who would put loyalty to an institution ahead of loyalty to the laity' (i.e. to the customers). According to this view it produced an environment of 'blame dodging, cowardice and the illusion of power' (Brown, 2010).

To take a very different situation, the US Air Force outperformed the Japanese in the Second World War because US pilots could use their discretion in combat whereas the Japanese fliers had to stick rigidly to a set of predetermined rules.

There are exceptions to this picture of local delivery. In some companies there is a local representational role to be played with government, regulators, educational institutions or industry bodies where the organization will want to speak with one voice. In highly unionized companies, employee relations may be both geographically devolved and of critical importance. So there have to be senior and experienced HR professionals in place to deal with these matters. The skill-set here is obvious with a high value being placed on influencing, negotiating, networking – a wide gamut of interpersonal skills.

BUSINESS MANAGEMENT

An increasing number of organizations have chosen to create a service management function under various names. These are quintessentially corporate roles because their purpose is one of integration and oversight. Yet even here there are design choices. Some organizations intentionally keep teams small and tight to minimize overheads and focus activity on key tasks in coordination and audit. Others are larger through taking on performance metrics and workforce analytics, especially from shared services (perhaps because of worries about or experience of shared service centre weaknesses in this area).

A more important question perhaps is whether the business management role sits outside the service delivery model or has responsibilities within it. SAP and RBS have chosen to include responsibility for HR shared services under their COO/CAO to drive higher performance and greater integration. By contrast, other organizations fear that this will compromise the independence of their audit/oversight role.

REPORTING LINES AND CAREER PATHS

There are implications of these developments both for HR structures and associated career paths. We have already discussed reporting lines for shared services and business partners in terms of whether they are to the function or to the business, and whether they are local, regional or global. The further interesting structural question is to whom do the country based HR people report. If there is a simple alignment between geography and business activity, which is unlikely, they could report to the business unit business partner. As shown in the boxed example, Shell has chosen in its latest HR configuration to ask country HR leads to report to a business partner with a geographic responsibility. In many other organizations they will report (at least functionally) to a (sub)regional HR director. This makes most sense where a) the region is an important construct in the way business is delivered (and for particular regions whether there is the scale of operations to justify it) and/or b) the region is reasonably homogeneous in language, culture, legal system, etc. In Siemens, for example, the country HR directors report to the cluster HR director.

In Shell, following the business model, the three biggest business partner roles each have a regionally determined group of country operational HR work to oversee. Thus there is Upstream Americas (Americas), Downstream (Europe and Africa excluding West Africa) & Upstream International (Rest of the World including West Africa). The other two lines of business (Projects and Technology and Global Functions) have no geographically linked accountabilities. This 'built-in interdependence' means that the business partners not only have to focus on their business units, but they have to be aware of all the operating HR work within their territory, for all business activity not just what happens in their own. It is noteworthy that this is not a way of interposing an additional regional level (these were removed some years before), but a conglomeration of country based activities.

Nonetheless, the previously reported (e.g. Tamkin et al., 2006) problems in developing the careers of HR staff can be exacerbated by the operation of the new structures in a global setting. Shared service centres may be even more remote than before, making it even less likely that staff will move through to other roles in the function (unless they are, say, mobile graduates working in a contact centre as their first assignment). Those working in global centres of expertise will be requiring even higher levels of knowledge, skills and experience, making jobs that were already tough to fill even harder. How many reward specialists are there who are competent in executive remuneration, expatriate compensation and global programmes? OD people are hard to find even without specifying that they must have cross-cultural, international expertise.

The same issues present themselves for business partners – getting globally experienced and successful staff drawn not just from the home base or those locations that are most culturally proximate. The challenge remains how do you build this capability inside the firm, as opposed to hiring it in from other companies that have done the development? As we suggested in the last book, there are ways of testing people out through short-term assignments, projects and absence cover, but the best approach is to build in developmental roles such as Assistant Business Partner or Junior Specialist. This is more challenging in widely dispersed operations and will get a lot harder if the function finds itself squeezing out the numbers to meet the HR:employee ratio or some arbitrary cost constraint. Having a local presence of HR people may help but this is where the narrowness of these roles may be seen as a disadvantage, not providing a wide enough experience base. Moreover, these staff may well have to be mobile if they are to take up corporate positions, thereby significantly changing the personal profile of incumbents.

At Procter & Gamble an aspiring HR manager is expected either to take a job in a plant or to work alongside a key-account executive to learn about a business unit and win the confidence of its managers. Coca-Cola Enterprises rotates top-performing line managers into HR positions for two or three years to build the business skills of its HR professionals and to make the function more credible to the business units (Guthridge et al., 2008).

An important aspect of career development is that a wide range of staff need international exposure if they are to do their jobs effectively. It is not just those in obvious positions, like business partners and experts who need to understand global people management, but also those in key service delivery roles. This is not necessarily going to be achieved by a full expatriate assignment, but through project working, extended visits and networking with the international community. The aim is for HR staff to obtain a feed for global HR issues so that they can support, advise and challenge manager-customers in an appropriate manner.

It is likely, as we said, that those filling business management positions will enter HR from other functions. However, it is important that 'regular' HR people pick up the skills the incomers bring with them. Greater interest in and facility with performance and reporting methodologies will stand HR people in good stead both to be more effective in their own roles, but also to offer opportunities outside the function. A company like

SAP has operations management teams in all its business functions, thereby offering the chance of a different career path.

Concluding Words

We wrote this book to see whether the globalization of business and trade has impacted HR, leading to a globalization of the function's activities. From our discussions with organizations, the conclusion we have come to is that there is a sense of inevitable development to this end. However, the speed and depth of the change is affected by the business model, sector and past history/present ambitions. This means that there are pressures to create a global brand, universal organizational culture, corporately driven talent management approach and global service delivery model. As such we see the components of HR transformation, consolidation, standardization and automation being pushed from the corporate centre in many organizations towards a common set of HR policies and processes, held together by a governance structure that seeks to minimize difference and maximize commonality. Whilst the western business model, and associated culture, is dominant, we have seen important variations from the east that reflect either a stage of development or a preference for a more hands-off approach to organizational management. The greater pluralism in operation fits also with a desire to get as close as possible to the countries in which they operate – a philosophy which is consistent with family ownership.

If this sounds overly determinist, we would stress again that our own intellectual preference is for best fit over best practice. There are still lots of choices in how organizations build their brands, influence their cultures, manage talent or create their service delivery model. Our general observation is that in the van of globalization are companies that are perhaps pushing too hard towards a standardized HR approach that both neglects important local differences and can appear to ignore or depreciate them. The risk is that there will be a backlash against this kind of centralization that will mean that the pendulum will swing back towards the 'small is beautiful' end of the spectrum.

To avoid these violent oscillations we suggest that organizations proceed more slowly, involving managers more in the design of the HR model, taking more of a case-by-case approach rather than an all embracing transformation. Some readers may feel that we are knocking down a straw man because there is no such intention towards a monolithic solution. It may be that the words said exaggerate the actual practice, but all one has to do is to go to conferences to hear practitioners extolling the virtues of 'oneness'. As we particularly observed in Chapter 4 on diversity, there appears little scope for difference or uniqueness unless the country is so small as to be irrelevant.

We do not want to return to the debate about HR's existential crisis, but as with other aspects of HR's role (especially its relationship to employees), the globalization of the HR function poses further questions about what HR seeks to achieve. The globalization imperative together with the impact of the recession have seemingly forced HR back to the corporate policeman role. Is that where HR wants to be: remote from its customers, only in electronic contact, ensuring that all follow the party line and arresting deviants? This is of course an exaggeration, but it is the outcome that current developments are leading many in HR towards.

An alternative destiny could be for HR to be encouraging the organization to understand its diverse culture, celebrate its benefits and see how best to reconcile the understandable wish for oneness and commonality with the flexibility to respond to the variegated circumstances within which it operates.

References

ADP and HROA (2008) *Global HR Transformation Report*.

Allouche, J., Domenach, J-L., Froissart, C., Gilbert, P. and Le Boulaire, M. (2008) *French Companies in China: the political environment, socio-economic issues and management practices*, Paris: Entreprise&Personnel.

Antila, E.M. and Kakkonen, A. (2008) 'Factors affecting the role of HR managers in international mergers and acquisitions,' *Personnel Review*, 37 (3).

Ashton, C. and Lambert, A. (2005) *The Future of HR: creating a fit for purpose function*, London: CRF Publishing.

Attar, R. (2009) 'Looking back at the end of history,' *BBC History Magazine*, November.

Aycan, Z., Kanungo, R.N., Mendonca, M., Yu, K., Deller, J., Stahl, G. and Khursid, A. (2000) 'Impact of culture on human resource management practices: a ten country comparison,' *Applied Psychology: An International Review*, 49 (1).

Baeten, X. (2010) 'Global compensation and benefits management: the need for communication and coordination,' *Compensation and Benefits Review*, September/October.

Bartlett, C.A. and Ghosal, S. (1989) *Managing Across Borders: the transnational solution*, Boston: Harvard Business School.

Bate, C. (2010) *WWWD – What Would the Web Do? An information systems strategy*, Atos Origin.

BBC (2010) 'A history of the world in 100 objects,' *Radio 4*, 22 February.

Birkinshaw, J., Bouquet, C. and Ambos, T. (2006) 'Attention HQ,' *Business Strategy Review*, Autumn, 17 (3).

Booz Allen Hamilton (1998) 'Shared services: management fad or real value', Viewpoint.

Boudreau, J.W. and Ramstad, P.M. (2007) *Beyond HR: the new science of human capital*, Boston, MA: Harvard Business School Press.

Brocket, S. (2004) 'Becoming a business partner: HR at Coca-Cola Enterprises,' *Strategic HR Review*, 3 (2), January/February.

Brookfield Global Relocation Services (2010) *Global Relocation Trends*, Chicago.

Brown, A. (2010) 'The pontiff is not so potent,' *The Guardian*, 30 March.

Budhwar, P. (2010) 'Management of Human Resources in foreign firms operating in India: the role of country-specific HR centre.' Paper for Work, Employment and Society Conference, 7–9 September, Brighton.

Budhwar, P.S. and Bhatnagar, J. (eds) (2009) *The Changing Face of People Management in India*, London: Routledge.

Business Week Research Services (2007) *New Era for HR Shared Services*.

Cappelli, P. (2008) 'Talent management for the twenty-first century,' *Harvard Business Review*, March.

Chandler, G. (2002) 'Let's not fool each other with the business case,' *Ethical Performance*, 4 (1), May.

Chartered Institute of Personnel and Development (2010a) *Talent Development in the BRIC Countries*, London.

Chartered Institute of Personnel and Development (2010b) *Learning and Talent Development, Annual Survey*, London.

Chartered Institute of Personnel and Development (2010c) *Next Generation HR*, London.

Chubb, C., Reilly, P. and Usher, T. (2010) *Learning from the Downturn: key messages from the downturn*, Report 476, Brighton: The Institute for Employment Studies.

Chubb, L. (2008) 'Tata takeover puts HR in the driving seat of change,' *People Management*, 3 April.

Churchyard, C. (2010) 'Europe-wide HR system helps Aviva branch out,' *People Management*, 16 September.

Classen, M. and Reilly, P. (2007) 'Shrinking differences,' *People Management*, 14 June.

Collings, D.G. and Scullion, H. (2006) 'Approaches to international staffing,' in Scullion, H. and Collings, D.J. (eds) *Global Staffing*, London: Routledge.

Colvin, G. (1997) 'Value-driven: the most valuable quality in a manager,' *Fortune* (European edn), 136 (12).

Conference Board (2007) *HR's Role in Company Transformation*, New York, 28 November.

Cooke, F.L. (2010) 'The changing face of human resource management in China,' in Rowley, C. and Cooke, F.L. (eds) *The Changing Face of Chinese Management*, Routledge 'Working in Asia' series, London: Routledge.

Cope, F. (1998) 'HR Planning: HR planning current issues in selecting high potentials,' *Human Resource Planning*, 21.

Corporate Leadership Council (2005) *Realizing the Full Potential of Rising Talent Volume I: A Quantitative Analysis of the Identification and Development of High-Potential Employees*, Arlington, VA.

Davis, G.F. (2009) 'The rise and fall of finance and the end of the society of organizations,' *Academy of Management Perspectives*, 23.

De Meuse, K.P., Dai, G., Hallenbeck, G.S. and Tang, K.Y. (2009) *Global Talent Management: using learning agility to identify high potentials around the world*, Los Angeles: The Korn Ferry Institute.

Deal, T.E. and Kennedy, A.A. (1982) *Corporate Cultures: the rites and rituals of corporate life*, London: Penguin Books.

Deloitte Consulting (2006) *Global HR Transformation*.

Deloitte Consulting (2009) *From the Ground Up: building an HR infrastructure to support future growth*.

Department for Innovation and Skills (2009) *Engaging for Success: enhancing performance through employee engagement*. Report to Government by David MacLeod and Nita Clarke, http://www.bis.gov.uk/files/file52215.pdf.

Devine, M. and Hirsh, W. (1998) *Mergers and Acquisitions: getting the people bit right*, Horsham: Roffey Park Institute.

Dyer, L. and Ericksen, J. (2007) 'Dynamic organisations: achieving marketplace agility through workforce scalability,' in Storey, J. (ed.) *Human Resource Management: a critical text*, London: Thomson.

Edwards, T., Budjanovcanin, A. and Woollard, S. (2008) *International Mergers and Acquisitions*, April, CIPD.

Entreprise&Personnel (2006) *Succeeding in China: the human issues and how to manage them*, China symposium, 14 June, Paris.

Eversheds (2011) *The Eversheds Board Report: measuring the impact of board composition on board performance*, London.

Freidman, T.L. (2000) *The Lexus and the Olive Tree*, New York: Anchor Books.

Fukuyama, F. (1992) *The End of History and the Last Man*, New York: The Free Press.

Furnham, A. (2010) 'Six learning experiences that shape all top people,' *The Sunday Times*, 10 October.

Garton Ash, T. (2010) 'This Nobel prize was bold and right but hits China's most sensitive nerve,' *The Guardian*, 14 October.

Gladwell, M. (2002) 'The talent myth,' *New Yorker*, 22 July.

Griffiths, J. (2004) 'Global expansion needs strategic HR,' *People Management*, 2 September.

Groysberg, B., Nanda, A. and Nohria, N. (2004) 'The risky business of hiring stars,' *Harvard Business Review*, May–June.

Guthridge, M. and Lawson, E. (2008) 'Divide and survive,' *People Management*, 18 September.

Guthridge, M., Komm, A.B. and Lawson, E. (2008) 'Making talent a strategic priority,' *McKinsey Quarterly*, January.

Haldane, A.G. (2009) 'Rethinking the financial network.' Speech delivered at the Financial Student Association, Amsterdam, April.

Hampden-Turner, C. and Trompenaars, F. (1993) *Seven Cultures of Capitalism*, New York: Doubleday.

Handy, C. (1992) 'Balancing corporate power: a new Federalist paper,' *Harvard Business Review*, November–December.

Harry, W. (2007) 'East and East,' *People Management*, 29 November.

Harvey, M. and Novicevic, M.M. (2003) 'Strategic global Human Resource Management: its role in global networks,' *Research and Practice in Human Resource Management*, 11 (2).

Hay Group (2010) *The Changing Face of Reward*.

Henry, C. (2008) 'How to ... lend HR expertise to mergers,' *People Management*, 21 February.

Hewitt (2007) *HR Shared Service Centres: into the next generation*.

Hewitt (2009a) *Managing HR on a Global Scale: findings from Hewitt's 2009 Global HR Study*.

Hewitt (2009b) *Fourth European HR Barometer Trends and Perspectives on the Human Resources Function in Europe*.

Hirsh, W. (2010) 'Positive career development for leaders,' in Storey, J. (ed.) *Leadership in Organizations: current issues and key trends* (2nd edn), London: Routledge.

Hirsh, W. and Jackson, C. (1996) *Strategies for Career Development: promise, practice and pretence*, IES Report 305, Brighton: Institute for Employment Studies.

Hofstede, G. (1991) *Culture and Organizations: software for the mind*, London: McGraw-Hill.

Honey, P. (2008) 'Cultural differences are a breeding ground for generalisations,' *Training Journal*, September.

House, R.J., Hanges, P.J., Ruiz-Quntanilla, S.A., Dorfman, P.W., Dickson, M.W. and Javidan, M. (1999) 'Culture, leadership, and organizational practices,' in Mobley, W.H. (ed.) *Advances in Global Leadership*, Bingley: JAI Press.

Hulks, S. (2009) 'The talent management paradox,' *HR Director*, January.

Hytner, D. (2010) 'Cash won't win you the title, Kalou warns Manchester City,' *The Guardian*, 3 August.

Industrial Relations Services (1999) 'IBM delivers international HR,' *Employment Trends*, No. 689, October.

Interdean (2011) *2011 Mobility Survey Report*.

Institute of Personnel and Development (1999) *The IPD Guide On International Recruitment, Selection And Assessment*, London.

Johnson, R. (2008) 'Recovery position,' *People Management*, 4 September.

Jonsen, K. and Bryant, B. (2008) 'Stretch target,' *People Management*, 21 August.

Judt, A. (1997) *A Grand Illusion? An Essay on Europe*, London: Penguin Books.

Kates, A. (2006) '(Re)Designing the HR organisation,' *Human Resource Planning*, 29 (2).

Keith, A. (2010) *Globalisation: The view to 2025*, London: Outsights.

Kenexa Research Institute (2010) *Exploring Leadership and Managerial Effectiveness: A Kenexa Research Institute Work Trends Report*, www.kenexaresearchinstitute.com.

Kettle, M. (2010) 'Trapped in the Anglosphere, we've lost sight of next door,' *The Guardian*, 20 August.

Kock, R. and Burke, M. (2008) 'Managing talent in the South African public service,' *Public Personnel Management: special issue on talent management*, IPMA, 37 (4), Winter.

Kotter, J.P. (2006) *Leading Change*, Boston, MA: Harvard Business School Press.

Larson, P.S. (2008) 'HR partnering in a global world.' Presentation to CIPD Annual Conference, Harrogate, 17 September.

Larsson, S. (2008) *The Girl with the Dragon Tattoo*, London: Quercus.

Le Boulaire, M. (2005) *Managing Diversity: how business is responding to new societal issues*, Paris: Entreprise&Personnel.

Lewis, R. E. and Heckman, R. J. (2006) 'Talent management: a critical review,' *Human Resource Management Review*, 16 (2)

Lievens, F., Harris, M.M., Van Keer, E. and Bisqueret, C. (2003) 'Predicting cross-cultural training performance: the validity of personality, cognitive ability, and dimensions measured by an assessment center and a behaviour description interview, *Journal of Applied Psychology*, 88 (3).

Lombardo, M.M. and Eichinger, R.W. (2002) 'The leadership machine: architecture to develop leaders of any future', Minneapolis: Lominger.

Maatman, M., Bondarouk, T. and Looise, J.C. (2010) 'Conceptualising the capabilities and value creation of HRM shared service models,' *Human Resource Management Review*, 20 (4).

Manpower (2009) *The Global Talent Crunch: why employer branding matters now*, Milwaukee, WI.

Marsden, D. and Belfield, R. (2009) 'Institutions and the management of human resources: incentive pay systems in France and Great Britain,' CEP Discussion Paper 941. Centre for Analysis of Social Exclusion, London School of Economics and Political Science, London.

Martin, G. (2006) *Managing People and Organizations in Changing Contexts*, Oxford: Butterworth Heinemann.

Martin, G. (2010) 'A corporate governance lens on Strategic Human Resources Management.' Paper submitted to the Strategic Management Society Conference, Florida, 29 June.

Martin, G. and Beaumont, P. (2003) *Branding and People Management: what's in a name?*, London: Chartered Institute of Personnel and Development.

Martin, G. and Hetrick, S. (2006) *Corporate Reputations, Branding and People Management: a strategic approach*, Oxford: Butterworth Heinemann.

Martin, G. and McGoldrick, J. (2011) 'Theorising the links between HRM, governance and corporate reputations,' in Young, S. (ed.) *Contemporary Issues in International Corporate Governance*, Prahran, Victoria, Australia: Tilde University Press.

Martin, G. Gollan, P. and Grigg K. (2009) 'A future for employer branding? Dealing with negative capabilities in Strategic Human Resource Management (SHRM).' Paper presented to the 15th World Congress of the International Industrial Relations Association Annual Conference, 24–27 August, Sydney, Australia.

Mayrhofer W., Morley, M. and Brewster, C. (2004) 'Convergence, stasis or divergence,' in Brewster, C., Mayrhofer, W. and Morley, M. *Human Resource Management in Europe: evidence of convergence*, London: Elsevier.

McCauley, C. D. (2008) 'Leader development: a review of research,' Center for Creative Leadership, September.

McCrae, R.R. and Terraciano, A. (2005) 'Personality profiles of culture: aggregate personality traits,' *Journal of Personality and Social Psychology*, 89 (3).

McCrum, R. (2010) *Globish: how the English language became the world's language*, New York: Viking.

McKinsey (2010) *Women at the Top of Corporations: making it happen*.

McSweeney, B. (2002) 'Hofstede's model of national cultural differences and their consequences: a triumph of faith: a failure of analysis,' *Human Relations*, 55 (1), January.

Mercer (2003) *Why HR Governance Matters: managing the HR function for superior performance*, New York.

Mercer (2010) *HR Transformation in Europe*, New York.

Michaels, E., Handfield-Jones, H. and Axelrod, B. (2001) *The War for Talent*, Boston, MA: Harvard Business School Press.

Minchington, B. (2010) 'Why would someone want to work for you?' *Journal of Corporate Recruiting Leadership*, October.

Millmore, M., Lewis, P., Saunders M., Thornhill, A. and Morrow, T. (2007) *Strategic Human Resource Management: contemporary issues*, FT Prentice Hall: Harlow.

Montana, P. and Charnov, B. (2008) *Management* (4th edn), New York: Barrons Educational Series, Hauppauge.

Morris, I (2010) 'Why the West rules for now,' *BBC History Magazine*, December.

O'Donnell, A. and Capblanc, P. (2004) *Mergers and Acquisitions: HR's role prior to integration*, Paris: Entreprise&Personnel.

Oertig, M. (2009) 'Die Rollen des HRM für eine gute Corporate Governance,' *HR Today*, 7 August.

Ostler, N. (2010) *The Last Lingua Franca: English until the return of Babel*, London: Allen Lane.

Overman, S. (2006) 'Show off your brand,' *Staffing Management*, 2 (2), April.

People Management (2009) 'Keeping Eastern promises,' 21 May.

Porter, M.E. and Kramer, M.R. (2006) 'Strategy and society: the link between competitive advantage and corporate social responsibility,' *Harvard Business Review*, December.

Purcell, J. and Hutchinson, S. (2007) *Rewarding Work: the vital role of line managers*, London: Chartered Institute of Personnel and Development.

Purcell, J., Kinnie, N., Hutchinson, S., Rayton, B. and Swart, J. (2003) *Understanding the People and Performance Link: Unlocking the Black Box*, London: Chartered Institute of Personnel and Development.

Raisch, S. and Birkinshaw, J. (2008) 'Organizational ambidexterity: antecedents, outcomes, and moderators,' *Journal of Management*, June, 34 (3).

Reilly, P. (1999) *Back Office or Shared Service and the Re-alignment of HR*, Report 368, Brighton: Institute for Employment Studies.

Reilly, P. (2010) 'Learning from abroad,' *HR News*, IPMA-HR, Alexandria, VA , April.

Reilly, P., Tamkin, P. and Broughton, A. (2007) *The Changing HR Function: transforming HR?* London: Chartered Institute of Personnel and Development, Research into Practice.

Reilly, P. and Williams, T. (2003) *How to Get Best Value from HR: the shared services option*, Aldershot: Gower.

Reilly, P. and Williams, T. (2006) *Strategic HR: building the capability to deliver*, Aldershot: Gower.

Roberts, J. (2004) *The Modern Firm: organizational design for performance and growth*, Oxford: Oxford University Press.

Roberts, M. (2006) *Change Management Excellence: putting NLP to work in the 21st century*, Carmarthen: Crown House.

Schein, E.H. (1985) *Organisational Culture and Leadership*, San Francisco: Jossey Bass.

Schuler, R.S. and Jackson, S.E. (2001) 'HR issues and activities in mergers and acquisitions,' *European Management Journal*, 19 (3).

Schwartz, S.H. (1994) 'Are there universal aspects in the content and structure of values?' *Journal of Social Issues*, 50.

Sennett, R (2008) *The Craftsman*, London: Allen Lane.

Sierk, Y. and Hyunghae, B. (2009) 'Cultivating cultural differences in asymmetric power relations,' *International Journal of Cross Cultural Management*, 9.

Silverstein, A.J. (2010) *Islamic History: a very short introduction*, Oxford: Oxford University Press.

Smedley, T. (2011) 'On my agenda', People Management, September

Sparrow, P. (2009) 'When is talent not talent?' *Talent Management Review*, Autumn.

Sparrow, P., Brewster, C. and Harris, H. (2004) *Globalizing Human Resource Management*, London: Routledge.

spring Messe Management (2010) 'International joint venture: building high performance teams.' Press release, 26 August.

Stahl, G.K., Björkman, I., Farndale, E., Morris, S.S., Paauwe, J., Stiles, P., Trevor, J. and Wright, P.M. (2007) 'Global talent management: how leading multinational build and sustain their talent pipeline,' INSEAD Faculty and Research Working Papers, 24/OB.

Stajkovic, A.D. and Luthans, F., (1998) 'Self-efficacy and work-related performance: a meta-analysis,' *Psychological Bulletin*, American Psychological Association, volume 124.

Stern, S. (2009) 'Living strategy and the death of the five-year plan,' *Financial Times*, 27 October.

Stiles, P. (2007) 'A world of difference,' *People Management*, 15 November.

Sun, S. (2007) 'The clay soldiers speak of the good and bad of absolute rule,' *The Guardian*, 8 November.

Tamkin, P. Reilly, P. and Hirsh, W. (2006) *Managing HR Careers: Emerging Trends and Issues*, London: CIPD.

Tamkin, P., Cowling, M. and Hunt, W. (2008) *People and the Bottom Line*, Report 448, Brighton: The Institute for Employment Studies and the Work Foundation.

Tamkin, P., Pearson, G., Hirsh, W. and Constable, S. (2010) *Exceeding Expectations; the principles of outstanding leadership*, London: The Work Foundation.

The Boston Consulting Group (2009) *Creating People Advantage: how to tackle the major HR challenges during the crisis and beyond*, Boston, MA.

The Boston Consulting Group (2010) *Creating People Advantage: how companies can adapt their HR Practices for volatile times*, Boston, MA.

The Grapevine (2010a) 'Gambling on talent,' September.

The Grapevine (2010b) 'Panasonic Talent innovation,' February.

The Hackett Group (2007) 'Shared services can reduce HR process cost cuts by up to 80%; while driving improved satisfaction, productivity, and quality,' Research Alerts & Press Releases, 30 January.

The Hackett Group (2010) 'HR focus,' March.

The Hackett Group (2009) 'Metric of the month,' November.

Towers Perrin (2005) 'Winning strategies for a global workforce: attracting and engaging employees for competitive advantage.'

Topcu, K. (2005) 'Theory and Practice of Culture Standard Research in Austro-Hungarian Management Interactions; an Analysis from a Hungarian Point of View', unpublished PhD, Budapest.

Trompenaars, F. (1993) *Riding the Waves of Culture: understanding cultural diversity in business*, London: Economist Books.

Trompenaars, F. and Woolliams, P. (1999) 'First class accommodation,' *People Management*, 22 April.

Ulrich, D., Allen, J., Brockbank, W., Younger, J. and Nyman, M. (2009b) *HR Transformation: building human resources from the outside in*, New York: McGraw Professional.

Ulrich, S., Rogovsky, N. and Lamotte, D. (2009a) *Promoting Responsible and Sustainable Enterprise-Level Practices at Times of Crisis: a guide for policy-makers and social partners*, International Labour Organisation: Geneva.

United Nations (2005) *Unlocking the Human Potential for Public Sector Performance, World Public Sector Report 2005*, New York: Department of Economic and Social Affairs.

Waterman, R., Waterman, J. and Collard, B. (1994) 'Towards a career resilient workforce,' *Harvard Business Review*, July–August.

Wickens, P. (1987) *The Road to Nissan: flexibility, quality and teamwork*, Basingstoke: Macmillan.

Withers, M., Williamson, M. and Reddington, M. (2010) *Transforming HR: creating value through people* (2nd edn), Oxford: Elsevier.

World Bank (1999) *Corporate Governance: A Framework for Implementation*, Washington.

Zwingle, E. (1999) 'Globalization,' *National Geographic*, August.

Index

If you have found this book useful you may be interested in other titles from Gower

Developing HR Talent:
Building a Strategic Partnership with the Business
Kirsty Saddler and Jan Hills
Paperback: 978-0-566-08829-2
e-book: 978-0-7546-8167-0

Going Global:
Managing the HR Function Across Countries and Cultures
Cat Rickard, Jodi Baker and Yonca Crew
Paperback: 978-0-566-08823-0
e-book: 978-0-7546-8134-2

Strategic HR:
Building the Capability to Deliver
Peter Reilly and Tony Williams
Hardback: 978-0-566-08674-8
e-book: 978-0-7546-8312-4

Working Together:
Organizational Transactional Analysis
and Business Performance
Anita Mountain and Chris Davidson
Hardback: 978-0-566-08846-9
e-book: 978-1-4094-3156-5

GOWER

How To Get Best Value From HR:
The Shared Services Option
Peter Reilly and Tony Williams
Hardback: 978-0-566-08495-9
e-book: 978-0-566-08964-0

The Global Business Handbook:
The Eight Dimensions of International Management
Edited by
David Newlands and Mark J. Hooper
Hardback: 978-0-566-08747-9
e-book: 978-0-7546-8137-3

Gower Handbook of Internal Communication
Edited by
Marc Wright
Hardback: 978-0-566-08689-2
e-book: 978-0-7546-9097-9

Human Resources or Human Capital?
Managing People as Assets
Andrew Mayo
Hardback: 978-1-4094-2285-3
e-book: 978-1-4094-2286-0

Visit **www.gowerpublishing.com** and

- search the entire catalogue of Gower books in print
- order titles online at 10% discount
- take advantage of special offers
- sign up for our monthly e-mail update service
- download free sample chapters from all recent titles
- download or order our catalogue